The One Year®
Daily Acts of Kindness Devotional

THE ONE YEAR®

DAILY ACTS OF
Kindness
DEVOTIONAL

*365 Inspiring Ideas to
Reveal, Give, and Find God's Love*

Julie Fisk | Kendra Roehl | Kristin Demery

TYNDALE
MOMENTUM™

*The nonfiction imprint of
Tyndale House Publishers, Inc.*

Visit Tyndale online at www.tyndale.com.

Visit Tyndale Momentum online at www.tyndalemomentum.com.

Visit the authors' website at www.theruthexperience.com.

TYNDALE, *Tyndale Momentum*, Tyndale's quill logo, *The One Year*, and *One Year* are registered trademarks of Tyndale House Publishers, Inc. The Tyndale Momentum logo and the One Year logo are trademarks of Tyndale House Publishers, Inc. Tyndale Momentum is the nonfiction imprint of Tyndale House Publishers, Inc., Carol Stream, Illinois.

The One Year Daily Acts of Kindness Devotional: 365 Inspiring Ideas to Reveal, Give, and Find God's Love

Designed by Eva Winters

Edited by Brittany Bergman

For information about special discounts for bulk purchases, please contact Tyndale House Publishers at csresponse@tyndale.com, or call 1-800-323-9400.

ISBN 978-1-4964-2161-6

Printed in the United States of America

23 22 21 20 19 18
 7   6   5   4   3

Introduction

One year as we approached Christmas, we found ourselves frustrated with our kids' attitudes. We were tired of our children whining about Christmas, tired of hearing them say "I want that" each time a commercial came on television, tired of them complaining about how other children had things they wanted. As mothers, we wanted to find a way to change their attitudes from self-centered to others-centered by refocusing them on the love of God.

So we proposed an experiment during the month of December: we'd perform one kind act each day, then post about it on social media to encourage others to join us. What began as a parenting whim to reclaim Christmas evolved into a year-long experiment in generosity.

When we joined together, it was simply to push back a little against the materialism that seemed to be consuming our families, but the end result was far more than we ever anticipated. After continuing our habit of showing kindness every day for an entire year, we found that our own lives and our thoughts toward others had changed. Instead of being quick to judge others, we realized our hearts had softened as we saw God reflected in the faces of people around us. And the changes didn't begin and end with us: we saw our families—and more specifically, our children—change and grow too. They're now much more aware of the needs of those around them, and they've grown in their passion for specific issues affecting people around the world. We all have a newfound desire to live lives marked by intentional giving, serving, and advocating for the least of these (Matthew 25:40).

Perhaps most importantly, we came to realize that the idea of grace—the idea on which we base our faith—hinges on *kindness*. Jesus' command to love God and love others is impossible without kindness. Kindness teaches humility, is the antithesis of selfishness and pride, and leads to matchless grace. Throughout our year of kindness, we saw our relationships with God flourish as we put our faith into action and as we witnessed the love of God—who hears the cries of his people—demonstrated in tangible ways.

If you've found yourself stagnant in your faith, wondering if there's more to life than just the daily routine, or if you've been frustrated with your kids' (or your own) selfish attitudes, this book will help you and your family see beyond your own four walls and into the community around you. We are so delighted that you would consider joining with us on this adventure we've begun. It is our greatest hope and prayer that these daily reflections will be both an inspiration and a call to action on your own journey to find and give away the love of Jesus.

— Julie, Kendra, and Kristin

January

A Crazy Idea

*Do not conform to the pattern of this world, but be
transformed by the renewing of your mind.*
ROMANS 12:2, NIV

I had no idea my New Year's Day would end with a stranger and her son living in my basement.

My husband, Tim, and I had awakened with a rare sense of freedom. Our two- and four-year-old daughters were, surprisingly, still asleep. With no work commitments to fulfill, we were looking forward to a lazy holiday at home.

Within an hour of waking up, however, Tim's expression clued me in to the fact that our plans had changed. Lips quirked, brow furrowed, thumbs clicking furiously on his phone, he paced the confines of our bedroom, stopping periodically to chew on his thumbnail while he waited for a response.

A mom and her young son needed a place to stay until a unit opened up in their new apartment building. They had been sleeping at our friend's house, but that was no longer a feasible situation, and they were looking for an alternative.

Tim looked at me, an unspoken question in his eyes: *Could we be that option?*

It wasn't a new situation for us; we had hosted a homeless mom and her two daughters for three months that previous summer. But since the request came on the heels of a whirlwind December, I hesitated. *I'm used to girls,* I thought. *I don't know if I can handle a little boy. What if we say yes and wish we hadn't?*

There was a very real chance I would live to regret my action. But sometimes it's the crazy ideas, the ones that open us up to uncertainty, that end up teaching us the most. Paul reminds us in Romans 12:2, "Do not conform to the pattern of this world, but be transformed by the renewing of your mind. Then you will be able to test and approve what God's will is—his good, pleasing and perfect will" (NIV). Sometimes we're led to take a step of faith that may look crazy to the world and trust that God will help us work our way through it.

— *Kristin*

— Today's Act of Kindness —

Start the new year by resolving to look for opportunities
to extend kindness to others, even in small ways.

Up Close and Personal

*Do to others whatever you would like them to do to you. This is the
essence of all that is taught in the law and the prophets.*
MATTHEW 7:12

That New Year's Day, when my family was faced with the decision of temporarily hosting a homeless woman and her son, I felt torn. After all, two of my friends and our families had spent the month leading up to Christmas performing acts of kindness each day: cooking a meal for a pregnant mom on bed rest, leaving treats for our mail carrier, filling a gas tank for a military serviceperson. We had documented them on social media and invited others to join with us. One night, recalling the amazing things we'd experienced during our month of kindness, I had thrown out the challenge at dinner: *What would happen if we committed to doing one kind act each day for a whole year?*

Now, on the first day of our commitment, I was already being challenged to rethink what a year of kindness would mean for our family. A month of kindness required forethought but didn't demand too much else. It's one thing to spend an afternoon making baked ziti for someone, casually dropping it off while running errands. But to let someone see me in ratty pajamas before I've had a chance to brush my teeth? To let someone see me in the mess of my regular life—nagging my kids for sticking out their tongues, aiming dirty looks at my husband for checking sports scores instead of clearing dinner, failing to clean up crumbs lingering in cobwebbed corners—felt like a much greater challenge.

Yet in that moment, I was reminded of the Golden Rule: "Do to others whatever you would like them to do to you." If I truly believe that an essential part of my faith is living this truth out daily, surely I'm also called to do more than live a comfortable, easy life. Allowing someone to see my imperfections is a small price to pay in the face of another's need.

That afternoon, as I nervously opened my door to two strangers, I knew saying yes to trusting God in this situation was the right thing to do.

— *Kristin*

— Today's Act of Kindness —

How can you stretch beyond your comfort zone to
reach those in need? Think of one small step you can
take today to go beyond yourself, then do it.

Piano Man

*[God] will not forget how hard you have worked for him and how you have
shown your love to him by caring for other believers, as you still do.*
HEBREWS 6:10

As I walked through one of many parking lots at Mayo Clinic, my eyes widened. License plates from practically every state were represented on the cars in the nearly full lot. While I told my three-year-old son that we were going on a big adventure, we were actually there for specialized testing. As we waited for the test results, my heart was in my throat and my eyes burned bright with unshed tears.

Walking through the rotunda while we waited, we were drawn to the sounds of an older gentleman playing a grand piano. Everyone is especially kind to children at Mayo, and this man was no exception. He smiled gently as my son wandered over to stand next to him, and the man leaned down to whisper that he had a special song just for my son coming up next. As the notes for "Jesus Loves Me" began to fill the air, he struck up a quiet conversation with me—asking me how often we come to Mayo and telling me that he volunteers to play every Wednesday at noon.

In this stranger, I recognized the love of my Savior. He faithfully comes to play, to smile, to whisper words of encouragement in this place where nearly every visitor walks the hallways in the midst of a medical crisis; good news and bad all mixed together.

His sacrifice of time, his musical gift, and his kind words brought peace and reassurance to my heart that no matter the test results that awaited us, my son was loved by not just my husband and me but by our Savior.

While I cannot remember the Piano Man's real name, my memory of him is vivid, and I think of him often as a faithful example of someone who shone with the love of Christ in a place where desperation and hope, despair and joy, and mourning and rejoicing so often walk the hallways side by side.

— Julie

— Today's Act of Kindness —

Pray about how you can use your gifts and talents to
reveal the love of Christ. Find one small step you can take
toward using your gifts to encourage and serve others.

Everyone Is Welcome Here

The Son of Man came eating and drinking, and you say, "Here is a glutton and a drunkard, a friend of tax collectors and sinners."
LUKE 7:34, NIV

When I sit scrolling through social media outlets, I see posts as varied as the people represented there. I try to look for the good, and I am encouraged by people who choose to speak about love and grace and mercy.

My eyes wander to our dining room wall, where we recently hung a print of a favorite quote of mine I came across last fall. It says, "Come on in, there is always room at the table for you." It's a welcome beacon over my dining room table, reminding me of what I, as a Christian, am called to do.

Love my neighbor.

I think about Jesus' life on earth, how he invited people into community who were very different from him. I remember that he was called a drunkard and a glutton—not because he was those things, but because he chose to hang around people who were. I'm reminded of the words my pastor so frequently offers us: "You can belong here before you believe."

I wonder how many of the conversations we see on our social media feeds would change if we would be willing to invite people into our lives. If we would gather around our tables and have conversations, face to face. If we started seeing what makes us alike, not just what makes us different.

I wonder what would happen if we chose to see the humanity in one another. If we embraced one another even when we don't embrace the same beliefs. Rather than speaking in generalizations or feeling that sharing our opinions is the same as sharing our faith, perhaps we need to do more. We need to be willing to put in the time and energy to love people right where they are. This is not an easy task, I know. We may even be questioned by others, but we can rest assured knowing that this is the work that Jesus calls us to do.

— Kendra

— Today's Act of Kindness —

When given the opportunity to speak ill of a person
or people group, instead pray blessing on them.

Legacy

Since we are surrounded by such a huge crowd of witnesses to the life of faith, let us strip off every weight that slows us down, especially the sin that so easily trips us up. And let us run with endurance the race God has set before us.

HEBREWS 12:1

I've got a milestone birthday looming. Instead of bemoaning the addition of a few more laugh lines, I've been pondering the notion of legacy. While legacy doesn't feel relevant as I navigate the parenting trenches of elementary school, I realize that if we aren't thinking about legacy now, then we're doing something wrong.

It is my heart's desire to leave a legacy of faith—that I would be remembered for reflecting Jesus to my children, my coworkers, and my neighbors. Not that I lived perfectly, but that I loved God and loved others to the best of my ability in the little moments and in the big moments.

Intentional kindness is an integral part of my legacy of faith. Kindness, especially when it is not the expected response to a situation, is how I tangibly reveal Christ's love in action. It is built through the quiet pouring out of time and resources into the lives of those around me and by living a life that looks beyond my own interests to the interests of others.

Hebrews 12:1 reminds us that our earthly lives are a race and that we are cheered on by the faithful Christians who have gone before us. We don't get to wait to build our legacy; we are building it every minute of every day, whether we want to admit it or not.

Wherever you are in your faith race, be encouraged! Our call to a legacy of faith is a marathon not a sprint. It is something that is built over a lifetime, not overnight. Just don't put it off, thinking that you are too busy and that you'll get around to it later. Your legacy is built day by day, small step by small step.

— Julie

— *Today's Act of Kindness* —

Prayerfully consider the legacy you are currently creating and take one small step toward the legacy you want to create.

Why Be Kind?

Do not be overcome by evil, but overcome evil with good.
ROMANS 12:21, NIV

Tim and I tumbled through the door of the coffee shop together on a chilly winter morning. We were on the cusp of our proposed year of kindness, and I was determined to get off to a good start.

As we looked around the shop for someone to bless, we spotted him. Fully dressed in his state trooper uniform, he sat at a corner table with a mug cupped between work-worn hands, visiting quietly with a woman. "Let's get him a gift card," I suggested. Nodding, Tim strolled to the counter and purchased the gift card and our drinks, then headed toward the trooper.

Finding a seat at another table, heart thumping, I glanced over to see my usually unflappable husband's smile falter a bit. Eventually, he made his way to me. Excited to hear how the conversation went, I was instantly deflated when Tim told me the trooper seemed dismissive of the gift, accepting it only after my husband insisted. The rejection stung.

His casual dismissal could have thrown us off track as we began our year of kindness. In that moment, it would have been easy to think, *Well, if that's the way it's going to be . . . forget it. I don't need the humiliation of a stranger's rejection.*

Though I've never turned down a gift card, I know I've rejected other acts of kindness. I've deflected compliments and turned down offers of help. In our moment of rejection, as uncomfortable as it felt, we were forced to ask ourselves the question: *Why be kind?*

As I thought about the question later, I was reminded of this truth: "Do not be overcome by evil, but overcome evil with good." Our willingness to be kind shouldn't be predicated on how someone else will respond; rather, it should stem simply from knowing that God desires for us to be kind. God sees our hearts, and our kindness is pleasing to him.

— Kristin

— Today's Act of Kindness —

Think of a time when you didn't thank someone
for a kindness he or she extended to you. If you
can, reach out and thank this person now.

Monthly Habit #1: Encourage

Encourage each other and build each other up, just as you are already doing.
1 THESSALONIANS 5:11

Sometimes in the busyness of life, creating an ongoing habit can be challenging. To battle this, our family decided that each month, along with doing small daily kind acts, we would focus on four kindness habits. We posted these four habits on our kitchen chalkboard, and we talked about them during our dinner times. Our first monthly habit was to offer encouragement to someone.

One evening when I asked for suggestions of who might need to be encouraged, my older son told us about another student in his class who had a debilitating illness. The boy was not a close friend of my son, but he had noticed that this boy had missed a number of days from school recently because of his illness. My son asked if we could offer him some cheer.

We agreed this would be a great idea, and the kids discussed what might encourage the boy. They decided that sending him movie tickets and a card would be the best thing to do, so my older son took out a card and the kids wrote words of encouragement and comfort to a young man they hardly knew.

The next morning my son took the note and gift card to school, explained to the secretaries what we were doing, and asked if they would mind sending it on to the boy and his family. They readily agreed and thanked my son for his thoughtfulness. When he came home he told us about his experience and how he felt good for offering encouragement to someone in need of a little support.

Encouraging one another and building one another up can be such a simple thing, but it requires us to intentionally recognize the needs around us. Just like my son did, we can stop each month to send a little note, to make a phone call, or even just to text someone to let them know that someone cares and has considered their needs.

— *Kendra*

— Today's Act of Kindness —

Write an encouraging note to someone
who may need a pick-me-up.

Monthly Habit #2: Thank

Give thanks to the LORD and proclaim his greatness.
Let the whole world know what he has done.
PSALM 105:1

The second monthly habit for keeping kindness at the forefront of my family's thoughts each month is to thank someone. We always try to come up with people who don't receive many thank-yous for what they do. For example, my children have thanked custodians at their school for keeping the bathrooms clean, our neighbors for helping us with our driveway in the winter, and our pastor for his messages that he works so hard on each week.

Each time we write a thank-you card, we try to think about all the ways we are grateful for these people and list the ways we've been blessed by their hard work. My children take responsibility for writing the cards themselves, and they hand them out when appropriate. It has become a fun challenge for us to look around for others who deserve thanks but rarely receive it. This in turn has fostered gratitude in our family for all the ways the work of others has blessed us.

It can be so easy to rush through our days without seeing the ways that others have helped our lives or bettered our communities. In fact, when our kids gave a handwritten thank-you note to the custodian at their school, he was so impressed, telling them it was the first time someone had written him one. When we take the time to notice what others do, especially behind the scenes, it reminds us of how grateful we are for the community of people around us and all the ways we benefit from a job done well. It is just another way we can give praise to the Lord, proclaiming and making known the things he has done.

— *Kendra*

— Today's Act of Kindness —

Notice the hard work of someone in your life, and send this person a thank-you note listing all the ways you are grateful for his or her hard work.

Monthly Habit #3: Bless

The generous will prosper; those who refresh others will themselves be refreshed.
PROVERBS 11:25

The third habit that helps us focus on kindness throughout the month is choosing to bless someone. This blessing can take many forms, anything from sending flowers to a neighbor who lost a loved one, buying stocking stuffers for kids who utilize our local food shelf, picking up extra school supplies in the fall, or volunteering at a local homeless shelter. There really is no limit to whom you can bless or what you can do to bless others each month.

Sometimes my children will do simple things to bless others, such as including a child who doesn't normally get picked to play a game or sharing their toys with a sibling. We as adults have paid for another person's lunch, given someone a ride, and spent time with a friend who just needed to talk. There are lots of ways to bless others, and teaching ourselves and our children to notice needs and act on them is another way we are all learning to be kind each month. If we aren't sure where to start or what to do, we'll often ask our kids (and ourselves): What have others done that has blessed us? Is there someone else we could pass that blessing on to?

Blessing others can be done in tangible ways, like buying someone a cup of coffee or a meal, or it can be offered through our words, simply letting someone know how they've benefited our lives. We don't always have to spend money to show kindness toward others. Sometimes the most thoughtful thing we can do is to show up and be present for the people around us. It's also good to remember that our kind acts don't benefit just others, but they benefit us as well. Proverbs 11 tells us that a generous person will prosper; whoever refreshes others will be refreshed. What a wonderful benefit we can receive by simply being a blessing to others!

— *Kendra*

— Today's Act of Kindness —

Find someone you can bless, and see if it doesn't
bring refreshment to your own life.

Monthly Habit #4: Serve

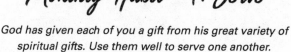

God has given each of you a gift from his great variety of
spiritual gifts. Use them well to serve one another.
1 PETER 4:10

The fourth habit of serving others is one that takes a bit of intentionality, but it also has the potential to be one of the most memorable of all the habits because it requires a sacrifice of time or resources.

My family has incorporated serving others into our daily acts of kindness by shoveling a neighbor's driveway in the winter or taking care of someone's house while they're gone on vacation. Throughout the year we try to find activities, either through church or a nonprofit organization in our community, that we can partner with in service to others. We've volunteered at homeless shelters, cleaned up local parks, painted community centers and schools, and washed windows at a local nursing home.

There are so many creative ways you can serve others. It can be done formally, like volunteering at a shelter, or informally, like helping out a neighbor. Along with being genuinely kind, serving others reminds us to consider putting someone else's needs before our own. It increases our desire to do something to help others out.

Serving is the action of kindness, the outward expression of linking ourselves to others, allowing us to use the gifts God has given us. Once we begin to notice needs in our neighborhoods or communities, it's hard to stop noticing—and even harder not to do anything about them. The habit of serving is one that becomes ingrained in us the more we do it.

These four monthly habits described in the last few devotions can be done as daily acts of kindness or in addition to what you are already doing. The point is that we want to establish these four habits firmly in our lives and not get stuck doing only familiar things. Kindness habits help us to make kindness a daily practice rather than one-off, occasional gestures.

— *Kendra*

— Today's Act of Kindness —

Find a simple way to serve someone in your life,
or take a small step toward a larger project you'd
like to accomplish in your community.

Be Still

Be still, and know that I am God; I will be exalted among
the nations, I will be exalted in the earth.
PSALM 46:10, NIV

In my mind, rest is one of the biggest ways we can be kind to ourselves. When God says, "Be still, and know that I am God," I take that literally. One evening as I sat rocking my seven-month-old, I thought about the idea of stillness. It had been a relentlessly busy month in our household, and I couldn't wait for a break. My husband had four out-of-town work trips within a two-week time span. I spent a weekend helping with one conference, closely followed by several days attending a different conference out of state.

Finally home again, I felt ready to drop.

I finished feeding my daughter. Normally, I would be in a hurry to get her back into bed, but instead I paused. I smoothed my palm over her back, felt her soft hair on my neck, heard her noisy breaths whiffling in chorus with her white-noise machine.

She's my third child, and I think this time more than any other, I've learned how to revel in her babyhood. My five-year-old still sits in my lap sometimes, but her coltish arms and legs sprawl haphazardly. There is no way to tuck her in close to my chest as I can the baby. So I know that these moments of rest, late at night, are fleeting. It's the stillness of these moments that gives them significance.

Here in this moment, there is only peace. I'm struck by the idea that maybe the reason my stillness is significant to God is because in the regular pace of life, stillness is rare. It is precious. The God of the universe revels in the moments when he can hold me close to his heart, because he knows that pretty soon, I'll be off and running again. But while this season of stillness lasts, I'll cherish it.

— *Kristin*

— Today's Act of Kindness —

Be kind to yourself by taking some time to rest, even if
it's just for a few moments. Lock yourself in the bathroom
to escape, if you have to! Enjoy the stillness.

Snowblown

Don't forget to do good and to share with those in need.
These are the sacrifices that please God.
HEBREWS 13:16

Bleary-eyed, I raised my head off the pillow as my husband attempted to move stealthily across our bedroom and out the door extra early one morning. The forecast had promised at least a foot of snow overnight, and he was getting up to snowblow a path out before we had to get to school-bus stops and jobs.

I got the kids up and moving, made coffee, and fed everyone breakfast, and after all that, I realized Aaron was still gone. I peered out the living room window and saw nothing but a freshly cleared, empty driveway. Turning my head, I spotted him—a snow-dusted figure slowly plowing his way down the sidewalks—headed toward our widowed neighbor's driveway.

This is not an uncommon sight during winter. When my husband heads out the door to take care of the snow, I'm never quite sure how long he will be gone. Once he gets started, more often than not he does a few extra sidewalks and driveways around our cul-de-sac, especially when he knows that someone has not been well or has a lot on their plate. In our snowy Minnesota climate, this is an easy way to bestow a tangible kindness on those around us.

Truth be told, it's a contagious kindness. Several people with snowblowers on our end of the neighborhood have started wandering past their own driveways and onto the sidewalks and driveways of neighbors nearby, ours included. It has become a give-and-take among neighbors—each of us keeping an eye out for one another on snowy days—and has deepened our sense of community.

And it all started because my husband simply took action. There were no elaborate plans, no discussions, no grand schemes behind it—he just started serving where he was and with what he had. These small sacrifices have served to pull our neighborhood closer together, and they are, undoubtedly, pleasing to God.

— Julie

— Today's Act of Kindness —

Serve someone else unexpectedly
with a sacrifice of your time.

When Kindness Flies High

Always be humble and gentle. Be patient with each other.
EPHESIANS 4:2

My husband flies to Arizona frequently for work. One particularly cold Minnesota winter, we decided we'd take our four kids and spend a week in Phoenix since my husband would need to be there for business anyway. I was a little nervous to take four children through airports and security lines, especially when our youngest was just a little over a year old and at a stage where she did not want to be held, preferring to explore the world around her.

I planned and prepared as much as I could ahead of time—we showed up that morning with sippy cups, snacks, books, and other activities to keep the kids entertained. The check-in lines were especially long that day, and as we printed off our tickets, I wondered how the kids would do. I needn't have worried as an airport security officer waved to our family, hurrying us through a family line while making conversation with our kids about where we were going and if they were excited. My kids paid no attention to the machines as they told him of their excitement for warmer weather and the promise of a pool to swim in each day. He smiled and nodded, handing them each a sticker and wishing us a safe and happy flight. As we gathered our things and headed for our plane, I was overwhelmed with gratitude for the kindness of this stranger.

We get to choose each day whom we will show kindness toward. We get to decide whether or not we show kindness to strangers who will never be able to repay us and, most likely, we will never see again. The question is, what will we do when being kind has no benefit to us? Will we still be patient, gentle, and humble? This security officer went out of his way to show my family patience when we needed it, even though it wasn't required of him. We should never underestimate the power of being gentle and kind to strangers.

— Kendra

— Today's Act of Kindness —

Go out of your way to show kindness to someone
who will never be able to repay you.

When You Just Don't Want to Do It

Jesus replied, "'You must love the LORD your God with all your heart, all your soul, and all your mind.' This is the first and greatest commandment. A second is equally important: 'Love your neighbor as yourself.'"

MATTHEW 22:37-39

Standing outside the elevator in my suit and heels, I sighed loudly. I was late for a free legal-advice meeting that I didn't want to host. I was simply too busy, and my attitude was the result of other more pressing issues vying for my attention that afternoon.

After grousing during the entire drive, I parked and then sat in the car a moment longer than necessary. I gave myself a silent shake about bad attitudes and said a quick prayer. I prayed that this time I was about to spend—time that felt like such a waste—would be used for good. I asked for forgiveness for my bad attitude and handed the time over to God.

I marched into the building and discovered my appointment waiting for me in the meeting room, tears streaming down her face. As I walked back out of the building a long time later, having stayed longer than I intended, having done far more than what was technically necessary, I shed a tear or two of my own.

Because of my bad attitude, I almost missed an opportunity to use my skills to help someone else. Because I was busy complaining, I almost missed out on the best part of my day. Because I was so focused on what I wanted to accomplish, I almost missed what God wanted to accomplish.

We are called to love God with our whole hearts, souls, and minds, and to love our neighbors as ourselves. Opportunities to love others often come shrouded in inconvenience and, when measured by the world's standards, may look like a complete waste of time. Do not be fooled into thinking that slowing down and setting aside your own agenda to show love to another is wasted effort. God will use us to change the world, one person at a time, if only we let him.

— Julie

— Today's Act of Kindness —

Is there something you are grumbling about doing?
Ask God to use that thing to bless someone else.

When Kindness Is a Listening Ear

My dear brothers and sisters, take note of this: Everyone should be quick to listen, slow to speak.
JAMES 1:19, NIV

"I am just so sorry. I don't know what else to say, but I'm sorry."

These words were spoken to me by a dear friend over dinner just days after I had gotten the news that my sister's cancer had returned more fiercely than before and her prognosis was poor.

Although no one around me would verbalize the thought, I knew everyone was thinking the same thing: she might not make it this time. By contrast, the things people said aloud sounded flat and superficial. They meant well, I knew, with their kind words like "God's in control" and "She'll be okay."

I appreciated the sentiment, but I wasn't so sure. As I sat across from my friend and the world swirled around us, life going on as usual, she listened as I once again explained what had happened to my sister.

And then I waited for her to respond like so many others had before, filling up the air with kind thoughts. But she didn't. Instead she looked at me, tears in her eyes, and simply said, "I am just so sorry. I don't know what else to say, but I'm sorry. Sorry this is happening to you, your sister, your family." And then she was quiet, allowing the sadness of it all to be there in our midst, offering no pat answers or token encouragement. It was just what I needed after one of the hardest weeks of my life: someone willing to just sit and be with me in the sadness.

There's something to be said about being able to be present with someone in the midst of their pain. To be able to stop—to take a break from the distractions of life—and acknowledge someone's suffering. To join them in their pain.

Be quick to listen and slow to speak. Your silence may be just the comfort someone else needs.

— Kendra

— Today's Act of Kindness —

Take a few minutes to listen to someone who is going through a hard time, without offering advice or platitudes. Instead, offer to pray for them.

Willing Hands

*From [Christ] the whole body, joined and held together by every supporting
ligament, grows and builds itself up in love, as each part does its work.*
EPHESIANS 4:16, NIV

I'm going to be honest in saying I'm not really a "kid person." Oh, I love my own kids, and there's a special place in my heart for my nieces and nephews and other children I know. But generally, I'm still not a kid person. I did a good job baby-sitting when I was a teenager because I didn't want to let anyone down, but my heart wasn't really in it. And God bless preschool teachers and day-care providers, because the thought of working either of those jobs makes me want to break out in hives.

This is why I was surprised to find myself, every other week, volunteering in the toddler room at church. It started out of necessity—my church needed more volunteers, and as a parent with children that age, it seemed like a given that I would help out. But as the weeks went on, I found myself actually enjoying it. I didn't mind the messes. I liked snuggling kids until they were confident enough to leave my arms and venture off to find a toy. And I loved watching kids grow and change from when they started with us at eighteen months old until the time they "graduated" to the next class at thirty-six months. Even though they weren't "my" kids, it was still fun to see their unique personalities emerge.

Sometimes we're asked to use our gifts to serve God and others. But other times, we're asked to just use our hands—no special gifts required. Being part of a community means that sometimes we need to put the needs of the collective body above our own, working together as the body of Christ. When we honor God and others by stepping in to serve, we find unexpected benefits, like snuggles from sweet kids, camaraderie with the other volunteers, and friendships with new families in the church.

Consider how God might be asking you to serve in an area where you are not particularly gifted but you have able hands ready to do the work.

— Kristin

— Today's Act of Kindness —

Spend an hour serving someone else, regardless of whether
or not the skills required are part of your gifting.

Use Your Gifts

In his grace, God has given us different gifts for doing certain things well.
ROMANS 12:6

My husband is a drummer. You will often find him absentmindedly tapping out rhythms on any available surface as he concentrates on whatever task is before him. Music, to him, is like oxygen to the rest of us. He creates playlists for every possible occasion, and his musical selections are both wide-ranging and of impeccable taste.

It was years ago when he first put together a playlist for someone outside our immediate family. We did not know her well, but she was going through a difficult time, and my husband gifted her a playlist of worship music. Over the years, my husband has quietly slipped individually curated playlists of worship music to people he has met in a variety of settings.

He is bold in sharing his love of Jesus through music in a way I've never seen anyone else do and would never have contemplated doing myself. When he discovered that a new coworker was battling cancer early this past fall, he sent her a playlist and an encouraging note. She died this past December, and my husband attended the wake. As he was standing in the long and winding receiving line, he tuned in to the music playing softly in the background. He found himself enjoying the music and then realized it was the playlist he had put together for her.

In speaking with her family, he learned how much she had loved the music he gave her, how she had played and replayed that playlist in the months before she died, and how she had selected that music for her wake.

As my husband quietly relayed the story to me that evening, I realized, once again, that God uses my husband's love of music to enable him to share his faith in a way that is beautifully unique. Romans 12:6 reminds us that God gives us different gifts for our various roles in his Kingdom. The question is, how are you using your God-given gifts to further his Kingdom?

— *Julie*

— Today's Act of Kindness —

Think about what you love to do, and identify one way
you can use it to show Jesus' love to someone else.

What's Wrong with This Picture?

Therefore, I urge you, brothers and sisters, in view of God's mercy, to offer your bodies as a living sacrifice, holy and pleasing to God—this is your true and proper worship.
ROMANS 12:1, NIV

I have a confession: I don't take a lot of selfies. But when I do, I have to take about a million until I get one I deem acceptable. The other day, I was trying to take a picture I liked, and it took *forever*. I switched from side to side; I tried smiling with my mouth open and then closed. As I looked through them, the running "what's wrong with this picture" thinking just wouldn't quit—my hair was out of place, my smile looked awkward, or the lighting was wrong.

That running dialogue can be heartbreakingly negative. After all, the things I deem "unacceptable" are all facets of me. It can make me feel as though *I'm* the unacceptable one. What's harder still is that these are photos of me at my best. Hair done, makeup on, perfectly posed. The truth is, there are many days when I wear my glasses all day, shove my hair into a ponytail, and wear workout pants I don't even bother working out in.

Sometimes the hardest acts of kindness are the ones we show ourselves. Yet I'm reminded that the Bible asks us to "offer [our] bodies as a living sacrifice, holy and pleasing to God—this is [our] true and proper worship." God doesn't make mistakes, and he sees us as lovely and pleasing. Why shouldn't we view ourselves the way he does?

That not-quite-put-together woman? She's me too. She's the woman my husband married, the one he wakes up next to each day and kisses before he leaves for work. She's the one who comforts our children when they wake up scared or sick, the one who rocks the baby to sleep. In those moments, she has no thought for makeup or hair, no concern over whether what she's wearing is fashionable.

She is lovely because she is real. She's a wife, a mom, a daughter, a sister, a friend. She's you, too. You are loved and accepted and acceptable just as you are.

— *Kristin*

— Today's Act of Kindness —

Whenever you catch yourself saying something negative about yourself, even in your head, remind yourself of how God sees you and choose to say something kind about yourself instead.

The Football Fan

"What should we do then?" the crowd asked. John answered,
"Anyone who has two shirts should share with the one who has
none, and anyone who has food should do the same."
LUKE 3:10-11, NIV

My husband, Tim, is a huge football fan. More specifically, as a native of Denver, he's a huge Broncos fan. It's not unusual to see us as a family wearing Broncos colors to church during football season. In fact, our children learned early on to identify blue and orange as Broncos colors.

Because he is such a fan, my husband has a variety of pieces of Broncos apparel that he wears quite often. One evening while Tim was serving a meal at our local homeless shelter, a man coming through the dinner line struck up a conversation with him.

"Hey, Broncos! I love the Broncos! You think this is it, their year?" he asked, smiling as they continued to talk stats and Super Bowl odds. As the night progressed, any time this man and Tim ran across each other, the man would light up and they'd share a smile.

Finally, toward the end of the night, Tim searched for the man. Finding him, he pulled off his Broncos shirt and threw it to the guy, retaining his undershirt. Clearly, he takes the whole give-someone-the-shirt-off-your-back message of Luke 3 literally, sharing both food and his shirt with the man over the course of the evening. And although the man had a shirt of his own, he seemed touched that Tim cared enough to give him something he loved.

"Are you serious?" the man asked, shocked. "Are you sure?"

The two hugged each other like long-lost best friends, and Tim headed out for the night. But the next night, when Tim showed up to drop off some gifts for an event, he saw the man again. Lo and behold, he was wearing the Broncos shirt.

— Kristin

— Today's Act of Kindness —

Share something you love with someone else. This
could take many forms but can be as simple as making
your favorite dessert and sharing it with neighbors.

Passing Kindness On

Don't be selfish; don't try to impress others. Be humble, thinking of others as better than yourselves. Don't look out only for your own interests, but take an interest in others, too.

PHILIPPIANS 2:3-4

This is the first winter our kids are becoming proficient skiers, and my husband has been taking them up the ski lifts and sending them down the easier runs on their own at the small ski hill near our house. My daughter, our most adventurous child, has embraced confidence and freedom as she grows more experienced and skilled.

It was over a cozy dinner after their most recent ski outing that the story came tumbling out. My children attend school in a Mandarin-immersion program, and their classroom assistants include teachers from China who are visiting as part of an international teaching program. Our daughter recognized one of the visiting teachers out on the slopes struggling by herself.

In a blink, my daughter skied over and invited the teacher to join our family for the afternoon. She saw someone in need and met that need—with zero coaching from her dad. My husband later told me how proud he was to watch as our daughter spent her afternoon sticking close to the teacher and sharing tips and tricks as the woman learned to ski.

My daughter's invitation became a precious and vivid memory for the teacher as she recounted her version of the story to me months later. Being greeted in her native language in the midst of a frustrating struggle, followed by an invitation to join our family, was profoundly touching. While my daughter may not have been thinking of Philippians 2:3-4 when faced with the choice of skiing independently or setting aside an afternoon to encourage one of her teachers, she certainly embodied the spirit and intent of today's verse in her choice.

While there are days when my husband and I wonder whether we are striking the right balance on this parenting journey, it is moments like these—when we realize that keeping our eyes and ears open for opportunities to help others is rubbing off on our children—that we are encouraged by what God is doing in our family.

— Julie

— Today's Act of Kindness —

Look for someone you can offer assistance to, and then do it.

Saying a Simple Yes

One person gives freely, yet gains even more; another
withholds unduly, but comes to poverty.
PROVERBS 11:24, NIV

Sometimes I feel like I can't make it out of a checkout line without someone asking me for a donation. Whether it be to support a children's hospital or to fund a local ice rink, it's commonplace to get asked to round up your change to the nearest dollar or donate extra money to a worthy cause.

For years, I felt awkward about this part of the exchange. Did I have to say yes? Was it rude if I said no? Would the cashier judge me if I didn't support the cause? Then a few years ago, I saw a news segment where the commentator argued that checkout donations only really help big corporations. "They're just another write-off for the company," he argued. "It's not like *you* get the credit for that donation." His argument made sense to me, so the next time a cashier asked if I'd like to donate to their cause of the week, I blithely said no. I didn't feel bad or awkward at all.

Fast-forward to our year of kindness. Suddenly, in my search for ways to practice one act of kindness each day, rounding up my change at the checkout or shelling out an extra dollar seemed like a pretty good idea. Instead of saying no, I began to say yes each time I was asked.

What I've come to realize is that neither response is inherently bad or wrong. The news commentator had a point, and yet I've decided to err on the side of saying yes. Why? Because we're called to "give freely." Because for me, it's an easy way to cultivate a habit of kindness. Because I've found that when I'm willing to say yes daily in small ways, like a checkout decision, I'm more apt to say yes to bigger acts of kindness too.

— *Kristin*

— Today's Act of Kindness —

The next time you're in a checkout line and the cashier asks if you'd like to round up your change or donate a dollar, say yes.

Wimpy Kindness

Each time he said, "My grace is all you need. My power works best in weakness." So now I am glad to boast about my weaknesses, so that the power of Christ can work through me. That's why I take pleasure in my weaknesses, and in the insults, hardships, persecutions, and troubles that I suffer for Christ. For when I am weak, then I am strong.

2 CORINTHIANS 12:9-10

There is a sizable community of Somali refugees that has relocated to my town. In the past decade and particularly in the past year, my community has struggled with assimilation on a number of issues involving racism, religion, and "otherness." Several residents, Christian and Muslim, have joined together to create a nonprofit to find common ground and spark dialogue about how to make our community safe and welcoming for everyone.

When I discovered that refugee families were arriving in our community in the dead of winter without coats and boots and warm clothes, I leapt at the chance to bring a national, abstract conversation to life in a tangible, personal way for my family.

And that is how I found myself huddled around the open trunk of my car with the two founding members of this nonprofit on a particularly cold and blustery winter day. My friends and I were donating warm clothes for a newly arrived refugee family, and the stares and smirks on faces of passersby stung momentarily as it occurred to me that we must have looked silly as we shifted bags of clothes between vehicles.

Being kind is frequently perceived as foolish and weak rather than as an admirable trait. Let's face it: being kind may never be viewed as powerful or strong; sometimes it may even be viewed as ridiculous.

Even so, we are commanded to love others and to be kind to those around us. Jesus provided the example, and he has called us to follow. Remember the exhortation of 2 Corinthians 12:9-10, and do not be dismayed or put off by the perception that your kindness is weakness. Being kind changes lives in ways that power cannot.

— Julie

— Today's Act of Kindness —

What preconceived notions of kindness as weakness or as foolishness do you believe? Ask God to help you let go of these misconceptions about helping others.

The Dressing-Room Disaster

O people, the LORD has told you what is good, and this is what he requires of you: to do what is right, to love mercy, and to walk humbly with your God.
MICAH 6:8

My feet thudded on the pavement. Heart pounding, I arrived at the door of the store, out of breath as I reached the dressing rooms.

My sister Katrina lay on the ground, her head nestled in a stranger's lap as the woman crooned softly to her, stroking her arm. She had collapsed in the dressing room, knocked unconscious by her battle with cancer and the effects it had ravaged on her body. She lay pale and still, her eyes half closed as she continued to recover from the faint, when I arrived flushed and breathless.

To be honest, I barely noticed the stranger in my haste to see my sister. Her indistinct features, soothing voice, and assurance that she was an off-duty nurse barely registered in the midst of my panic. As we waited for an ambulance and I gathered my sister to myself, I simply forgot about the woman.

For many years, my memory of that day was eclipsed by my anguish, knowing that even as Katrina lay there, disoriented and alone, multiple strangers stepped over her in their haste to try on sweaters and jeans. I forgot all about that stranger's kindness. I forgot that someone, an off-duty nurse, *did* care. She took the time to set aside her clothing items and simply help. She recognized what had happened to Katrina, knew the confusion she would feel upon regaining consciousness, and treated her gently.

Looking back now, I'm so grateful for that stranger. I'm so thankful she took the words of Micah 6:8 to heart as she showed mercy and compassion for another. Because of her kindness, I've been able to reframe my memories, seeing that difficult time not only through a haze of remembered pain but also through a lens of remembered kindness.

— Kristin

— Today's Act of Kindness —

Show a stranger kindness, even if it's as simple as opening the
door for them or putting their shopping cart back in the cart corral.

The Practice of Written Prayer

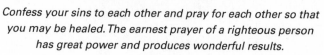

*Confess your sins to each other and pray for each other so that
you may be healed. The earnest prayer of a righteous person
has great power and produces wonderful results.*

JAMES 5:16

It was a decade ago when my friend sent out a New Year's prayer e-mail to our group of girlfriends. She incorporated a paragraph for each of us individually, praying over the tough things in our lives and speaking a blessing over our lives in the year to come.

Those written words touched me profoundly, and I realized the incredible impact of written prayer—it's a gift to have the ability to reread the prayer and secretly soak in the words, to fold it up and carry it around in my pocket. It's one thing for someone to tell you that they are praying for you, but it is something else entirely to hold in your hands the actual prayer that someone has prayed over you.

I toyed with this idea of written prayer for a few years and would occasionally send an e-mail or a handwritten note to someone I knew was walking through a difficult time. The response was always overwhelmingly positive. It wasn't until two years ago that I adopted the practice of written prayer sent as text messages. Someone I love was struggling on a daily basis, and I began texting her quick prayers several times a week. It was quick and easy for me, and it reached her immediately and effortlessly.

We both loved texting as a way to send prayers to one another so much that we expanded our text prayer correspondence to include a group text of women who would all pray for one another. As today's verse in James reminds us, our prayers for others are both powerful and effective. Sometimes when life looks impossibly difficult, the biggest blessing you can give another is the gift of a prayer written in the spirit of James 5:16.

— Julie

— Today's Act of Kindness —

Encourage someone through a written prayer
via text, e-mail, or social media.

Do Small Things with Great Love

Do everything with love.
1 CORINTHIANS 16:14

When she was just fourteen, my mom experienced the loss of her own mother. My mom was the youngest of four children, and her older siblings were already grown, so she lived alone with her dad.

When the time came to bring a dish to a gathering of the Luther League at her church, my mom confided in a good friend that she didn't know what to do; all her friends' mothers would be doing the cooking, and my mom didn't know how to make the Jell-O she was supposed to bring. The friend went home and told her mother about my mom's predicament. In response, that friend's mother took the time to write out three pages of Jell-O recipes, front and back, so my mom would have ideas of different things to bring to church anytime there was a function.

The funny thing about those pages of recipes is that my mom still has all of them, now yellowed with age. They still show the kindness of a mother to a young woman who needed help. One recipe that includes strawberries and Cool Whip has even become a family favorite of ours over the years.

As I listen to my mom tell this story, as I watch her pull out the recipes and run her hands over the worn pages, I'm sure that the other mother did not realize that fifty years later, those recipes would still matter to my mom. She never knew that those handwritten pages would become a reminder of the kindness of another during a difficult time.

When we do everything in love, we'll begin to see and notice the small ways we can have a big impact on someone's day. Who knows? Maybe fifty years from now, someone else will tell their own story of our kindness to them, just when they needed it most.

— Kendra

— Today's Act of Kindness —

Take time to listen for a simple need that someone
has, and then take a step to meet that need.

Turning Scraps into Treasure

Don't look out only for your own interests, but take an interest in others, too.
PHILIPPIANS 2:4

When I picked up my daughter from piano lessons, her teacher pulled me aside for an extra moment to show me a beautiful blanket. It was hand knit by a woman who, keeping needles and yarn by her side constantly, spends all her spare minutes with knitting needles flying. The blankets she knits are gorgeous, and she drops them off at Karen's house, knowing that our school's music teacher will quietly gift them to school families who need a helping hand.

Running my hands over the perfect stitches and the multihued chevron design, tears sprang to my eyes because of the love and the time I knew she poured into such a gift. Karen then said, "But Julie, you haven't seen the best part—look at what she does with the scraps."

Setting one blanket down, I shifted my attention across the room as the stunning creation was unfurled. It was the same chevron pattern, but this version was knit from all the pieces of leftover yarn—the scraps—and it was a magnificent riot of colors whose crazy combination of hues somehow blended into a one-of-a-kind masterpiece.

That blanket was knit from the scraps—the little ends and pieces that most would have discarded as worthless, as too small to make a difference, as a waste of time. But all knitted together, they became the most beautiful blanket I've ever seen. This idea has been banging around my head since I held that blanket: what we consider "scraps"—those things about us that are less than perfect—can be used by God in the most glorious ways.

As we lift our lives to God with open hands, let's ask him how we can be used to pour into those around us. Let's pray for opportunities to look beyond our own interests and instead respond to the needs and interests of those we meet. May we listen carefully for how God might want to use the scraps of our lives. It is often the things we deem worthless about ourselves that are used by God to provide immense blessing to others.

— Julie

— Today's Act of Kindness —

Spend time in prayer offering God the "scraps" of your life and asking him to use them to bless someone else immeasurably.

Starting Conversations about Kindness

Never let loyalty and kindness leave you! Tie them around your neck as a reminder. Write them deep within your heart.
PROVERBS 3:3

Suppertime at our house is a gathering time for our family. It's when we discuss the events of the day, activities that are happening, and how everyone is doing. It's also the time when we pray together, share needs, and talk about how to incorporate kindness into our everyday lives. As a parent, I find these meals to be especially meaningful as they have become a way for our family to connect with one another and to convey our family values on a regular basis.

These days, I am regularly struck by my family's ability to notice when there is opportunity to show kindness toward others and to note when others have been kind to them. For example, my kids have mentioned the child at school who was left out, and then they made sure to include him in activities. They've remembered the neighbors they like to visit regularly just to say hello. These acts are seemingly small and easily dismissible individually, but collectively they are creating habits of kindness in each of us.

Creating habits of kindness can start with daily or even weekly conversations. Start small and simple by asking questions like these: Who did you show kindness to today? Who showed kindness to you? Do you know someone who has been going through a hard time lately? What could you do to help?

By initiating conversations *about* kindness with others, we will begin to become more aware of ways we can *show* kindness to others. Again, these do not have to be big things—simple and small is the way to start. Did you hold the door open for the person behind you, smile and say hello to a stranger, or encourage a coworker? All these things matter. No kind act is too small to count, and talking about it with others is the first step in making kind acts a regular habit—a practical way to bind them around your neck and write them on your hearts.

— Kendra

— Today's Act of Kindness —

Ask your child, your spouse, or a friend how they
showed kindness today and what it meant to them.

When You've Been Scammed

One of them, when he saw that he was healed, came back to Jesus, shouting, "Praise God!" He fell to the ground at Jesus' feet, thanking him for what he had done. This man was a Samaritan. Jesus asked, "Didn't I heal ten men? Where are the other nine? Has no one returned to give glory to God except this foreigner?"

LUKE 17:15-18

Snookered. That's how I felt exactly three seconds after I handed five dollars to a young woman standing at the transit station who told me she was raising money for Feed My Starving Children.

To be fair, I was utterly distracted. My kids and I were in downtown Minneapolis, and I was trying to read a map, buy train tickets, and herd the kids to the correct side of the platform when she approached with a flyer and her request. My suspicions were confirmed when this young woman and her cronies crowded into the same train car. I overheard enough conversation to realize that they were on their way to the Mall of America and were hopping out at various stops to scam people into giving them cash.

Clearly, there was something about me that marked me as a target, and that burned more than losing my money. Rather than confronting her angrily, I prayed over the young woman and whatever had encouraged her to scam five dollars for a trip to the mall. I prayed that her current trajectory would be intersected by God in a mighty way.

After I prayed, I let it go. After all, how many of the ten lepers thanked Jesus when he healed them? Exactly one—and he was a despised Samaritan. And didn't Jesus know that would happen before he healed them? Jesus reached out anyway, fully knowing the result ahead of time. While being scammed was an excellent reminder to be smarter about the clues and the context in which I help someone out, it will not stop me from responding to someone's need in the future.

— *Julie*

— Today's Act of Kindness —

Consider a time when you felt duped by helping someone else.
Let it go, and then pray for the person who has scammed you.

Looking for the Good

*Be kind to each other, tenderhearted, forgiving one another,
just as God through Christ has forgiven you.*
EPHESIANS 4:32

My friend and I used the same doctor to assess our children's asthma, and each of us came out with a completely different experience. She found the doctor to be belligerent and smug, unwilling to listen to her. My family's experience was the complete opposite: the doctor found what others had missed among my daughter's breathing problems and treated her with compassion, encouraging her and giving her hope for better health. I wondered, *Whose opinion of this doctor was more correct?*

Some time later, another friend and I were talking about a mutual acquaintance who, from her perspective, had been harsh and uncaring toward another. While I could see how this person could respond in such a way, I knew that she also had the personality to vehemently defend things and people she believed in. She was a fighter. Again, I asked myself, *Whose assessment of this person is more correct?*

I believe the answer lies in the fact that each of us was equally fair in our evaluation and each opinion was equally correct. Who of us is completely good and right all the time? None of us, unfortunately. Who of us is mean spirited, smug, or incorrect in word or deed? All of us, at times. The truth is that we can be all these things—kind one day, unkind the next. Forgiving in one instance, holding a grudge in another. Although it is easy to find fault in others, how much better would it be to look for the good in those around us?

When we are faced with unpleasant people, we have a choice: we can be kind and compassionate, forgiving them as we remember how Christ forgave us, or we can hang on to anger and bitterness. Although healthy boundaries may need to be put in place so we do not allow ourselves to continually be hurt by another, we ultimately have the choice to forgive and move on.

— Kendra

— Today's Act of Kindness —

Instead of retaliating when someone has been unkind to you,
choose to respond with kindness, remembering the times when
you have acted out of character and needed some grace.

A Meal on the Doorstep

If someone has enough money to live well and sees a brother or sister in need but shows no compassion—how can God's love be in that person?
1 JOHN 3:17

I was sick and miserable, so weak that I wondered how I could walk up the stairs by myself, much less chase after my young children. After leaving a message asking for prayers for a quick recovery on the Facebook page for women in our church, I was inundated by comments that folks were praying and by offers to help out. While I appreciated each of the messages, a text from a friend spoke the loudest: "Can I bring you a meal?"

A few minutes later, I had yet to respond, but she had already texted again: "Never mind. I am bringing you a meal today! If you aren't able to answer the door, it's okay. I'll leave it outside."

All too often, I find myself saying to those who are struggling with a hardship, "Let me know if you need anything." Although my words are sincere, if I'm honest, they aren't always helpful. People don't really want to impose, and asking for help can be hard. Yet if we see someone in need and do nothing to help, how can the love we claim to have for God appear to be anything but hypocritical?

Instead, ask those who are struggling with an illness or emergency if you can do specific, concrete things to make life a little easier. There are simple, nonpushy ways to ask if you can help out: "What day could I bring a meal for you this week?" "I'm going to the grocery store this morning, what can I pick up for you?" "My girls would love to see your kids for a playdate. Could I come pick up your kids for a few hours on Saturday to give you a break?"

Your little act of kindness will go a long way to make someone who is struggling feel loved, cared for, and blessed.

— *Kristin*

— Today's Act of Kindness —

Think of someone you know who is struggling, and instead of saying "Let me know if you need anything," find a tangible way to meet their need.

The Forgotten Note

I urge you, first of all, to pray for all people. Ask God to help them; intercede on their behalf, and give thanks for them.
1 TIMOTHY 2:1

As the keynote speaker at a professional women's networking luncheon finished her last sentences, everyone around me slipped on their winter coats and made a beeline for the door. Having arrived late, I was seated at a hastily erected table in the back corner. The woman next to me, also a late arrival, leaned over and asked if, almost eight years ago, my daughter had attended a local day care.

As this woman's story unfolded, tears began pooling in my eyes.

Our daughters, roughly the same age, once attended the same day care center. Her daughter, they discovered, had something seriously wrong with her spine and was set to undergo a scary operation. I heard of her ordeal and sent an encouraging note through the day care staff, praying for her daughter and for their family. We had never met. I never heard what had happened to her daughter, and, honestly, I'd forgotten all about that note.

Recognizing my name on my luncheon name tag, this woman told me how beautifully the surgery had gone and how her daughter is now a healthy, thriving young girl. We spent several minutes catching up on our daughters before we each slipped back into our work days. Before we parted ways, she told me that my simple note, sent in that hard moment, meant so much to her that she has it still, eight years later.

As I left that luncheon, I said a little prayer of thanksgiving to God for reminding me of how a small act of kindness can profoundly impact someone else's life. Just as today's verse in 1 Timothy reminds us, we are to be generous in praying for others. God so often shines through us when we go out of our way with small kindnesses toward people we barely know.

— Julie

— Today's Act of Kindness —

Drop an old-fashioned note in the mail letting an acquaintance know that you are praying for them.

February

Hello, My Name Is Martha

But Martha was distracted by the big dinner she was preparing. She came to Jesus and said, "Lord, doesn't it seem unfair to you that my sister just sits here while I do all the work? Tell her to come and help me." But the Lord said to her, "My dear Martha, you are worried and upset over all these details! There is only one thing worth being concerned about. Mary has discovered it, and it will not be taken away from her."

LUKE 10:40-42

When I think of the name *Martha*, I think of two women: Martha Stewart and Martha, sister of Mary, friend of Jesus. In fact, I imagine that the Martha of the New Testament was similar to Ms. Stewart: efficient, organized, and living in a home without a mote of dust to be found. And while all of these could be considered good things, it was Martha, not Mary, whom Jesus gently admonished.

Lately I've been too much Martha and not enough Mary. Life has been so busy that I've missed the main course—the joy of simply being, of simply worshiping, of making time to quietly seek my Savior. It is so easy, at least for me, to fall into the Martha trap. I love to help others, to solve problems, to feel useful. It isn't bad to be a Martha. Marthas are essential. But it *is* bad to be a Martha all the time, because that's when I find myself striving out of my own energy and strength. Left to my own devices, being intentionally kind can leave me feeling drained and frustrated, especially when I'm faced with responding kindly to people or to situations that have me feeling decidedly unkind.

So I make sure I'm spending time in Scripture, filling my house with worship music, and praying regularly. Because I have a young family, I often find that those in-between moments in the shower or while I'm driving between activities are perfect moments to spend in prayer or to turn on a favorite worship song. When I spend time in God's presence, I'm better able to meet the day's events refreshed and encouraged and with a kind response, regardless of the response I may feel someone deserves.

— *Julie*

— Today's Act of Kindness —

Examine your own Mary-Martha balance. If you need to make an adjustment in the amount of time you are spending at the feet of Jesus, take a moment to write down what you are going to change.

The Forgotten Gift

*God demonstrates his own love for us in this: While
we were still sinners, Christ died for us.*
ROMANS 5:8, NIV

The year I met and married my husband, my future mother-in-law sent me a lovely box full of blue-and-silver wrapping paper and gift boxes. She knew they were my favorite colors, and she went out of her way to purchase them, package them up, and mail them across a distance of several states. Yet as wrapped up as I was in wedding plans, the box got lost in the maelstrom of wedding gifts, only to be recovered again months later. She must have thought I was so ungrateful!

Although I did drop the proverbial ball with my mother-in-law, our ingratitude as humans isn't really unexpected. After all, our sinful nature is the most ungrateful of all when it comes to receiving acts of kindness. Here's the ultimate demonstration of kindness: Christ gave us the gift of his death on the cross to cleanse us of our sins. Yet often our first response is, "Thanks, but you really didn't have to. I'm okay without it."

So many of us reject Christ and his gift of salvation, or diminish what a great gift it truly is by acting like it means less than it does. And what is his response? Does he say, "Well, if that's the way it's going to be . . . forget them!"? Thankfully, no. His response illustrates the love he has for us in spite of our sinful nature: he died for us even though we continue to sin.

Christ's mercy in the face of our ingratitude sets a new bar for us. Rather than focusing on how others *should* receive our kind acts, thereby souring our attitude when things go awry, let's focus on loving others despite their ingratitude, extending grace and kindness even if they don't deserve it.

Have you been hurt by someone's ingratitude? How can your expectations alter your attitude the next time a similar situation arises?

— *Kristin*

— Today's Act of Kindness —

Go out of your way to extend kindness to someone who may not deserve it, remembering that we don't deserve the gift Christ has given us. You could send them a note, give them a genuine compliment, or buy them a coffee.

Armed and Dangerous

Blessing and cursing come pouring out of the same mouth. Surely, my brothers and sisters, this is not right! Does a spring of water bubble out with both fresh water and bitter water? Does a fig tree produce olives, or a grapevine produce figs? No, and you can't draw fresh water from a salty spring.

JAMES 3:10-12

Our culture encourages sharp tongues. Reality TV is filled with women who thrive on the clever verbal smackdown, whose entire relevance is based on their razor-sharp tongues. Snarky disdain and smugness have become a national pastime, and social media is filled with trolls and name calling.

Despite how much we try to resist them, these verbal habits can seep into our churches, into our families, and into our daily interactions with friends, coworkers, and strangers. With a sharp comment or a snarky observation, we expose fellow women in their moments of need, instead of extending them mercy and grace by refusing to participate in the sarcasm circus.

We wield tremendous power through our words. I know women who have mastered the fine art of death by a thousand verbal cuts, and I know women who speak the language of encouragement and hope and empowerment. We have the power to choose daily, hourly, and even moment by moment which woman we will be. Scripture tells us that we cannot choose both: our words will be either salty or refreshing, deadly or life giving.

Watching our words is a continuous process that takes intentionality. I failed in this area last week—and even as the words of complaint about that other woman left my mouth, I was wishing I could pull them back. I was frustrated, and this person had hurt my feelings. While my words weren't vicious, they were enough to make me wince in regret and vow to do better.

We must be vigilant to guard our words and watch our tongues. If we aren't careful, it is easy to use words as a deadly weapon, often against other women and against the people we love most.

— *Julie*

— Today's Act of Kindness —

Guard your tongue, letting nothing mean-spirited, snarky, or smug cross your lips.

FEBRUARY 4

A Touching Celebration

Share each other's burdens, and in this way obey the law of Christ.
GALATIANS 6:2

When my daughter was first placed with us as a foster child, we were told it might not be permanent. Being foster parents, we knew our role was often to care for kids in the interim while parents got the help they needed or until another family member came forward to care for the child.

Jasmine was just so different. We loved her deeply and in a different way, and we secretly hoped we'd be able to keep her in our family. When she came to us, I was working full time and then found out I was also pregnant (surprise)! My coworkers and boss were incredibly supportive of me during this time. I had many doctor's appointments and social worker visits on my schedule, and the people I worked with did what they could to help me and support me.

Months later, when we finally got word that we would be able to adopt Jasmine, my coworkers were some of the first to celebrate with us. At the office baby shower for my soon-to-be-born son, Abram, I walked into the room, completely surprised that my coworkers had secretly turned it into a double baby shower for both Abram and Jasmine. The presents they gave us to celebrate these two children coming into our home and family were much more than just things; they represented an understanding of all of the uncertainty we had walked through the past several months in regard to whether Jasmine would get to stay in our home, and what a big deal it was to finally be able to keep Jasmine and celebrate her becoming a part of our family.

When we take the time to put ourselves in another's shoes and understand where they are coming from or what they are experiencing, we give them the gift of kindness through our compassion and empathy. It may seem like a small thing to do, but to the recipient it can be life changing. Never underestimate what a little empathy, a carrying or sharing of another's burdens and exemplifying Christ's life and behavior, may mean to someone else.

— *Kendra*

— Today's Act of Kindness —

Really listen to someone, empathize with them, and offer support for their current circumstances.

Lent Remixed

For forty days and forty nights he fasted and became very hungry.
During that time the devil came and said to him, "If you are the
Son of God, tell these stones to become loaves of bread."

MATTHEW 4:2-3

For years I struggled with how to pull Christ back into the center of our Easter celebration. After prayerful consideration, my family, along with Kendra's and Kristin's families, adopted what we call Lent Remixed.

Lent is the (roughly) forty-day period leading up to Easter, during which some Christian denominations pray and abstain from meat and other items. Although it is not a biblical command, there is spiritual significance to the number forty as a time of preparation, praying, and fasting before hearing from God.

Both Moses (Exodus 34:28) and Elijah (1 Kings 19:2-13) fasted and waited forty days before they received instruction from God. Jesus fasted and prayed for forty days and forty nights in the desert before he was tempted by Satan and, standing firm, began his public ministry (Matthew 4:2-3).

And so, in the tradition of Moses, Elijah, and Christ himself, many Christians observe Lent for the forty days (not counting Sundays) before Easter by preparing, fasting, and praying as they wait to celebrate the resurrection of our Lord and Savior, Jesus Christ.

I so love the significance and symbolism behind the Lenten tradition that my family now observes Lent but with a twist: we pick a different item to fast from each week. As we fast, we pray for a specific cause and do something tangible to meet needs related to that cause. For example, we might fast from electronics, pray about human trafficking, and make a donation to International Justice Mission during one of the weeks.

What I love is that the weekly fasting and prayerful focus on global, national, and local issues, when combined with tangible acts of kindness, prepares our hearts and minds for the somber, joyous, devastating beauty of Holy Week like nothing else we've ever done.

Lent Remixed, for my family, is an antidote to Easter-bunny overload during this season.

— Julie

— Today's Act of Kindness —

How might acts of kindness be worked into your own
traditions as you prepare to enter the Easter season?

When a Kind Act Does a Big Belly Flop

So let's not get tired of doing what is good. At just the right time
we will reap a harvest of blessing if we don't give up.

GALATIANS 6:9

"Well, that was a disaster," I muttered as my husband, Kyle, and I started cleaning up dinner.

We had just attempted to facilitate a devotion with our children during our family dinnertime. But thwarting our sober conversation, the baby decided it would be a good time to scream in her high chair, and my youngest son could not refrain from making inappropriate comments, inciting giggles from the other kids.

The meaningful conversation I'd planned to have during our supper quickly spiraled downward, right along with the food thrown on the floor. My patience wore thin, and I told the kids to hurry up so I could clean up in quiet. The loud sigh that followed was an all-too-obvious signal that I was tired and had had enough.

Not everything we plan to do works out. Not every act of kindness becomes a teachable moment. My kids are compassionate and loving, but they are still kids who sometimes throw tantrums, yell, get angry, and act greedy.

So why do I try? Why continue trying to teach kindness?

Because my kids need to know they are not the center of the universe. Kind acts toward others have taught my family about gratitude and compassion, grace and humility, in a way that little else has. And so, even when I mess up or my kids just don't get it, I won't stop or quit. I won't become weary in doing good, because I know God promises a harvest of blessing if I don't give up. I'm beginning to understand that a life without kindness is akin to a life without Christ. And when it comes right down to it, I want my children to see these acts of kindness—even the screw-ups—as acts of Christ, a little bit of heaven brought to earth.

— Kendra

— Today's Act of Kindness —

Think about the last kind act you did that didn't turn out how you had hoped. Instead of getting discouraged, think about what you learned through the experience.

Lying to Myself

I satisfy the weary ones and refresh everyone who languishes.
JEREMIAH 31:25, NASB

I lied twice in one Sunday. Then I lied again on the next Tuesday.

When a friend asked how I was doing that Sunday—with my husband's month-long recovery from surgery, with the pressure of doing all the household chores and daily care for our three children, including a newborn—I gave her a pat answer. As the words "I'm fine" tumbled insincerely from between frozen lips, I felt sick with the guilt weighing heavily in my stomach.

After my initial response, my friend questioned me further but then dropped it. On Tuesday, the woman I was visiting with called me out on my fib. "You're lying," she said, her laughter removing the sting of her words. "I remember those days."

My friend saw right through my forced words and canned reply. Honestly, it was a relief to have her tell me what I already knew, and I felt reassured that she saw me in the midst of a struggle yet didn't judge me for the pretense. I hadn't been lying just to others; I'd been lying to myself. I like to be in control. I like to hold things together, and I'll do it even if it's with Scotch tape and Band-Aids. When life gets hard and messy and ugly, I will fake it until I make it.

That week, I lied to my friends because I wanted to lie to myself. I wanted things to be okay, but they weren't. Most of all, I lied because my foolish pride wouldn't let me ask for help.

Sometimes we are the ones in need of a little kindness, a little care, and a little comfort.

Feeling humbled, I wiped tears from my eyes and prayed for forgiveness. *Lord, forgive my arrogance. Help me to realize that it's okay to ask for help and not feel ashamed or embarrassed by doing so. Help me to remember that you satisfy and refresh me when I am weary.*

— *Kristin*

— Today's Act of Kindness —

The next time a trusted friend asks how you're doing, answer them honestly. If you're in need of a little help, ask for it.

An Unexpected Kindness

I recall all you have done, O LORD; I remember your wonderful deeds of long ago.
PSALM 77:11

My husband, Kyle, had just lost his job. I was six months pregnant with our second child, and we were fostering two children. I was planning to stay home full time with the kids once our son was born. Kyle's job loss completely derailed our plans, making us unsure of what to do next. We began to ask ourselves questions: *Can I still quit my job? Would it be irresponsible to do so? What is the best thing for us to do financially? What is God asking of us?* These questions, along with the uncertainty of our future, left me feeling worried. Many nights I would lie in bed praying for my husband to find work and wondering what I should do about my job. I knew I wanted to make a wise decision—one that would honor the Lord and be the best thing for our growing family.

At the time, we were renting a house from friends of ours. The week after Kyle lost his job, my friend sent me a little note offering encouragement and letting me know they wouldn't be collecting a rent check for the following month. A gift, she said, to help alleviate any financial concerns while Kyle looked for another job.

That unexpected kindness was enough to carry us through the next couple of months' bills without too much concern, and it became a continual reminder of God's faithfulness when worry would start to creep in.

Kindness is a two-way street, something we give and something we receive from others. Psalm 77 tells us to remember all the ways we've been shown kindness and seen miracles over the years as an example of God's faithfulness in our lives. When we remember and are grateful for all the ways God has shown favor toward us, it can help us to more easily show kindness toward others.

— *Kendra*

— Today's Act of Kindness —

Offer some encouragement or support to someone
who may be going through a financial hardship.

Helping Hands

Now finish the work, so that your eager willingness to do it may be matched by your completion of it, according to your means. For if the willingness is there, the gift is acceptable according to what one has, not according to what one does not have.

2 CORINTHIANS 8:11-12, NIV

"Who is that?" someone asked my then-six-year-old niece Madeline. Looking around, she saw the woman this person was referring to and said casually, "Oh, her? That's our maid."

The funny thing was, this woman wasn't a maid. My niece wasn't trying to be rude or flippant in her assessment; it was true that Carol cleaned their home each week. Rather than a paid professional, however, she was simply a wonderful friend, one who volunteered her time to clean my sister Katrina's home. At the time, Katrina was sick with cancer. Between her brutal, draining treatments and caring for her two young children, she simply didn't have the energy or ability to keep up with cleaning the house.

Knowing this, Carol offered to help. She began to visit regularly, arriving on my sister's doorstep with buckets and cleaning supplies in hand. Each week, she spent several hours scrubbing and washing and cleaning the house from top to bottom. Vacuuming, dusting, scrubbing showers and toilets—all the thankless jobs that are part of housecleaning she did faithfully and with a smile for a period of several months.

It's easy to say to someone, "I'd like to help." But going the extra mile to follow through is the true measure of whether our good intentions actually materialize into kind actions. Scripture says that we are all given gifts in order to contribute to God's Kingdom, but just as important as the gifts themselves is our willingness and eagerness to use our gifts to serve. Even just a pair of hands, outstretched to help someone in need, can make all the difference.

— Kristin

— Today's Act of Kindness —

Giving your time to others is a gift. Volunteer an hour
of your time to help meet another person's need.

Saying Yes to Possibilities

*Jesus looked at them intently and said, "Humanly speaking, it
is impossible. But with God everything is possible."*

MATTHEW 19:26

As a mom, I say no a lot. "No, you can't climb up on the kitchen counter." "No, you can't hit your sister." "No, you can't come wandering out of your bedroom at 11 p.m. without a reason."

Sometimes, though, I say no because I'm feeling lazy or inconvenienced. Saying yes sometimes means making a mess, and often I'm just too tired of nagging my children to clean up, or I don't want to face more dirty laundry or dishes.

I'm not saying it's always a bad thing to say no. But sometimes, I've found that the easiest way to model kindness to my children is by showing them the possibilities of yes. As a child of God, I see the world as full of infinite possibilities. If the main word in my lexicon is *no*, is it possible for my children to see the world this way? We belong to a God of possibility—as Scripture says, with him, *everything* is possible—so I want to be a mom of possibility.

Now I try to say yes more often. "Yes, you can make toast with four different jellies striped across it." "Yes, we can get the paints out." "Yes, it can be Taco Tuesday." Yes, yes, yes.

Don't get me wrong, I still say no to plenty of things. But I'm working on saying yes more often because I not only want my kids to say yes to me, but I also want them to say yes to God. I want them to see that he is the God of infinite possibilities and unlimited chances, and that his mercies are new every morning. I want them to know that, as his children, they can experience the freedom of those truths.

— *Kristin*

— Today's Act of Kindness —

Look for opportunities to say yes. Say yes to one request—
be it from a coworker, a friend, or a child—that you would
normally say no to because it's inconvenient or messy.

Choosing Kindness over Condemnation

Dear friends, let us continue to love one another, for love comes from God. Anyone who loves is a child of God and knows God. But anyone who does not love does not know God, for God is love.

1 JOHN 4:7-8

A good friend of mine has an extended family member who has not always made wise choices. Years of addiction and chaos have led to several burned bridges within their family. This person will do well for a while and then inevitably take several steps backward in his recovery. It's happened more times than my friend can count.

But even with all his faults, he has had shining moments of compassion and care for my friend and others in her family, which remind her that he is still a human being with thoughts and feelings, who is deserving of kindness.

Just last winter my friend found out this person's heat was about to be shut off, and she and a few of her family members decided they would pay for the gas to heat his house through the rest of the winter months. Without a word to her relative, they simply took care of the need, while also taking care of him, showing once again the love that they have for him.

Loving others is not always easy. Often we do not see an obvious return on our investment of kindness or care. Although I am a huge advocate of appropriate boundaries, especially with family members who may try to use or abuse us, there are also times when we may be called to give a little more than we receive in a relationship. When that happens, we can remind ourselves of how much God has given to each of us. As 1 John reminds us, love comes first from God, and anyone who loves others is a child of God. When we remember God's love and grace for us, how can we not extend that same kindness toward others?

— Kendra

— Today's Act of Kindness —

Pray for a family member whom you may need to be reconciled with, and, if appropriate, ask God to show you one way you could extend kindness toward this person.

The Day I Got Nothing Done

Offer hospitality to one another without grumbling.
1 PETER 4:9, NIV

I thought she was stopping by to get a book, a quick blip on our morning radar, something to cross off my long to-do list. When she appeared at our door, son in tow, I stepped back and invited them in. They removed their shoes and traveled down my in-need-of-cleaning hallway to our dining room, settling in at our kitchen island, and I realized the quick stop I had envisioned was instead going to be a lengthier visit. As I found myself making coffee and pouring water, supervising kids and making small talk, I settled into the visit, putting my agenda on the back burner.

I'd had plans for the day, you see. But as our visit turned into one hour, then two, then three, I realized the day might not turn out as I had planned.

When they left that afternoon, I began to make dinner. But as we sat down at the table, my husband and I received text messages simultaneously, and I knew the day had changed yet again.

Resignedly, I gave up my plans for a quiet movie night with just the two of us. Instead, another friend and her son came to visit, and they settled onto our couch as she dealt with the fallout of a family crisis. As she made phone call after phone call, grief and worry etched in the lines of her face, I played quietly with her son so that she could talk, free of distraction.

When they finally left, I sat down, marveling at how my day had changed so markedly from my expectations. Though I got "nothing" done—no cleaning, no work, nothing crossed off my to-do list—at the end of the day, my *nothing* was someone else's *everything*. By offering hospitality without grumbling, I had done exactly what I needed to do that day. Sometimes all that kindness requires is our presence and undivided attention.

— *Kristin*

— Today's Act of Kindness —

Who needs the kindness of your attention?
Give it to them undividedly.

Kindness to a Kid

Jesus said, "Let the children come to me. Don't stop them! For the
Kingdom of Heaven belongs to those who are like these children."
MATTHEW 19:14

As a child, my experience with adults was oftentimes that they would spend a few minutes with us kids, then move on to more-adult companions and conversations, leaving us to play. My uncle Jimmy was different. He had a love for life and for people, especially kids, like few others my little eyes had seen. He was always glad to see me, seemingly never tired of the silliness of kids. Even though he worked long hours at a paper mill and was often tired, he would always take time to saddle the horses so we kids could go for a ride or to sit in the living room and tell us stories until late into the evening.

Looking back now, I realize the sacrifice it was for him to make time for us. He never made us feel like he didn't want us around, and he always had time to spend with us. It wasn't one big thing that he did but just small acts of kindness that added up over the years.

It's often the little things, rather than the big events, that make the most meaningful memories of our lives. My uncle lived out Jesus' teaching about how children are to be cherished. Uncle Jimmy, whether he knew it or not, consistently showed up in this little girl's life and made her feel like he had time for her and that she mattered. Looking back as an adult, I realize that his simple kindness formed one of the most meaningful relationships in my childhood. He didn't make any grand gestures. He just continued to show up, year after year.

Looking back on your life, who had a big impact on you? Whose words or actions made all the difference to you? Was it something big that they did, or was it little things over time? Remembering how we have been treated can give us insight into how to treat those around us today.

— Kendra

— Today's Act of Kindness —

Give some extra attention to a child in your life.

The Very Best Valentine

I am convinced that nothing can ever separate us from God's love. Neither death nor life, neither angels nor demons, neither our fears for today nor our worries about tomorrow—not even the powers of hell can separate us from God's love. No power in the sky above or in the earth below—indeed, nothing in all creation will ever be able to separate us from the love of God that is revealed in Christ Jesus our Lord.

ROMANS 8:38-39

My husband and I were going through a challenging time with one of our children. After a particularly difficult day, I knelt down until I was at eye level with my child's little face. I whispered to this little soul, "Do you know what? *I love you.* Nothing you can do will ever make me stop loving you."

As I spoke those words to the heart of my child, I could hear them echoing inside my own heart, from my Savior to me: *I love you without condition, without strings, without regard for your lists of regrets or accomplishments. I love you.*

How often do we allow something we've done—or something we've left undone—to determine our value? We so easily forget that value based on achievements is a worldly definition and has nothing to do with Christ. We need not strive, need not prove ourselves worthy of his love—because, quite honestly, we can't.

Friend, you are loved by God. You have no say in the matter, and you can do nothing to stop him from loving you. There is no place that you can go to escape his love, and there is no one who can separate us from God's love. Isn't that realization comforting?

No matter where you find yourself, no matter the dark valleys you may walk through, you are loved by God. You are loved so deeply that his only Son, Jesus, willingly went to his death on a cross for you—before you were born, before you knew of him, and regardless of whether you would ever choose to love him in return.

— Julie

— Today's Act of Kindness —

On this Hallmark holiday celebrating romantic love, unexpectedly shower someone besides your significant other with the overwhelming love of our Savior.

Love That Covers

*Most important of all, continue to show deep love for
each other, for love covers a multitude of sins.*
1 PETER 4:8

I was hurt and angry. Some women from my church had said unkind things about me, and I was ready to retaliate. I'd spent all day thinking up what I would say to each one of them.

I was in the right, and their actions were wrong—I was sure of it.

As I laid out in my mind the list of reasons why they were wrong and should be sorry for their words, I was taken aback by a fleeting thought I can attribute only to God, because it was so unlike anything else I was thinking about at the time:

Kendra, you can be so right, you're wrong.

Well, that's not what I wanted to hear, I thought.

As I began to ponder the idea, I realized that my heart toward the women who had hurt me wasn't right. I began to see that what I really wanted was retaliation (and some vindication) for the way I had been treated. Instead of owning the hurt I felt, I wanted to lash out in anger with an "I'm right and you're wrong" mentality. In reality, that line of thinking would have done little to repair the relationship I had with these women. If anything, it would only make things worse. I decided to take my heartache to the Lord, let him deal with the women and their harsh words, and not say anything I would possibly regret. I was reminded that sometimes "love covers a multitude of sins."

Sometimes wisdom and kindness lead us to confront others over their unfair words and actions, and sometimes they lead us to let things go. Discerning the best approach depends largely on the attitude of your heart. Before deciding what to do, examine your heart by asking yourself these questions: *Do I feel the urge to say something because I genuinely care about this person? Or am I trying to hurt them back by putting them in their place?* Our attitudes can make all the difference in approaching and handling challenging relationships with grace.

— *Kendra*

— Today's Act of Kindness —

Are you feeling hurt by someone? Choose your actions and your
words wisely as you deal with this challenging relationship.

The Road Less Traveled

Peter called to him, "Lord, if it's really you, tell me to come to you, walking on the water." "Yes, come," Jesus said. So Peter went over the side of the boat and walked on the water toward Jesus.

MATTHEW 14:28-29

When I was a tween, my dad decided to take a dirt road "shortcut" in western South Dakota on our way to Mount Rushmore. As the dirt road gradually faded into two dirt tracks with grass growing down the middle, we traveled through pastures and over cattle guards before our car came to a chugalugging stop at the top of a small, desolate hill.

With the car's hood open, my family milled around while my dad repeatedly banged the clogged air filter against a nearby rock. When one of my brothers directed our attention to the horizon, we glanced skyward and froze. Two fighter jets streaked silently overhead, flying fast and extremely low directly over us. It wasn't until the jets had almost disappeared over the horizon that we were blasted by the sonic boom.

My parents shared a silent look. We had obviously stumbled somewhere we did not belong. Dad hurriedly finished clearing the air filter, and we left the way we came, continuing our journey without further delay.

Adventure has a tendency to find my dad. He has a penchant for taking dirt roads wherever he goes. Because of it, our family road trips growing up were filled with beautiful sights, crazy adventures, and fond memories.

The same goes for following God. When you say yes to intentionally incorporating kindness into every part of your life, you'll often find yourself on the road less traveled. You'll be asked to trust God in difficult circumstances when everyone else doubts, to step forward when others step back, and to share when others hold tightly to what they have. The Gospels are filled with examples of Jesus encouraging his followers to step out in faith, just as he invited Peter to step out onto the water. Peter's lack of faith aside, he was brave enough to take the step, something no one else in the boat managed to do. Peter took the road less traveled, and Jesus asks us to do the same.

— Julie

— Today's Act of Kindness —

Prayerfully consider which of your comfort zones God might be asking you to step out of. Then take a step.

Go Tell It

Let us think of ways to motivate one another to acts of love and good works.
HEBREWS 10:24

A professor and mentor of mine once described the Victorian era's attitude toward acts of charity as one in which secrecy was paramount. Rather than seeking public approval, British citizens believed that hiding their good deeds increased the legitimacy of what they were doing—if people found out, the generosity didn't really "count."

It's that same entwining of secrecy and generosity that's addressed in Matthew 6:2-4: "When you give to someone in need, don't do as the hypocrites do—blowing trumpets in the synagogues and streets to call attention to their acts of charity! . . . When you give to someone in need, don't let your left hand know what your right hand is doing. Give your gifts in private, and your Father, who sees everything, will reward you."

Yet I struggle with this idea. There are many times when friends have posted about a charity or a cause they believe in, asking for donations or help, and I'm moved to do as they ask. Is it a bad thing to talk about organizations we believe in, have helped, and want others to help as well? How is this any different from what the hypocritical do-gooders from Matthew did?

I think it's more of a heart issue—one that's addressed in Hebrews, where we are told to "motivate one another to acts of love and good works." The folks parading their good deeds in the street did it with false humility—"See what I did for these poor people!"—rather than out of a genuine concern for those in need. If our own selfish pride is at the heart of our motivation, we're in trouble. But touting worthy causes out of a genuine belief that others need help and we can do something about it is never a bad idea.

Do you struggle to tell others of your good deeds? Recognize that there is a fine line between bragging on yourself and spurring others to do good works. Ask God to help you distinguish the difference so you can honor him as you go about his work.

— *Kristin*

— Today's Act of Kindness —

Post on social media or send an e-mail to some friends
about an organization you care deeply about, encouraging
them to consider supporting this ministry.

Mentoring as Kindness

One generation commends your works to another; they tell of your mighty acts.

PSALM 145:4, NIV

I always felt like I was in way over my head at my first job out of college. At just twenty-one years old, working with hospice patients and their families was a bit overwhelming and intimidating for me. One person who helped me get through that tough first year was my supervisor. As a wiser, older woman who had spent many years in the field, she knew I'd need support, and she spent hours with me each month talking through cases and offering me support, both professionally and personally. Looking back now, I realize the importance of her taking the time to mentor me as a young person in the workforce.

Just recently at a Bible study I attend, a fellow mom shared about how an older couple in her church has taken her and her family under their wing. My friend was not raised in a Christian environment, and this has put her in the predicament of having a lot of questions when it comes to Christlike parenting. Her older, wiser friends are there to offer her wisdom, love, and support anytime she needs them.

At any stage of life, we have the ability to mentor others. If we are young in our professions, we can mentor teenagers who are still deciding what they want to do with their lives. If we're well into our careers, we can take under our wings the new recruits who come into our offices. Even once we've retired, we can offer wisdom to the younger generations—wisdom that comes only from walking through many years of life's challenges.

Mentoring others is one way we can honor God's command in Psalm 145: we are to commend God's works to one another and tell of his mighty acts. We all have something to offer, and when we pass on our wisdom to others, we not only extend kindness to the person we're helping, but we honor God as well.

— Kendra

— Today's Act of Kindness —

Take a little time to mentor someone who may need
a little encouragement, instruction, or wisdom.

Choosing Peace

Real wisdom, God's wisdom, begins with a holy life and is characterized by getting along with others. It is gentle and reasonable, overflowing with mercy and blessings, not hot one day and cold the next, not two-faced. You can develop a healthy, robust community that lives right with God and enjoy its results only if you do the hard work of getting along with each other, treating each other with dignity and honor.
JAMES 3:17-18, MSG

It happened years ago, but the memory is still vivid. The preschool teacher pulled me aside during pickup to tell me that my then-three-year-old son had spit on another child during a disagreement.

My husband and I, horrified, invoked consequences. Still, I wasn't prepared for what I heard the next morning as I dropped my children off. The victim's words were a knife through my heart: "My mom says I can't be Jon's friend anymore." He wasn't saying it to be mean; he was simply repeating the instructions his mother gave him.

One of the things I love most about my husband is that he is not afraid to apologize. When my husband walked in the door that night, he handed me a Hallmark card with a sad puppy on the front and asked if I would help our son write an apology.

I set the card at the edge of the table, immediately knowing that I should also write a note to the other mom. I wrote my son's message, and he "signed" it . . . and then the card sat on the corner of the table for an additional three hours. I just didn't know what to say and how to say it in a way that the other mom would know that I truly meant my words. What if she didn't believe me?

It finally occurred to me that my extension of a sincere apology was all that was required on my part. I could not control how she would respond; I could only control my own attitude and actions. Just as today's verses state, that is all God asks us to do—to be gentle and reasonable and to try to make peace. The other person's response is up to them.

— Julie

— Today's Act of Kindness —

Do you need to apologize to someone? Don't let the sun set without reaching out with an apology.

Mercy after Meltdowns

If we confess our sins to him, he is faithful and just to forgive us our sins.

1 JOHN 1:9

It was a mama meltdown, an epic freak-out of gargantuan proportions. As if from a distance, I could hear myself shouting at my children to "Stop! *Just stop!*" But instead of stopping, my two-year-old continued screaming and my four-year-old looked at me with desolation in her eyes and burst into tears, and I couldn't help but follow suit. As I stopped the car on the side of the road, I soothingly told them, "Mommy was just frustrated and didn't mean to make you sad. Everything is okay." Yet inside, a little voice whispered to me, *Surely no "good" parent has days like this.*

The next day, as I was enjoying the rare pleasure of midday coffee with a friend, the topic arose—how hard it is to have our children inside all day during the unforgiving winter. Listening to her, I heard my own thoughts echoed: "I just get to the point where I don't even like myself and the way that I'm acting." I grabbed my coffee from the table, gulping down tears and the overwhelming feeling that I was doing everything wrong.

I think as parents we need to manage our expectations. As a child, I thought my parents were invincible. Part of growing up meant realizing that parents are people, too. We don't always know what to do. We feel hurt and lonely and scared, but we hide it so our children feel safe and loved.

As parents, we lavish our children with generosity. Yet we are inherently stingy with ourselves, forgetting that grace isn't available just on Sundays. Are you kind to yourself when you make mistakes, or do you berate yourself unendingly? Whether you're a parent or not, forgiving yourself just as God forgives you and resolving to do better tomorrow is one of the greatest kindnesses you can show yourself.

— *Kristin*

— Today's Act of Kindness —

Thank God for the mercy and forgiveness he extends
to us, then forgive yourself for an action you did,
an attitude you had, or words you said.

When Kindness Makes Time

By this everyone will know that you are my disciples, if you love one another.
JOHN 13:35, NIV

My oldest "child"—a young woman who lived with my family during her last two years of high school and is now in her early twenties—is still very close to our family. We continue to have a wonderful relationship with her and are so proud of the woman she has become. She calls and texts often and will stop by on a moment's notice. Although most of the time this is completely fine with me, there are days when my to-do list seems more important than taking the time to stop and visit. There are moments when it feels inconvenient because of my own schedule and agenda.

Here's the deal: sometimes kindness is inconvenient. Sometimes it takes time or money or both. Sometimes it involves stopping what we are doing and intentionally being with another person. Sometimes kindness is hard because it isn't always tangible. I can't always cross something off my list after showing kindness.

Just this week, a group I'm a part of had a discussion about the idea of legacy and what we'd like others to say about us when we're seventy-five years old. We all wrote down things we would want people to say about who we were, not what we did. We wanted them to say we were kind, loving, caring, good listeners—all things that involve how we treat other people. Not one of us said we hoped our friends would think we had really clean houses or manicured lawns. None of us said we wanted others to acknowledge how well we could cross things off our to-do lists, because the truth is, although tasks can certainly be important, they are not the *most* important thing, and they are not what we want to be remembered for.

John 13 reminds us of God's command to love one another: this is how we'll be known as Jesus' disciples. It may not always be the easy choice, and it certainly may not result in us crossing something off our to-do lists, but stopping to love others is always our best choice.

— *Kendra*

— Today's Act of Kindness —

When you're faced with the choice to get something
done or to stop and love someone, choose to love.

Embracing Imperfection

*Keep on loving each other as brothers and sisters. Don't forget to
show hospitality to strangers, for some who have done this have
entertained angels without realizing it!*

HEBREWS 13:1-2

I have a confession: my bathrooms are covered in wallpaper circa 1989. You know the kind—dusty-blue wagon wheels with the mauve highlights? Yep. I just need a few beribboned geese hanging on the wall to make the look complete. I've removed the wallpaper from my kitchen walls, but the cabinets, knobs, and countertops all suggest that my kitchen is in that odd historical spot—dated, but not quite dated enough to be considered endearingly vintage or even retro.

Sigh. And while other parts of my house have been updated, my decor will never be worthy of Pinterest.

Despite my uglyish kitchen and the "vintage" wallpaper, my husband and I regularly throw open our doors and invite people into our house, into our imperfect lives. Being real, being authentic, and inviting people to journey alongside us without any pretense of perfection is, honestly, so much easier than trying to be something we are not. I've discovered that when I'm willing to let my real self be the person others meet, they almost always respond in kind. And wouldn't you know that the real person is the most interesting and most delightful part of anyone I've ever met?

I would rather snort-laugh and ugly-cry with a new friend over hopes dashed, dreams dreamed, and everything in between, all while holding coffee mugs as we're curled up in the armchairs of my living room, than sip champagne, smile politely, and mingle in cocktail dresses over small talk with a room full of Important People.

Life is too short not to be authentic. Please don't let all the imperfect things in your life convince you to put off inviting others into your home and your life for another moment. As Christians, we are called to hospitality and to sharing our lives—including with strangers. Don't wait until your house, your family, and your life are perfect, because then you'll never do it.

– Julie

– Today's Act of Kindness –

Invite someone over this week for dinner, coffee, or an ice-cream
cone, and resist the urge to clean up before this person arrives.

Put-Ups

A good man brings good things out of the good stored up in his heart, and an evil man brings evil things out of the evil stored up in his heart. For the mouth speaks what the heart is full of.

LUKE 6:45, NIV

Not a day goes by that I don't struggle with negative self-talk. My thoughts run the gamut, critiquing everything from my parenting skills to my body to the social shyness that sometimes emerges. For example,

> *I can't wear this shirt; people can see my squishy mom arms. I need to work out.*
> *Ugh, I can't believe I said that to him. I sounded like an idiot.*
> *I forgot to put her library book in her backpack again. I'm such a bad mom.*

No matter the topic of internal dialogue, it is often easier to skew toward the negative than toward the positive. Being hard on ourselves seems to come more naturally to us than does reflecting on the things we like about ourselves. One day at work I was bemoaning something I didn't like about myself, and a coworker told me she needed to hear me say some "put-ups." *What in the world is that?* I thought. *Is it some new kind of diaper?*

Actually, put-ups are the antithesis of put-downs. So now in our house, when we hear someone say a negative statement about themselves, we have that person follow it up with three put-ups: *I'm a really fast reader. I'm amazing at Boggle. I'm creative.*

It's a mental exercise that may sound silly but is actually quite useful in our quest to be kind to ourselves. Because we require three put-ups to offset every one put-down, the overall focus is on the positive parts of ourselves: the best things, the fun things, the silly things.

Scripture says that "the mouth speaks what the heart is full of," so changing our internal dialogue is key to influencing our external dialogue: the ways in which we talk about ourselves and others.

— *Kristin*

— *Today's Act of Kindness* —

Show yourself some kindness by thinking of
three put-ups you can say about yourself.

Passion plus Knowledge

They delight in the law of the Lord, meditating on it day and night.
They are like trees planted along the riverbank, bearing fruit each
season. Their leaves never wither, and they prosper in all they do.

PSALM 1:2-3

As a novice gardener one especially warm spring a decade ago, I planted my tomato plants in March because I assumed the nursery selling them knew what it was doing. My poor plants were stunted by the cold soil and died. I had to buy new seedlings to replant in early June—at the same time that every other Minnesotan plants tomatoes.

I had passion, but I lacked knowledge. I enrolled in a gardening class and started hanging out with long-time gardeners. I began applying my new knowledge and experience against the information on the plant tags in the local nurseries. As I gained knowledge, I found myself less and less susceptible to being snookered.

My faith in Christ is not so different from my development as a gardener.

As a new Christian, I had a lot of passion but lacked knowledge. Passion without knowledge, in any subject, makes people vulnerable. It is only when a person has both passion and knowledge that they can carefully consider information, opinions, and ideas and then determine whether the information is accurate—or if, perhaps, something important has been omitted from the message.

As Christians, we have a biblical mandate to balance our passion and zeal with knowledge. It is easy to have passion; it takes intentionality and commitment and dedication to gain knowledge. Passion is not enough; we need a firm foundation in Scripture in order to navigate difficult people and difficult circumstances. Apart from Jesus, we are nothing, and nothing we do has any eternal value. Just as today's reading encourages us, our meditations on God's Word are what sustain our faith and help us reflect Jesus to others.

— Julie

— Today's Act of Kindness —

Are you consistently spending time in Scripture? If not,
take a moment to prayerfully consider how to make this
a daily habit. Start by reading the rest of Psalm 1.

When the World Doesn't Look Very Kind

If you are faithful in little things, you will be faithful in large ones. But if you are dishonest in little things, you won't be honest with greater responsibilities.

LUKE 16:10

Sometimes being kind feels as though we are swimming against the current of the world. It can be easy to get discouraged or overwhelmed when we're constantly being inundated with news of war, violence, poverty, and hunger. The list of needs in our world seems endless and daunting. It can be easy to give up on kindness because we wonder if our small acts even matter in such a broken world.

I've questioned this at times too. Then I remember how it felt to be a social worker holding the hand of a man who was dying while in hospice care. I recall how listening to him talk of his love for his children was priceless, and how looking into the eyes of someone who'd loved well for decades was comforting. How the ordinary moments of life—the simple smiles, hugs, and affection shown in words or deeds—were what made all the difference in the end.

The kind words we speak—these small acts of love—have ripple effects beyond just today. They continue to spread, creating a current of kind acts, loving gestures, and sweet memories. They carry on in our relationships with those around us, reminding us that being faithful in the small things is just as important to God as being faithful in the large ones.

Sometimes the best way to combat all the bad things that are happening around you is to do just one kind act in response. Don't underestimate how far it may go—it could have an effect far larger than you will ever know. And if you find yourself discouraged today as you think about everything that's happening around the world, choose to look for the good instead.

— *Kendra*

— Today's Act of Kindness —

Smile and say hello to others you pass as you go about your day. You never know what a kind word will do to change someone's day.

The Ministry of Meals

These three remain: faith, hope and love. But the greatest of these is love.
1 CORINTHIANS 13:13, NIV

I would consider myself to be a mediocre cook at best. I try to add new recipes to my repertoire, and my family seems happy enough with our daily fare, but spaghetti and tacos still seem to make the rounds at our house at least once a week.

Yet one of the consistent needs that arises in our church is for meals. Meals for parents with new babies, meals for someone who underwent surgery and is recovering, meals for those who are bereaved or struggling to cope with a medical diagnosis. Providing food is an easy way to show that we value love above all else. So during our year of kindness, I found myself making a lot of meals to drop off at others' homes. Thirteen, to be exact. Of those, four of them were in a two-week time span!

Meals are such a practical, tangible way to help, but sharing them with others doesn't have to be a daunting task. Find what works for you. I keep it simple by having a couple of go-to meals that I make for these situations. Another great option is to double a meal that you were already planning to make for your family, then freeze it until it's needed. Are you not a cook at all? No problem. Order a pizza or have sandwiches delivered from a local restaurant.

Providing a meal doesn't have to be complicated, but it does make an impact. I can still tell you the names of each of the families who took the time to bring us meals after my husband's neck surgery and after the births of our three children. In our times of need, their simple kindness resonated long after the table was cleared and the dishes were washed. Genuine kindness is not about doing grand gestures; rather, as Mother Teresa expressed, it is all about doing "small things with great love."

— *Kristin*

— Today's Act of Kindness —

Think of someone who could use a meal, then schedule
a day to bring it to them within the next week.

Stop and See

The Heavens declare the glory of God; the skies proclaim the work of his hands.
PSALM 19:1, NIV

"Hey, Hon. You awake?" I whispered it into the darkness, standing by the edge of the bed. I heard a groggy "Yeah" from my husband, buried beneath the blankets. "Great! Come with me," I said as I turned and trotted out of the bedroom. I heard his slightly incredulous voice following me down the hall: "Are we going outside?"

It was 2:30 a.m., and Aaron and I were at a cabin nestled deep in a pine forest, overlooking a lake. We stumbled about, gathering coats and shoes before cracking open the door and stepping out into darkness. We gingerly navigated the forty-three steps down to the lake, emerged from the pine forest onto the dock, and looked up.

Stars. Billions of them. Orion. The Seven Sisters. The Big Dipper. The Milky Way glittered like a million diamonds in the sky. We drew in a breath and stared upward. There were no man-made lights to compete with the splendor arrayed above us, and the night sky was breathtaking.

I mused, *I sleep through all this beauty every night? We all sleep through it? Who is this beauty for?* And then I remembered Psalm 19: "The Heavens declare the glory of God; the skies proclaim the work of his hands" (NIV).

This magnificence was but a tiny, breathtaking glimpse of the glory of God. I could not fully wrap my brain around the thought that there is something infinitely more glorious than what I was seeing in that moment. Deep within, I felt a stirring to *wake up* and *see* instead of stumbling and sleepwalking through the days, through the obligations, through life itself.

While we are called to think of and care for others, we cannot do that for long without experiencing our own refreshment and renewal. Worship plays an important role in how I refresh and renew my soul, and besides singing, spending time quietly awed by creation is my favorite way to worship God.

— Julie

— Today's Act of Kindness —

Stop and really see the beauty of God's creation. Spend
time reflecting on what it means to be surrounded
by his glory. Remember that God created this beauty
for you to enjoy as an act of love and kindness.

Remembering Others in Grief

God blesses those who mourn, for they will be comforted.
MATTHEW 5:4

My widowered neighbor, who lives alone, lost his sister recently. They were very close. He would visit her weekly at the nursing home where she lived and take her to doctor appointments. Her death was a bit of a surprise, made even worse by the fact that, because of a snowstorm, he didn't get to see her one last time.

As soon as we heard the news, my family visited him, bringing him handmade cards and store-bought cookies. We sent flowers to the funeral and attended the wake to show our support to a man who had come to mean so much to us. We had conversations with our other neighbors about who would visit him and when, to make sure he felt loved and supported over the next several days. Our kids continued to visit him in the weeks that followed to make sure he was doing all right.

Remembering those we've lost and the kindness shown to us during our grief can help us reach out to those who are grieving as well. I once had a friend tell me she got an anonymous card offering encouragement each month for a year after her father died. She told me how comforting it was to receive each one, especially during holidays and special times of the year like anniversaries and birthdays. She was touched that someone would remember her each month. I think about what a wonderful show of support this was to my friend. Although simple, it took intention on the part of the giver to remember to do this each month.

Kindness shown toward those experiencing a loss can be especially valuable, particularly after the initial condolences have quieted down. Letting others know that we are there for them, even long after the loss, is one way we can help offer comfort to those who mourn.

— Kendra

— Today's Act of Kindness —

Think of someone who has lost a loved one, either recently or in years past, and send them a note offering comfort and encouragement.

March

A Life-Changing Mistake

No, dear brothers and sisters, I have not achieved it, but I focus on this one thing: Forgetting the past and looking forward to what lies ahead.
PHILIPPIANS 3:13

When I asked my husband if I could share this story, he cringed a little. It's not very flattering, rehashing a mistake made long ago. But it's become a turning point for his life.

As a young man he was out carousing with his friends. The group was sitting in the outside patio section of a pizza parlor when they were approached by a man who asked them for pizza or money to buy some.

"Dude, I haven't eaten in, like, three hours," my now-husband said carelessly, straight faced, as his friends laughed.

The next day, every meal he ate sat heavy in his gut. Feeling ashamed of his flippant response the night before, he went looking for the man. He spent hours searching for him, driving the streets, but never found him.

Knowing my husband now, I'm still a little shocked by the story. Because if there's one population of people that he loves to help, it's the homeless. He has organized groups of people to serve meals at our local shelter; he has baked the brownies we serve there. Each December, he's been the impetus behind adopting homeless families and singles for Christmas, shopping for presents and helping to wrap them before dropping them off. He's the one who fills our vehicle with new items for homeless or at-risk kids to give to their siblings and parents for Christmas. I've even watched him literally give a homeless man the shirt off his back.

Shame over our past actions can serve a purpose, if we use the lesson we've learned to influence our future. Jesus' love for us is a narrative of redemption. He longs for us to acknowledge our mistakes and then use them for his glory.

— *Kristin*

— Today's Act of Kindness —

Think of a time when you were unkind. Maybe it was the way you treated a family member, coworker, friend, or stranger. Consider how you might redeem that past situation, then take one step toward doing so.

Giving with No Strings Attached

Give your gifts in private, and your Father, who sees everything, will reward you.
MATTHEW 6:4

A few years ago, my husband read a book by a pastor whose church would close its doors on a Sunday morning several times a year and instead go out and serve in the community. This struck such a chord with Kyle that he brought the idea to our pastor and church family.

Everyone loved the idea, and since then, we have adopted it as our own. We've washed the windows of a local nursing home and brought gifts for its residents; we've landscaped a yard for an elderly woman who was unable to do the work herself; and we've cleaned up and painted local playgrounds around our city.

We do all this with little fanfare or praise; often, the people we help don't even know we are a church group. Our goal is simply to help others outside of our church community, with no strings attached. We follow God's command to give our gifts in secret so that our Father who sees would be the one to reward us. We want to see the needs around us and work to meet them because we love Jesus, not because we want glory for ourselves. We've found that we show this love best by loving others through our actions, especially toward those who could never repay us.

Although we may not all be part of a church or organization that regularly does service projects in our communities, we probably all know people who need our assistance, if we'll only take the time to notice. Bringing a meal to a friend who has just had surgery, mowing an elderly neighbor's lawn, or buying a meal for a homeless person are all ways that we can show kindness and give to others quietly, even anonymously, with no strings attached.

— *Kendra*

— Today's Act of Kindness —

Do something in secret for someone who cannot repay you.

Actions Speak Louder Than Intentions

*Don't just listen to God's word. You must do what it says.
Otherwise, you are only fooling yourselves.*

JAMES 1:22

There is an old adage that comes to mind as I contemplate what it means to be an intentional doer of good: "The road to hell is paved with good intentions."

How many times have I felt a nudge in my soul to call someone who is going through a rough time and to give to them out of my resources—time, energy, or money—only to blow it off? Probably more times than I would care to admit.

Let's face it: it's often inconvenient to take time and energy out of our already too-busy days and nights and weekends to answer those nudges. I've been there too often, I'll admit it. But whenever I answer those nudges—when I say *yes* and stop in the midst of my busy life to meet someone else in a moment of need—I never, ever regret it.

It is not enough to have good intentions; we must practice putting Scripture into action, as James warns us. We must follow through on our intentions and translate our thoughts into physical, tangible deeds. If we don't, we deceive ourselves into thinking that we are living scripturally. It's not always easy to put kindness into action, but it can certainly be simple.

We are each called to be a light upon the hill. We are called to be salt and light to the world and to be generous with our lives. When we get that nudge to help someone else, we have the choice to ignore it. But our intentional, positive response to that nudge may well be a defining moment in the life of another. We may be invited to be the reflection of Christ to that *one* person, in that *one* moment. Often it is not grand gestures that change the world, but the small things—the heart-to-heart, one-on-one moments—that have the most profound impact.

— *Julie*

— Today's Act of Kindness —

What have you been thinking or talking about
doing lately? Put those intentions into action.

The Neighbors

The whole law can be summed up in this one command:
"Love your neighbor as yourself."
GALATIANS 5:14

My husband and I are admittedly inept homeowners. We're the ones who had to use fire extinguishers on two different grills after they each started on fire, the ones who had sparks shooting from the microwave when we turned it on with nothing inside it. Yep, we're *those* people.

Thank goodness we moved into a nice neighborhood. Oh, I don't mean that the houses are pretty or the lawns are well kept, although that is true. I mean that we have incredibly kind neighbors. They're the folks we call when my husband gets locked in our basement while I'm at the movie theater and not responding to his frantic messages, or when there's a suspicious gas smell in the garage. They also graciously tolerate our wild, hooligan children racing through their lawns or talking to them incessantly while they work in their gardens.

Our previous neighborhood was very different. Most days I would come home from work, drive the car into the garage, and close the door before going inside. Although a couple of families were kind enough to invite us to dinner, Tim and I didn't make an effort to get to know many people. I'm ashamed to admit that I wouldn't be able to pick most of them out in a crowd.

Why is this neighborhood so different? It's not the quality of the houses or the nature of the people, in my opinion—the neighbors we did know in our old neighborhood were certainly kind. In my mind, the difference has been in the intention. Our current neighbors invite our family to do things, and if we say no, they still invite us the next time. They take the time to visit or wave to us and our children. They've brought us baby gifts, meals, and jars of Christmas goodies. They truly live out the idea of loving your neighbor as yourself. In turn, we've found ourselves reaching back to them, engaging in acts of kindness throughout the year that let them know we care.

— *Kristin*

— Today's Act of Kindness —

Reach out to a neighbor in an intentional way. Drop off cookies, have your children make them a card, or simply give them your time and attention when you see them outside.

Our Source of Strength

God is our refuge and strength, always ready to help in times of trouble.
PSALM 46:1

A few months ago, the son of a high school friend was buried. I went to his funeral hesitantly. I was alone and unsure of what to expect. Having not been to my hometown in several years, I had a bit of anxiety over whom I would see and how I should act.

As I pulled into the already overfilled parking lot, my anxiety continued to rise. I took a deep breath, exited my car, and quickly entered my old high school. The gym was almost completely full, and I hurried to the back corner, head down, to find a place to sit. A few minutes later, a dear friend from high school started up the bleacher steps, immediately recognized me, and took the seat next to me. She said she was grateful to find someone she knew, and I told her I felt the same.

The family took their places, and I watched as this brave mother sat through the ceremony to say good-bye to her only child. I grieved as I thought about how hard this must be for her. I quietly prayed for her as tears streamed down my cheeks.

As I headed back to my car for the hour-long ride home, I was still upset but also glad that I had decided to come. Since the ceremony, I have continued to pray for my friend who lost her child and have sent her messages of love, prayer, and encouragement.

Sometimes I just want to hide from the pain of this world. It's in these painful moments that we can find comfort in Scriptures that remind us that God is our refuge and strength. We are reminded that we do not carry our burdens alone, and anytime we or those we love are hurting, we can bring our pain to God, and he will carry us.

— Kendra

— Today's Act of Kindness —

Pray for someone you know who is grieving or walking through a difficult season in life. Then let that person know you are thinking about them.

A Giving Spirit

Give, and you will receive. Your gift will return to you in full—pressed down, shaken together to make room for more, running over, and poured into your lap. The amount you give will determine the amount you get back.

LUKE 6:38

"Hey, wanna join me on a radio show after lunch?"

I froze, my eyes growing round as I stared at my friend.

My friend is extravagantly generous and completely random like that. She is the executive director of a small nonprofit in town and had been given the opportunity to share on our local talk-radio station about how assistive technology could keep senior citizens in their homes longer.

Her invitation was sincere, and later that day I found myself being introduced to the radio host and settling myself into a corner of the on-air studio, assuming that my role would be small and that of a supporting character in the interview. As it turned out, the host introduced me and my law firm each time we broke for sponsors and again as we returned to the air—which was easily hundreds of dollars in free radio advertising.

Though I was initially hesitant because I'd had no time to prep and I felt nervous about being on live radio, it all went fine, and my friend and I shared one last chuckle in the parking lot afterward before we slipped into our cars and went back to our respective offices. As I recounted the unexpected adventure to my husband that evening, my thoughts turned again to the value of the radio time my friend shared without hesitation.

While we don't often have the chance to work together, my friend is a consistent cheerleader in my life. She is a strong leader, and she is always looking for ways that everyone can win. There is no competition with this friend; she is unabashedly and wholeheartedly collaborative in everything she does. She is a beautiful example of a woman who embodies the giving spirit described in Luke 6:38. Her generosity with her time, her talents, and her resources has impacted thousands of lives, and I strive to be more like her.

— Julie

— Today's Act of Kindness —

Consider what resource you can share
with someone, and then do it.

We Reap What We Sow

Whoever sows sparingly will also reap sparingly, and whoever sows generously will also reap generously.

2 CORINTHIANS 9:6, NIV

Kindness is not always a quality we come by naturally. Often it's one we have to cultivate over time. The busyness of life, harshness of others, or even just our never-ending to-do lists can hinder our desire to extend kindness. Sometimes we just don't feel like doing things for others. It's in those moments that kindness toward others takes practice and intentionality.

There are many times when I don't feel like being kind—when I get angry with my kids or my husband, or when I feel upset when someone cuts me off in traffic or is rude to me in the checkout line. When kindness is not a habit, I can feel powerless to be kind in those moments, finding myself snapping instead. But I do have a choice in how I will respond, and cultivating a habit of kindness makes that choice easier in difficult circumstances.

In the tough moments, we can remember that Scripture says when we plant sparingly we will also reap sparingly, but if we plant generously we will reap generously. This also applies to the kindness we extend toward others, encouraging us to plant more of what we'd like returned to us in our own lives. It's simple, really: if we want others to be kind to us, then we need to be willing to show kindness first and not wait for others to extend it to us.

Do you find yourself overwhelmed with busyness and struggling to be kind? Have you struggled to make kindness a regular habit rather than a onetime event? Remember that kindness does not have to be grand; a habit of kindness is built one tiny action at a time. It just takes a bit of intentionality. Be generous with your kindness today, even if you don't feel like it.

— Kendra

— Today's Act of Kindness —

Choose to extend kindness to someone
else in a frustrating moment.

I'm Offended!

Go ahead and be angry. You do well to be angry—but don't use your anger as fuel for revenge. And don't stay angry. Don't go to bed angry. Don't give the Devil that kind of foothold in your life.
EPHESIANS 4:26-27, MSG

As she was speaking, I felt my blood pressure starting to build, and I wondered whether she would soon see steam curling out of my ears. Her words were unfair and unkind to someone I love deeply, and I was angry and hurt on behalf of my loved one.

Because I've learned that speaking in anger rarely results in anything positive, I managed to hold my tongue, but I spent a good portion of that evening and the next day locked in an internal battle. I wanted to stomp back and tell this woman that she was being extraordinarily unfair. Every time I started down that mental path, though, I felt a tugging backward from the edge of that angry cliff and an urge to stand still. I felt an invitation to hand over that jumbled-up ball of emotions to Jesus. And so, *finally*, I did. In fact, I handed it to him several times—every time a new argument started in my head about why this person was wrong, I stopped and handed it over anew.

My mind returned to some wise words spoken to me by a friend years ago: "Taking up an offense on someone else's behalf rarely ends positively."

So I heeded my friend's words and the advice from Ephesians 4. While anger is a legitimate emotional response, we are warned to be very careful about using anger to fuel revenge and are advised not to go to bed angry. When we dwell on our anger, we risk giving the devil a foothold in our lives.

As I set aside the angry emotions, I began to see solutions to the problem that didn't involve me stomping angrily or severing a relationship. When I kept my lips zipped in that angry moment and went to Jesus first with my anger, the Lord worked in my heart to show me a winning solution for this woman, my loved one, and me.

— *Julie*

— Today's Act of Kindness —

If you are holding a grudge against someone,
take it to Jesus and then release it. If you need to
seek reconciliation with this person, do it.

Obedient to Grace

Out of his fullness we have all received grace in place of grace already given.
JOHN 1:16, NIV

A few years ago, my husband stopped at a street corner to talk to a homeless man. The man said he was an Iraq War veteran who hadn't had much luck at local shelters and just needed to purchase a bus ticket to get to another city. Moved by his story, my husband gave him some money to help purchase the ticket.

On his way home, he called Pastor Carol, the director of one of our local shelters—who also happens to be a friend—and related the story. She paused and then asked what he looked like. When he described the man, Pastor Carol immediately knew who my husband was talking about and that the man's story about his past, however moving, was false.

Disappointed, Tim felt bothered that he had believed the man's fabrication. Pastor Carol's response, however, resonated with him: "You're not responsible for his response or his truthfulness. You need to be faithful to do what God asks you to do and trust that he will take care of it. You can't let someone else's response dictate your giving."

At the end of the day, the lesson we learned wasn't about the man and his lie, it was about ourselves. Although we always try to give wisely, our larger purpose is to give and *let it go*. After all, we are responsible only for our obedience in responding to God's guidance in giving. There's no sense in worrying after the fact about whether the person deserved the gift. Rather than trying to find some arbitrary definition of what makes someone truly in need of help, let's let God judge the appropriateness of their response. After all, as John 1:16 reminds us, haven't we all been given more than we deserve?

— *Kristin*

— Today's Act of Kindness —

Practice giving without judgment by doing an act of
kindness for someone whose circumstances are beyond
your knowledge. For example, you could pay for the person
in the car behind you in the coffee shop drive-thru lane.

Our Inherent Worth in Christ

You also are complete through your union with Christ.

COLOSSIANS 2:10

Over coffee, I listened quietly as my friend poured out her heart. Accustomed to being the one who gives, who quietly provides, who meets needs, she has found herself suddenly in a season of life where she simply doesn't have the resources to do what she has always done. She has been stripped down and laid bare financially, emotionally, physically. She has found herself in the position of needing assistance, and it's hard.

As we talked, it became clear that part of her identity and her worth was wrapped up in what she could do for others and in what she believed she could do for Christ.

This view of God and this need to prove our worthiness is a common trap so many fall into. It can be easy to allow our identity to get wrapped up in what we *think* we bring to the table for God. We begin to believe that God needs us, our resources, and our talents. This line of thinking, when flipped, logically leads to the opposite thought: if we fail, make a mistake, or hit a rough spot in our lives—if we suddenly find ourselves in a position of needing to receive instead of give—then we've lost our value to God and have become worthless. Nothing could be further from the truth.

We are complete through our union with Christ—there is no striving, no earning, no buying into his favor. In fact, there is nothing we have that was not originally given to us by God. There is nothing you can do—or fail to do—that will diminish God's love for you.

I love living this adventure of being intentionally kind, and I believe we are called to live out kindness as part of our Christian walk. However, my worth in Christ is not dependent on what I do, and it has nothing to do with my kindness scorecard from week to week. It is purely the result of unearned grace and unmerited favor.

— Julie

— Today's Act of Kindness —

Show yourself kindness by prayerfully reflecting on the ways you may be mixing up your identity in Christ with what you believe you bring to the table. Ask God to remind you of your true worth.

Tongue-Tied

Fire goes out without wood, and quarrels disappear when gossip stops.
PROVERBS 26:20

I'm in the midst of an intentional, ongoing effort to be the person who lets gossip die rather than passing it on.

Don't get me wrong, it's not the big stuff that trips me up. I hold on to secrets and confidences without any problem. It's the little things—the stuff that seems harmless, meaningless—that I catch myself passing on without a thought. While I've never thought of myself as a stereotypical gossip, it's surprising how tempting it is to pass on that little morsel of interesting information I learned in the break room, in the church lobby, or while chatting with girlfriends, especially when others are doing the same. It's a trap that I trip into suddenly and unexpectedly, and, more often than not, even as the words cross my lips I start wishing that I could reach out and grab them and stuff them back in.

My goal is this: what I hear or see going on around me doesn't get repeated if it isn't kind or necessary. (Please don't misunderstand: anything that endangers bodies, minds, or spirits must be exposed and stopped.) I'm not perfect, and I've discovered that this effort to curb my unruly tongue is a journey, not a destination. But my determination not to gossip, even in the small things, has helped me zip my lips and lift my fingers away from the send button on more than one occasion. As time has passed, I find it increasingly easier to curb my tongue.

Sometimes the kindest thing you can do for someone else is to refuse to participate in a behind-their-back discussion of their character or their life. As the verse in Proverbs states, removing the fuel puts the fire out. So often, it takes only one person to gently steer the conversation away from gossip and on to a more productive topic.

— *Julie*

— Today's Act of Kindness —

For the next week, refuse to pass on comments that are neither necessary nor kind. See if you're not less tempted to gossip as you build your strength in biting your tongue.

Eyes to See

[Jesus] told them, "Go into all the world and preach the Good News to everyone."
MARK 16:15

I went on my first mission trip as a young married woman. My husband and I were youth leaders in our church and were asked if we'd be willing to take a group of kids to Mexico to encourage some smaller, remote churches within our denomination. We agreed, and soon I found myself leading a bundle of kids across the border, unsure of what to expect.

Along with ministering to the churches there, we visited many of the slums and, essentially, dumps, where people who were too poor to afford anything else lived. We prayed with people, handed out supplies, and spent time with the families who lived there. We made connections through smiles and hugs, even when our language skills fell a little flat. It was one of the best trips I've ever taken, because it challenged me to see the needs of others, especially when I returned home. The experience increased my sensitivity to others I come across in my daily life—like the homeless person standing on the street corner, the one I used to quickly avert my eyes from, or the neighbor I would politely wave hello to but never really stop to get to know.

Sometimes stepping outside of our everyday environments and our comfort zones can be a good thing. It can allow us to see the world and the people who live in it with fresh eyes. It can also stir in us a desire to help others who are less fortunate than we are.

We may not all be able to go to another country, but obeying God's command to "go into all the world and preach the Good News" can start with going to new places right in our own communities and reaching out to people who live nearby. It doesn't matter where you live; there is always someone who has a need. Whether it is with food or clothing, transportation, or even just encouragement to get through the day, we can start by helping those who are right around us.

— *Kendra*

— *Today's Act of Kindness* —

Pray that God would give you eyes to see a need in your
own community, and then take a small step to help.

Toxic Loneliness

Father to the fatherless, defender of widows—this is God, whose dwelling
is holy. God places the lonely in families; he sets the prisoners free and
gives them joy. But he makes the rebellious live in a sun-scorched land.

PSALM 68:5-6

Did you know that loneliness is toxic?

I was listening to the radio one day and was amazed to hear about a study that found that loneliness can be a danger to your health—just as dangerous as being obese. Researchers from Brigham Young University analyzed data on lifestyles and health from three million adults. They found that the link between loneliness and premature death was even stronger than the link of obesity.[*]

Frankly, I was astonished. I'd heard admonishments to eat a healthy diet and take care of my body, but no one had ever talked about trying to avoid loneliness. But it makes sense—loneliness seems to stick to our bones the way a bad meal settles heavily in our stomachs.

Scripture talks about how God is "father to the fatherless" and a "defender of widows," but I'm struck even more by what follows: "God places the lonely in families." To me, that hits home (pun intended). As a mom, I am surrounded by a loving husband and (usually loving) children. I have a good relationship with my own parents, and I count my sister as one of my very best friends. Yet I also have friends I've met over the years with whom the bond goes so deep that they feel like sisters and brothers to me. We don't need to be born into perfect families to be part of a loving, thriving community. God places us in the families we find ourselves in, whether we are related by blood or by common interest. His intention is for us to live in community with others.

— Kristin

— Today's Act of Kindness —

Who do you know that may be lonely? Perhaps it's an elderly
person, a single parent, or a teenager struggling at school.
Reach out to this person and let them know they aren't alone.

---

[*] Julianne Holt-Lunstad, Timothy B. Smith, Mark Baker, Tyler Harris, and David Stephenson, "Loneliness and Social Isolation as Risk Factors for Mortality: A Meta-Analytic Review," *Perspectives on Psychological Science* 10, no. 2 (2015): 227-37, http://pps.sagepub.com/content/10/2/227.abstract.

Love each other with genuine affection, and take delight in honoring each other.
ROMANS 12:10

My husband sometimes travels for business, and among all the things I miss about him when he's not home, I miss the cup of coffee he brews me every morning the most. He not only brews it, but he walks it upstairs to our room and hands it to me with a smile and a twinkle in his eye—a little nudge to get up and get moving. When he hands me that steaming cup of coffee each morning, it feels like he's handing me a small, unspoken love note.

Marriage is made up of thousands of tiny interactions, and while grand gestures and fancy dinners are nice on occasion, it is the way we treat one another in the small, ordinary moments that so often slowly builds or destroys the love between spouses.

While practicing kindness is often considered something we do for a stranger or for someone who is going through a rough patch, I'd argue that practicing true kindness begins at home with our closest, most intimate relationships. It feels easy to skimp on kindness with our loved ones, because there is a tendency to take for granted our most intimate relationships—whether they are spouses, parents, children, or deep friendships. Let's be honest: sometimes, practicing kindness toward our spouses is far more challenging than buying a stranger a cup of coffee on our way through the coffee-shop drive-thru.

While it is satisfying to shower kindness on a random stranger, the kindness we intentionally pour into our most intimate relationships will enrich and deepen our lives and the lives around us in ways far beyond our investment of time and energy. Kindness builds strong marriages and strong relationships one small act at a time. If you want the love between you and your spouse to be based on showing genuine affection and taking delight in honoring each other, start by quietly doing small intentional acts of kindness on a daily, weekly, and monthly basis. You may be pleasantly surprised by the response.

— Julie

— Today's Act of Kindness —

Who in your family needs an unspoken love note? Show
that person a small act of kindness and love today.

Circles of Influence

Walk with the wise and become wise; associate with fools and get in trouble.
PROVERBS 13:20

My son is fourteen and in the throes of his teen years. He's a good kid who tries hard and loves to be involved in activities. He has a tender heart and wants to get along well with others, and while this has afforded him many benefits—he's well liked by his teachers and peers—it comes with one small weakness: he can lean toward pleasing people, even when it means doing something he knows is wrong.

I've had many conversations with my son about choosing wisely whom he spends his time with and whom he lets influence his life. This mama knows all too well how hard it is not to just go along with everyone else, especially when you want to be liked. I've struggled in my own life with the same desire to please others. But I'm committed to teaching him that sometimes we need to be discerning with friendships. That we are always kind to others, no matter who they are, but we don't have to let others have influence over us, especially those who could potentially lead us into sin or danger.

The people we choose to allow into our circles of influence will show us who we will become. If we spend most of our time with people who are negative and judgmental, we'll most likely end up being the same. But the opposite is true as well: if we surround ourselves with people who desire, as we do, to love others well, to believe the best about people, and to serve those around them, we'll end up doing more of those things as well. This, in turn, grows our ability and desire to be kind.

Whom have you given influence in your life? Have you been wise to pick people who are wise themselves?

— *Kendra*

— Today's Act of Kindness —

Evaluate whom you allow to influence your life. If you don't currently surround yourself with kind, wise influencers, identify someone whom you'd like to let into your circle of influence.

A Community of Kindness

Owe nothing to anyone—except for your obligation to love one another. If you love your neighbor, you will fulfill the requirements of God's law.
ROMANS 13:8

My house is tucked into the very back of my neighborhood with just a few other homes, with room to spare between our group of houses and the ones that sit just down the road. Even though there's not much of a separation from the rest of the neighborhood, our "hood" has evolved into a small community of its own.

I love the way the neighbors wave hello when I go out to get the mail and the sweet gift of their assistance when I need a helping hand. Yet I know that's not the case in every neighborhood. If you want to cultivate a community of kindness, there are some practical things you can do:

- Find a way to communicate. For instance, we use a private Facebook group that includes only our neighbors.
- Help in times of trouble. Send over meals, magazines, or movies when a neighbor is ill or injured.
- Have a party. Invite your neighbors over to your next New Year's Eve, Super Bowl, or birthday party.
- Share an evening together. Host a bonfire or use a projector on someone's garage door to watch a movie together.
- Plan a special event. One summer, some of the couples in the neighborhood went on a dinner cruise together.
- Begin a tradition. You could start a neighborhood Secret Santa gift exchange, and then have brunch together to celebrate the season.

Loving your neighbors fulfills God's law, yes, but it shouldn't be considered a hardship. There are many fun, practical ways to reach out to your neighbors and show them God's love. You'll find that when you begin to intentionally create a sense of community on a smaller scale, your love for the community beyond your immediate neighborhood will expand too.

— Kristin

— Today's Act of Kindness —

Think of one tangible thing you can do to begin creating community among your neighbors. It could be as simple as saying hello to someone while you're taking out the trash and being open to where the conversation might lead.

Seasons of Kindness

Commit yourselves wholeheartedly to these words of mine. Tie them to your hands and wear them on your forehead as reminders. Teach them to your children. Talk about them when you are at home and when you are on the road, when you are going to bed and when you are getting up.
DEUTERONOMY 11:18-19

"How do you participate in acts of kindness when you have young kids?"

This was the endearingly honest question a mom of two young kids asked me after hearing a talk I gave on showing acts of kindness. She wanted to incorporate kind practices into her family's life, but with such young children, she had the very valid concerns of how to include them and find the time to do it.

I told her that I understood and that it's okay to participate at varying levels depending on what season of life we are in. I encouraged her to start with what her family could manage and grow each year as her kids did. She told me she would love to help serve the homeless at our local shelter but that her kids were too young to bring along, so we brainstormed ways she could go once a month while arranging for someone to stay home with her kids. Finally, I told her she should always come home and talk to her kids about what she had done and why.

These conversations allow our kids to see the motivation behind our kindness toward others in tangible ways, and thus they see our faith lived out through our actions and in our lives. In turn, they come to see acts of kindness as a normal part of everyday life and begin to copy our behavior.

Don't forget to talk with your kids or other family members about acts of kindness you're doing. It will encourage and spur them on to do the same as they see you putting God's word into action.

— *Kendra*

— Today's Act of Kindness —

Do one small act of kindness for someone, and then tell your kids or other family members what you did and why.

A Home Away from Home

Cheerfully share your home with those who need a meal or a place to stay.
1 PETER 4:9

My parents moved away from Litchfield, my hometown, in the fall of my freshman year of college. Although I saw them often at the town house they bought as part of their downsizing, I missed my childhood home, especially since I still made frequent trips to Litchfield.

At the time, I was dating someone who lived there, and I visited him just about every weekend. Knowing that I didn't have anywhere to stay overnight, a dear friend from high school offered to let me stay at her parents' home, even on the weekends when she was away at college.

That's how I found myself, time and again, surreptitiously opening the back door to let myself in to her big, quiet house. Their family had a gorgeous historic home that reminded me of my own childhood home with its big staircases and wooden floors that I would tiptoe across in the dark. More often than not, when I arrived, her parents would already be in bed or at least out of sight, but there were always towels laid out in "my" bedroom whenever they knew I was coming.

Though I appreciated their kindness at the time, I marvel at it even more now. I needed a place to stay, and they invited me in, no strings attached. Although I always tried to chat with them in the morning before I left, sometimes I wouldn't see them at all. They certainly didn't have to let the teenage friend of their daughter stay at their house. Living on a busy street, they could have been worried about making sure their doors were locked tightly against possible intruders, but instead they left them open and left the light on for me.

It's been many years since I made these trips into their house in the dark of night. But now, with teenagers of my own who steal into the house late at night, when I hear the door creaking and footsteps falling softly on the hardwood floors, I'm reminded of my friend's sweet parents and find that I don't mind at all.

— Kristin

— Today's Act of Kindness —

Invite someone to use your home, no strings attached.
You could invite your children's friends over or allow
a friend to stay while you're out of town.

Birthday Party Reboot

You should remember the words of the Lord Jesus:
"It is more blessed to give than to receive."
ACTS 20:35

Several years ago, my husband and I intentionally scaled back on presents for our children during Christmas and Easter in exchange for being slightly more celebratory on their birthdays. After we explained that Christmas and Easter are holidays about Jesus, our children bought into our logic and were generally happy with the arrangement.

I, too, was perfectly satisfied with this plan until my children were old enough to have friend parties. After our first friend birthday party, I found myself struggling against the tidal wave of additional presents and a fear that we were headed in the wrong direction with birthdays.

After a lot of discussion, my husband and I implemented a "no gifts please" rule for friend parties. We still do fun things, give out little goody bags, and try to find ways to send the kids home pleasantly worn out, but we intentionally shifted the focus onto friendships and away from gifts.

Our kids have gone along without complaint, and they are generally so busy having fun with their friends that they truly don't miss the presents. As my children get older, I'm slowly shifting them away from friend parties at the local gymnastics studio or bounce-house company and toward birthdays that involve serving others.

To date, my favorite birthday party was the one we threw for my daughter's fourth birthday at our local humane society. My daughter and her friends toured the shelter, played with kittens, and "helped" groom a dog before finishing the party with eating cupcakes and opening presents that each child brought for the animals. The kids left the party happy, sugared up, and full of stories.

My husband and I are continually trying to tuck the truth of today's verse into the hearts of our children—that we are often far more blessed when we give than when we receive. We're always looking for tangible ways to make this truth come to life, especially around holidays and birthdays.

— Julie

— Today's Act of Kindness —

Consider how you might turn your next gift-getting event into a giving event instead.

Acknowledging Service

Encourage each other and build each other up, just as you are already doing.
1 THESSALONIANS 5:11

My father served in the navy during the Vietnam War. Upon his return he realized pretty quickly that public opinion over his service was not always so favorable. Without any fanfare or accolades, he quietly assimilated back into society, usually not telling anyone of his years of service. He went on to college, married my mother, and started a family, all with little time spent thinking about or talking about those years in the navy.

It wasn't until almost thirty years later, when he attended a men's conference, that he was reminded again of his years of service. During the program, one of the speakers asked if there were any Vietnam vets in the room, and if so, would they please stand so they could be acknowledged. My dad hesitantly stood up and looked around as many more men joined him. Suddenly a slow roar of applause moved across the stadium as the other men in the room began to clap and cheer. My dad stood there, tears streaming down his cheeks over the simple acknowledgment of his service from all those years before—service that had never been recognized until that day.

We might never know the impact our acknowledgment of another's actions may have or what our encouraging words may mean to someone. Perhaps someone has served for years without anyone noticing. Maybe someone has worked tirelessly without any acknowledgment or has continued to take on work for others to lessen their loads or alleviate their burdens. It can be easy to accidentally overlook quiet, humble servants—but they are deserving of our recognition and appreciation. When we take the time to commend or thank another person, it could be just the encouragement they need to keep going, to feel valued, or to sense that what they do truly matters.

— Kendra

— Today's Act of Kindness —

Do you know someone who is happy to serve quietly?
Take time to acknowledge this person for their
hard work that may have been overlooked.

A Professor's Encouragement

Kind words are like honey—sweet to the soul and healthy for the body.
PROVERBS 16:24

My heart pounded in my chest, its thumps in time with my quiet knocks on the door of my journalism professor's office. A gruff man who was roughly the age of my parents, he called out in a deep voice inviting me inside. As I sat down in one of the chairs, scanning the diplomas on the walls, one from the University of North Dakota caught my eye. We chatted briefly about how he and my father had both attended the school, and I found myself relaxing.

As we moved on to other topics and began to talk about the class of his that I was currently enrolled in, he spoke words that would have a profound effect on me for years to come: "Your copyediting test was excellent. Really good. In fact, I think you should try out for the student newspaper. Have you thought about doing that at all?"

To be honest, I hadn't. As an English major, I thought a minor in mass communications would be a practical way to boost my résumé. I knew I loved reading and writing, but I didn't have firm plans for a career path. Yet his simple words of praise and encouragement—kind words that were sweet to my soul—were just the impetus I needed to pursue a new path. Within a few days, I was working for the college newspaper. After graduation, I worked for several years at our local daily newspaper, a time in my life that I treasure.

One man's single comment had a profound impact on me, an impact that influenced many years of my life. I will always be grateful for his kind words and how he went out of his way to encourage me to pursue a path I hadn't considered.

— Kristin

— Today's Act of Kindness —

Speak a word of encouragement into the life of someone around you. Do you see a talent or gift in them that they have not recognized in themselves? Tell them what you see.

Early Delivery

Whenever we have the opportunity, we should do good to everyone—especially to those in the family of faith.

GALATIANS 6:10

I love coffee. While I clearly have a caffeine addiction, I've discovered that I am in love with the ritual of coffee more than with the energy jolt it provides. I love to start each workday with my hands wrapped around my favorite handmade coffee cup while I let the hot liquid inside slowly warm my fingers. This little ritual fills me with peace as I peruse my e-mail inbox, listen to my voice mails, and start tackling my daily to-do list.

One day, I arrived at the office earlier than normal. I was the first coffee drinker on my side of the building to arrive, so when I rounded the corner to the closest kiosk, I discovered that no one had made coffee yet. I started brewing the first pot and walked away, leaving my cup sitting there with the intention of coming back soon. Upon returning to my office, I became so engrossed in preparing for an early-morning meeting that my cup and my java jolt were forgotten.

Hearing a soft knock at my door, I looked up to see a coworker I don't know well standing in the doorway, holding my coffee mug. She entered, handed me the freshly brewed beverage, and said, "I know you love coffee, so I thought I'd bring you your cup."

In the grand scheme of things, it was a small gesture. She simply filled my mug and walked it to my office. But it was so unexpected that it was spectacularly sweet, and it made my entire morning. In fact, it made my entire day.

Scripture calls us to do good to people every time we have the opportunity. Sometimes this takes being on the lookout for little moments to bless someone. On that morning, my coworker saw an opportunity to care for someone else, and she went out of her way to do something small that had a very large impact.

— Julie

— Today's Act of Kindness —

Find a small, completely unexpected way to bless someone.

Treat Yourself Kindly

You, O Lord, are a God of compassion and mercy, slow to get angry and filled with unfailing love and faithfulness.

PSALM 86:15

It may seem like a selfish act, but showing kindness to yourself is actually a wonderful way to start showing kindness toward others. Kind acts start as kind thoughts, and if we are constantly thinking negatively about ourselves, it can be hard to think kind thoughts about others, which in turn makes it hard to actually do kind actions.

I have a friend who can be highly critical and wary of others' motives. She has a tendency to initially believe that others are simply out to take advantage of her, so in turn, she rarely finds a reason to help other people, especially strangers. I was somewhat taken aback by her assumptions and judgments of others until I heard her start talking about herself and her own faults and imperfections. I realized her negative thoughts toward others were simply a reflection of the same negativity she felt toward herself. When I realized where her thoughts had originated from and how she was thinking about (and treating) herself, I felt compassion for her.

When it comes to kindness, how we treat ourselves first will have an effect on how we view and treat others. If you have a hard time thinking about doing a kind act toward others each day, start by pondering what kind of thoughts you have toward yourself. Are you critical of yourself when you make mistakes? Do you berate yourself for your past? Do you wish you had a different life, childhood, or personality?

When we spend our mental energy speaking unkind words to ourselves, we will have a hard time showing kindness to others. Scripture reminds us over and over that God is compassionate and gracious toward us, filled with unfailing love. In the face of such kindness, how can we not be willing to follow his example by extending this same grace to ourselves? Kindness needs to start in our own hearts and minds before we can give it away to others.

— Kendra

— Today's Act of Kindness —

Be aware of your thoughts toward yourself. When you hear yourself being critical, stop and instead remind yourself how loved you are by God.

The Prom-Dress Shop

Love each other with genuine affection, and take delight in honoring each other.
ROMANS 12:10

Racks of hundreds of donated sparkling, brightly colored dresses edged the room, and star-shaped balloons bobbed overhead, listing their sizes. Dressing rooms were in one area, snacks in another. Seamstresses were on hand for alterations. The prom for students with special needs was more than a month away, but the prom-dress shop—an event in its own right—had arrived.

As the girls filtered in to the pop-up dress shop, they were paired with personal shoppers who listened to their preferences and suggested dresses to try on. Some girls, despite being in their late teens and early twenties, had no idea what size formal gown would fit them. They'd never attended a prom before, never had an occasion like this for which to buy a formal dress. Whenever a girl finished trying on all her options and finally chose the dress she deemed to be the perfect fit, she would return to the front and ring the bell, while everyone else in the room cheered and clapped.

It was a day of celebration. And as the day wore on, it became profoundly clear that the parents were overwhelmed with how the event catered to their daughters, aiming to make them feel like princesses for a day. As the parents wiped away tears, their comments could be overheard:

"She looks so beautiful."
"I never thought she'd be able to go to prom."
"I can't believe you guys are doing this."
"Thank you so, so much."

For the girls who visited the prom-dress shop, it wasn't just the dresses that made them feel magical. It was the way in which the people at the shop went out of their way to make them feel special and valued. All the workers were volunteers, and it was clear that they cared for the girls with genuine affection, and they delighted in honoring their very special guests.

— *Kristin*

— Today's Act of Kindness —

How can you make someone feel special? Through your words or actions, go out of your way to make their joy your aim.

Dumplings for Dinner

You are the light of the world—like a city on a hilltop that cannot be hidden. No one lights a lamp and then puts it under a basket. Instead, a lamp is placed on a stand, where it gives light to everyone in the house. In the same way, let your good deeds shine out for all to see, so that everyone will praise your heavenly Father.

MATTHEW 5:14-16

We stumbled onto Thursday Night Dinner Buddies quite by accident. It was while I was volunteering at an after-school activity that one of the visiting Chinese scholars from our school's immersion program kindly insisted on coming to our house that night to make my family dumplings as a way to share her culture. I graciously accepted her offer and then rushed home, calling my husband to rearrange schedules and obligations so that we could make space for her friendship.

Over good conversation, laughter, and a shared meal, we realized that our friend had never eaten steak fresh off the grill or so many other meals that are considered typical American fare. What started as my husband and me quietly and quickly making space for this person in our house one Thursday night has turned into a weekly coming together of cultures. We take turns sharing new foods, and we find our conversations wide-ranging and engaging.

These Thursday nights have become the new normal in our house, and I suspect they have become a new way of life altogether. Knowing that our doors will be thrown open every Thursday night eliminates the stress and anxiety of trying to plan one-off events. We know what to expect, and we invite our friend and her son to do life together with us.

In order to be that city on the hill or the light on a stand instead of under a basket, we have to throw open our doors and our lives and invite others to journey alongside us. When you trust God enough to open your life to people he brings across your path, you can know that he is trustworthy enough to guide the conversation, eventually, back to him.

— *Julie*

— Today's Act of Kindness —

Prayerfully consider how you might throw open your doors and your life to others. You can start by inviting someone to your home for a low-stress dinner.

An Average Life

*My God will meet all your needs according to the riches
of his glory in Christ Jesus.*
PHILIPPIANS 4:19, NIV

Shivering against the cold, I hugged my toddler against me as I headed toward my sister Kendra, who was standing in the shadowed doorway of our local homeless shelter. Together, we walked up the stairs and headed into a hallway that was brightly lit by newly hung chandeliers, the smell of paint and varnish assaulting our noses.

We were just two weeks out from dedicating the newly refinished women's floor at Place of Hope, and I surveyed the dressers and mattresses still crowding the floor, the tarps laid down. The unfinished rooms held a silent, waiting quality. Even as we chose prints for the walls and dragged toys into the children's room, I knew that in a few weeks the place would look and sound wildly different, as the fourteen rooms of the newly named Katie's Wing became home to women and their families.

Despite the disarray, I marveled over how my sister Katrina's legacy was evolving yet again. The foundation created when she passed away from breast cancer was now able to help fund the creation of a wing that would change the lives of countless women. Eleven years ago when my family said yes to God in creating the foundation, we had no idea that it would go to help homeless women, many of whom have escaped domestic-assault situations or have been victims of human trafficking.

Katrina would probably be astonished to see the legacy that has emerged since her passing, because in her mind, she lived an average life. "Come and see what the Lord has done in this average housewife's life," she once wrote in her journal to her children. That's how she saw herself, as average, nothing special—but other people saw her as so much more. But now the Lord is using her legacy to meet so many needs.

At the dedication of Katie's Wing, my brother-in-law Jim echoed Katrina's words: "Any family could do this," he said. "With the Lord's help, any family could do something like this."

No matter your circumstances or your background, God can use you. When we rely on God's riches, he will meet our needs and the needs of others as we seek to show kindness.

— Kristin

— Today's Act of Kindness —

As you do an act of kindness today, pray that God would
meet both your needs and the recipient's needs.

Responding with Compassion

Beware that you don't look down on any of these little ones. For I tell you that in heaven their angels are always in the presence of my heavenly Father.

MATTHEW 18:10

My husband and I provided foster care for more than six years to children in our county. During that time period, we took in approximately twenty kids. Some stayed with us a few weeks; others stayed months or even a year; and two we adopted, keeping them forever as a part of our family.

Often the children who arrived on our doorstep had hard exteriors. Life experiences had taught them that to get what they wanted or needed, they had to be aggressive and angry and show no fear. On the surface, these kids seemed unapproachable, and at times they would act out with behaviors that would push most people away.

Understanding that for many of the children, these behaviors were just defense mechanisms, my husband and I would try to respond in a way that was completely opposite from what the child expected: when they yelled, we'd whisper a response; when they pushed us away, we'd sit close by to show we cared. One child would scream and cry as I held her, as I let her know she was safe from any harm. Although change didn't come overnight, these compassionate responses to the children in our care eventually led to small changes in their behavior and in their reactions to us.

We may not fully understand the life experiences that someone else has walked through, the events that made them who they are today. Some may have faced hardships we've never even dreamed of understanding. A compassionate response to others can disarm even the hardest of hearts, allowing us to better understand or relate to where they are coming from and helping us not to look down on anyone. We know that God cares deeply for each of the children we've taken in, and it's our job to reflect that love to them.

— Kendra

— Today's Act of Kindness —

Think of someone whom you have a hard time getting along with, and consider what may have led the person to act the way they do. Then pray that God would give you compassion for them.

Failed Expectations

*Direct your children onto the right path, and when
they are older, they will not leave it.*
PROVERBS 22:6

In my mind, it was a grand idea. A kid's clothing store had great deals on fleece pants and pullovers, and we had several families in our city in need of basics, including warm clothes.

I packed up the kids, gave them some money, and explained the game plan: we were buying warm clothes for other kids. It seemed so simple. Fast-forward to ten minutes later, and I had one child lying on the floor, so completely *done* with the experience. I was beyond frustrated that the vision in my head wasn't playing out the way I had intended.

Argh!

I wish I could say that I was calm, cool, and collected as I watched my good intentions implode, but I wasn't. I felt myself getting anxious, uptight, and slightly snappy. As we grabbed our selections and headed to the checkout counter to make our purchases, I made the wise decision to just let go of the experience, for now. I knew we would circle back to it in a conversation when my kids delivered the clothing to the local nonprofit organization handling distribution.

Teaching kids to be generous and to think bigger and beyond themselves is a journey, not a onetime event. If your grand plan doesn't work, regroup and try again later. When I think about the processes of forming habits and training minds, I realize they both occur over time through education and hands-on experiences. The best training is repetitive and ongoing and allows us to flail, fail, and slowly figure it out through repetition and practice.

If you're a parent, you're in this apprenticeship program for the long haul. Don't get discouraged. Keep at it. God encourages us that the battle will be worth it and that children trained up and discipled into faith will not depart from it. That is something I cling to on the rough days, knowing that God is doing something bigger in my children than I could ever do on my own.

— Julie

— Today's Act of Kindness —

Include your children in a random act of kindness,
and let them pick the kind act.

"Worthy" of Kindness

The earth is the LORD's, and everything in it, the world, and all who live in it.
PSALM 24:1, NIV

My husband works in the financial services industry. Throughout the years, he's heard stories about clients who reveal the best and worst parts of human nature. Siblings who fight over their inheritance following the death of their parents, leading to disputes that dissolve the family. A wealthy couple who have made millions, yet wonder if their $1,000 donation to charity the previous year was "too much."

In my opinion, possessiveness can only lead to unhappiness. When I start thinking about things as *mine*—*my* money, *my* resources, *my* time, *my* talents—that inward focus can lead to dissatisfaction in giving.

Have you ever heard of someone who was in need and immediately you wanted to judge whether or not the person was truly "worthy" of the gift? I'm sad to admit that I've done this too. I don't want to give something that's *mine* to someone who might waste it or use it foolishly.

I'm not advocating being a poor steward of your resources, but we should remember that we have been given *all* things from the Lord—all our resources, all the possessions we cling to so tightly. We were born in this era, in this country, with all the advantages and opportunities that engenders, by God's design.

What if, instead, God gave us resources based on our gratitude, humility, or frugality? Many of us might be poorer, both in spirit and in resources, if that were the case! Rather than possessively holding on to what we've deemed ours, miserly giving it only to those who seem worthy, perhaps we should consider all we have to be an outpouring of God's blessings. In a way, we're simply giving back to him—so a standard of "worthiness" really isn't for us to decide.

What's more important than the recipient being worthy of kindness is my heart's motivation behind the action: Is it for my glory or for God's? When we act out of a desire to honor God, we will find deeper satisfaction in our giving.

— Kristin

— Today's Act of Kindness —

Prayerfully do something kind for someone
you've judged or considered unworthy.

Shutting Down the Green-Eyed Monster

*Don't be selfish; don't try to impress others. Be humble,
thinking of others as better than yourselves.*

PHILIPPIANS 2:3

I was jealous. Although that doesn't happen very often, when it does, I'm ashamed to admit it. Jealousy is not an attractive emotion, but every now and then it rears its ugly head in me.

It happened just the other day when Julie and I applied to speak at a local gathering of women. Confident we would be included in the group because we had been the year before, we were surprised when we got a reply politely declining our application.

I knew I shouldn't be jealous of the women who had been accepted, but for a moment I couldn't help myself. I looked through their biographies and credentials, wondering what made them better than us or more qualified to share. Was this a bit immature on my part? Yes, it was.

I finally shut down my computer and took my feelings in prayer to God. I realized that my jealousy stemmed from wondering if I measured up against others who were chosen when I was not.

God reminded me that my value comes from him, not from acceptance by other people. I was reminded of his love for me and how the plans he has for me are both good and different from the plans he has for other people. I was also reminded that I will never be happy if I'm doing things out of selfishness or a desire to impress others. I ended my time by praying for the women who would be sharing at the gathering, that God would bless their lives and their messages.

It's easy to get consumed by jealousy when we focus too much on what those around us have instead of on what God has in store for each of us. Keeping a tally of what others have and being angry about what we don't have is no way to live. When we place our focus on God, we begin to see the plan he has for us individually, and the need to measure up against others begins to dissipate.

— *Kendra*

— Today's Act of Kindness —

When you find yourself being jealous of someone else's talents, gifts, or things, remind yourself of what God has given to you, and then pray a prayer of blessing for the other person.

Bridge Building

God blesses those who work for peace, for they will
be called the children of God.
MATTHEW 5:9

Years ago, a single conversation helped correct a misunderstanding between two professionals within my community.

All told, it took five minutes from my day. I gained nothing from it. I simply noticed the misunderstanding unfolding and quietly approached one of the individuals, Bruce, with a quick explanation and a suggestion that he extend a lunch invitation to the other person. He listened to my advice, and over lunch the misunderstanding was smoothed out. Bruce has ended up working closely with the other person on several projects in the years since that conversation.

I thought nothing more of it, and honestly, I forgot all about it until I started a new job. I felt off kilter and uncertain that first week as I struggled to learn the new software, figure out the phone system, and remember names of my new coworkers. I didn't know it yet, but Bruce was a friend of my new boss and a person with influence in my new organization. It wasn't until after the third person (the human resources manager, no less) swung by my office that first week to mention that Bruce had been raving about me during a recent lunch that I really stopped to think.

I was suddenly reaping the benefit of my simple words, my willingness to step forward as a peacemaker all those years ago, at just the moment when I felt a little vulnerable and exposed. As the third person left my office that day, I smiled secretly as I turned back to my work. I thanked Jesus for the great wisdom contained in Scripture and for so clearly being with me as I started this new job.

In a world filled with instigators and individuals who fan the flames of controversy, we need peacemakers. We need people who encourage others to seek out common ground, who build bridges, who build community.

— Julie

— Today's Act of Kindness —

Pray that God would give you eyes to see how you can serve
as a peacemaker. The next time you notice a conflict arise,
however small, gently suggest steps toward reconciliation.

April

My Grandmother's Earrings

*For God is not unjust. He will not forget how hard you
have worked for him and how you have shown your love
to him by caring for other believers, as you still do.*
HEBREWS 6:10

My paternal grandmother died when I was seven, and I inherited a pair of her clip-on costume-jewelry earrings. They were drop earrings, each one a soft-pink faceted bead the size of a grape, with just a glimmer of shimmery iridescence.

I did not know my Grandmother Brotzler well, and I regret that our lives did not overlap by more years so that I might have known and remembered her personally instead of relying solely upon the stories others told. She was a woman of substance, fun, faith, unending strength, and unconditional love.

I tucked those earrings away, and as I grew, I all but forgot them—until I met my friend Jenna for lunch. I immediately noticed her earrings; they were an exact replica (only pierced instead of clip-on) of mine. I admired her earrings, telling her about my Grandma Brotzler and how I inherited her earrings and had always felt beautiful when I wore them.

As I opened my front door the next morning on my way to work, a small package propped against the door fell inside and landed at my feet. Retrieving it, I found Jenna's earrings and a little note of encouragement.

I cried at her thoughtfulness. I've intentionally worn those earrings on days and to events when I need just a little extra boost of self-confidence. They remind me of my grandmother, my heritage, and the generosity of a friend who believes in me. They have become a symbol of the woman I strive to be.

I've often watched as Jenna's loving actions toward others beautifully reflect her faith in God. She makes taking care of others a central part of her daily life, and I know that God sees and does not forget how she cares for others, believers and nonbelievers alike.

— Julie

— Today's Act of Kindness —

Choose to do an act of kindness in which the sentimental
value for the recipient far exceeds any financial value.

The Gift of Memory

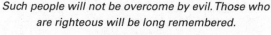

Such people will not be overcome by evil. Those who
are righteous will be long remembered.

PSALM 112:6

"Wait, are you Katrina's sister?" The question, asked casually at a Tuesday-morning meeting of moms from the surrounding area, stopped me in my tracks.

I replied yes, my heart pounding a little. I'd just talked about my past, my sister's cancer, and how I still struggled to overcome my grief from her death at the age of twenty-eight. The things I had shared with the other ladies from my table had left me feeling a little uncertain and a lot vulnerable.

Sympathetic, the woman looked me straight in the eyes. I didn't know her well, but I knew she was a nurse. She said words I'll never forget: "Kristin, she is remembered. Your sister is remembered. There are nurses on the cancer floor at the hospital who still talk about her to this day."

I thanked her, blinking back tears, then rushed to get my children from their classrooms and hurried to the parking lot. Then, in the front seat of my car, I started to sob.

Losing my sister Katrina was, in many ways, a defining moment in my life. I treasure my memories of our time together and mourn the years we didn't get to have. Yet as the years have passed, I've been burdened in a new way with the thought that she might be forgotten by others, even as she remains vibrant in my memory.

Scripture says that "those who are righteous will be long remembered," and on that Tuesday morning, I was reminded of that promise. Those few words spoken to me by the mom at my table, the gift of memory she so kindly passed on to me, were a priceless treasure I've never forgotten.

— *Kristin*

— Today's Act of Kindness —

Think of someone who has experienced loss. Reach
out to this person and share a memory or two that you
have of the loved one they lost. Let them know that their
loved one may be gone but has not been forgotten.

Use Your Gifts

All who are skilled among you are to come and make
everything the LORD has commanded.
EXODUS 35:10, NIV

My daughter Jasmine loves, among many things, to sing. At just seven years old she is already making up her own songs, practicing tunes on the piano, and performing them regularly for my husband and me. Seeing the passion she has, we are sure to encourage her writing and performing.

One spring she asked our pastor if she could sing during a service, then she bravely got up and shared her song with our church community, who praised her for her courage. Another time, when we'd invited our neighbors over for dinner, she again asked if they'd like to hear her song. They agreed, and once she was done, one of our neighbors was so touched that she asked if Jasmine would sing it again. My neighbor later told me how moved she was by Jasmine's little song, and I just nodded, struck by how my daughter's words had meant so much to her.

As I've thought more about Jasmine's songs and the impact they've had on others, I've realized that what is most moving to people is not just her talent but the sincerity and the heart behind what she shares. In a world that can often be insincere and fake, people notice when we are passionate and genuine in our words and actions. She sincerely and unashamedly uses her gifts to bless others.

It is no accident that we are all gifted in unique ways. God asks each of us to use our gifts and talents and skills for him, not from an attitude of pride in ourselves, but humbly, in a way that brings glory to him. When we operate out of the gifts God has given to each of us, we honor him and bless others by being living examples of his goodness and kindness.

— Kendra

— Today's Act of Kindness —

What gifts or talents has God given you? Instead of being
ashamed or hiding them, use them to bless someone else.

Do Our Actions Even Matter?

God is not unjust. He will not forget how hard you have worked for him and how you have shown your love to him by caring for other believers, as you still do.
HEBREWS 6:10

One day as I was driving my kids to school, I unexpectedly cracked. As I pondered the crazy onslaught of obligations in the upcoming weeks and months, I suddenly felt crushed beneath their weight.

Once the kids were safely delivered to school, I started sobbing—the loud, uncontrollable, ugly kind of crying that comes from overwhelming emotion. Without thinking, I looked to the sky and cried out: "Does any of this actually make a difference?"

Whoops. I hadn't meant to shout. The words poured out when my guard was down and my emotions were raw. I half expected a lightning bolt to turn me into a crispy critter as I murmured an apology for shouting at the God of the universe and continued my drive to work.

It was midmorning when my friend called to tell me about a person who had been deeply touched by a project I had helped on. I laughed ruefully and confessed exactly what I had shouted at God that morning. My friend chuckled and stated the obvious—God heard me and responded.

Later that day, another friend sent me an e-mail describing a breakthrough in a terribly difficult situation for which many people have been praying. I smiled a bit bigger. God heard and responded. Before the day was done, I heard from a third person who had received an answer to prayer in a situation that was beyond her control. God reminded me that I am a tiny part of something bigger, and my actions do matter.

I stopped and thanked God for loving me enough to answer my tantrum with grace and for reminding me that when we partner with him, our actions do matter and we do make a difference—regardless of whether we ever see it. God does not forget us as we do his work.

— Julie

— Today's Act of Kindness —

Consider a time when you were the recipient of kindness.
Reach out to the person who showed you kindness and let
them know just how much their actions meant to you.

The Diva Boutique

Clothe yourselves with love, which binds us all together in perfect harmony.
COLOSSIANS 3:14, NIV

I love clothes. In fact, my closet resembles nothing so much as a messy explosion of colors and textures, usually draped on top of each other. (I don't love to clean as much as I love clothes, clearly.) So participating in the Diva Boutique at the retreat for single moms combines my love of giving with my love of clothes.

The Diva Boutique is a place where women can "shop" for clothing items—jeans, scarves, shirts, bras, you name it—for free. The donations are collected statewide in the months leading up to the event, and volunteers sort and organize the items by size and type, and truck them to the retreat. Then they set everything up, decorate the shop, and open for business.

The response is overwhelmingly positive. And for me, it's fun. I worked in retail for many years, so my favorite job is to hang out by the dressing rooms. It's not as creepy as it sounds, really. I love to see women emerge to model their clothes. For some, it's been so long since they've shopped for themselves that they've forgotten what size they wear. Others need something specific—clothes for work, a dress for church or a wedding—and it's a pleasure to help them hunt down the perfect item. I love finding pieces that reflect their inner beauty and personality, honoring them and showing them love in tangible ways.

Some of my favorite moments are the quietest moments, the ones where no one else is paying attention. Sometimes a woman has six items instead of the allotted five, and I have the privilege of whispering, "Go ahead and take all six." Seeing her smile and hearing her hesitant, "Are you sure?" makes me feel wealthy beyond measure, simply by choosing to give away more than expected.

That feeling of unity, of usefulness, of giving something of value to someone else is also a gift to myself. The long hours of preparation, the physical toll of the weekend, and my aching feet are a small price to pay for the internal satisfaction and deep gratitude I feel and the simple reminder of how we're called to love others.

— *Kristin*

— Today's Act of Kindness —

Find something extra in your house and give it away
to someone who would appreciate it, either a person
you know or an organization in your community.

Turning an Aching Heart into a Kind Heart

*Since God chose you to be the holy people he loves, you must clothe yourselves
with tenderhearted mercy, kindness, humility, gentleness, and patience.*
COLOSSIANS 3:12

"Mom. My class voted for who should be Snow White in our class play, and I am
the only person who voted for me."

My eyes remained focused on the freeway, but my attention was on the young
voice in the back seat.

"Not one person voted for me. *No one likes me.*" Her voice quivered before she
dissolved into heart-wrenching sobs.

My heart broke. I was hoping my daughter would be a bit older before she
had to navigate the difference between her intrinsic worth and the thoughts and
opinions of people around her.

Oh, how I wish I could keep her safe from the hurts of this world . . . but I
know I cannot and should not. We cannot completely shield our children from
heartache and still expect them to respond compassionately to those who are hurting around them.

So often, our determination to reach those who most desperately need to see
the love of Christ stems from an intimate understanding of heartache ourselves.
Showing intentional kindness means that we will get our hands dirty, we will cry
hard tears, we will see suffering instead of glossing over it and pretending it doesn't
exist. Oftentimes, learning to be truly merciful, kind, humble, patient, and gentle
requires us to experience the opposite, so that we can know and understand the
pain inflicted by careless words and actions.

While my heart aches when my children feel the sting of rejection, I want it to
happen when they are living under my roof, so my husband and I can counter the
lies before they get buried into our kids' hearts. We want to show our kids biblical
truth about God's unending love for them and his good plans for their lives.

— Julie

— Today's Act of Kindness —

Where have you been hurt, believed lies, or felt the sting of
rejection? As you come across someone in your life who is
hurting, channel those memories so you can respond in empathy,
showing them tender kindness and gentle truth in their pain.

The Truth about God

I am confident I will see the LORD's goodness while
I am here in the land of the living.
PSALM 27:13

"I have a really hard time seeing God as my Father, since my earthly father was so distant."

I heard this admission from a woman at a Bible study I attend. At best, she has a rocky relationship with her father—when they are speaking at all. She has been a Christian for years, but she still struggles with believing that God is a loving Father, since the earthly example she was given is just *not*. Nodding in agreement over our friend's struggle, many other women shared ways that they have mistakenly viewed God because of their own relationships and life experiences.

We all see God through the lens of our experiences, and we all struggle with what we believe about him and his character. Our experiences can skew the way we view God. Often we don't even realize this is happening.

So what do we do when we aren't sure what is true about God? We can start by reading the Bible and finding truth there. When we wonder if God loves us, we can start by searching for Scripture that tells us that he does (such as John 3:16). When we worry about the future and if God can be trusted, then we can look for Scripture that reminds us of his care and concern for us (such as 1 Peter 5:7).

Whatever we are facing, we can find a promise or a truth about God and his character that will sustain us. This is important, because if we don't believe that God is kind and loving, how can we extend kindness and love to others? We have to trust in God's goodness so that we will be able to freely give it away to others. We need to have the confidence to say, "I will see the LORD's goodness."

— *Kendra*

— Today's Act of Kindness —

Spend some time thinking about what misconceptions
you have believed about God. Find a verse of Scripture
to remind you of who he truly is, then text that
verse to a friend who may need to hear it too.

A Wrecked Life

*If someone has enough money to live well and sees a brother or sister in
need but shows no compassion—how can God's love be in that person?*

1 JOHN 3:17

My friend Danielle was living an ordinary life in the US when she and her husband read the book *Red Letters: Living a Faith that Bleeds*, by Tom Davis. In it, this former CEO of Children's HopeChest (a nonprofit organization serving underprivileged children worldwide) talks about the role the HIV epidemic has played in the African country of Swaziland and the thousands of orphaned and vulnerable children left to fend for themselves in the wake of its deadly effects.

As parents themselves, Danielle and her husband, Michael, felt immediate concern and compassion for the children of Swaziland, and they resolved to find ways, even small ones, to help. First, they sponsored a young girl through Children's HopeChest. Next, they became sponsorship coordinators, helping connect other children in need with sponsors. Finally, they spent a week in the girl's community, living among her friends and neighbors. It was at this point that they were radically changed.

"We were wrecked," Danielle told me later. "Wrecked for the ordinary. Wrecked for living for ourselves. Wrecked for these little ones who need advocates to stand up and say, 'Yes! I will pray. I will give. I will go.'"

When Danielle arrived home, she began coming up with more ways their family could help the community in Swaziland flourish: creating and selling T-shirts and bracelets; sharing during speaking and writing opportunities. Whatever she could do to support the children in Swaziland, she began doing. Despite her comfortable life, she was moved to do even more.

Not only does Danielle model a life of generosity, but she invites others to do the same. The passion someone has for giving can inspire others to give more generously as well. Cheerful giving is contagious—how might you spread it today?

— Kristin

— Today's Act of Kindness —

Think of a cause that "wrecks" you. Is it human trafficking,
hunger, homelessness, or something else? Once you've
identified it, take one simple step toward supporting solutions.

Left Out but Not Counted Out

All of you together are Christ's body, and each of you is a part of it.
1 CORINTHIANS 12:27

When I was a little girl, I looked up to and admired my older sister Katrina. A born leader, Katrina drew people into her circle of friends quite naturally. So naturally, in fact, that my parents tell stories of family trips or vacations when, even as a child, Katrina would gather all the other kids in the pool for a shared game or activity. They even coined a term for these group activities: Katie's Clubs.

My father also likes to remind me that although I was always very willing to go along with Katrina as the leader and was happy just being a part of the group, I also had a unique gift of seeing the one child who didn't quite fit in or who couldn't keep up with the rest of the kids. My dad says I would often notice and befriend this child, going off to play one-on-one, ensuring that no one was ever left out.

We all have the responsibility and the privilege of including others at work, at school, at church, or in our neighborhoods. It doesn't really matter if you're outgoing like Katrina, leading a large group, or if you're more introverted like me, seeing the needs of just one person. God uses all of us to show his kindness and love toward others, and no one person's role is greater or more important than another's. We were uniquely made to fulfill individual roles, and we were also meant to complement each other as a part of Christ's body. Don't be afraid to step out with whatever personality style God has given you. There's no need to wish you were more like someone else and, by doing so, inadvertently dismiss the people God asks you to bring his kindness and love to. You may just be the best person for the job.

— Kendra

— Today's Act of Kindness —

Choose to include someone who may be feeling left out,
whether it's as part of a large group or one-on-one.

God's Redeeming Kindness

Whoever finds me finds life and receives favor from the LORD.
PROVERBS 8:35

Erin, a girl in my social circles in college, brought me to tears more times than I'd care to admit. Her talent was the subtle snub, communicating superiority with a raised eyebrow and a slight sneer, and I was a favorite target. After a time, just hearing her name formed a knot in the pit of my stomach and filled my heart with anxiety.

Eventually, I took my pain to Jesus, asking him to remove my anxiety and to help me forgive Erin. After that prayer, every time I heard her name spoken and felt anxiety rising up, I'd hand the situation back to Jesus—asking him to take my anxiety and to help me forgive all over again.

A few weeks into my new habit, I heard someone shout "Erin!" across my college campus, trying to catch the attention of a friend. Bracing for the anxiety, I felt nothing. After a few more Erin run-ins with zero anxiety, I realized that my prayer had been answered. Praising God, I moved on with my life.

It was when I was in law school three years later that I met the love of my life. He is my best friend, my biggest fan, and the person who knows my worst self and loves me anyway. Can you guess his name?

Aaron.

When I took my pain to Jesus and asked for his help with extending forgiveness instead of continuing to struggle alone, he took the name that caused me stomach-churning anxiety and turned it into a name that fills my heart to overflowing.

I sometimes temporarily forget that Jesus is intimately kind to us in ways that can take our breath away. We find joy and redemption when we listen to his voice, when we watch for him, and when we wait on him. God promises life and favor to those who find him, especially when we seek him and find him in the midst of a painful situation. He alone can redeem our pain, weaving it into a blessing beyond comprehension.

— Julie

— Today's Act of Kindness —

Is there a source of pain or a grudge you're still hanging on to? The next time you're faced with the situation, ask for God's help to forgive the person and ask him to redeem the pain.

Celebrate with Those Who Celebrate

Rejoice with those who rejoice; mourn with those who mourn.
ROMANS 12:15, NIV

It was a rare date night out for Tim and me, and as a stay-at-home mom, I was looking forward to visiting with other adults. We made our way to the table, sat down with the two other couples, and started chatting, perusing the menu, and ordering appetizers.

As our dinner progressed, a sudden movement caught our eyes. A few tables over, a man was getting down on one knee, a ring box outstretched toward the woman across from him. Though I didn't hear his words, it was obvious that he was asking the woman to marry him. As she nodded and smiled and wiped tears from her eyes, I found myself looking away for a moment, overcome by the intimacy of such a private moment. Other than participating in my own proposal, I'd never seen someone get engaged, and even as an observer, it was an emotional experience. Blinking my own tears away, I joined the other diners as they burst into spontaneous applause while the couple embraced.

I whispered to Tim that we should send over a bottle of champagne to congratulate them, and he quietly signaled to the waiter and put in our anonymous request. As we stole glances at the happy couple throughout the night, I felt my own joy at the occasion mirroring the faces of the newly engaged pair as they raised their glasses to toast each other.

Sometimes kindness requires us to grieve with those who grieve, but it's just as important to enjoy this life and celebrate with those who have something to celebrate. Celebration is a gift from God, and honoring the special moments and momentous occasions of friends and neighbors is a great opportunity to show them the kindness of your attention.

— *Kristin*

— Today's Act of Kindness —

Think of someone who has reason to celebrate—
a promotion, an engagement, or a new baby—and find
a way to celebrate with them. Bake a cake, take them
to lunch, or leave an encouraging voice mail.

She Will Be My Friend!

*[Ruth replied,] "Wherever you go, I will go; wherever you live, I will live.
Your people will be my people, and your God will be my God."*

RUTH 1:16

Several years ago I went on a girls' weekend with a handful of friends. A new woman who had just moved to our area, and who also happened to be the youth pastor's wife, was invited to come with us. It was a lovely weekend of connecting with other women, having fun, and enjoying a break from our usual lives.

On the second morning, as the new woman, Jenny, showered, my sister Katrina proclaimed to those of us in the room, "She *will* be my friend!" We all looked at her and giggled at the proclamation, as someone else asked, "And what about us? We'd like to be her friends too!" Laughing, Katrina responded that of course we could all be friends with Jenny.

And that is exactly what happened. Katrina intentionally pursued a relationship with Jenny, who, over the years, became one of her closest friends and confidantes, walking with her through some of the hardest days of her life.

Developing friendships is not always easy. Often it takes a willingness to put ourselves out there and even be intentional and vulnerable about pursuing a relationship with another person. Katrina's example is one that I still emulate today whenever I meet a new woman whom I really connect with and think, *She will be my friend.* Just as Ruth pledged herself to Naomi in today's Scripture, we can allow others into our lives as a purposeful act of kindness that bonds us to them. It's an act that takes time and a willingness to openly and honestly share ourselves with others. So many people are in need of a good friend, and if you take the time to notice others, you may just be the answer to someone's prayer for friendship.

— Kendra

— Today's Act of Kindness —

Look for someone who may be lonely or in need of a
friend. Be intentional about extending a hand of kindness
and an invitation of friendship toward them.

A Legacy of Kindness

*Let your good deeds shine out for all to see, so that
everyone will praise your heavenly Father.*
MATTHEW 5:16

My aunt and uncle were foster parents for twenty years, and during that time, they took in fifteen kids long term and adopted four. As a young girl, I watched how they took care of kids, loving them through challenging and joyful circumstances. They never made any grand speeches or gave any sermons to us kids about loving others; they just showed us by their lives, day in and day out, what it means to love others.

It was a lesson I carried into my adulthood as my husband and I talked about starting our own family. When I mentioned that I'd like to provide foster care for kids and told him of my experience watching my aunt and uncle all those years earlier, he readily agreed. For six years we, too, took in kids who needed a home, caring for twenty children and adopting two into our family forever.

I often think of my upbringing, how being kind and loving others were *shown* even more often than they were talked about. This example challenges me with my own family now to not just speak to my children about how they should behave but to also lead them with my actions. Kindness is not just a thought or an idea; it's how we live out our very lives for others to see. I know my aunt and uncle would never have thought I'd follow their example by providing foster care; they just did what came naturally for them. But that kindness was passed on, not only to the kids in their home, but to me as well.

When we consider our lives and what we hope to pass on to others, what examples are we setting through our everyday lives and actions that would make someone else want to emulate us or follow in our footsteps? Are we letting our good deeds shine out for all to see, so that everyone will praise our heavenly Father? What acts of kindness can we do today, to benefit not only the recipient but also others who may be watching our example?

— *Kendra*

— Today's Act of Kindness —

Show an act of kindness toward someone in front
of your spouse, your kids, or a friend—not out of a
desire to be praised, but to set an example you would
want to be remembered for years from now.

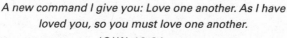

APRIL 14

The Gift of Giving

A new command I give you: Love one another. As I have
loved you, so you must love one another.

JOHN 13:34, NIV

We've all heard that it's better to give than it is to receive, but did you know that research confirms it? Biologically speaking, kind people have better health and tend to live longer.

In an article entitled "What We Get When We Give," sociologist Christine Carter gives an overview of some of the myriad health benefits of living a life of kindness.

> People who volunteer tend to experience fewer aches and pains. Giving help to others protects overall health twice as much as aspirin protects against heart disease. People 55 and older who volunteer for two or more organizations have an impressive 44 percent lower likelihood of dying— and that's after sifting out every other contributing factor, including physical health, exercise, gender, habits like smoking, marital status, and many more. This is a stronger effect than exercising four times a week.*

Since I loathe exercising, this is good news for me. A lot of these positive side effects are attributed to what's often referred to as a "helper's high." Carter notes that in one study, many of the participants felt calmer and happier, reporting feelings of greater self-worth and higher energy levels after helping someone else.** Helping someone in need stimulates our brains to reward us by releasing the feel-good chemical dopamine.

It reminds me of giving Christmas presents—I'm often more excited to see someone else's response to a gift I've carefully chosen for them than I am to open anything placed under the tree for me. When God tells us to "love one another," it's a command that, when lived out, can give us just as much pleasure (and good health!) as it gives to those we're aiming to help.

— *Kristin*

— Today's Act of Kindness —

Is there an organization or cause that you believe in? If so, maybe it's time to take the next step and volunteer with them on a regular basis.

---

* Christine L. Carter, "What We Get When We Give," *Psychology Today*, February 19, 2010,
http://www.psychologytoday.com/blog/raising-happiness/201002/what-we-get-when-we-give.
** Ibid.

Craving the Son

[Jesus] said, "I am the light of the world. If you follow me, you won't have to walk in darkness, because you will have the light that leads to life."

JOHN 8:12

The first week in April is always seed-starting week at my house. A small corner of my kitchen converts to a greenhouse as I nurture flats of tiny seedlings under fluorescent bulbs. Most springs, I move my plants outside and into the sun as soon as I can—letting them grow during the day and tucking them safely into the house during the chilly early-spring nights.

One spring was remarkably different. The miserably unrelenting snow, gray skies, and freezing temperatures had trapped my tender seedlings under artificial light and kept them from the sun's strong rays far longer than what is healthy.

And then, finally, the sun came out for a few days one week. As I moved my flats of plants onto the front porch and into the warm rays of the sun, I closely examined my seedlings—pale and a little spindly from too much time under artificial lights, despite my best efforts.

During my perusal, I lifted my head from my little plants, and I noticed my other "seedlings"— my children—as they leaped and danced and ran through the yard in their swimsuits. (Yes. Swimsuits.) They twirled like tiny windmills in the bright sunshine.

As I felt the sun warm my skin and lift my mood, I thought, *The sun is good for all of us.* Immediately, my next thought was, *The Son is good for all of us.*

Isn't it fascinating that we call that golden orb that gives life and warmth to our cold planet the "sun," and we call Christ, who came and gave light to our lives, the "Son"? Life without the sun or the Son is cold and miserable and gray. But when we live life in the sun and in the Son, life pulses with warmth.

Just like those seedlings, we can only expend so much energy without nourishment. Living a life of intentional kindness requires us to soak up life-giving energy from the Son on a regular basis through spending time in his presence and in his Word.

— Julie

— Today's Act of Kindness —

Set aside thirty minutes to bask in the presence of our Savior. By doing so now, you'll be better equipped to pour out kindness later.

Giving Others the Benefit of the Doubt

Most important of all, continue to show deep love for each other, for love covers a multitude of sins.

1 PETER 4:8

I've been told that when I was young, I would often side with the underdog in any given situation, and that when someone I loved was making poor choices, I could still find the good in who they were as a person.

Much of my response to others was shaped by my father. Many times after someone had spoken harshly or been unkind, he would tell me, "You never know what they're going through. Maybe they're facing something really hard in their own lives." Although my parents never allowed others to take advantage of them or be cruel, I continually heard and watched them give others the benefit of the doubt. They always reminded us children that not long ago they, too, were not very loving or kind people, until God changed their lives and their hearts.

We have a choice in how we think about and treat other people. Oftentimes what we see on the surface may not be all of what someone is experiencing. We often don't see the secret pain or hurt that others are feeling in their lives. We should recognize that we all face hurts, obstacles, and challenges in life, which help remind us to extend grace and kindness toward others. Even when others may not deserve it, we need to remember that love covers a multitude of sins and it's up to us to extend this love.

We can always control the things we say and the way we respond to people, no matter their words or actions. We can give others the benefit of the doubt by considering what may lie beneath the surface and imagining all that a person may be facing. This, in turn, will give us the grace to withhold an unkind response and instead speak blessings over that person's life.

— Kendra

— Today's Act of Kindness —

When faced with the option of speaking unkindly in response to someone's harsh words, choose to bless and encourage them instead.

Willing to Do

I heard the Lord asking, "Whom should I send as a messenger to this people? Who will go for us?" I said, "Here I am. Send me."
ISAIAH 6:8

Justice. As a lawyer, I navigate this concept on a daily basis. I pick up the phone and suddenly find myself having deeply personal conversations with individuals about what our legal system is able to do—and what it cannot. Although I know in my head that life is not fair, that there is no guarantee of justice in a legal system run by fallible human beings, I cried particularly bitter tears on my way home from a hearing one afternoon.

Vulnerable people were left exposed and exploited, and the ones with the power to make a change told me there was nothing they could do. Tears streamed down my face as my car ate up the miles on the long drive home. Anger burned as my frustration turned into feelings of helplessness.

What can we do when we believe we are helpless? I know what we cannot, must not do: turn away, willfully ignoring the wrongs we see around us. We must never get to the point where we choose to overlook injustice because it hurts too much, because it is too exhausting, because we are just one tiny life in a sea of billions, and because we think our caring couldn't possibly matter.

Let's not numb ourselves with the distractions of life that have no eternal value, to the point that we do nothing else. Let's not hit "like" on social media and think that making a single click is the same as truly taking action. You can speak up if you see a stranger being verbally abused. You can volunteer with a nonprofit organization that specifically works with disadvantaged groups. You can financially support overseas ministries that are involved in advocating for human rights, ending human trafficking, or another issue close to your heart.

Let us not give up before we've even begun, convinced that what we do does not matter.

What you do matters. Helping even one person has ripple effects far beyond what you will ever know this side of heaven. God is looking for people he can trust to send into a broken, messed-up world with the message of redemption and salvation. He is looking for people who are willing to step forward and say, "Here I am, send me," who will show Christ's love in both words and deeds.

— Julie

— Today's Act of Kindness —

The next time you're faced with an opportunity to stand up to an injustice, ask God how you can take action, then do it.

Messy Kindness

Don't forget to do good and to share with those in need.
These are the sacrifices that please God.
HEBREWS 13:16

I peered at the directions on my phone as I wound my way farther into the countryside. Pulling up to my destination, I saw a garage door opening, the space inside filled with piles of garbage bags. As I exited my car, my friend Jen opened her front door and led me downstairs to what looked like an episode of *Hoarders*—a basement filled to the brim with clothes, some stacked on the table neatly, others on the floor haphazardly, with signs taped above them to announce their sizes.

"We got a lot done yesterday," she said, looking around at the mess optimistically. "This actually looks a lot better than it did."

Jen is in charge of the Diva Boutique, where single moms can "shop" for free. She'd spent the past many months collecting clothes for the shop, and on this day she was sorting items at her home before they were transferred to the event. This particular year, there were about seven thousand items. Each item would be looked over carefully. The ones that weren't up to the standards of "gently used" would be removed, while the others would be put on hangers or folded up neatly and placed in garbage bags. In a couple of weeks, the volunteers would drive the items to a camp and use them to turn a conference room into a beautiful boutique full of clothes and accessories.

As I left that day after working for a few hours, I thought about how, so often, kindness isn't glamorous. Sometimes it's messy and it means sacrificing your personal space. It can require hours of backbreaking work. Yet it's this behind-the-scenes kindness that can be the *most* important. It's unseen, often thankless. There's no spotlight to bask in, just the heartfelt thank-yous from women who will never know how many hours you spent thinking about and praying for them while sorting clothes.

My friend Jen is an unsung hero. She's proof that showing kindness is *work*. It's intentional. Doing good and sharing with those in need is often a sacrifice—and these sacrifices please God.

— *Kristin*

— Today's Act of Kindness —

Choose to do an activity that requires you to sacrifice in some
way—with no promise of reward or even a "thank you."

A Simple Invitation

I was a stranger, and you invited me into your home.
MATTHEW 25:35

Sitting in the pew, I just knew this wasn't where I'd be regularly attending services. At only twenty-two years old, I was determined to make my own way in town but had agreed to join my sister at her church, just this once, before finding a place of my own.

As I was exiting the sanctuary, a young woman came up and greeted me and asked who I was, before sharing a bit about herself. She immediately went on to tell me about a young-adult progressive dinner that was coming up the following week. One course was being hosted at her house, and she asked if I'd like to help her. She was so kind, and since I had very few friends in the area, I said yes. That was the start of a beautiful friendship, one that also brought me into a community of friends I so desperately needed. (I also never ended up leaving that little community to look for another church.)

I often think about her invitation—how my life would be different had she not invited me to her house. How such a small act of kindness had such a profound impact on my life. As a part of that church community, I found friendship and growth in my faith that was vital to those early adult years. I am forever grateful for her willingness to step outside of her own comfort zone, say hello to a stranger, and invite me into her group of friends.

We just never know what can happen if we're willing to open up our lives to those around us. Being willing to be the first to greet a new person, whether at work, at church, or in some other group, may start a friendship, or at the very least, allow someone who is a little lonely to feel welcomed. Jesus reminded us that when we invite the stranger in, we are inviting in Christ himself. When we acknowledge those who need a friend, it's as if we are extending the very love and kindness of Jesus toward that person. And that is no small act.

— Kendra

— Today's Act of Kindness —

The next time you see someone new at work, at church,
or in your neighborhood, greet them and welcome
them into your friendship circle or community.

Kindness in the Silence

*I urge you, first of all, to pray for all people. Ask God to help
them; intercede on their behalf, and give thanks for them.*
1 TIMOTHY 2:1

"I've prayed all these years, and God has never once answered."

The weight of those words hung in the air between us. As much as I wanted to disagree, to remind her of all the ways God had provided, I remained silent, choosing to simply listen.

My therapist friends have taught me the power of silence, of allowing someone to think aloud, of allowing a person to grapple with emotions in the sacred space of uninterrupted companionship.

We both knew her words weren't true, but, in that moment, that was her *felt* truth. And feelings can be honest and raw and different from reality because they represent our *perceptions*—right or wrong, factual or not. In a world of perfectly posed Instagram photos, it takes courage to admit that everything isn't okay, that life feels unbearably hard, that God seems to be silent. When someone bravely whispers that things aren't perfect—she received a dreaded medical diagnosis, her marriage is on the rocks, or whatever hard thing she whispers across that quiet space—what is it that we can do?

How do we respond to those whispered needs—needs whose solutions seem so much more complex and less tangible than a bag of groceries secretly left on the porch? Sometimes silent companionship is the best way to show the love of Christ without coming across as insincere—with answers that are too simplistic or with a distracted pat on the head as we quickly change the subject.

And we can pray. We are called to intercede in prayer on behalf of others, asking for God to help in their circumstances. There is such power in prayer, and sometimes our role, our best way to help, is to faithfully and quietly pray for our friends when they are too tired, too weary to pray for themselves. God is good. He hears our prayers and is moved to respond (see Matthew 7:7-11), even when life is hard—*especially* when life is hard.

— Julie

— Today's Act of Kindness —

Is there someone in your life who needs the gift of
listening? Pray silently for that person's struggles,
and then offer a quiet mouth and a listening ear.

Kindness Steps In

Ask me for anything in my name, and I will do it!
JOHN 14:14

The message was posted on the Facebook page for women in our church one Friday. A single mom and her four kids had been evicted from the home they were living in and were desperately seeking a place to stay. They were hoping to enter a local church-of-the-week program the following Monday, which would at least give them rotating but regular housing, but in the meantime, they didn't have anywhere to go over the weekend.

My heart broke a little, imagining the mom's worry. How helpless would I feel in that situation if the roles were reversed? Each of us is only one action or accident away from facing a challenge like hers. When I finished reading the message, I forwarded it to my husband, as I often do when situations like this arise. Knowing he'd want to help, I called him to follow up.

After we chatted briefly about the situation, we hung up, and he immediately called our church's leaders to say we'd be more than happy to take on the cost of putting the family in a hotel over the weekend, until they could enter the program on Monday. The fact that we didn't know the family personally was insignificant. A mom and her babies had nowhere to go—that is the *only* fact I needed to know to move me to help.

Scripture tells us that when we ask for anything in Jesus' name, God will take care of it. When we ask God for help, he hears and is moved to take action. As Christians who seek to mirror the character of Christ, how can we do any less? When we see a need we know we can fill, taking a few minutes out of our days or a few dollars out of our bank accounts to help can make all the difference to someone else.

— *Kristin*

— Today's Act of Kindness —

Sometimes kindness requires us to simply see a need and act immediately—like carrying someone's groceries to their car or rounding up stray carts in the parking lot. Be on the lookout for a need you can meet, and meet it without hesitation.

Loving Others like Family

God places the lonely in families.

PSALM 68:6

When I was growing up, my parents loved to have my friends over to our house. They made sure snacks were stocked, and they even finished off a room in our basement where we could watch TV and hang out. They made sure to get to know the kids I was spending time with, but not just out of politeness—my parents truly cared for my friends and loved them as much as I did.

When I was a teenager, my dad loved to make a game out of answering the door before my friends would knock. With almost comical gusto he'd open the door, offering a warm welcome and often a hug to anyone on the other side. I watched my dad's example as he loved well the people his children loved. My mother, although not quite as exuberant, was always a quiet supporter, offering a listening ear when we needed it and loving my girlfriends like she was their second mom.

Now as an adult, I recognize and appreciate the kindness my parents intentionally invested through their time, attention, and thoughtfulness, not only in my life but also in my friends' lives.

We can all open our homes and our circles of influence to include those around us, regardless of whether we have children or not. If we pay attention, we'll see people every day at work, school, or church who are lonely and in need of community. Psalm 68 says that God places the lonely in families, and so often, he uses us to do it. To this end, we can all ask ourselves on a regular basis: *Who in my life may be in need of a friend, and how can I open up my life and my home to that person? Who in my community could use some extra support and care, and what can I do to provide it?*

— *Kendra*

— Today's Act of Kindness —

Look for someone in your community who may be lonely or in need of a friend. Invite them into your home for a meal or a cup of coffee.

When Your No Should Be Yes

*Work willingly at whatever you do, as though you were working for the
Lord rather than for people. Remember that the Lord will give you an
inheritance as your reward, and that the Master you are serving is Christ.*

COLOSSIANS 3:23-24

I have the privilege of serving alongside female ministry leaders from churches big and small, across denominational lines, and from every corner of Minnesota. I left one of our meetings recently pondering one small part of the evening's conversation. Two leaders were discussing the "epidemic of no"—this chorus of voices encouraging women to say no to any activity that doesn't "fill them up" or renew their spirits or meet a specific need of their own.

"Based on this, who would ever clean the toilets?" one woman asked with a sigh as the conversation ended and our meeting began.

Her words bounced around in my brain for weeks after that meeting.

Believe me, as a person who loves to please others, I understand the need to say no to some obligations so that there is enough of me to say yes to the things and people who matter most. However, I've begun to wonder if perhaps we're swinging too far in the other direction. Sometimes someone simply needs to clean the proverbial toilets—regardless of whether it is God alone who sees us bent over, scrubbing filth.

I'd rather do the dirty, unacknowledged task God has set before me, witnessed only by my Savior's eyes, than the glamorous, fun task acknowledged by humans, but with my heart misguidedly seeking their approval and applause. It is our attitudes as we work that are far more important than any earthly recognition—remembering that we are working for God, not for people, and that he is the one who gives us our inheritance.

And let's be honest, some of the most eternally important work is the stuff no one else wants to do, the stuff done without fanfare and in the shadows—the stuff that quietly supports another who gets the public glory. Are you prayerfully considering the requests on your time, talent, and treasure before saying yes or no?

— *Julie*

— Today's Act of Kindness —

When you're asked to do something you would normally say
no to, pray about what God wants you to do, and then obey.

Journey Bags

Imitate God, therefore, in everything you do, because you are his dear children. Live a life filled with love, following the example of Christ.

EPHESIANS 5:1-2

I have a sweet friend with a heart for foster care. Even before she and her husband began taking tiny babies into their home to care for them alongside their own children, she went out of her way to support foster parents and children. She even made freezer meals for my sister, who was a busy foster mom for many years.

One day, as we were chatting about organizations that could benefit from the help of our small women's group, she told us about The Forgotten Initiative, an organization that seeks to aid and support foster parents and children. One of their projects is providing "Journey Bags"—new backpacks filled with age-appropriate pajamas, books, and care items—to foster children entering a new home.

After hearing my friend's stories about how many foster care children arrive at their new homes with very few items, often hastily thrown into plastic shopping bags, I couldn't help but compare their circumstances to those of my own children. Sure, my girls love to lug around backpacks, but they are filled with Care Bears, not clothes. My daughters have stable lives and are never worried about what they might wear, what they'll eat, or where they will live. In the midst of my own comfort, my heart aches for the upheaval many children face.

And so, together in our pursuit to "live a life filled with love," this group of women agreed to gather items to put into backpacks. Throughout the week, I picked up some of my favorite children's books; warm, cozy pajamas; and teething toys. Then one Saturday morning we gathered together to fill up rows of backpacks with items for the children in our community, praying that our small effort would help smooth their transitions.

— Kristin

— Today's Act of Kindness —

Think of one thing you can do for the children in your community—whether it's helping a single mom with childcare or volunteering in your church's nursery—and then do it.

Love the Person in Front of You

*The LORD said to Moses, "Look, I'm going to rain down food
from heaven for you. Each day the people can go out and
pick up as much food as they need for that day."*

EXODUS 16:4

I love social media. It has become an easy way for me to reconnect with family members and friends who don't live close by, allowing me to still feel like I am a part of their lives. It has allowed me to rekindle relationships with old friends and given me a sense of community.

But there is also a side to social media that I find ugly. Opinionated posts, unkind comments, and banter about who is "right" in all aspects of life can sometimes leave me feeling a little overwhelmed. Sometimes I just don't know what to do with all of the information that is constantly streaming my way.

One morning, feeling like it was all a bit too much, I shut down all my devices and opened my Bible. I read about how God fed the Israelites and asked that they take only what they needed for that day—not worrying about tomorrow, but believing that God would continue to give them what they needed each day. I sat and thought about my schedule, shutting out everything else, and prayed, *What is most important for me to do today?* I felt like the answer was simply for me to love whomever was in front of me, right in that moment. If it was my child in front of me, I needed to stop and show them love. My husband over dinner: love. The person at the checkout counter: love. My coworker in the morning: love. I've come to realize that not worrying about tomorrow but simply focusing on who is in front of me today can shift my focus and help me remember that smaller and simpler is sometimes better. Just like he did for the Israelites, God will rain down his bread from heaven, giving me just what I need for this day.

— Kendra

— Today's Act of Kindness —

Instead of allowing yourself to feel overwhelmed by the world's
problems, think about who is right in front of you. Focus
on showing those people some extra love and kindness.

Convicted Kindness

You say you have faith, for you believe that there is one God. Good for you! Even the demons believe this, and they tremble in terror. How foolish! Can't you see that faith without good deeds is useless?

JAMES 2:19-20

The sometimes-frustrating side effect of trying to live a life of intentional kindness is that twinge I feel in my spirit when I do something that is not kind, is not helpful, or is not how I know I should have responded in a situation. More often than ever before, I find myself wincing over an opportunity that I've blown in some way and wishing I'd responded differently.

Being on this intentional journey of kindness seems to shine an especially bright spotlight on my less-than-perfect moments—the ones I'd rather forget, sweep under the rug, or justify in my mind with a lousy excuse. While I know that my salvation does not depend upon how many good deeds I accomplish during my years on earth, I also know that my faith, if it is authentic, must reveal itself in my actions.

The Bible reminds us that even the demons acknowledge the authority of God. It is in our *actions* that we reveal our true faith. In other words, our intangible faith (or lack thereof) is made tangible by how we live our lives and the small actions we take every day.

As I feel those twinges of conviction over whatever action I took (or did not take), I thank God that he's helping me to recognize my weak spots and learn from my mistakes. Without conviction, there is no improvement, no growth, no desire to do and be better. And that is my greatest desire—to love God with my whole heart, my whole soul, and my whole mind, and to love my neighbors as myself (Matthew 22:37-39). I cannot grow in my ability to love and be kind without recognizing my mistakes and learning from them.

— Julie

— Today's Act of Kindness —

Pray that God would convict you the next time you miss the mark of kindness. When you feel that twinge of conviction, ask God for a second chance, and if necessary, apologize and ask for forgiveness.

Give Them a Break

Share each other's burdens, and in this way obey the law of Christ.

GALATIANS 6:2

As she entered the conference room, lugging a baby carrier and a bag full of diapers and teething toys, her smile was tired but happy. The group of women gathered around her as she unbuckled the baby and lifted her out. The baby's eyes blinked in the light, and she had dark, downy hair and a serious expression. Conversations about motherhood, nursing, and a lack of sleep ebbed and flowed around the table as the group grabbed plates of food from the buffet and sat down for a combined baby shower and meeting.

I asked the new mom if I could help by holding the baby for a bit so she could eat her dinner in peace, and she gratefully accepted. As I rocked and jiggled the baby, standing and bouncing her quietly in the corner, I breathed in her sweet baby scent and felt only a little envious that everyone else was eating chocolate cupcakes without me. I watched as the mother relaxed into the warmth of the conversation and said quiet thank-yous as she opened gift bags filled with tiny outfits and soft blankets.

Even though I know that this mom wouldn't trade her new child for anything in the world, I also know that sometimes, all we really want is just a little break. When life revolves around the eating and sleeping patterns of a tiny tyrant, sweet though they may be, it takes a few months for things to turn right side up again. Though the birth of a child is a joyful event, it also brings a lot of upheaval. As Christians, we are called to share one another's burdens, and sometimes stepping in to give someone else a moment to relax can be the sweetest gift of all.

— *Kristin*

— Today's Act of Kindness —

Who do you know that needs a break? Maybe it's a new parent, a single parent, or a caregiver. Reach out to them and set up a time for you to give them a break.

APRIL 28

Are They Worthy of Kindness?

*Whatever you do, whether in word or deed, do it all in the name of
the Lord Jesus, giving thanks to God the Father through him.*
COLOSSIANS 3:17, NIV

"Don't you worry that they'll use your gift inappropriately?" an acquaintance innocently asked as I told her about the kind acts my family was doing. It's a question I've heard more than once when sharing about ways we've given to meet the needs of others.

Being kind can, at times, appear to be weak or naive. Kindness is not often associated with power or strength. Yet the Bible is filled with reminders to care for the poor, for those without a voice, and for those who have needs, and that is what we remind ourselves of as we continue to plan acts of kindness.

My responsibility is to listen to what I believe God is asking me to do or give and to let him worry about how the other person manages the gift. Should we be responsible to research organizations or situations before we give? Absolutely. But it's *God's* responsibility to take my gift and use it in whatever way he deems fit.

If I've done my part with a pure heart, then I won't be so worried about the worthiness of the person who receives the gift. This is the place where my faith steps in and believes that God will use whatever small thing I give or do for his glory. Because in all honesty, our kindness toward others is simply a response to God's kindness toward us and his command that we do all things in Jesus' name. Remembering that he is ultimately the reason I show kindness toward others removes my need to constantly know how the gift is being used.

The truth is, there may be times when others misuse or waste our gifts. It is in those moments that I remember the kindness and grace God extends to me each day. How often do I waste the gifts God so freely gives? I won't let a few people's negative actions deter me from extending kindness toward others and cultivating a heart of gratitude toward God.

— Kendra

— Today's Act of Kindness —

Is there someone in your life that you avoid showing
kindness to—possibly because you disapprove of them?
Go out of your way to show that person kindness.

On the Outskirts

Whether you eat or drink, or whatever you do, do it all for the glory of God.
1 CORINTHIANS 10:31

Standing behind a table decorated with rows of silver gift bags, I chatted with other workers as we greeted a stream of parents entering the building, directing them to the festivities. Inside the gym, the prom for students with special needs was in full swing, with students dancing and laughing as music blared from overhead speakers.

The lobby, on the other hand, was a cool, quiet oasis. My husband asked me later, "Didn't you feel like you missed out, not being in the gym? You didn't get to be in there with the students."

It's true, my interaction with our honored guests was minimal. But I'm always happiest on the outskirts, looking in. I was able to marvel at how hours of work culminated in this event, one unlike any other in the area. And I had the opportunity to chat with the parents of these sweet students, which, in my mind, is equally rewarding. These are folks who don't always get a lot of support. They told me, with tears in their eyes, how they never thought their child would get to experience this teenage rite of passage. How blown away they were that the community had jumped on board to provide everything—dresses and tuxes, limos, food, a party—all at no cost to them. Again and again, their thank-yous were a highlight of my night.

I couldn't help but think, *This is why we do this.* This is why I roped my childhood best friend into making ninety-three gift bags when she came to visit me. This is why my mom and I spent hours making centerpieces full of lollipops and gum balls. This is why I sent countless e-mails, attended meetings, and had brainstorming sessions with my coleader that left us both a little exhausted. Because at the end of the day, it was so worth it.

What you do today matters, and the kindness that you show someone else is *always* worth it. Whatever we do, we are to do it all for the glory of God—because when we do, our actions can resonate and ripple far beyond the moment.

— *Kristin*

— Today's Act of Kindness —

Find something on the outskirts that you can do,
whether it's stuffing envelopes for a charity you believe
in or volunteering to decorate for an event.

Beautiful Words

No one can tame the tongue. It is restless and evil. . . . Sometimes it praises
our Lord and Father, and sometimes it curses those who have been made
in the image of God. And so blessing and cursing come pouring out of
the same mouth. Surely, my brothers and sisters, this is not right!
JAMES 3:8-10

I watched yesterday as a woman rejected a compliment about her creativity. She is talented, so there is no doubt in my mind that the compliment was both genuine and deserved. Why is our first instinct to deny life-affirming words genuinely and truthfully spoken over us, while at the same time we secretly accept, repeat, and even nurture ugly words that have sliced us deeply, often through to our very soul?

Although I now recognize this trap when I see other women stumble into it, I continue to fall into the same trap myself. My first instinct is to reject or downplay anything beautiful that's spoken about me. I secretly lay claim to ugly words about myself that, more often than not, have never actually been spoken aloud by another person. They've been whispered by only that small internal voice that would have me believe I am a failure in so many areas of my life. How I long for every woman to know and recognize her worth!

As I've thought and prayed about how to intentionally break this cycle, I've discovered the joy of intentionally speaking words of life and affirmation into the lives of people around me. Too often we allow our tongues to wag freely, speaking both blessings and curses over people created in God's image. We must stop cursing ourselves and others with our words.

So now, I make an extra effort to genuinely compliment others. If I find myself quietly admiring another woman's ability, her talent, or her scarf (or earrings or fingernail polish or whatever), I tell her, even if I've never met her before, even if she doesn't look insecure or like she needs to be complimented. I choose to share life-giving words freely and without reservation.

— Julie

— Today's Act of Kindness —

Give a genuine compliment to someone you meet—
whether it's a loved one or a complete stranger.

May

The Gift of Groceries

Keep putting into practice all you learned and received from me—everything
you heard from me and saw me doing. Then the God of peace will be with you.
PHILIPPIANS 4:9

It was years ago that our friend, then a young youth pastor, stood in the checkout lane of his local grocery store. His cart was filled with diapers, formula, and baby food for his twin sons, and he sighed internally as he did the math. He and his wife were struggling financially, and, while diapers and formula were important, they were not what he wanted to spend their hard-earned money on.

The gentleman in front of him in line interrupted his thoughts when he told the store clerk that he would be paying for my friend's groceries. He saw what the youth pastor was buying, and he wanted to help out. This man refused to identify himself, and once the transaction was complete, he quietly slipped away.

As our families sat around the dinner table listening to the story being recounted more than a decade later, our friend ended by saying, "Someday, I will buy someone's groceries and pay that forward."

What I wanted to say, and should have said in response, was that his family has paid that kindness forward a thousand times over. Their family strives to live out the New Testament's command to love God and love others. Their home is constantly filled with neighborhood children, their twins' teenage friends, and a whole host of people who ebb and flow through their lives. They are generous with their time and their resources. While life gets chaotic, the peace of God permeates their home and their souls. You cannot help but feel that peace when you sit in conversation with our friends.

There is no question that they strive to put into practice what they've seen and heard about first-century Christians in the New Testament. They practice living as Christ has called all of us to live. The result is peace in the midst of chaos and a calmness in their souls that calms those around them.

— Julie

— Today's Act of Kindness —

The next time you're at the grocery store, consider
quietly purchasing someone else's groceries.
You never know how it might bless them.

MAY 2

Special Delivery

A cheerful heart is good medicine.
PROVERBS 17:22

My friend told me she had been sick for months—and I hadn't even realized how much time had passed. Although I consider her a close friend, our visits are infrequent since we don't live in the same town. Something had settled into her lungs, and she was coughing constantly, in pain, and at her wits' end about how to get well.

My friend had two children already and a third on the way, and I could sense her frustration even though she was trying to make the best of it. She knew her kids desperately wanted to get out of the house, but she just didn't feel well enough to take them anywhere. After chatting with her, I had an idea: what if I had some boredom busters delivered to her door?

I enlisted my oldest daughter's help because she wants to be an artist (and an astronaut and a dancer) when she grows up. In pursuit of this goal, Elise is constantly drawing pictures of rainbows, painting canvases in the garage, using up all the stickers in the house, and asking for new projects to fill her time. I have a closet that's overflowing with art supplies stacked in precariously messy piles, and despite the disorder, those supplies sure do come in handy when my children need a distraction.

So after talking to Elise about our friends, I sat down with her at the computer and picked out all the craft supplies and projects we thought they might like, then had them delivered to the family. We couldn't do anything to help my friend overcome her health challenge, but we knew we could do something to cheer her up and let her know that we loved and cared for her.

— Kristin

— Today's Act of Kindness —

Who can you send a care package to? Maybe it's an elderly person, a college student, or a friend who is struggling with an illness. Let them know you're thinking of them by mailing them a special treat.

The Yellow Shirt

*Jesus took the loaves, gave thanks to God, and distributed
them to the people. Afterward he did the same with the
fish. And they all ate as much as they wanted.*
JOHN 6:11

Several years ago I attended a women's conference where the organizers shared about an upcoming retreat for single moms that they would be putting on the next month. They asked us if we'd be willing to donate new clothes for the moms who would be attending, explaining that single moms are often so busy taking care of their kids that they put themselves last. The retreat was being put on not only to encourage these women but also to give them some very practical things, like new clothes, that they could use in their everyday lives.

I sat listening, moved by their plea for clothing. I immediately thought of the new yellow shirt I had just bought that afternoon and felt a small nudge to donate it. I put it out of my mind, thinking it was such a small thing. Immediately I felt God impress this question upon my heart: *But can you obey me in the small things?* In that moment I knew I needed to give the shirt away, and the next morning, as I came back for the second day of the conference, I did just that.

The funny thing about the shirt I gave? This *small* thing? Because it was yellow, a color I normally don't wear, it stood out in my mind. All summer long, as I would take walks and spend time outside, I would remember that shirt and pray for the single mom who received it.

God can use even the smallest of things to fill a need. God is not concerned with our actions only but also with the motives of our hearts. Just like the boy who gave his small lunch to Jesus as an act of obedience could've never known that it would actually, miraculously, feed over five thousand people, we never know how God will multiply our small acts of kindness each day. Don't miss God in the small things.

— *Kendra*

— Today's Act of Kindness —

When you're tempted to write off an act of kindness as too small
or insignificant, pray that God would use it, and then do it anyway.

The Intentional Neighbor

We can make our plans, but the LORD determines our steps.
PROVERBS 16:9

He's a familiar stranger. I see him often, sometimes more than once a day. It took me a while to figure out where exactly he lives in the sprawl of our neighborhood—I always seemed to see him in different areas, whether he was out for a walk, doing small jobs in someone else's yard, or chatting with people on the street corner.

He has short, gray hair and a stocky build, and I'm not sure I've ever seen him smile. But he is the most intentional neighbor I know. Each time I drive by him—rain or shine, snow or sleet, without fail—he stops what he's doing and waves. Yesterday, as I drove past in my car full of noisy kids, I saw him as he was crossing the street carrying a small dog. Even though his back was originally toward me, he stopped walking, pivoted, waved to me, then turned back around to continue on his way.

We've never been introduced, but I feel like I know him. Not because he's become a close friend to the family, but simply because he *always* waves. He is an intentional waver, and each time I pass him I wave back. It's simple, but it sends the message: *I see you. Safe travels. Welcome home.*

He shows the same respect to everyone, regardless of who it may be. His intentionality is admirable. Sometimes it's easier to pretend you don't see someone, or that you're busy on your phone or with your children, than it is to stop and acknowledge that person. I've found myself "not noticing" acquaintances when I'm at the grocery store or the mall, simply because I don't want to take time from my schedule to stop and chat. I'm trying to let go of my own plans and let God determine my actions and steps. It can take effort to be intentionally open and kind, but when we are, people notice.

— *Kristin*

— Today's Act of Kindness —

Go out of your way to be intentional with your neighbors
in the way you act by waving, smiling, or saying hello.

A Second Mom

Feed the hungry, and help those in trouble. Then your light will shine out from the darkness, and the darkness around you will be as bright as noon.
ISAIAH 58:10

The music teacher at my daughter's public school is our school's "second mom." Our immersion teachers call her their American mom; she is often the first person on this continent to hear the news of engagements and pregnancies for our young teachers who crave a mothering figure in their lives on this side of the ocean.

She knows the names of her students, their siblings, and their parents. She stands outside the school doors on chilly mornings, keeping students company as they wait for the bell to ring and the doors to open.

A whirlwind of activity, she is constantly meeting needs quietly and rallying the parental troops around worthy causes. Her home, a block from the school, is filled with kids and families on afternoons and weekends for piano lessons, and her entryway is always filled with donations of food, snow boots, or winter jackets—because parents know she will get the items to someone who needs them. She is a trustworthy person who can be called with questions, and she'll always know the right people to talk to in order to find answers.

My love for her tender heart and generous spirit has only grown over the past year that my daughter has been enrolled as one of her piano students. She knows my daughter's strengths and weaknesses, and she knows when to push and when to encourage. She is my daughter's biggest fan—just as she is every child's biggest fan.

My kids, while clearly loved by her, are just two of thousands of children on whom she has poured out equal measures of love, affection, and guidance during their elementary years and even beyond. Her faith is quiet, yet her actions speak so clearly of Christ's love. She feeds the hungry and helps those in trouble, and her light shines in the darkness. I can think of no other person who fits today's verse in so many areas of her life, and she is a shining example that I strive to be more like.

— Julie

— Today's Act of Kindness —

Is there someone in your life who lives out today's verse?
Consider some ways you might pattern your life after theirs,
and let them know how they've made an impact on you.

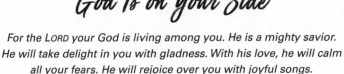

God Is on Your Side

For the LORD your God is living among you. He is a mighty savior.
He will take delight in you with gladness. With his love, he will calm
all your fears. He will rejoice over you with joyful songs.
ZEPHANIAH 3:17

Public speaking is a skill I've had to develop over the years. Since I'm an introvert by nature, getting up in front of others was terrifying at first. At the same time, I've also had a desire to share God's Word with others, and so when opportunities arose to speak, I'd take them, despite my fears. I wanted to do a good job, one that would make God proud.

A few years ago, as I was once again preparing a message, I prayed that God would be pleased with my words and that I wouldn't mess up badly enough to embarrass him. Immediately I was flooded by an overwhelming feeling of love and a sense that he was already proud of me just for trying. Since then I have thought more about this idea that I need to do well for God to be pleased with me. Although I grew up being told that God's love is unconditional, for some reason I still felt I needed to perform perfectly to prove myself to him.

Do you know what I've since discovered? This is simply not true. God is not testing me as I take steps of faith to honor what I believe he's asked me to do. God is more like a proud father who delights in me because he loves me, whether I do really well or fall flat on my face. He rejoices over me with a love that never changes.

Have you wondered if you measure up to the task God is asking of you? Scripture tells us that God takes delight in us with gladness, that he calms our fears and rejoices over us with joyful songs. This sounds to me like he's a God who is pleased with us just as we are. Rest in the truth of his great love and kindness toward you today.

— Kendra

— Today's Act of Kindness —

Take time to thank God for all he has done and ask him to give you courage to continue to pursue the plans he has for you. Remember that he sees you through eyes of kindness.

The Gift of Time

Love is patient and kind. Love is not jealous or boastful or
proud or rude. It does not demand its own way. It is not
irritable, and it keeps no record of being wronged.

1 CORINTHIANS 13:4-5

Recently, as I sat on an airplane, I glanced down the row and was met with the smiling faces of my husband and six dear friends—three other couples—all of us headed out for a celebration of big wedding anniversaries. We were celebrating twenty years, fifteen years, almost fifteen years, and thirteen years of marriage by flying halfway across the country to spend five days on the West Coast.

My husband and I had never spent so many nights away from our kids, and honestly, he and I needed this time. We *all* needed this time. The hustle and bustle of busy lives, left unchecked, can take a toll on a marriage. This was going to be a time of refreshment and renewal with some of my favorite people on the planet.

My kids were in the loving hands of my mother-in-law, a woman who is generous and kind, and whose willingness to move into our crazy, loud household for the week was the reason my husband and I were able to steal away for some precious time of reconnecting.

Her generous pouring of herself into our lives and into the lives of our children sometimes moves me to tears. My children know their Grandma Connie as the woman who comes bearing craft projects and banana bread, who takes them to the park, and who always stops at McDonald's to buy them shakes on the way back home. She sees my children when they are less than perfect and loves them fiercely anyway.

Her gift of time is absolutely precious. Having grown up without involved grandparents due to advanced age and distance, I understand how fortunate my children are to have a grandparent so lovingly and tangibly involved. And we aren't the only ones who benefit: Connie is generous with her time with a multitude of family members and friends. She is a wonderful example of the unconditional love described in Scripture: not proud or selfish, but patient and kind.

— Julie

— Today's Act of Kindness —

Whom has God given you to pour time and love into? Maybe it's
your spouse, a friend, your children, or your nieces and nephews.
Give them the gift of your time and undivided attention.

Rolling Out the Red Carpet

Love each other with genuine affection, and
take delight in honoring each other.
ROMANS 12:10

One spring, Tim and I helped organize a prom for students with special needs. The event was free for participants, and businesses and volunteers offered time and money to make it happen. When the day arrived, I was mostly tied up, helping take care of the decor, gift bags, and some other logistical items. But I managed to sneak away to see the students walk the red carpet.

Each honored guest rode to the prom in a limo (or other transportation, if they needed additional help), and when they arrived at the high school, they were treated like VIPs. The red carpet stretched from the curb to the door, with canopies hanging over the top. Throngs of family members and folks from the community, emergency personnel (just in case), and even Minnesota Vikings cheerleaders crowded the sides. After exiting the limo, the students got the chance to strut down the red carpet while "paparazzi" took photos, the announcer boomed their names over the loudspeaker, and the audience roared their approval.

Watching the students, I felt their joy reflected in myself, but it wasn't until I witnessed the silent applause that I found myself in tears. For some of the students, too much noise can feel overwhelming, so in those cases the audience cheered silently by waving their hands in the air and smiling broadly.

It reminded me of watching a sporting event after something solemn has happened in the world. The announcer asks for a moment of silence, and the crowd goes still. It's a moment of honor, one in which silence reigns and the gravity of the moment can be felt.

The silent clap held that same, solemn weight of honor, but it was somehow more. The weight of silence was balanced by the joy of celebration, seen in raised hands—hands lifted to say, "I honor you, and I celebrate you."

As I wiped tears away, seeing tears in the eyes of those around me as well, I thought about how when Scripture asks us to "take delight in honoring each other," this is exactly the sort of thing it means.

— Kristin

— Today's Act of Kindness —

Think of someone you can honor. Write this person a note, or call
to let them know how much you admire them, just for being them.

More Than a Gesture

Three things will last forever—faith, hope, and love—
and the greatest of these is love.
1 CORINTHIANS 13:13

Kyle and I were foster parents for six years. During that time we took in many kids and worked with a lot of parents, and each situation was unique. We found that many parents really loved their kids, but they had struggles such as addiction or mental illness that made it difficult for them to care for their children.

That was the case with the twin boys who came to us at just seven months old. We immediately bonded with the babies, and we had a deep affection for their mom, who we could see was doing her best to work through her addiction and provide for her children. For several months we watched her work hard, put her kids and their needs first, and love them every chance she got.

Eventually we knew our time with the twins would be ending, and we wanted to celebrate with this mom as she would be regaining full custody of her kids. As their first birthday approached, I realized that she would probably love pictures of her kids to commemorate this milestone. So one afternoon I put the boys in new outfits and brought them to a local photographer, who took some of the most beautiful pictures I'd ever seen.

A few weeks later I brought those pictures along with the twins for our last visit. We gave her the pictures and a few other gifts. She cried; we cried. She said no one had ever done anything that nice for her. We left feeling privileged to have known this family, even just for a season.

God tells us that of all the things that will last forever, the greatest is love. Extending kind acts toward others, especially those walking through hard times, goes beyond just kind gestures: it's a display of God's grace and mercy, an encouragement to the discouraged, an offering of hope and peace.

— Kendra

— Today's Act of Kindness —

Who in your life is going through a hard time and could
use some encouragement? Do an act of kindness that
will remind them of God's goodness and love.

Ring and Run

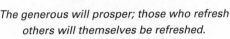

The generous will prosper; those who refresh
others will themselves be refreshed.
PROVERBS 11:25

Our church has a wonderful Mother's Day tradition. The church buys coffee gift cards and candles and lines them up along the front of the sanctuary. Midservice, each mom is invited to come forward and select one (or several) of the candles and gift cards—the only requirement being that she must prayerfully gift her choice to another mother in her life.

I *love* this tradition. It is an opportunity for mothers to bless other mothers, and the stories that trickle back are priceless. These gifts have found their way to grieving moms, single moms, brave moms, and moms who simply needed to know that they are loved.

This year, my daughter asked if she could help me select a candle, and so we both walked forward to sniff and giggle and collect our candle loot. Upon arriving home, I put the candles on the small table between my living room and kitchen—at the busiest intersection in my house—so that I would be continually reminded to pray about who should receive the gifts.

My friend's face floated into my mind as I walked down our steps and caught a glimpse of the candles. This friend is a gracious, loving woman who'd had a tough winter and needed some encouragement. I packaged the candles and gift card in a cute gift bag, wrote her a note of encouragement and prayer, and then slipped into my car to make a clandestine delivery.

I pulled into the back alley of her house, hoping to hang the bag on her doorknob and slip away without being caught. Alas, her son rounded the corner of the house in the midst of some imaginary game and busted me, letting his mom know that I was in their backyard.

As my friend and I chatted on her back steps, we chuckled about my foiled attempt at a "ring and run"—a phrase I'd never heard before but that perfectly summed up my attempt to be sneaky.

I didn't stay long, but our chat warmed my heart as I hopped back into my car and went about a busy day. Providing refreshment to others often results in my feeling just as refreshed.

— Julie

— Today's Act of Kindness —

Surprise a friend with a "ring and run" act of kindness.

Look for the Good

*[Jesus said,] "You are the light of the world—like a
city on a hilltop that cannot be hidden."*
MATTHEW 5:14

Maybe it's all those years I spent working at the copydesk in a newsroom, designing front pages and tweaking photos and text on the "Life" section covers, but I love anything that's well designed: interior decor, children's clothing, someone's hairstyle. If it has style and panache, I'm apt to notice and admire it. Part of being "the light of the world" means that we express our God-given creativity, and when people follow through on that, I think it should be celebrated.

There's a scene in the movie *Pollyanna* where a character shares these convicting words: "When you look for the bad in mankind, expecting to find it, you surely will." Obviously, the opposite is true too, so I've resolved to always look for the good. When you look for the good in people, you will surely find it. It can completely change your attitude and outlook when you focus on the good.

One day while trawling lazily online, I ran across a small web developer. She was a new college graduate, and while her portfolio was thin, it was amazing. I thought her designs were truly dazzling, and on a whim, I wrote out a quick message and told her so. Despite the fact that she was a stranger, I wanted her to know that someone had noticed the work she was doing and admired her for the creativity and effort that was obvious in her designs.

Have you noticed any good things lately? Maybe you've seen someone do a stellar job at work. Perhaps you've admired a neighbor's flowers but never mentioned it. In what ways can you begin to not just notice the good things in life but to also celebrate them?

— Kristin

— Today's Act of Kindness —

Take the time to compliment someone's creativity or
hard work today—call, send a message, or stop by to
chat in person to tell them they're doing a good job.

Just One Thing

Don't be concerned for your own good but for the good of others.

1 CORINTHIANS 10:24

It can get a little discouraging at times to think about intentionally incorporating acts of kindness into your life every day. Kristin, Julie, and I often get asked how to do so on a consistent basis, and our response is always to just *start where you are.* We encourage people to look at the flow of their everyday lives and to begin incorporating kind acts into what they are already doing, at the places they normally go and with people they already know. It's perfectly fine to start small, and this can empower you to do even more.

Once you've begun to see how easily kind acts can be accomplished with just a little intentionality, ask yourself these questions: *Where do my passions lie? What stories move me? What issues make my heart beat fast?* Maybe for some it's combating hunger; for others it's issues such as homelessness, child abuse, clean water, refugees, orphans, or education. The list of things we could be passionate about is endless, and each of these issues is dear to God's heart.

God has given each of us a desire to see the world become a better place, but it can be overwhelming if we try to care about everything at once. Start with just one cause or concern, something you are already passionate about, and go from there.

Thinking of others is God's intention as well, as he tells us not to be concerned for our own good but for the good of others. God may even surprise us with what he'll do if we're willing to just take the first step toward intentional kindness right where we are. When we begin to put the concerns of others at the forefront of our minds, we open the door for God to work through us. Who knows where it may lead?

— Kendra

— Today's Act of Kindness —

Do one act of kindness that is already within the flow of your everyday life or that utilizes a passion you already have.

A New Perspective

*Direct your children onto the right path, and when
they are older, they will not leave it.*
PROVERBS 22:6

It was as I was snuggling Peanut, our sweet poodle-mix dog, that I noticed a weird white film in one of his eyes. Concerned, I took him to see our vet. Cataracts was the diagnosis, and the prognosis wasn't great: he was going to go blind. My heart sank as I spoke with the vet about options. He explained the good news that cataracts aren't painful, but it turned out that treatment options were prohibitively expensive for my family.

While having a dog with a disability wasn't something we'd anticipated, my husband and I have embraced this unexpected opportunity to help our children gain a deeper understanding of kindness and unconditional love as we make adjustments in our family and in our home for Peanut.

As Peanut's eyesight has gotten progressively worse, we've had ongoing conversations with our kids asking them to consider how he might feel when they get too rowdy with friends and why he startles when we leave something unexpected in his path. When he wandered away from home and into the next neighborhood one weekend after being left outside unattended, we spoke of what it must feel like to be alone, unable to see, and unable to find the way home. While these are all ideas that adults can understand in the abstract, framing it from Peanut's perspective has given my children the opportunity to grasp these concerns in very tangible, real ways.

Peanut's blindness has given my children an opportunity they might not otherwise have had—an opportunity to practice empathy by seeing another's perspective and caring for them accordingly. They are putting into practice the conversations we have about what it means to be both children of God and people who take care of those around them. As with so many other parts of our faith walk, my husband and I pray that these words, these experiences, and these opportunities to reveal Christ through kindness are being soaked up by our children, so that when they are faced with choosing their own path in life, they will fulfill the promise of Scripture and not depart from the path God has set before them.

— Julie

— Today's Act of Kindness —

If you are responsible for children—whether you're a parent, a
teacher, or a church-nursery volunteer—consider how you can
start conversations about helping others in more tangible ways.

More Than a Vacation

I am giving you a new commandment: Love each other. Just as I have loved you, you should love each other.
JOHN 13:34

She was on her way to Disney World with her young children when she got the devastating phone call: her husband, who wasn't able to come with them, had died unexpectedly. After turning the car around, she spent the next week doing what she had never expected—planning a funeral rather than riding roller coasters with her kids.

Tim and I met her a few years later. My husband loves Disney World—it's probably his favorite place in the world—and hearing her story, knowing that she'd never gotten the chance to experience the magic of Disney, struck a chord. Now that she was a single mom, money was tight and left little margin for things like trips.

So my husband and some of our good friends rallied a few local families around this idea: we'd pool our resources and buy her family a trip to Disney World. One of our friends bought the mom a card and put all the trip information inside. At church one Sunday, our friend passed the envelope to the mom and waited to hear what happened.

Thinking it was just a note, the mom didn't open the card until she was in the parking lot. When she did, she just sat there and cried, and then she cried some more. Her daughter had just commented earlier that week that it would have been her dad's fortieth birthday and he would have wanted them to take that trip eventually—but in the mom's mind, it was out of reach.

For us, this act wasn't so much about sending her on vacation as it was about letting her know that she was loved, that she mattered. We wanted her to know that although her husband had died and life had taken a turn she hadn't expected, it didn't mean that she or her dreams—for the future, for her children, or even for vacations to Disney World—had disappeared with him.

— *Kristin*

— Today's Act of Kindness —

Is someone in your life grieving? Think of a way to honor them tangibly, then reach out to them in love.

A Child's Compassion

Blessed are those who are generous, because they feed the poor.
PROVERBS 22:9

My oldest son has always had a heart for the homeless population in our community. Whenever we ask how he'd like to extend kindness, he usually picks something geared toward the homeless. As a result, our family has bought food, served meals, and given gift cards to homeless men and women in our town.

When our missional community from church decided to assemble gift bags for the homeless as a service project, my son loved the idea. Each family collected basic supplies such as socks, toothbrushes, bottled water, soap, granola bars, gift cards, and more to be put together in gallon-sized bags to be distributed to the homeless around town. We set up an assembly line of people and supplies, explained to our children what we were doing and why, and then asked the older kids to pray over our supplies and the people who would receive them.

After we bagged all the supplies, each family took several bags to keep in their vehicles and hand out whenever they came across a homeless person. My kids were excited to give their bags away, and just a few days later we had the opportunity to hand out several of them. Things went well, and my family felt good about the way we'd been able to give to those who needed help in our city.

Although the project is complete, my son continues to remind me of the needs of the homeless in our area. He now has a greater understanding that the generous will themselves be blessed. He is quick to jump in and help, and his heart for those who are without a home has spurred my husband and me to continue helping the homeless as well.

Do you know someone whose passion for a certain cause or people group has moved you to action as well? Are there concerns or needs nearby that you could help alleviate? We all have something to give when we remember that no gift is too small.

— Kendra

— Today's Act of Kindness —

Think of a need in your community and give something you
have—a skill, time, money, or a physical resource—toward it.

Bittersweet Milestones

A friend is always loyal, and a brother is born to help in time of need.
PROVERBS 17:17

Upon receiving the invitation from my friend for her son's high school graduation, I winced.

The invitation reminded me that these years truly do fly by, and I wondered how my friend was handling the bittersweet experience of launching her child. While she has every reason to be proud and delighted by the young man she has raised, my mama heart empathized, and I leaked a tear or three on her behalf over the thought of sending her son off into the great big world.

As I picked up a card for the new graduate, I couldn't help but also pick up a card for my friend. I got her a coffee gift card and a wonderful-smelling candle and put together a pink, frilly gift bag just for her, along with a note of encouragement and prayer as she prepares to move into a new season in her life and her marriage.

I'm discovering that many celebrations in the life of a child also contain a bittersweet sting for moms and dads as firsts are often also followed closely by lasts—and we often don't know when the last time (last bottle, last diaper, last cuddle in your lap) is *the* last time.

Because of this, I try to acknowledge these moments in the lives of friends with a little note and a small gift. It lets them know that the millions of sacrifices, large and small, they have made over the years have been noticed and have mattered. Having loyal friends who stick with us is like having a brother or a sister in times of need. We all need people who *see* us, especially in the moments when we are smiling big while also feeling the sadness of life moving forward.

— *Julie*

— Today's Act of Kindness —

Is there a parent in your circle of friends who could use a little encouragement in the face of a bittersweet milestone? Surprise him or her with a handwritten note and a coffee gift card.

Responding with Peace

God blesses those who work for peace, for they
will be called the children of God.
MATTHEW 5:9

I have the privilege of volunteering with a Christian women's ministry that spans the state of Minnesota. The organization offers support to women through its blog, ministries, and conferences each year. The director, a seasoned woman who is older than I am, leads women from all backgrounds with grace and dignity.

As we were planning a conference several years ago, one of our leaders was struggling to complete her duties. Feelings of failure overwhelmed her, and she lashed out in anger at the director—who was a close friend of mine—insulting her leadership and abilities. Later, as I talked to my friend, my own feelings of defensiveness on her behalf began to emerge. Quick to disarm them, she told me she was not offended and then asked, "How can we make this a win for her?"

I was taken aback. This woman who had just been berated by another was asking how she could help make the angry woman feel successful in her role. She wisely saw below the surface to a woman who was struggling and compassionately asked how she could help. We devised a plan at once in which the hurt woman could reengage with the project and successfully fulfill her role. This situation taught me an important lesson about seeking godly wisdom.

When faced with unkindness from others, it is easy to want to respond in the same way we've been treated or to take up an offense for someone else who has been mistreated. The Bible is clear that God blesses those who work for peace. Often when we choose to step back and ask God for wisdom, he will lead us to the correct response. Although we may need to be firm or create healthy boundaries, we can still respond with compassion rather than with anger or defensiveness.

— Kendra

— Today's Act of Kindness —

Think of someone who has been unkind toward you
or someone you love. Pray for them and ask God to
give you wisdom in how to deal with them. Then reach
out to that person with a gesture of support.

Working within Your Gifts

May he equip you with all you need for doing his will. May he produce in you, through the power of Jesus Christ, every good thing that is pleasing to him. All glory to him forever and ever! Amen.

HEBREWS 13:21

According to Gary Chapman, author of *The Five Love Languages*, the five ways of expressing love are acts of service, quality time, words of affirmation, physical touch, and receiving gifts.* I think it's safe to say that receiving gifts is one of my love languages, which is why I also enjoy giving gifts to others whenever I have the opportunity. For my purposes, "gifts" translate into "gift baskets."

I love *themed* gift baskets in particular. For instance, this year I was making several baskets for speakers and leaders at a women's conference, and I decided to use Hebrews 6:19 as my inspiration, which says, "We have this hope as an anchor for the soul, firm and secure" (NIV). I bought personalized, anchor-themed canvas bags; pretty, framed prints of this Scripture; anchor bracelets; and anchor mugs. I even tucked in a bag of popcorn that had an anchor on the front of the package.

What I love about intentional kindness is that so often we can use our gifts and talents to express it. I'm not as good at affirming people through words, and as an introvert, I prefer to spend time alone rather than always spending quality time with others. So acts of kindness centered around words and quality time are a lot harder for me. Giving thoughtful gifts, on the other hand, is something I revel in. The cost itself may be nominal—I can just as easily give someone a gift by passing along a book I read and enjoyed, or by making them my favorite kind of cookies—but it's the intentional thoughtfulness that matters most.

Scripture says that we are equipped with all we need for doing God's will, and it's my belief that there's no greater way to do that than by utilizing the love language hardwired within us to show love and kindness to others.

— Kristin

— Today's Act of Kindness —

Do you know your love language? If not, find out what it is, and then use your love language to show someone kindness.

---

*Gary D. Chapman, *The Five Love Languages: The Secret to Love that Lasts* (Chicago: Northfield Publishing, 2015).

Loving Your Neighbor

Love your neighbor as yourself.
MARK 12:31

"What if Jesus actually meant that we should love our literal neighbor?"

This was the question and challenge presented by our pastor one Sunday morning several years ago, as we studied this passage of Scripture from Mark 12. As my husband and I drove home in silence, we knew this was a challenge we would want to approach together.

We had already lived in our neighborhood for several years when we felt compelled to get to know and love those around us—we had never made a big effort to reach out before. We decided to start by saying hello and spending time with our neighbors when we would see them outside. We then invited them to a neighborhood party and then other barbecues when the weather was nice. It was awkward at first, but over time, it became easier to do.

What started as a challenge to extend Christ's love toward others by loving our neighbor as ourselves has benefited us more than we could have ever known. Our neighbors are some of the kindest and most generous people we know, and they have taken an interest in us and our kids—attending piano recitals and baseball games, celebrating with us and inviting us into their homes and lives.

As I think back on how we were first challenged years ago, I realize that I had no idea that we'd *receive* such blessing by loving our neighbors. They have become some of our greatest supporters and friends.

Reaching out to people around us who are strangers can be hard, especially when we need to take the initiative to start the relationship. But we never know what God may do through us until we're willing to open ourselves up to the possibility of friendship with those around us, including our neighbors.

— *Kendra*

— Today's Act of Kindness —

Greet or start a conversation with a neighbor you do not know very well. Don't put unnecessary pressure on the conversation; just get to know this person a bit better and see where it leads.

Love Your Enemies

Love your enemies! Do good to them. Lend to them without expecting to be repaid. Then your reward from heaven will be very great, and you will truly be acting as children of the Most High, for he is kind to those who are unthankful and wicked.

LUKE 6:35

When I wandered into my garden last week, I stumbled upon a tiny baby bunny inside my supposedly secure perimeter rabbit fence. With my neighborhood brimming over with rascally rabbits every spring, it's a running joke in my family when I mutter teasing threats against those lettuce-munching critters in my best Elmer Fudd voice.

I called the kids over, and as they cooed over this tiny creature, the irony of the situation was not lost on me. The little fellow was the mortal enemy of my pea plants, and yet I could not help but ooh and aah over him before relocating him to my lilac hedge.

I continued to think about that baby bunny in the days after his relocation and about the idea of extending mercy and compassion toward those we might label as enemies. I think we are often too quick to define people who have hurt us as enemies. In the past, I've labeled someone an enemy, only to discover that she was facing her own personal crisis about which I knew nothing, and that her actions stemmed, in part, from that crisis. While this person's circumstances didn't excuse her actions, understanding them helped me realize that she wasn't an enemy. She was a hurting person making hurtful decisions.

What would happen if we were a bit slower to use the enemy label and quicker to consider that there might be something else going on underneath the offense? What if we were slower to make assumptions and quicker to show mercy and compassion?

That baby bunny got me thinking and praying about whether there was anyone in my life that I had labeled as an enemy and written off. I was encouraged to do exactly what Scripture says: to be kind to those I tend to think of as enemies.

— Julie

— Today's Act of Kindness —

Who have you labeled as an enemy? Prayerfully reconsider that label and ask God for wisdom about what may be going on in that person's life. Then, go out of your way to show them kindness.

Commend and Recommend

Don't use foul or abusive language. Let everything you say be good and helpful, so that your words will be an encouragement to those who hear them.
EPHESIANS 4:29

Spotting my friend at church one Sunday, I made a beeline for her. After exchanging greetings and pleasantries, I got to the point: the girl who used to nanny for my kids was looking for a job for the summer, and I knew this woman was searching for someone to watch her own two children. I told her how this teenager had started out as a babysitter but now felt more like a daughter to us. "My children love her," I raved, "and so do we. I'm sure she would do an amazing job for you." I sang her praises some more, and then, seeing that the service was about to begin, waved goodbye and continued on with my morning.

The girl got the job. Knowing how personable she is and what great rapport she has with kids, I'm sure she could have gotten the job by herself. Plus, my conversation was brief and took almost no effort. But when we recognize the talents and abilities someone else has, it never hurts to praise them, whether the words are spoken to them or to someone else. When we remember to "let everything [we] say be good and helpful," the purpose is clear: positive words are an encouragement to those who hear them. And they just might be the added push someone needs to move forward.

Whom can you recommend to someone else? It might not be for a job, so think outside the box. Is there someone whose leadership abilities you admire, who you think would make a great candidate for a role in a ministry or in an organization in your community? Did you see the child of a friend or neighbor doing something kind for someone else? You could tell their parents they are doing a good job. Open your eyes to the ways you can speak encouragement to and about the people you know.

— *Kristin*

— Today's Act of Kindness —

Intentionally praise someone's gifts or abilities to another person.

Dreaming Together

*Let us think of ways to motivate one another to acts of love
and good works. And let us not neglect our meeting together,
as some people do, but encourage one another.*
HEBREWS 10:24-25

Kristin, Julie, and I have been blogging, writing, and speaking together for the past several years. When we started out with the simple dream of writing a book, we never imagined it would take us this far. We never imagined after writing that first book together that there would be more books and a blog and speaking engagements and a writer's conference.

But here's what we've come to realize: we'd never have gotten this far on our own. Part of the fun of this dream is that it is a shared adventure, a joining together with one another, spurring each other on, celebrating joy and sorrow—all together. This community of three has been a stronger cord than any of us would have been on our own. I know that many people go it alone and write, blog, or speak individually—and they do it really well. But I would dare to say that even people who appear to be dreaming alone usually have a group of others with whom they share ideas and dreams, lending support and encouragement in community together.

This is one of the beautiful things about dreams: it's more fun to achieve them when there are others to do it with you. When you think about your life, who has encouraged your dreams? Who has pushed you beyond what you thought possible? Maybe that hasn't been your experience, and you don't have a group of people who support you or your dreams. If you find yourself in this situation, first, take your dreams to God and ask him to give you wisdom and encouragement as you pursue what he has placed on your heart. Second, ask him to bring someone who can offer you encouragement and support, and in return, someone you can listen to and spur on in love and in good deeds. This Christian life is meant to be lived together, so find your people—they need you as much as you need them.

— Kendra

— Today's Act of Kindness —

Take the time to listen to someone else's dreams
and offer some encouragement to them. Then
ask if you can share your dreams as well.

Looking past the Exterior

God does not show favoritism.
ROMANS 2:11

"What is *that*?" My aunt squealed as a tiny, scruffy bit of fluff scampered across our kitchen floor. My ten-year-old self scooped up the tiny kitten—the runt of the barn-cat litter—and snuggled her close, secretly terribly offended that my aunt could not see the beauty hidden beneath the scraggly exterior of my adorable (to me) new cat.

My childhood was spent on a farm, surrounded by pets. My dad was the public works director for our small town and was constantly dragging home some bedraggled, ragamuffin animal who needed a bowl of whole milk, some scrambled eggs, and the love of three rascally children. Our pets were almost always free and had usually been rescued by my dad as the last resort before being put down.

My mom was (and still is) a trooper—she opened her home and heart to a whole variety of scruffy pets with tiny hearts of gold. Some of our best pets were the ugliest ones—the ones that everyone else had formerly rejected as not meeting the physical requirements of pedigree and beauty. On more than one occasion, our rescued pets sparked conversation as people asked what breed our dog was (a purebred that looked nothing like the breed standards) or where on earth we found that cat.

My brothers and I learned from an early age to love a creature's heart, not its pedigree and certainly not a beautiful exterior. It's a lesson I've taken to heart, both with animals and humans.

It is so easy to judge whether someone is worth knowing, liking, or loving simply based on external factors. Yet Jesus warned us firmly that God does not show favoritism. As I move through my days, I am recommitted to seeing others through God's eyes. Have you ever been guilty of determining someone's worth based on the exterior?

— Julie

— Today's Act of Kindness —

The next time you find yourself judging someone's exterior,
recommit to looking at others through Jesus' eyes, and
then find a way to get to know that person's heart.

Waiting on Island Time

Be kind to each other, tenderhearted, forgiving one another,
just as God through Christ has forgiven you.
EPHESIANS 4:32

We waited. In the fading twilight, the stillness of the evening was broken by the sound of horses' hooves clip-clopping along the deserted Mackinac Island street. I shivered, pulling my jacket closer while simultaneously hugging my seven-month-old daughter. It was almost 9:00 p.m., and my exhausted baby squirmed in my arms while my two-year-old jumped up and down on the pier.

No cars are allowed on the island, and horses and bikes are the main sources of transportation. So where was *our* horse-drawn taxi? Annoyed, I counted each minute until the carriage finally arrived. It was charming, really, but as we squeezed on with two other families, I was distracted. We hadn't planned—or packed—well. We didn't really think through the logistics of having to lug everything we had brought to our hotel. In our car, the overflowing luggage, toys, and portable crib looked reasonable. Piled on the pier, it all looked absurd. Feeling embarrassed that our luggage bordered on the ridiculous, that our children were cranky and acting like hooligans, and that others were there to bear witness to it all, I just wanted to go home.

Although I expected the other passengers to be annoyed with us, I was met with only kindness. When Elise threw her teddy at a man across from us in the carriage, he smiled good-naturedly and proceeded to play "Where's teddy?" the remainder of the ride. She squealed, laughing uproariously every time he wiggled its head or threw it back to her. The other passengers smiled indulgently, and I found myself relaxing a little. As we arrived at our hotel and exited the carriage, I smiled with gratitude at our fellow travelers, who went out of their way to soothe a stranger's frazzled nerves.

As Christians, we're called to be kind, tenderhearted, and forgiving toward one another. Sometimes that means actively doing something for another person, but oftentimes all it requires is that we regard with compassion those who are struggling and show them mercy in their distress. The strangers in the taxi reminded me that a little compassion can go a long way.

— *Kristin*

— Today's Act of Kindness —

Go out of your way to be kind to a parent who is dealing with a recalcitrant child, whether it's on a plane or at the grocery store.

Creating Community

You have been called to live in freedom, my brothers and sisters. But don't use your freedom to satisfy your sinful nature. Instead, use your freedom to serve one another in love.

GALATIANS 5:13

At a church I used to attend, my small group of girlfriends became the informal baby-shower committee. Every woman got one baby shower at our church—regardless of whether it was her first baby or her tenth. If it was her first baby while attending at our church, we showered her.

We had shower hosting down to a science. We rotated hosting duties, and I have fond memories of showers when my small house was packed to overflowing with women, gifts, and pastel-colored decor. The host would clean and decorate, and the rest of our friends would bring the food. We spread the burden evenly among ourselves, and our showers became fun social events in our church.

An experienced mom would share a short devotional, and we always ended the shower by praying over the soon-to-be mom, her child, and her family. These two pieces became sacred, precious parts of our showers.

A majority of the women in the congregation made it a point to attend the showers. We had women from every generation participating, and I especially loved watching women bring their elementary-aged daughters to witness the example of Christian motherhood, Christian womanhood, and Christian community you would find at our gatherings. As Christians, we are called to support, lift up, and shower hospitality on other Christians. We are specifically called to use our freedom to serve one another in love.

Today's Scripture is specifically calling Christians to serve other Christians. I've seen Christians get it wrong both ways. Some focus so much on meeting needs inside the church that they never look beyond the church walls to their neighbors, their coworkers, and others. Other Christians focus so much on meeting needs outside the church that they forget the importance of building Christian community. We are called to *balance* in serving the Christian community while also seeing those who do not yet know Christ and showing them his love in tangible ways.

— *Julie*

— Today's Act of Kindness —

How are you building up your Christian friends?
Meet with another Christian for coffee or a
meal, and encourage them in their faith.

Little Ripples Become Big Splashes

Do not despise these small beginnings, for the LORD rejoices to see the work begin.
ZECHARIAH 4:10

Not long ago I met with some dear ladies on the patio of a local restaurant to plan for a fall retreat. While the sun shone on our backs, we dreamed of themes and promotions, our excitement increasing as we shared new ideas, encouraged each other, and built upon the work we'd already done.

I looked around the table of women, a bit in awe to be a part of this group. Many years earlier, my sisters and I attended the conferences put on by this same organization. Every year we would look forward to attending. Even after my sister was diagnosed with cancer, we made a point of going. As she struggled in the midst of her illness, her life's motto became "choose joy," a theme taken from one of the conferences we attended. The work of these women I now sat beside rippled out, multiplying and blessing us, even when we were strangers.

I told them about the impact each year's conference had on me and my sisters, how it spurred us on in our own faith and lives. I shared how, after my sister's death, the phrase "choose joy" became the tagline for Katie's Club, the fund set up in her name—a fund that offers girls and women a chance for hope in their lives through financial support for things such as education, housing, and job training. The conference was a ripple from all those years earlier, creating a bigger splash in the lives of those helped by Katie's Club.

Then one woman said, "You just never know what a difference you can make. You may never know, until heaven, whose life you've affected."

I left thinking about how often our small acts of obedience, kindness, and love can impact others. My life may not be anything exceptional, but the small ripples I make could be enough to spur someone else to make a large splash in their own life, impacting other people I will never know. God can use our small beginnings to bless our families, our friends, and even strangers we may never meet face-to-face.

— *Kendra*

— Today's Act of Kindness —

As you go about your regular day, pray over the small actions and decisions you make, asking God to use these small kindnesses to create a ripple effect in others' lives.

Incremental Kindness

Don't look out only for your own interests, but take an interest in others, too.
PHILIPPIANS 2:4

As a mom, I make a lot of trips to Target. It's pretty much my happy place, especially if I don't have kids begging me to buy the new Barbie movie or trying to surreptitiously sneak treats into the cart. Give me a caffè mocha and an empty cart, and I will gladly wander that wonderland for hours.

Throughout our year of kindness, I specifically wanted to find ways to help others without breaking the bank. It's fun to give away big-ticket items, but it's not usually practical. Most folks can't afford to spend a lot of money every day giving to others, even if it's for a great cause.

Scripture says to "take an interest in others," which includes intentionally looking for ways to *consistently* help others—not just helping in big ways. What I found during the year was that, because I always had the premise of kindness in mind, I would find little ways to contribute to larger needs. For instance, we always try to have new socks stocked in the Diva Boutique at the retreat for single moms, where moms can shop for free from a room full of new and gently used clothing and accessories. So I made it my mission to stock up on socks to give away at the boutique.

For several months, each time I went to Target, I would try to pick up socks. They didn't cost a lot of money to begin with, and they were often on sale, too. Even though it didn't seem like much in my cart each time, as the year progressed, I found myself with a decent-sized bag full of socks waiting in my storeroom. Yet since I did this a little bit at a time, the cost was a tiny bump in my budget rather than a massive mountain.

Have you put pressure on yourself to do or give only in big ways? Remember that each small contribution makes a difference, and over time, small gifts add up to something great.

— *Kristin*

— *Today's Act of Kindness* —

Think of something you'd like to contribute to—whether it's donating food to the local food pantry or gathering school supplies for children in need—and begin your incremental kindness in pursuit of a larger goal.

Encouragement for the Journey

If your gift is to encourage others, be encouraging.
ROMANS 12:8

Each spring I attend a friendship coffee gathering at a local moms' group that I am a part of, during which we celebrate the end of another year of meeting weekly to grow in God's Word and support one another in our parenting. This year we celebrated the twenty-fifth anniversary of the group by bringing back many of the leaders who founded it all those years ago. The leaders shared how they began with just a few women, mainly because they were lonely and needed community. That small group of women is now a thriving group of well over one hundred moms who gather each week to support one another, grow in their faith, and pray for each other. Many weary moms have found hope and built lifelong friendships through the group.

But community isn't something that is needed only by parents. We all need support from people who understand us, no matter where we find ourselves in life. We were made to be in relationship with others, and finding those who are journeying similar paths as we are, who can understand us, show compassion and kindness, and spur us on can be so helpful, especially when we're discouraged.

We are called to encourage each other, and what better way to do that than by coming alongside someone who is in a situation similar to what we've experienced and offering them some kindness through our words or deeds? Maybe you have adopted a child and have wisdom to offer someone else who is considering adoption. Maybe you're working in a career where you can give advice to those thinking about entering the same field. Or maybe you're a grandparent who can offer a young couple some encouragement as they look to start their own family.

Wherever we find ourselves in life, we can look behind us and find others walking the same road. Let's take these opportunities to offer wisdom and encouragement. We're never too young or too old to offer kindness and hope to others.

— *Kendra*

— Today's Act of Kindness —

Think of someone who is going through a situation you've walked through before, and offer them some wisdom and encouragement for their journey.

Grace over Griping

May God, who gives this patience and encouragement, help you live in complete harmony with each other, as is fitting for followers of Christ Jesus.
ROMANS 15:5

I am a fixer. A problem solver. And I can get hung up on what could be, what *should* be, instead of being thankful for what simply *is*. When faced with the fragility and the shortcomings of those whose lives intersect my own, it is sometimes tempting to focus on their weakness instead of on the many gifts and talents they bring into my life.

As I fretted about a friendship this past week and about what I wished the relationship could be instead of what it was currently, God gently reminded me of my friend's wonderful qualities, her incredible strengths, and of all her good characteristics that far outweigh this one weakness. I realized that I needed to extend grace.

Grace chooses to cover another person's weakness instead of laying bare that person's vulnerabilities for all the world to see. Grace recognizes those things that may never be changed—and then it intentionally sets aside the frustrations in order to enjoy and celebrate those whose lives are interwoven with our own. Grace is a gift that has been freely given to each of us and is one of the most beautiful gifts that we can bestow upon one another.

Sometimes, living in complete harmony with one another means that God is calling us to extend grace regarding another's weaknesses and to focus on the strengths a person brings into our lives. God is the fixer, not us—and some things are best left completely to God.

As I thought about my friend, I quietly chose grace over griping, over trying to fix that which may never change. With that decision made, I have since discovered that my relationship with this particular friend has improved and harmony has been restored because I've stopped trying to fix something that is not my responsibility to fix.

— *Julie*

— Today's Act of Kindness —

Who in your life needs grace instead of fixing? Take one small step to restore harmony in that relationship by extending grace.

Childlike Kindness

The disciples came to Jesus and asked, "Who is greatest in the Kingdom of Heaven?" Jesus called a little child to him. . . . Then he said, "I tell you the truth, unless you turn from your sins and become like little children, you will never get into the Kingdom of Heaven. So anyone who becomes as humble as this little child is the greatest in the Kingdom of Heaven."

MATTHEW 18:1-4

My daughter had a friend in her class last year who has Down syndrome and was sick a lot during the school year. Many nights when we would ask the kids what they'd like to pray for, Jasmine would bring up her sweet friend who missed school so often.

This past summer, we ran into Jasmine's friend and her aide, who was with her daily at the splash pad. The aide came over to me and Jasmine with a huge smile on her face and told me what a blessing Jasmine had been, not only to the little girl in her class but also to the aide. Jasmine, unbeknownst to us, had made cards and written notes of encouragement throughout the year to her friend and to the aide, while also making sure to include the girl in classroom activities. This had touched the woman so deeply that she glowed as she talked about Jasmine's kindness. I watched as Jasmine's friend shyly smiled at her.

Later I asked Jasmine what caused her to befriend the girl in her class. She told me she felt sad that some of the other kids wouldn't include her, and she wanted to make sure this girl knew she had a friend. I couldn't have been more proud.

Including those who are different from us is important at any age. Finding commonalities even when faced with our differences is critical when showing kindness to others. Being aware of how we ourselves would like to be treated should be paramount when deciding whether to include another or extend a hand of friendship. As Scripture tells us, anyone who becomes as humble as this little child is the greatest in the Kingdom of Heaven.

— Kendra

— Today's Act of Kindness —

Find a way to extend kindness toward someone who, on the surface, may appear to be different from you.

A Broken Back

I was sick, and you cared for me.
MATTHEW 25:36

As the older-model vehicle careened around a corner on the country road one Memorial Day weekend, it hit loose gravel and spun out of control. With a sickening lurch, it hit a tree in the ditch and ended up lying on its side. Of the four teenage girls inside the car, I was the only one who ended up with a serious injury—two broken vertebrae. The others escaped relatively unscathed.

After surgery and a week in the hospital, I went home the summer after my junior year of high school to an altered reality: careful shifting in bed, limited movement, a back brace for three months, and no possibility of participating in marching band that summer or cheerleading in the fall.

I felt sad and angry. When I was in public, my back brace garnered looks from curious passersby. I can still remember one boy who almost tripped over his feet trying to see the apparatus.

Yet through it all, what stands out most in my memory now—besides achieving the best tan my Scandinavian skin will ever see, due to the countless hours I spent lying outside in the hot summer sun because I couldn't do much else—is the way my friends responded. Some visited me in the hospital, even though it was an hour away from home. One friend came to see me numerous times at my house, bringing me books and magazines. Another friend took me swimming (one of the few activities I could safely do) numerous evenings after she'd finished work for the day.

I easily could have felt alone and lonely, but my friends went out of their way to let me know they were thinking of me. They made the conscious decision to care for me when I was recovering, and it made a world of difference to me. The emotional support they provided was just as important as the soothing water of the lake and the books stacked next to my bed.

— *Kristin*

— Today's Act of Kindness —

How can you provide emotional support for someone struggling with a medical condition? Drop off a coffee or a magazine at their house, or send a message to let them know you're thinking of them.

June

More Than Mechanics

God has given each of you a gift from his great variety of
spiritual gifts. Use them well to serve one another.
1 PETER 4:10

There's a small group of people at our church who regularly volunteer their time to repair cars for people in the community. Those who benefit from the volunteers' skills don't need to be members of our church—just folks who could use a helping hand.

One week, a friend of my husband's contacted him and asked if the group had room for a friend of hers who was having trouble paying for a brake repair. Tim got in touch with the group leader, who said they would be happy to help and could get her car in first at their next session.

The following week, the car was dropped off and fixed. The woman picked it up, but about an hour later she returned. The group leader and his family watched as the now teary-eyed woman, her husband, and her son walked slowly up the driveway, a plate of cookies and a letter for the group in hand.

"Thank you so much for your incredible kindness," the letter said. "We are traveling through this very tough journey and have been very blessed." The letter went on to relate that the woman's husband had spent months in the hospital, only to receive a terminal diagnosis. They weren't sure he would live to see his son graduate from high school. Paying to have their car repaired simply wasn't something they could afford.

We are called to use our gifts to serve one another. This group of volunteers has the knowledge, skill, and desire to work on cars. They could spend their time working on their own vehicles, or offer to help a few select friends, but instead they sacrifice their time to put those skills to work for strangers. In doing so, they not only honor the people they serve, but they also honor God.

— *Kristin*

— Today's Act of Kindness —

Make a list of three skills or gifts you possess, then think of three individuals or groups who could benefit from your help. Choose one skill and one way to help and get started.

Making Space for Hospitality

Always be eager to practice hospitality.
ROMANS 12:13

Summertime at our house is a time of freedom, flexible schedules, and playtime. Our kids love playing outdoors, making up games, riding bikes, and running through the sprinkler.

All these things are fun, but the challenge for us as a family has become making time to show kindness even when it's not linked to a holiday or season. For us, kindness in the summer looks a bit different than other times of the year. Sometimes we get a little lax or forget to be intentional about doing kind acts or even talking about kindness.

To combat this challenge, one way we work to incorporate kindness is through playtime with other kids in our neighborhood. My kids are all extroverted and love to have friends over to our home. This is especially challenging for me, as I am not the mom who naturally loves playdates or having lots of kids in my house. I hate messes, and noise tends to get to me after a while, but I realize the importance of empowering my kids to incorporate kindness into their lives and relationships.

Keeping that in mind, I look for ways that they can have their friends over when it works for our calendar. I say yes when we've got a free day at home, and I don't feel bad when our schedule another day is too busy. I also have conversations about what activities my kids would like to do with their friends, what snacks they could offer, and how long their friends can stay. This teaches my kids how to be hospitable and how to welcome others into our home, a lesson I'm hoping they can carry into adulthood. It teaches us to be more flexible, to share, and to practice hospitality along with kindness, which is a good lesson for me, too.

— Kendra

— Today's Act of Kindness —

Invite someone over, even if it's just for a cup of coffee. If it's too uncomfortable to invite them to your house, start by inviting them to a local coffee shop or restaurant.

The Gray Swimsuit

*The Lord does not look at the things people look at. People look at
the outward appearance, but the Lord looks at the heart.*

1 SAMUEL 16:7, NIV

It was a Calvin Klein swimsuit that pushed me over the edge. Colored two shades of gray, it was lovely and understated and fit my best friend perfectly. As my thirteen-year-old self glanced down at my yellow swimsuit with bright purple flowers, I suddenly felt inadequate—my thighs too big, my chest too small. Without the armor of makeup and hair spray, I felt ugly and exposed, my enjoyment of the pool tainted.

It wasn't her fault that she was slim and pretty, but a thin ribbon of jealousy curled through my stomach as I noticed her artless laughter, her effortless beauty. Lying next to her on a pool lounger, I suddenly felt frumpy and graceless.

Even though it's been twenty years since that day, there are so many days when I feel like I'm thirteen again, measuring myself against someone else and falling short. That self-consciousness is something I haven't been able to rid myself of. Although I'm much more comfortable with myself at thirty-three than I ever was at thirteen, I still find myself brushing aside compliments about my post-baby body or lamenting my squishy stomach. If it doesn't *feel* beautiful, it must not *be* beautiful. Self-kindness is so often a struggle for me.

Recently, my mom and I had a conversation revolving around beauty and getting older. I was bemoaning some of the extreme measures I had seen people take in their efforts to turn back time.

Pausing, my mom simply said, "There is beauty in aging. But you have to look for it." And isn't that true? Though we may not always fit society's definitions of beauty, there is something infinitely precious and valuable in our "flaws." God sees our inward beauty, not the outside veneer we obsess over. The scars on my belly and the thin white streaks on my hips speak to babies delivered into this world, cradled and cared for by this "imperfect" woman. If God can look at me and see beauty, should I not be able to do the same?

— *Kristin*

— Today's Act of Kindness —

Communicate to someone else—your mother, sister,
daughter, or friend—that her "flaws" are beautiful.

The Drama Vortex

Watch your tongue and keep your mouth shut, and you will stay out of trouble.
PROVERBS 21:23

The message that popped up on Facebook reeked of drama—the unhealthy, suck-you-in-and-twist-you-up kind of vortex that I've disliked for my entire life, but have grown to especially hate this past year. I had found myself inadvertently drawn into a situation involving adults who, despite being well into their thirties and forties, were engaging in behaviors I can only liken to the mean-girl antics of seventh graders.

I've never been "good" at drama. My stomach clenches with anxiety when I find myself in the turbulent waters of hidden agendas, fake niceness, and people who say one thing and yet mean something completely different.

I've watched a fellow Christian respond to this situation with uncommon grace and genuine peacemaking gestures that are a beautiful reflection of Christ. Meanwhile, I've struggled mightily to be civil, let alone graciously Christlike, despite my head knowledge of Scripture and of the ways Jesus calls us to respond to those who are unkind. I'm prayerfully working on my attitude, but I find myself in the spot of having to remain silent and simply avoid the individuals involved in the drama for fear that my response in this emotional state will do more harm than good to the cause of Christ.

I want to be someone who is intentional about revealing Christ through my words and deeds. I'm discovering that I have to be equally intentional when faced with how I respond in situations where I know my emotions run high and have a tendency to bubble over in unhelpful ways, despite my best intentions. Sometimes the best way to stay out of trouble is to zip our lips and silence our tongues. And while I know my ideal response would be full of grace and mercy, I also know it has to be genuine and heartfelt. Until I can respond that way, my best response is no response at all.

— Julie

— Today's Act of Kindness —

Are you in the midst of an emotional storm that's tempting you
to react in a way that is unbecoming for a follower of Christ?
Choose instead to respond in a thoughtful, gracious way.

The Kindness of a Stranger

Do not let any unwholesome talk come out of your mouths,
but only what is helpful for building others up according
to their needs, that it may benefit those who listen.
EPHESIANS 4:29, NIV

It's a common experience for parents: you take your kids out to eat thinking this will be the day they are able to handle it, only to find yourself chasing a child who will not sit still, cleaning up spilled milk, and trying to stop little hands from throwing food. So much for a relaxing dinner out with family.

One night out, as I took my youngest to the bathroom with me—more as a distraction for her than anything—the two older ladies at the table next to us smiled and commented on "what beautiful children" we have. I nodded and thanked them while wrangling my daughter down the corridor to the bathroom.

On our way back, the two ladies were getting ready to leave, and as they walked past us, one stopped for a moment, told me again that I have great kids, and then said, "You're doing great; keep going, Mama!" Tears immediately sprang to my eyes, and I could have hugged her. She had the ability to see what I could not in the moment—that I do have beautiful kids and a wonderful family—and she encouraged me to keep going. Sometimes in the middle of the chaos I can forget my blessings. The kindness of a stranger in that moment was just the reminder I needed.

It seems so simple—a little encouragement from a stranger—taking no more than a few moments. When we put kindness into action, we see the needs, big and small, of those all around and then we attempt to meet those needs. How often do we see people who would benefit from our helpful words instead of our harsh glares, especially when they feel like they are failing or not doing a good job? Just think how much our kindness would build them up.

— Kendra

— Today's Act of Kindness —

Be conscious of someone who crosses your path who may be in need of a little encouragement. Take time to stop, notice, and offer encouragement to this person. It could make their whole day.

Investing in Fun

Wherever your treasure is, there the desires of your heart will also be.
LUKE 12:34

My husband loves movies. At night, you can usually find him lying in bed reading a movie synopsis or watching a movie trailer. As a young married couple, we used to have "bed days" where we'd make a big bed on the living room floor in front of the TV and watch movies all day long. Now that we are parents of three young children, those days of lying around doing nothing on a weekend are long gone, but we've adapted to the changes. Now as a family, it's become one of the things we all like to do together on evenings and weekends when we need a bit of a break: we crash on giant pillows on the floor, children tucked between adults, and watch movies about Barbies and LEGOs.

So it came as no surprise to me when Tim had an idea for a church event that would reach into our community: What if our church rented out the local movie theater on a Saturday morning and paid for everyone's movie tickets and popcorn? What if we invited our neighbors and folks in the community alongside the children from our church?

Our church leaders agreed to try it out, so we chose a family-friendly animated movie and began inviting people. For the children in our church, it became an incentive to learn their Bible verses and invite friends to church, which "earned" them the treat of attending a free movie. But for those outside our church community, there was no requirement or obligation. As a congregation, we just wanted them to relax and feel welcome in our midst. Our church has now done this event the past three summers, and every year hundreds of kids and their parents attend. It seems my husband isn't the only one who loves movies.

We're told in the Gospel of Luke that where we choose to put our treasure reveals our hearts. Sometimes I feel like I should only give to "big" or "important" things. Yet something like a community movie reminds me that choosing to invest in fun things—little moments that reveal our heart for others—can bless people too. You never know when these small moments will impact someone for eternity.

— *Kristin*

— Today's Act of Kindness —

Find a way to share a hobby or passion of yours
with someone else who would appreciate it.

Kindness Accountability

You are the salt of the earth. But what good is salt if it has lost its flavor? Can you make it salty again? It will be thrown out and trampled underfoot as worthless.

MATTHEW 5:13

Sitting around the living room, we watched as the last of the kids tossed their paper plates in the trash after the impromptu breakfast buffet before heading off to play. Our conversation slowly switched topics from general chitchat about our weeks to the reason for our gathering.

We are a group of Christians striving to live in a way that reflects God—through service, through relationships, through kindness—and we meet on a regular basis to encourage each other, to hold one another accountable, and to work together.

It is during these meetings that we ponder what it means to be Christians who live in the world but are still set apart from it. How do we remain salty, as described in today's verse in Matthew, while being friendly, accessible, and welcoming to those who think and act differently? How do we navigate the tension between wanting to share the gospel and wanting to form authentic relationships first, allowing us to have a credible, transforming voice in another's life?

These are the issues that my husband and I, that all our group members, wrestle with. Having a group of committed Christians who desire the same lifestyle—who want to be salt in the world, who strive to be known first by our actions, reflecting Christ before we utter a single word—has helped us stick to this journey.

While we don't always get it right, having others who pray for and encourage us and who are striving to live the same way has helped us stay the course. We read Scripture and discuss how the Word of God applies to the various circumstances we face. We read books on missional living and the missional message woven throughout the Gospels. And we frequently are found visiting in one another's kitchens, manning someone's grill during a barbecue, or helping one another clean house as we prepare for a neighborhood party—lightening the load that comes with entertaining others and inviting them into our homes and lives.

— *Julie*

— Today's Act of Kindness —

Think of someone you can join with as an accountability partner as you incorporate kindness into your everyday life. Reach out to that person to schedule a regular time to meet.

The Blessing Budget

*What good is it, dear brothers and sisters, if you say you
have faith but don't show it by your actions?*

JAMES 2:14

A few years ago, my husband and I went through a budgeting course and got our financial house in order. It felt good to know where our money was going each month, what we were paying off, and what we could afford. One area that has been a priority since the very beginning of our marriage is being generous with our finances, and it was with that idea in mind that my husband came up with the "blessing budget."

On a practical level, our blessing budget is a sinking fund, meaning we add to it each month and it builds up over time so that we're prepared for opportunities that arise to help those in need. It's a separate category from other giving, such as tithing, and is specifically designated for blessing others.

Of course, it's possible to help others in ways that don't cost any money at all. But for us, having a blessing budget gives us the freedom to help as needs arise without wondering if we really have the funds to do so. Living out our faith means that we're willing to live it out in our actions, and sometimes that means helping in areas of need by providing material goods or services. And, honestly, it's fun.

I keep an ongoing list of what we give, and every once in a while we read through it. Each time we do, we are amazed at the ways God has been able to use that little seed money, and we marvel at how it always seems to go further than we'd imagined. Through it, we've been able to pay for appliances for people who need them, plane tickets for folks who haven't seen their loved ones in way too long, car repairs, medical bills, supplies for newborns, food for the homeless, rent, electric bills, and more.

— *Kristin*

— Today's Act of Kindness —

Put together a plan of action for building your own blessing
budget. Begin to set aside funds, even small amounts,
that you can use to help others in their time of need.

Cheering Each Other On

Be happy with those who are happy.
ROMANS 12:15

When Kristin, Julie, and I found out we were going to write and publish a book, we were *so* excited. After writing together for the past several years on our blog, we were finally seeing a bigger dream of ours come true. When we told a few of our close friends, who had seen all the hard work we'd done over the years, their responses were priceless. They were beyond excited, cheering with us and even jumping up and down in celebration. They rejoiced in our success, and it felt so good to share this accomplishment with others who were happy for us.

Not long after this, I was reminded of a friend I had in junior high who had accomplished a goal she'd set for herself. I remember that I hugged her, congratulated her, and asked, "How can we celebrate together?" She looked at me and, with surprise on her face, said, "I've never had a friend who was happy for me when I did well." I found this odd, thinking, *Why wouldn't I be happy for my friend who has tried so hard and done so well?* But as the years have gone on, I've realized that we don't always do a good job of celebrating one another's successes or cheering others on in their pursuits.

In a world filled with competition, we can sometimes forget that celebrating others' accomplishments and rejoicing with them matters. We shouldn't let our own personal goals or even our insecurities hinder us from telling others, "I'm proud of you" or "You did a really good job." But the truth is, one person achieving their goals doesn't mean you can't achieve yours—there is room for everyone, and God has a plan for each of us individually. Since we are called to "be happy with those who are happy," what better way to show kindness to those around us than by celebrating with them in the joys of life?

— Kendra

— Today's Act of Kindness —

Take the time to acknowledge and celebrate with someone who is experiencing a success or has accomplished a goal recently.

The Pet Foster Family

*If someone has enough money to live well and sees a brother or sister in
need but shows no compassion—how can God's love be in that person?*

1 JOHN 3:17

"Honey," I asked, "can we be a foster home for Scampi?" My husband raised his
eyebrow suspiciously: "Scampi?"

Scampi is a gray-and-white tabby cat who is what I affectionately call a cat-dog.
Unlike many cats, he is cuddly and friendly, and he is one of the most delightful cats
I've ever had the pleasure of knowing. His owner was a single mom working hard
to provide a better life for her son, and she was faced with having to temporarily
move to an apartment where Scampi was not welcome. This cat had been a part of
her family for many years, and she was heartbroken at the thought of losing him. I
don't remember if she asked or if I offered, but I found myself asking my husband
to consider becoming a cat foster parent for Scampi—it was just for nine months!

Scampi joined our home soon thereafter and quickly became a familiar companion, joining me every time I sat down and curling up at the foot of our bed
in the evenings. He was sweet and friendly, and he quickly wove himself into the
fabric of our family.

As the months passed, we stayed in touch with Scampi's owner, giving her
updates and assuring her that all was well. When she contacted me midspring of
the following year with the exciting news that she was moving to a new place and
that she would be picking up Scampi next weekend, I couldn't help but feel a tiny
bit sad for us while feeling joy for her.

We are called to have a compassionate response when we see a brother or sister
in need. Providing a safe spot for Scampi to live while his owner transitioned into a
safer housing arrangement was the perfect compassionate response in that situation.
Where might God be asking you to show compassion?

— Julie

— Today's Act of Kindness —

Many women's shelters seek foster homes for pets
while their owners transition into safer homes and
environments. Consider becoming a pet foster family.

A Ripple Effect

Let us consider how we may spur one another on toward love and good deeds.
HEBREWS 10:24, NIV

For several months, the ALS Ice Bucket Challenge was all the rage on social media. Folks were videotaping themselves as they pledged funds to help the ALS Association, dumping vats of ice-cold water on their heads and nominating others to do the same. For a while, it seemed like everyone was doing it: celebrities, family, friends, neighbors. There were even outtakes and gag reels on YouTube about "fails" where challenges went awry, such as when people tried dumping buckets from high above and knocked themselves down or missed entirely.

Sure, it was fun to watch people soak themselves. Yet what was most intriguing, at least to me, was the idea that we can spur one another on to more good. In 2009, CNN reported that an anonymous twenty-eight-year-old man donated a kidney to a stranger. This person's action set off a ripple effect that resulted in ten people receiving new kidneys, all as a consequence of that single, anonymous donation.* One single person. That's it! What an encouragement for us on our quest for kindness—our actions are never wasted, and sometimes they can reach far beyond our wildest hopes.

Perhaps donating a kidney is out of reach, but there are lots of other ways to pay it forward. For instance, one day I was at our local Goodwill purchasing curtains and curtain rods. The older lady in front of me said hello to my children, and we chatted for a few minutes about the weather while she checked out. A few minutes later, when I reached the register myself, I was astonished to find that she had left money to pay for part of my bill. She didn't know it, but the purchases I was making that day were going toward a new women's wing at our local homeless shelter. Through her generosity, she had unknowingly been part of a two-fold act of kindness that extended far beyond our single encounter. Her desire to pay it forward set off a chain reaction. Even our small actions can cause giant ripples of kindness.

— *Kristin*

— Today's Act of Kindness —

Think of one way you can pay kindness forward.

* Anne Harding, "Donation Chain Has Led to 10 Kidney Transplants," *CNN.com*, March 11, 2009, http://www.cnn.com/2009/HEALTH/03/11/kidney.ten.transplants/.

Leaving Your Comfort Zone

I heard the Lord asking, "Whom should I send as a messenger to this people? Who will go for us?" I said, "Here I am. Send me."

ISAIAH 6:8

Sitting at the large table in my favorite coffee shop, I mostly listened as conversation ebbed and flowed among the women who had joined me to discuss the turmoil my community has faced this past year with respect to refugees, religious differences, and race.

Different countries of origin. Different religions. Different cultures. I quietly tallied up more differences than similarities among most of us. As conversation veered into topics touching on race and religion, with perspectives and experiences vastly different from my own, I found myself slightly uncomfortable, definitely out of my element, and exactly where I wanted to be.

The longer I've walked with Jesus, the more I recognize that God works best when I'm in over my head and beyond my skills, when I'm fully reliant on him. I've learned that God does the most amazing things only after I've stepped beyond my comfort zone and into a space that makes me feel stretched, twitchy, and more than a little uneasy.

Life is far too short to be lived lulled into a sense of false security. Regardless of what others might tell you, we rarely change the world from the safety of our recliners via Facebook or Instagram. God asks us to step out, step up, and get our hands dirty. World changing usually includes careful listening, sometimes involves broken hearts, and almost always requires a pouring out of ourselves into the lives around us.

How can Christ's transforming love shine through us if we are afraid of building genuine, authentic relationships with those who are different from us? In order to fully live out Scripture and be messengers of the Good News, we have to actively be involved in spaces and places where others do not yet believe. Instead of always hanging out with our brothers and sisters of faith, we must be willing to be sent as representatives of Christ.

— Julie

— Today's Act of Kindness —

Reach out to someone in your life who has a different culture, religion, or worldview, and ask them to meet you for coffee or a meal. If no one springs to mind, prayerfully consider how you can open your life to better engage others who are different from you.

Broken to Beautiful

The one sitting on the throne said, "Look, I am making everything new!"
REVELATION 21:5

My daughter Jasmine's birth mother passed away one winter, and we decided together that we'd like to do something to remember her by. I knew of a woman who made necklaces out of broken pieces of glass, demonstrating the idea that God takes things that are broken and makes them beautiful again. I asked Jasmine if we should have a necklace made in memory of her birth mother. Jasmine agreed and decided that she'd like to have a cross necklace. She picked out the colors, and then we decided to order them not only for us but also for Jasmine's two birth aunts as a way for them to remember their sister.

After the necklaces were made, we brought them with us to a family reception that we were invited to. While playing at the pool, Jasmine stopped to pull out the crosses, and she shyly explained to her aunts the meaning behind them. I had tears in my eyes as I proudly watched my daughter tell her aunts that she picked the Scripture in which God says he is making all things new as the inspiration for the necklaces. The aunts whispered thanks and words of love as they each put on their gifts. Later, we took pictures of them all together, affirming the unity between Jasmine and her birth family.

God really does make all things new. It may not be the way that we would want or expect, but he can take things that are broken and make something beautiful out of the pieces. This is a promise we can cling to, even when we are unsure of the outcome. This truth of God's heart for redemption reminds us that kindness is not just something we do or say at the surface level. Instead, it can be a show of solidarity and strength as we sit with those who are hurting or in pain, a way for us to show them the hope we find in God.

— *Kendra*

— Today's Act of Kindness —

Offer hope to someone who desperately needs it,
through your words, your actions, or a gift.

Extravagant Generosity

Each of you should give what you have decided in your heart to give,
not reluctantly or under compulsion, for God loves a cheerful giver.
2 CORINTHIANS 9:7, NIV

Kindness was the reason I married my husband. Oh sure, I loved his blue eyes and his bear hugs and his snappy wit, too, but his generosity was what originally piqued my interest.

I met Tim the year after my sister had died from a five-year cancer battle. To honor her memory, my family started a foundation that benefited girls and women. We decided that our big fund-raiser for the foundation would be a mountain climb in Colorado. Since Tim had been a business associate of my dad's for several years and my dad knew Tim was from Colorado, he invited him to come along to climb the Mount of the Holy Cross, a fourteen-thousand-foot peak located near Minturn, Colorado.

The climb itself was a long, exhausting success, one our family would repeat on other "fourteeners" for several years to come. But the day after the climb, we celebrated by meeting up with all of the folks who climbed with us, as well as with their families, for breakfast at a local restaurant. As the meal came to a close, Tim graciously picked up the tab for all of us.

I was already intrigued by Tim's personality and charm, but his generosity? *That* won me over. Moved by his thoughtfulness, I sent him an e-mail after we arrived home, thanking him for his kindness. We were married less than a year later.

What Tim displayed on that day many years ago is a quality that I've come to appreciate more and more as time goes on. Scripture says that God loves a cheerful giver, and I've found that I do too. The people who impress me the most—the ones I want to have as friends and whom I choose to surround myself with—aren't impressive because of their wealth, status, or good looks, but because they love to give. They are extravagantly generous to those in need, and their cheerful attitudes are contagious. Like Tim, they have learned the value of giving cheerfully.

— Kristin

— Today's Act of Kindness —

What act of outrageous generosity can you do?
It doesn't have to be monetary. Bless someone
beyond what they would or could expect.

Kindness at the Office

Do all that you can to live in peace with everyone.
ROMANS 12:18

I am fortunate to work for a company that values community and group activities. Every year my office holds a food drive for our local food shelf, puts together thank-you dinners for our volunteers, and comes together to help when someone is in need.

Recently, one of my coworkers was injured and had to take several weeks off of work. The office staff immediately began brainstorming ways we could help, including running errands and dropping off dinners to her family for the next several weeks. Kind acts such as these have created a cohesive community that ensures no one feels alone or unsupported.

I know that not every work environment is as supportive as mine is, and I've worked in environments that were less than friendly. But I also know that we all have a choice in how we approach our work and our coworkers. Are we quick to offer assistance to others who need our help? Do we keep ourselves out of drama and squabbles between staff? Are we actively trying to live out God's command to "do all that [we] can to live in peace with everyone"? Do we show kindness toward everyone?

It's so easy to get sucked into workplace drama, especially when we work in environments that don't promote teamwork or collaboration. We can feel powerless to change a whole culture as just one person. Although we may not be able to control others' words or actions, we can certainly control our responses. Oftentimes it takes just one person to start a wave of kindness toward others, which in turn can change the whole environment. We have the ability to have a positive impact on those we work with, as well as those in our community, if we're willing to take the first step.

— Kendra

— Today's Act of Kindness —

Plan a simple act of kindness that you and your coworkers
could do together—something that will create community
and require a team effort so everyone can join in.

No Toilets? No Problem

*Don't forget to show hospitality to strangers, for some who have
done this have entertained angels without realizing it!*
HEBREWS 13:2

Aaron and I live near a large park that hosts, on one Friday every June, thousands of people for an outdoor concert. Our house is close enough to the park that we can set chairs out in our shady backyard and enjoy the music without the crowds and the unrelenting sun, and one year we talked about inviting our friends and people from the neighborhood to bring a chair and join us in the backyard.

Of course, that was while we had toilets. In the weeks after that conversation, we undertook what I thought would be a simple remodeling project in two of our three bathrooms—resulting in a house that was in disarray and had only one working toilet the week of the event. This improvement project wasn't supposed to interfere with our party, but life isn't always predictable.

As Aaron worked to get the tiki torches installed, I wandered outside to revisit our party plans. "Honey, I've been rethinking this party," I began. He turned to me with a slight grin. "Don't you turn into an introvert on me!" When I reminded him that we were down to one toilet and had a house that felt like it had been flipped upside down and inside out, he softly said, "I think we should go ahead anyway."

He was right. Life is unpredictable. There will never be a perfect time to invite others into our homes and into our lives. If we wait until the time feels just right, we will be waiting forever and missing valuable opportunities to love others in the meantime. When we practice hospitality by opening up our lives and homes to those around us, including people outside our normal circles of friends, we allow God to do a work in our midst. And as Hebrews 13:2 tells us, we might even be entertaining angels unwittingly.

— Julie

— Today's Act of Kindness —

What invitation have you been putting off because you've been
waiting for the "perfect" time? Prayerfully reconsider your timing
as compared to God's timing, and extend the invitation anyway.

Late-Night Letters

The words of the godly encourage many.
PROVERBS 10:21

Sometimes a year can feel like a whole lot of days. In the course of our determination to spend 365 days doing one act of kindness each day, there were some days when I would have to scramble to do something late at night. Either I hadn't had time for it earlier in the day, or it had simply slipped my mind until I was climbing into bed.

One easy—and free—idea that I had in mind for these moments was to write notes to the people I encountered throughout the day. Accordingly, I began writing out notes, usually sent via e-mail or Facebook message, but sometimes dropped in the mail, letting people know that I was thinking of them. Some were short and others were long, but as I began to write them, I realized they fell into several predictable categories.

If you're searching for inspiration, here are some ideas for folks you can focus on sending a note to:

- Someone who needs encouragement.
- Someone who is doing a good job and needs to hear that it has been noticed.
- Someone who is facing a medical crisis or long illness, either their own or someone else's.
- Someone who may be lonely.
- Someone you've lost touch with—maybe even someone you haven't talked to in years—but would like the chance to reconnect with.
- Someone who needs to hear an apology from you.
- Someone you wish you knew better.
- Someone you're proud of but haven't told them so lately.

Scripture says that our words have the potential to encourage many. Whom can you intentionally impact with the power of your kind words?

— *Kristin*

— Today's Act of Kindness —

Going off the list above, think of one person in each category. Write one note today, and then resolve to write the rest of the notes as you have time.

Removing the Log

*[Jesus said,] "Why worry about a speck in your friend's eye when you
have a log in your own? . . . First get rid of the log in your own eye; then
you will see well enough to deal with the speck in your friend's eye.*

MATTHEW 7:3-5

This last year, Kyle and I had an episode with our teenage son and one of his social media accounts. Some of our son's school friends tagged him in several posts that were not at all in line with our family's shared beliefs and faith. We talked to our son about setting appropriate boundaries, but when that failed to work, we shut his social media accounts down for a season. We explained how guilt by association worked and how, even as an "innocent" participant, he was still just that—a participant. We also explained how he could end up in the same trouble these boys were likely to find themselves in if they continued with their destructive posts.

In the days that followed I found myself not able to shake my anger toward these young men. How could they be so ignorant and mean? And then I was reminded of some foolish things I did as a teenager—things I would never do today. I felt a small tug of conviction in my heart over the way I'd been thinking and feeling toward my son's friends.

Part of grace is offering others forgiveness—while not condoning or allowing inappropriate behavior—because we've been forgiven for much. Did I set boundaries for my son with social media? Absolutely. But *my* heart changed when I decided to forgive those boys and let go of my anger over their foolishness.

Oftentimes it's easier to judge others without acknowledging our own sin and foolishness than it is to first assess our own behavior. But Matthew reminds us that we are to take care of the logs in our own eyes before we worry about anyone else. Kindness comes in many forms, and offering forgiveness is just one way we can choose to extend kindness toward others.

— *Kendra*

— Today's Act of Kindness —

Do you have someone you've been unforgiving
toward? Choose to forgive that person without
compromising appropriate boundaries.

The Joy of Sharing

*Let everyone see that you are considerate in all you
do. Remember, the Lord is coming soon.*
PHILIPPIANS 4:5

Rushing through Target's front doors at 6:48 p.m., I scanned the crowd even as my feet slowed from a brisk walk to a gentler gait. I was three minutes late for my arranged meeting time with a young married couple from China—two teachers in my children's immersion school—and we had big plans for the evening.

They were pregnant with their first child, and the parents in our program asked if we could throw them an American-style baby shower, complete with the obligatory baby registry. My shower cohostess and I quickly realized that this young couple was overwhelmed by all the American baby paraphernalia and was unsure of how to even begin deciding what was necessary in those first months after birth, so I volunteered to tackle the baby aisles with them.

That night, we had such fun. We laughed as we tried to figure out how to collapse the strollers, we cooed over the tiniest of hats, and we debated the pros and cons of the bigger swing versus the travel swing. I steered them away from the gimmicks and helped them discern which items were a priority. They, in turn, gave me the gift of a stroll down memory lane as I shared in their excitement of anticipating new life and new beginnings.

As we hugged goodbye in the middle of the diaper aisle, they thanked me for sharing my wisdom and experience with them, and I thanked them for allowing me to be a part of their great joy on the cusp of this grand new adventure.

As I practically skipped my way back out of the store, I thanked God for the opportunity to use my parenting experience and knowledge to bless someone else who is just starting the journey. When we are intentionally considerate of others, it reveals God at work in us. How we act and how we treat others reveals God to the world without a single word.

— Julie

— Today's Act of Kindness —

Think of an area where you have the wisdom of experience.
Use your knowledge and experience to help someone else.

Encouraging Potential

Let everything you say be good and helpful, so that your words
will be an encouragement to those who hear them.
EPHESIANS 4:29

One of my dear friends once told me how as a child she would usually get Cs in school. Her mother always said that Cs were good enough. My friend believed her mother's words and continued to get Cs until an eighth-grade teacher told her, "You know, you're really an A student. I know you get Cs, but you are smart enough to be getting As."

This teacher's comment had a profound impact on her, opening the doors of possibility in her own mind for her to believe she actually *could* do better. From that point on, she always got As in school. All it took was someone who was willing to tell her that she was actually capable of achieving more and truly believed that she could.

Why is it often so much easier to see the potential in others than it is to see it in ourselves? Sometimes a little push of encouragement from someone else is just what we need in order to believe that we can accomplish the task before us or to see a possibility we hadn't seen before.

We are instructed to share good and helpful words that will encourage those who hear them, even though we may never know the impact our words will have. I'm sure that teacher didn't realize the profound impact she would have on my friend and how her words would completely change the trajectory of her education and life. When we see opportunities to share words of encouragement with someone else, we should speak up willingly, trusting that God will use our words to accomplish his purposes.

Has someone spoken encouraging words to you that have totally changed the course of your life? Ask God to show you how he might want you to encourage someone else in a big way.

— Kendra

— Today's Act of Kindness —

Encourage someone who has been struggling lately, and
be sure to point out the potential you see in them.

The Gift of Pampering

Encourage each other and build each other up, just as you are already doing.
1 THESSALONIANS 5:11

Despite the fact that my babies are long past diapers and strollers and swaddling, there are a few things about those first few weeks and months when they were teeny tiny and newly home with my husband and me that are forever etched in my heart and in my mind. One of the hardest things was knowing that I was on maternity leave and that my time at home was limited and short.

I vividly remember silently ticking off the days and weeks of maternity leave with dread and sadness as I nursed my tiny babies in the early, predawn hours. The knowledge that I had only a few precious weeks hovered always in the back of my mind, and every Monday morning was another week gone.

Over the years, I've seen those same feelings reflected in the eyes of other moms as they quietly speak about maternity leave. Emotions run high those first few days back at work, and countless new moms I know have put on a brave face in front of their colleagues while confessing to friends about tears spilled in cars, outside of day care, and in office bathrooms.

When a friend went back to work after the birth of her daughter a few months prior, I put together the small present of a coffee gift card, flowers, and an encouraging note, and then my son and I stopped by her office toward closing time during her first week back. We whisked in, my son delivered the gift, and we whisked back out. We left her standing with a small smile on her face as she left one meeting and was about to enter another one.

Our gift was pure pampering, with nothing essential or useful—meant just for her, with nothing to do for her darling baby, her family, or anyone else. When we intentionally encourage and build someone up in the midst of a hard day, week, or season in their life with a kind word or a thoughtful gift, we live out Scripture in a beautifully tangible way.

— Julie

— Today's Act of Kindness —

Prayerfully consider who might need some extra
encouragement. Choose someone you can surprise with
a small, fun gift of encouragement and pampering.

A Memorable Mentor

Dear children, let's not merely say that we love each
other; let us show the truth by our actions.

1 JOHN 3:18

It was an ego blow, to be honest. I was ecstatic to see my acceptance letter to the graduate program, but my heart sank a little at the words "probationary status." I had just two classes to prove that my writing—deemed less than stellar by the committee—could survive the program.

Sure, I'd been out of the university environment for a while, and my writing skewed toward concise journalism rather than the evocative language of academia, but I was embarrassed at the idea of being "less than."

As the semester progressed, my uncertain status weighed heavily on me. What if I really wasn't good enough? What if my writing didn't improve? Other than the spectacular failure of my first on-the-road driver's license test, I had never truly failed at anything. The prospect was terrifying.

When I approached one of my professors midsemester and asked her to write a letter confirming my aptitude for the program's committee, she graciously obliged. I was so relieved. As my probationary status lifted, so did the weight on my heart.

A few years later, when I was choosing a mentor for my capstone essay, the same professor immediately came to mind. When she agreed to help, I was once again grateful for her feedback and guidance.

Yes, she was smart and insightful, but it was her kindness that won me over—taking time to write the letter, spending all those hours with me in coffee shops and her office. That mentoring was invaluable to me because of the underlying messages I heard from her, woven throughout our time together: *You matter. You're smart. Your ideas are worthwhile. You are a good writer. You can succeed at this. I believe in you.*

Those affirmations, some verbalized and others unspoken, might have rung hollow if her actions hadn't backed them up. But her actions, and what they meant to me, resonated far beyond the time we spent together.

— Kristin

— Today's Act of Kindness —

Do something that tangibly affirms your belief in someone
else—maybe it's writing a letter of recommendation, contributing
to their performance review at work, or even just sending
a personal note telling them they're doing a good job.

Remembering Her Legacy

Remember your leaders who taught you the word of God. Think of all the
good that has come from their lives, and follow the example of their faith.

HEBREWS 13:7

In the early part of the summer, my mother-in-law holds her annual garage sale. My sister-in-law and I join her every year to part with items from the past year— clothes that are now too small for our kids, toys that have been forgotten, and other household items that are no longer needed. The proceeds from the sale then fund our families' vacation budgets for the summer.

This past year a woman we hadn't seen in many years came through our sale. We spent a nice time visiting and chatting about our kids growing up, graduating from school, and getting jobs. It was a wonderful time of reminiscing and catching up. As she was about to leave, she paused, cocked her head to one side, and said to me, "You know, I just have to tell you, I still think about your sister Katrina so often." She then went on to say how impactful Katrina's life had been on her, how she still thinks of her regularly, and how she cherishes a book she received from my sister long ago. Tears sprang to my eyes, and she quietly hugged me. As she left, I felt comforted by her words and her remembrance of my sister who has been gone many years now.

Remembering those who've impacted our lives is so important, even if the person is no longer here. Let others know how their loved ones made an impact on you. It will encourage them to know that their loved one's life mattered and that who they were and what they did made a difference in someone's life. In doing so, we live out Scripture's encouragement to remember our leaders who modeled goodness and faith. Let's honor those, living and deceased, who've been examples of God's love and kindness toward us.

— Kendra

— Today's Act of Kindness —

Send a thank-you note to someone (or their loved ones) whose life had an impact on you.

The Cold-Caller

*If you favor some people over others, you are committing
a sin. You are guilty of breaking the law.*

JAMES 2:9

I absentmindedly answered the cell phone as I stirred dinner in the frying pan, forgetting to look to see who was calling before I picked up. As the unfamiliar woman's voice asked if I would please consider spending a few minutes taking a survey, I sighed inwardly at my mistake in answering in the first place. *Ugh. I hate cold calls, especially political ones during primary season,* I thought before reluctantly agreeing.

As we worked our way through the survey questions, I found myself starting to snicker at the obvious attempts to manipulate my answer. Politics have me feeling weary and jaded, and sometimes I'd cry if I didn't laugh. And these silly questions deserved a laugh.

I stopped her, apologized for laughing, and explained that I found the questions so ridiculous that they were funny, before breaking into another giggle. She paused before laughingly agreeing with me. We spent a few moments talking about how her company is hired to conduct the survey without any knowledge of who hired them, and how hard it sometimes is to be the neutral messenger, especially when the survey is political in nature.

As I finished the survey, she warmly thanked me for being a good sport and for being so nice to work with. Hanging up, I felt a twinge of regret for the times I've been frustrated with the poor soul on the other end of a cold call. Cold-calling is a difficult job, and while I don't have to do exactly what the caller wants me to, I can decline in a way that is considerate and polite. If I pick and choose whom I treat with kindness, then I'm committing a sin. We are not to favor some over others—we are to be nondiscriminatory and treat everyone equally, even the cold-caller at dinner time.

— Julie

— Today's Act of Kindness —

Does the way you treat cold-callers reflect Christ's
love? Decide now to respond with love and kindness
the next time you receive one of these calls.

The Benefit of the Doubt

Since God chose you to be the holy people he loves,
you must clothe yourselves with tenderhearted mercy,
kindness, humility, gentleness, and patience.

COLOSSIANS 3:12

There was a boy from elementary school whom I've never forgotten. His tantrums were legendary. One day, after he crushed a milk carton in the school cafeteria with his bare hands in a fit of rage, I went home and told my parents about it, in disbelief that someone would do something like that.

Solemnly, my dad said something to me that he would repeat often over the years: "You never know what their home life is like." His larger meaning was this: don't judge, because you never know the trauma or chaos a person may be experiencing in another area of their life.

Over the years, I saw my parents live out the words my dad expressed to me that day. Our home was always open to guests who lived on the fringes or appeared a little rough around the edges. My parents invited strangers to spend time with us, even on holidays, and kindly overlooked it when our guests lacked the ease of social graces. I watched my dad befriend a wheelchair-bound man who had serious medical issues and lived alone in a nursing home. I saw my mom buy work outfits for a young mother who struggled to raise her son alone. I watched them exemplify the gracious art of overlooking, of seeing a person's heart rather than the roughened surface they presented to the world.

Sometimes kindness requires us to look beyond the circumstances to recognize why someone may be acting in a certain way. Maybe they grew up in a home that was rife with abuse or neglect. They may be struggling with substance abuse. Perhaps there are things in their life that make them feel unworthy or unloved. We are called to extend mercy, kindness, humility, gentleness, and patience to others. Those characteristics are sometimes best demonstrated by simply offering someone the benefit of the doubt. Our attitude of mercy and perspective of grace can be a great kindness and a true act of love.

— Kristin

— Today's Act of Kindness —

When you are tempted to judge someone for their
actions, give them the benefit of the doubt by
considering what else may be going on in their life.

You Are So Normal

For we do not have a high priest [Jesus] who is unable
to empathize with our weaknesses.
HEBREWS 4:15, NIV

When I first became a mother I was overjoyed, but I was also a little (okay, a lot) overwhelmed. This may come as a shock, but motherhood was not everything I expected it to be. Don't get me wrong, I love my kids and am grateful for them, but parenting is really hard. I often wondered if I was doing it right, constantly questioning whether I could trust my judgment. Always wanting to do right by your kids can be stressful.

It was during this time that I found a group of moms in my area who surrounded me with love and support. As we met each week, I was relieved to learn that what I was feeling and experiencing as a mom was totally normal. That *I* was normal. They didn't give me all the answers to my problems, and I still went home and struggled with raising my kids, but it helped me to know that I wasn't alone. Other people had experienced and were experiencing the same things that I was. And somehow that was comforting.

Everyone goes through times in their lives when they wonder if they are the only one. One of the greatest acts of kindness we can extend toward others is letting them know they are not alone, that what they're experiencing is normal. Whether it's a life change like getting married or starting a family, moving to another part of the country, starting a new career, or dealing with a new health diagnosis, we all can feel a bit out of sorts at times, and being around others who've walked through a similar experience can be comforting.

Just as Jesus is able to empathize with our weaknesses and everything we experience in life, we can extend that same kindness toward others by letting them know that they are not alone.

— Kendra

— Today's Act of Kindness —

Encourage someone who is walking through an experience
similar to what you are facing now or have faced in
the past. Let them know they're not alone and that
what they're going through is completely normal.

The Gift of Guidance

Walk with the wise and become wise; associate with fools and get in trouble.
PROVERBS 13:20

With a big job change looming, I found myself sitting across the café table from a wise woman a decade or two my senior who has mentored me in my profession over the years. As we chatted, our conversation turned to change.

She spoke of significant career shifts she had experienced in her life—mourning the loss she experienced each time she started over in a new job, a new place, a new town while also embracing the opportunity to learn something new, to try something completely different. She told me that never in her wildest dreams did she think she would someday use all that knowledge, all that experience, all that history. Yet in her current position, she does exactly that. It is as if her new position was carved out especially for her, based exactly on her previous experiences. The experience she gained at past jobs she loved became an invaluable resource for where she finds herself now.

Her words were like a salve as I navigated my own job change. I recognized the biblical truth in the wisdom she shared, and it was encouraging to hear these words from someone who had walked my path not once but several times during her professional career.

While I love my friendships with women my own age, I especially treasure my friendships with women who are older than I am. Their perspective and wisdom gained through experience is invaluable, and I am grateful when they take time out of their busy lives to provide insight and guidance to me.

And that means that I, in turn, intentionally but informally mentor a smart and accomplished woman who is ten years my junior. Periodically she'll slip quietly into my office with a life question. Buying a house, navigating a tricky personal relationship, supporting her new husband's career (and vice versa)—we've discussed all of it and more. While I don't always have a perfect answer, I honestly and freely share what I've learned and help guide her decisions.

— Julie

— Today's Act of Kindness —

Find someone to mentor. It doesn't need to be a
formal thing; it could be a younger coworker, a mom,
or a friend from church. Just make it a point to be
available and encouraging to this person.

A New Washer

You must each decide in your heart how much to give. And don't give reluctantly or in response to pressure. "For God loves a person who gives cheerfully."

2 CORINTHIANS 9:7

I saw the request posted in one of the social media groups I'm in, sandwiched between prayer requests and questions about babysitters. "I have a friend who has been out of a job for over a year, and now her washer is broken," it read. "Anybody know of someone who would be willing to donate one to her? Prayers appreciated too."

Calling up Tim, I quietly asked him what the likelihood was that we could help. We have a "blessing budget" that we use throughout the year when situations like this arise, and I was hoping we could use some of it to purchase a new washing machine for this woman.

He agreed, and I reached out to our mutual acquaintance. She messaged me back, "Just so you know, this isn't a friend from church. I didn't want to mislead you." Reading her response, I chuckled a little and told her that it didn't matter to us that this woman didn't attend our church. My friend was thrilled. The woman in need, an older lady, had been out of work for a while and couldn't take another blow to her finances. A new washer, especially from a stranger, was a godsend.

I got the woman's address from my friend, and Tim and I called up the local appliance store and had them arrange delivery for her. We found out later that even the store employees enjoyed being in on this act of kindness and delivering good news to someone who needed it, which reminded me how fulfilling it is when we give not reluctantly but cheerfully.

So often in doing acts of kindness, especially anonymous ones, the impact our actions have is impossible to measure. Yet even this small glimpse of someone else's gratitude was a reminder of what a great privilege we have in showing God's love to others regardless of their background or circumstances.

— Kristin

— Today's Act of Kindness —

Make some time to review your finances and see if you can create some space for a blessing budget—it doesn't have to be a large amount. Then be on the lookout for who God might want you to bless with these funds.

Simple Obedience

Today when you hear his voice, don't harden your hearts.
HEBREWS 3:7-8

Making gift bags for the homeless is one of my children's favorite ways to help in our community. We usually have bags in our car, but during an unusually busy summer I found my car completely empty.

"No big deal," I thought, "I'll get some more supplies later."

A few days went by, and I found myself behind schedule, rushing around town to get to an appointment on time. I was already late when I drove by an intersection where a homeless man I did not recognize was standing on the corner. "Will work for food," his sign read. Arguing to myself about how I did not have time to stop and how we were out of our gift bags anyway, I quickly turned my head away so as not to make eye contact.

I hurriedly pulled out as the light turned green and then felt a small pang of conviction hit my heart. No, I did not have a gift bag, but there was a gift card in my purse I'd just received from a friend and a fresh, unopened bottle of water I'd taken with me when I'd rushed out the door. I quickly turned the next corner, deciding to go back and hand my meager gift to the very appreciative man on the corner.

Later on that night I told my kids what had happened, explaining to them that the small conviction I felt was from God and how important it is to be sensitive to respond when we feel like God is asking us to do something. My kids nodded their understanding as we prayed again for those experiencing homelessness in our community and asked God to help us be willing to obey what he asks of us.

Have you ever felt conviction over something you did or did not do? Listening to God's voice and being sensitive to what he is asking of us is an important part of our relationship with him. We should be careful to notice when we feel moved to do or say something—whether we're at home, at work, or even just driving down the street.

— Kendra

— Today's Act of Kindness —

Be sensitive to God's conviction. Listen for what he's
asking you to do, and then obey what he says.

The Gift of Distraction

As we have opportunity, let us do good to everyone, and especially to those who are of the household of faith.

GALATIANS 6:10, ESV

The thing about losing a loved one is that long after the frozen casseroles have been eaten and everyone has returned to their busy lives, the loss is still there, the pain waiting to ebb and flow.

Grief is a crazy, unpredictable thing that still rears its ugly head and moves me to random tears more than a decade after one of my best friends, Katrina, died of cancer at the tender age of twenty-eight. Although she was a mere six months older than me, she was more poised, more polished, and more put together then than I am now, a full decade later. I love her and miss her with unbearable poignancy at the most unpredictable times.

Even having lived through it, I struggle with speaking words of empathy to others who have lost a loved one—no words seem quite suitable. I've often wished I could contribute something better than another frozen casserole or memento to put on a shelf. This year, I found a better option—at least for one person.

A few months ago my cousin lost her husband suddenly and without warning to a massive heart attack. As her children and grandchildren gathered around, I couldn't help but think of the lonely nights she would face six months after the funeral—after friends and family had returned to their normal lives.

I prayerfully considered how my family could tangibly show our love in an enduring rather than fleeting way, one that could serve to distract on a lonely evening. I longed to remind her of Christ's immense love, even in the midst of deep sorrow. We are called to do good by encouraging and building up our fellow Christians, just as much as we are called to love strangers.

Inspiration struck midday; my cousin loves to quilt, and what better way to distract than to inspire her with new creativity for her hobby? I researched quilting magazines, secretly conferred with her mom, and then signed her up for a subscription. Then I wrote her a note and sent her my favorite devotional for when life feels impossibly hard. The gift may not be able to heal the pain, but I do trust that God will use it to keep her company on the hard nights.

— *Julie*

— Today's Act of Kindness —

Think of someone you know who is going through a hard time. Provide them with the gift of distraction through movie tickets, a spa gift card, or a magazine subscription.

July

Lost in Paris

Don't look out only for your own interests, but take an interest in others, too.
PHILIPPIANS 2:4

We were hopelessly lost. As two twentysomething Americans wearing jeans and battered tennis shoes, with backpacks slung over our shoulders as we walked the streets of Paris, we were clearly out of our element. Although we had successfully navigated the overnight train from Vienna to Paris and then the metro to our current location, the quiet, nontouristy streets were proving to be a challenge. Peering at the street signs, I could have sworn we were walking in circles as I checked our map yet again.

Then, from a street corner, an older woman beckoned to us. She had a bluish tint to her hair and clutched a battered suitcase in her wrinkled hands, but her dark eyes were sharp and alight with intelligence. She asked us something, but my single year of French was no match for her rapid-fire words, and I simply shrugged and looked helplessly at my equally confused companion. Pulling out the hotel address, I handed it to the woman, a wordless plea for help.

Nodding, she motioned sharply for us to follow, then proceeded to walk us to our hotel three blocks away. With a gracious smile and another little wave, she took her leave and continued on her way.

As we entered the lobby of our hotel, I marveled at this woman's kindness. The walk was clearly a challenge for her and required us to go slowly. Even more than that, we were strangers—Americans, in a time when our people were characterized as rude and aggressive tourists—and yet she overlooked stereotypes to help us. We, in turn, had been cautioned by fellow travelers that Parisians disliked Americans and merely tolerated their presence. Yet we experienced none of the disdain we had been led to expect. Instead, a stranger took the time to help us with no expectation of anything in return.

As Christians, we're asked to look beyond our own interests to help others, but all too often it can be easy to look the other way when a stranger needs help. Have you judged someone based on certain stereotypes? If so, how can you look beyond your preconceived notions to show them kindness?

— *Kristin*

— Today's Act of Kindness —

Go out of your way to be kind to someone
you may have judged in the past.

Use What You Know

God has given each of you a gift from his great variety of
spiritual gifts. Use them well to serve one another.

1 PETER 4:10

My kids have a hard time with reading. One year, as summer approached, I wondered how I could get my kids to read more. More than just that, I wanted to find books they really liked to read that would hold their interest. Unsure of what to suggest to them, I reached out to my husband's cousin Holly, who is an avid reader and a middle-school librarian. I asked for her help in finding books my kids would enjoy.

She quickly messaged me back with many book suggestions for each of my children, but then she offered something more than just her knowledge: she offered to bring books to my kids after she visited her school's library the next Tuesday. To say I was overjoyed was an understatement. I was *elated*. She came by the following Tuesday and spent time with my kids, telling them about the books she picked and why she thought they'd like these particular ones. My kids were sold, and later that afternoon I sent her a picture of them reading in the living room, along with a huge thank-you message.

She has since offered to come by each Tuesday to pick up the books my kids have finished and to bring them more. When I try to tell her how much I appreciate her kindness, she shrugs and says that getting kids to read is something she loves to do. That may be so, but it is still a huge kindness to this mom, and it's one of my favorite memories from that summer.

We don't always have to step outside of who we are or outside of our comfort zones to show kindness to others. Sometimes kindness starts with something we already know a lot about or that is very familiar to us. As Holly demonstrated, our passions or areas of expertise can be just the kindness someone else is in desperate need of. Scripture reminds us that God has given each of us gifts and we should use them to serve one another. What expertise do you have that you could share with another?

— *Kendra*

— Today's Act of Kindness —

Use something you are already passionate about
to show kindness toward someone else.

Listening Well

*Let everyone see that you are considerate in all you
do. Remember, the Lord is coming soon.*

PHILIPPIANS 4:5

It was the second day of a professional conference, and as I sat in the session after lunch, I noticed that many of my fellow attendees looked as ready for a nap as I felt. As I approached the speaker at the end of the session, his words surprised me. "Are you always such a good listener?" he asked. I paused, reflecting on my behavior during his session, wondering what I had done that drew his attention in a large room filled with other listeners.

While I'm not perfect, I strive to be an active listener. This means that I intentionally use nonverbal behavior (leaning in, head nodding in agreement, facial expressions) to reveal that I am not only hearing what is being said but also actively processing and reacting to the information. It was my nonverbal communication during the session that this particular speaker picked up on—and he appreciated what I was communicating in a room filled with tired, sleepy, distracted people.

As an attorney, mom, wife, and friend, I've learned that listening well is sometimes the best gift we can give to another. When the person talking feels heard and understood—even when we can't solve the problem—it releases anxiety, allows the speaker to think out loud, and often reveals a way forward that hasn't been previously considered.

While my daily goal is always to reveal the love of Christ in my actions as I go about my tasks, I sometimes forget that simply being considerate, especially when others are not, quietly reveals Christ in me—and that can be a powerful message, even in the midst of a crowd. As we await Christ's return we are his messengers both in word and in deed.

After wrapping up my conversation with the session speaker with an exchange of business cards, I said a silent prayer of thanks for the reminder of the importance of listening well in every situation—even when we are tempted to think that it doesn't really matter, especially when we are just one face in a crowded room.

— Julie

— Today's Act of Kindness —

Be an active listener in everything you do and
everywhere you go—whether you're in a meeting,
with your kids, or among friends.

Friendships Made through Heartache

Share each other's burdens, and in this way obey the law of Christ.

GALATIANS 6:2

I first got to know my friend Christa when she and her family decided to come on a hike with my family in honor of my sister Katrina, who had died of cancer. The hike was an annual event, put on to raise money for women and children who needed financial support and as a way to continue to remember and honor my sister.

I remember telling Christa about the hike that was coming up, what it meant to me, and where the money was being donated that year. She seemed interested and showed genuine empathy over the loss of my sister. A few days later I got a text saying that she and her family would like to join our team and hike with us. She had not known my sister and did not know me very well yet, so I was especially touched by her kindness.

As we continued over the next few months to talk about the hike, train for it together, and discuss all the practicalities of where we'd be staying and the activities surrounding the hike, I realized what a dear woman Christa was. She was a treasure, and as we hiked together on a perfect July day, a bond and friendship was created that has continued to this day.

Everyone needs to know what it is like to have others come alongside of them in their pain. Being willing to be present with another, listening, and offering empathy are just a few of the ways that we can share each other's burdens and thereby obey the law of Christ. Creating relationships and building friendships with others is one of the greatest joys in life, but to do this we must be willing to show kindness by engaging others and caring about what matters to them. Who do you know that could use a friend to come alongside them?

— Kendra

— Today's Act of Kindness —

Join in with someone else on an activity or outing that is important to them.

Home as a Resource

Cheerfully share your home with those who need a meal or a place to stay.
1 PETER 4:9

The group from a local nonprofit, along with a videographer, arrived a little after 9:00 a.m. By midmorning, my house had been turned upside down for a video shoot. My dining-room table, now covered in plastic and paper, was placed in my living room, while my couch was disassembled and trundled into two separate rooms. Coffee and conversation abounded, and the house was full of people and lights and craft projects. As someone turned to thank me for letting them use the space, I shrugged and said that I really didn't mind.

It was true, and yet it was for radically different reasons than they perhaps imagined. You see, I had experienced a major readjustment in my heart and attitude after hearing my friends' story about their own home. A few years ago, my friends decided that they would be fine with a smaller home and considered downsizing. However, after thinking about it further, they decided to remain where they were, but with a mind-set shift. No longer would they consider their home to be a possession; instead, they would think of it as a resource like any other. Instead of trying to protect it, they would use it to pursue community and offer it as a space to host meetings, meet new friends, and encourage and minister to others.

Hearing their story, my husband and I (especially me, with my sometimes hermit-like ways) felt convicted. How often had we opened our home to others in the past few months? And when we did, how often was it done begrudgingly rather than cheerfully, as Scripture calls us to show hospitality?

With their story fresh in my mind, the next time my husband asked if we could invite a new couple over to our home, I said yes. When opportunities arose to host gatherings, I began to say yes as often as I could. And when I was asked to host this video shoot, I said yes—cheerfully.

— *Kristin*

— Today's Act of Kindness —

Do you consider your home or living space a resource
or a possession? Use your personal space to encourage
or help someone else by inviting them in.

Local Heroes

*Show proper respect to everyone, love the family of
believers, fear God, honor the emperor.*
1 PETER 2:17, NIV

One of my husband's favorite acts of kindness we've done with our church community was when we put on a barbecue at our local fire department for Father's Day. We wanted it to serve as a thank-you for all the hard work the firefighters do to serve our community, especially on holidays when others don't have to work. We invited our local police officers to stop by as well.

It was a beautiful day for a barbecue, with the sun shining and a warm breeze blowing. As we talked with the firefighters, served them food, and thanked them for their service, they showed us their trucks, let the kids play with the hoses, and talked about what it's like to be a firefighter. My kids met local heroes that they continued to talk about all the way home, and I left feeling completely grateful for the men and women in my community who step up to help others, often putting themselves in danger to do so. I could not believe how kind they were to us. It gave me an even greater respect for all that they do every day.

Have you ever thanked a public servant in your community? We all have people around us who are serving selflessly. Things often run so smoothly that it can be easy to forget they are even there behind the scenes, helping to make our communities safe. The Bible tells us to show proper respect to everyone, and taking the time to thank your city's public servants is one way to do just that.

If you are blessed to live in a city or area with public services that improve your life, thank God for them—and look for ways to extend kindness and respect to these hardworking men and women.

— Kendra

— Today's Act of Kindness —

Write a thank-you note, bring a treat, or find some other
way to thank a public servant in your community.

A Sweet Invitation

I was hungry, and you fed me. I was thirsty, and you gave me a drink. I was a stranger, and you invited me into your home.

MATTHEW 25:35

Growing up, I was very quiet and reserved. I didn't make friends easily, and I often found myself happiest when I could observe from the sidelines before joining in on a group activity. While I've learned to act extroverted and be outgoing in business situations, the default in my personal life is still to feel slightly uncomfortable when meeting new people for the first time.

My husband, on the other hand, is a true extrovert. There is no difference between Aaron's work persona and his private persona, especially when it comes to meeting new people. I've heard childhood tales of his fearless befriending that make me, and everyone else in the room, chuckle when we realize that the warm, mischievous sparkle in his eyes has always been there and that he was clearly an outgoing, precocious little boy.

As houses have sold and new people have moved into our neighborhood these past few years, Aaron has taken on the role of the Fisk family greeter, despite the gender stereotypes that put that duty into my column. Shortly after someone new moves in, you'll find him in the kitchen whipping up a box of brownies (adding several extra cups of chocolate and peanut-butter chips, just for good measure) and then wandering across the street with the still-warm brownies in hand to meet the new neighbors. He'll be gone for fifteen minutes or so before ambling home with names, backgrounds, and all the details of whomever has just moved in.

My husband's gift of brownies and introduction continually sets the stage for us to extend further invitations into our home and into our lives. With the ice broken and a few details already exchanged, I find it easy to then pick up where he left off.

Regardless of whether we struggle or find it easy to take that first step, we are specifically called to show hospitality to strangers by sharing food and inviting them into our homes and our lives. That first step of turning a stranger into an acquaintance—who may someday become a friend—is often the hardest, and yet that is what Scripture encourages us to do.

— *Julie*

— Today's Act of Kindness —

Set up your own ritual for welcoming new neighbors into your neighborhood.

Is That Why You Do This?

Love your neighbor as yourself.

LUKE 10:27

He sat down next to me with a heavy sigh, bushy eyebrows peeking out from underneath the food-safety hairnet, the lower part of his face and the beard underneath it covered as well. The chatty, friendly woman across the table asked his name, and he told her it was Randy, then retreated into silence, concentrating on his task.

We, along with dozens of other volunteers, were in the midst of packaging meals for area residents. As I grabbed a large package of tomato basil pasta, measured out a meal's worth of pasta, put it in a bag, and then passed it along to Randy to be sealed, he broke his silence.

"I wish we'd had meals this good when I was in Vietnam," he said abruptly. Slowly, his story emerged: he had originally volunteered with this organization because he wanted to help other veterans like himself. He'd been in the army—special forces, to be exact. "So many veterans are homeless," he said. "I can't believe that twenty-two of them commit suicide every day." Though his demeanor was gruff, the passion in his voice was clear.

"Is that why you do this—why you're here?" the lady across the table asked.

"Yes," he said quietly. On the surface, it was a simple answer. He was taking time out of his day to show love to his neighbors because he himself had experienced hardship. Yet a little later on, the depth of his passion, generosity, and desire to help those in need was revealed when a woman and three children surrounded the table. As one, their high voices piped out the "Happy Birthday" song to Randy, their grandpa. When they finished, they took up some of the empty spaces around the table to serve alongside him. Randy was there, serving all day—from 9:00 a.m. until 9:00 p.m.—on his birthday, because the plight of others just like him moved him to do so.

Sometimes loving our neighbors means serving the people who literally live next door, and sometimes it means serving those who live in our neighborhood without homes of their own. When we become aware of the hardships of those around us, our compassion can spur us to meet our neighbors' basic needs with something as simple as a meal offered from a servant's heart.

— *Kristin*

— Today's Act of Kindness —

Make or purchase a meal for a neighbor who needs one.

Knowing Your Limitations

Come to me, all you who are weary and burdened, and I will give you rest.
MATTHEW 11:28, NIV

I was tired, and my husband and family knew it. After months of serving in a variety of settings and groups, I was feeling a bit overwhelmed and ready for a break. After praying about it one morning, I decided it was time to excuse myself from a few of the groups and activities I was a part of—not because they weren't good things to be doing, but simply because I needed to rest.

As I sent e-mails and made calls letting others know what I was doing, it was hard but also a bit freeing to know my limitations and to let others in on my need for a rest. The people I contacted responded with such grace, completely understanding my need to take a step back. As the next several months went on, I continued to say no to things that were good but perhaps were not the best things for me to be a part of for a while.

We all experience seasons of heavy activity in our lives and times when we need to step back and rest. Our culture pushes us to constantly be busy and do more, but that is not what God calls us to be and do. Jesus said, "Come to me, all you who are weary and burdened, and I will give you rest," which is quite different from what the world tells us. We're told that our identity is found in our ability to perform, but Jesus reminds us that our worth is found in him and that he alone provides true rest.

Extending kind acts toward others is not meant to be a burden or one more thing we have to do to please God, and that includes the kindness we show ourselves. Sometimes the best kindness we can show is toward ourselves, making time to take care of our own needs and finding our rest in Christ. If you have been feeling overwhelmed or pressured to be more or do more lately, know that is not from God. He is already pleased with you just as you are.

— *Kendra*

— Today's Act of Kindness —

Show kindness to yourself by saying no to something you don't feel like you should do and taking the time to rest in Christ instead.

Mentoring Friendships

Walk with the wise and become wise; associate with fools and get in trouble.
PROVERBS 13:20

While I love my friends who are close to my age and in roughly the same parenting stage that I am, I've discovered that we all tend to be flailing through life together. While these friends and I can (and do) give one another advice, I've grown to especially treasure the advice I receive from Rachael, a woman who is ten years my junior, and from Carol, who is roughly the same age as my mom.

Rachael is like the younger sister I never had and never knew I needed. I teasingly call her my fashion consultant, and she laughingly calls me her life coach. And it's true. She is my litmus test for what is going on in the heads and hearts of women in their twenties, and she also helps me to avoid mom jeans and sweetly offers her opinions when I anxiously text her pictures of outfits from the fitting room. Recently, she has started acting as my personal trainer as I've taken up running races, including a 10K in the not-too-distant future. She pushes me to try harder and do more than what I would do on my own. I, on the other hand, am just far enough ahead on the marriage and career paths to help her navigate pitfalls I've seen others (or myself) inadvertently stumble into.

On the other end of my friendship spectrum is Carol. She is a grandmother many times over and is the best leader I've ever had the privilege to follow. She is wise and steady and has walked with Jesus for so long that there is a sense of peace in her presence, regardless of the chaos that might be swirling in a situation. Her advice is always filled with the perspective of life experience that I just don't have and with an objectivity that my mother and mother-in-law can't always provide.

The beauty of a friendship that spans time and life stages is that the perspective of each person broadens the horizons of the other. When we seek out wise people, we are made wise, but when we hang out with fools, we can become foolish. My life is made richer and broader by these two women and the unique perspectives they so generously share with me, and their investments make me a better mother, wife, and follower of Christ.

— *Julie*

— Today's Act of Kindness —

Find someone at least ten years younger or older
than you, and start a mentoring friendship.

When Giving Is Hard

Don't forget to do good and to share with those in need.
These are the sacrifices that please God.
HEBREWS 13:16

"I don't want to give my toy up, Mom."

My daughter said this as she was faced with the reality of leaving a toy that she had picked out for another child to receive. I stooped down next to her and looked into her sad eyes. We'd discussed how we were picking out toys for kids who wouldn't otherwise be getting anything for their birthdays, and she'd been excited all the way to the store and while walking through the aisles. She'd made a careful decision about what toy she'd like to donate. All had gone well until we were at the drop-off site waiting to place her toy in the bin and walk away.

Sometimes giving is easy; sometimes it's not. Sometimes I can know the reason to give is good and still have a hard time choosing to be generous. Sometimes I'm happy about giving, right up until it's time to do it. Then I hesitate.

I told my daughter I understood her hesitation and reminded her why we were doing this. I told her we were extending kindness to others. I reminded her how happy the child would be who received her gift. I told her it's hardest when the gift is leaving our hands, but she'd feel good once we were done. With a determined nod of agreement, she walked over to the birthday bin and left her toy with the others. She turned and grinned as we walked out the door, wondering out loud who the child would be that received her gift.

It may not always be easy to give things away, but when we remember the blessing it is to do good and share with those in need, it can help us let go of what we want to keep for ourselves. These actions are pleasing to God. It's not always easy to be generous, but as my daughter and I are learning, it sure feels good when you do it.

— *Kendra*

— *Today's Act of Kindness* —

Find one thing in your house you could give to someone else.

Instagram Friends

Be encouraged and knit together by strong ties of love.
COLOSSIANS 2:2

In an effort to keep myself awake during my newborn daughter's nighttime feedings, I began idly scrolling through Instagram. As I did, I stumbled across small online-only shops selling resale women's or children's clothing. After purchasing from several of these shops, I had the idea that it would be fun to try online selling for myself. After doing some research, I launched my own small shop, selling items purged from my own closet or thrifted from area stores.

Although millions of people have Instagram accounts, the number of folks who have shops similar to mine is a smaller community. In an effort to increase exposure and sales, a group of sellers began to share each other's shops on our own pages. One day, the owner of one of the shops I admired invited me to join a group of sellers on a messenger app that would allow us to communicate more easily. Hoping to build my business and network, I readily agreed.

It wasn't long before my husband began teasing me about my newfound friends whom I'd never actually met. Ashley had been in the air force, and Emily's husband was currently in the military. Rose was married to a pastor, and Shelly, from Memphis, was my style twin. Karen lived in Oregon, while Jessica, Lauren, and Rachel all lived in California. We chatted daily, sharing more and more of our lives, including family photos and struggles with parenting and work, until I felt like they were truly friends. When Jen's mother passed away, we grieved her loss and sent flowers to the funeral. When Miclyn, Alicia, and Darby became pregnant, we rejoiced with them. When Rose had her baby, we sent small gifts to celebrate the new arrival.

The daily interaction I had with this group of women—despite our different ages, backgrounds, and life circumstances—became a source of support when the days were hard. In our age, it's more and more common to have online friendships. While perhaps not a replacement for in-real-life friendships, these relationships can bring very real connection and encouragement.

— Kristin

— Today's Act of Kindness —

Encourage an online friend by sending a thoughtful message.

Stingy Generosity

Give, and you will receive. Your gift will return to you in full—pressed down,
shaken together to make room for more, running over, and poured into
your lap. The amount you give will determine the amount you get back.

LUKE 6:38

At the beginning of each school year, I purchase school supplies for my children, and I buy extra sets of the same items to donate to our school. One year as I walked the aisles, my eye was drawn to the folders I knew my kids would love—puppies, Lisa Frank, fast cars, Ninja Turtles. While I splurged and bought the fun folders for my children, my generally frugal nature had me reaching for the fifty-cent solid-colored folders for the donated items.

Pausing, I remembered an article discussing the psychological difference it makes when kids receive donations of school supplies that consist of the "good stuff" instead of the very cheapest stuff. I realized that I was about to do the same thing that so frustrates me about stingy generosity—I was giving my children the good stuff and giving someone else's child the cheap stuff. Over the years, I've winced time and again when Christians have responded to a call for donations with inferior-quality items. While I'm not suggesting that donations need to come from the most expensive stores, I do think there's something to be said for providing what we ourselves would like to have.

I silently asked God for forgiveness. Instead of going over my budget, I made my kids part of the conversation. They got to choose a mix of the regular, solid-colored folders and the fun, fancy folders for themselves, and we set aside the same mix of regular and fun folders to donate. My children are learning the joy of giving the good stuff to others, not the leftovers, the rejects, the stuff that is not good enough for them.

We are called to be generous, cheerful givers, and we are told that the amount we give will determine what we receive. God has not been stingy with the blessings he has poured onto my family, and I cannot, if I am giving in accordance with Scripture, practice stingy generosity.

— *Julie*

— Today's Act of Kindness —

Consider whether you typically practice stingy generosity. The next time you're faced with the opportunity to give, do so generously.

Unlikely Friends

God created human beings in his own image. In the image of God he created them.
GENESIS 1:27

I recently read about a movement called the Human Library. This movement allows people to "check out" other people and to sit and talk with them for a few hours. The purpose is to gain knowledge of someone who is different from us and to achieve a better understanding of one another in order to see our commonalities as human beings, not just our differences.

It reminded me that I've met good friends in some of the most unlikely places, like at my first job after grad school. It was there that I met Trina, who on the surface was my exact opposite: Southern, raised by her grandma, and of a different race—no one would have thought that we would get along as well as we did. We may have been a little surprised ourselves, but as we got to know each other we realized we had more in common than not: both of us were raised in strict, loving homes where a strong faith and work ethic was instilled in us. We began running our therapy groups together and found that we were the perfect fit as cofacilitators, able to play off of one another and engage our clients in ways we'd never have done on our own. She became a great friend and one of my strongest supporters at work.

Sometimes appearances can be deceiving. In a world that increasingly wants to label and separate us from other people, we can be the ones to find the commonalities and build bridges to those who, at least on the surface, look different from us. Remembering that God created all human beings in his own image can help us extend kindness to everyone that we come in contact with, because everyone is equally valuable in the eyes of God.

— *Kendra*

— Today's Act of Kindness —

Think of someone who is different from you. Identify
a few commonalities, and then reach out with a
word of encouragement for that person.

Being Grateful in All Things

Give thanks for everything to God the Father in the name of our Lord Jesus Christ.
EPHESIANS 5:20

First my daughter had a meltdown because no one was sitting next to her in the backseat of the car. Then she had another meltdown when I wouldn't immediately show her a video of hot lava. "You're mean, and I don't like you!" she said. She smacked my leg with her hand while we walked into church, and as a result, lost out on her daily treat. It was only 9:30 a.m., and it was already a hard day.

Our responses to these events were different. She cried loudly all the way into church while friends gave us worried looks or uncertain smiles. I smiled widely and pretended it was fine: *Nothing to see here, folks; this is normal!* But I knew that, deep inside, we were both feeling a little fragile. As I listened to the sermon echo over the loudspeakers, I thought of a Brené Brown quote: "There is no joy without gratitude."

Often our ability to externally show kindness toward others is predicated on an internal grateful heart that is moved to compassion. Sometimes, before we can show kindness to others, we need to gauge the true state of our hearts and work on cultivating gratitude. Scripture says that we should give thanks always for all things. Yet how can I be thankful when my child jumps on my very last nerve?

I love how *The Message* paraphrases that same verse: "Sing praises over everything, any excuse for a song to God the Father." I try to take that to heart. When I'm feeling frustrated and just want to shout, I try to sing instead. Most often the songs that tumble from my lips are snatches of old hymns, like "Blest Be the Tie that Binds" or "In the Garden," my Grandma Jo's favorite. Whenever I sing like this, I notice my children's reaction: a lot of times they'll become wide eyed, staring at me as I hum or sing.

Our gratitude for everything in our lives—good things, messy things, even hard things—is an outward expression of the internal change in us and a reflection of God's love for us.

— Kristin

— Today's Act of Kindness —

Who or what are you grateful for? Verbally
express your gratitude to others.

Strings-Free Kindness

If you help the poor, you are lending to the LORD—and he will repay you!
PROVERBS 19:17

My friend Jen had always prided herself on being the person who gives to others, so she struggled when she suddenly found herself in a place of needing to receive. Her life circumstances had shifted, and she was finding it difficult to pay her bills. A friend encouraged Jen to contact a local church where this friend's father was on the committee overseeing a giving fund and to ask for help.

Setting aside her pride, Jen contacted the church. The committee told her they would help, but only if she started attending their church—despite the fact that she had a church home elsewhere and was clearly a believer.

As Jen relayed the story to me, I winced.

While we should be good stewards of resources, I've become extremely wary of the strings people attach to kindness, and I often wonder whether the manipulation does greater harm to the Kingdom of God than the intended kindness does good to the recipient.

My small church has a giving fund that is disproportionately large for the size of our congregation—landing somewhere between 40 and 50 percent of our weekly tithes and offerings. This fund is strictly no strings attached. We serve (both financially and with physical labor on projects) the local community: people from our church, people from other churches, people from no church. We ask for nothing in return and simply point to the love Christ showed when he walked this earth as our example.

Have we been taken advantage of? I'm sure we have. But the vast majority of gifts we give are received with overflowing gratitude, and we find ourselves having the most amazing conversations with astonished recipients when we give with no strings attached, conversations that we pray change lives in eternal ways.

Although others have warned us that such a radical approach will result in a bankrupt giving account, our fund grows faster than we can give it away. God multiplies what we freely give, and it has surprised us all. When we help others financially, we are "lending to the Lord." He has certainly repaid our small church both financially and in other blessings.

— Julie

— Today's Act of Kindness —

Have you attached strings to your kindness in the past? Find
someone you can bless without expectation of repayment.

A Lunch Lesson in Kindness

Love is patient.

1 CORINTHIANS 13:4

I recently stopped in at a local sandwich shop for lunch. It was obvious almost immediately that someone must not have showed up for their work shift, as one young man was behind the counter taking orders and making sandwiches as quickly as possible all by himself. Everyone going through the line seemed a bit impatient and curt, even though he met each person with an apology and a smile. Most simply ignored him, looking at their phones or out the window as he tried his best to quickly fulfill their orders.

When he got to me, I gave him my order while smiling and taking the time to look him in the eye, and then as I was paying, I said, "You're doing a really great job." He stopped for just a moment, looked me in the eye, and said, "Thanks," before moving on to the next person. It wasn't much of a conversation, but it was just enough to show him that he was noticed, that I saw how hard he was working and believed he was doing his best.

It can take just a minute to notice and tell someone they are doing a good job. Oftentimes people who work in service positions are overlooked, or even ignored, as they provide assistance to others. The Bible says that one of the attributes of love is that it is patient, and patience has become a challenging trait to acquire in our fast-paced, goal-oriented world. But it is still something that God sees as valuable.

The next time you are tempted to be impatient with someone, choose instead to notice the *person* and how they may be trying to quickly and accurately accomplish a task. (Even if they do not seem to be hurrying, we can still practice patience!) And through our patient responses to others, we can extend kindness to them that they may not receive very often.

— *Kendra*

— Today's Act of Kindness —

Take the time to notice, show patience toward,
and thank someone who is serving you.

A Simple Handshake

You, too, must show love to foreigners, for you yourselves
were once foreigners in the land of Egypt.
DEUTERONOMY 10:19

My brother-in-law Phil and sister-in-law Marlene were in Prague visiting their friend's parents, who split their time between living in California and the Czech Republic. It was during this trip that they heard the story of how this couple ended up in the United States several decades ago.

They escaped the Czech Republic (then known as Czechoslovakia) in 1968 with a mere one hundred dollars in their pockets, just as the Communists were taking over the area in which they lived. Although they both had college educations, they wondered how they would make ends meet once they arrived in the US. They landed in New York and, through the kindness of strangers, were sponsored by a private family and loaned enough money to rent an apartment and pay for their daily living expenses. This deal was struck with just a handshake.

The couple paid back the money within six months, and the husband went on to become an executive for Bank of America. Although the couple met the sponsoring family initially, they didn't keep in touch over the years. To this day, the husband still can't believe the sponsors trusted him with just a simple handshake. Relating the story to Phil and Marlene, he told them that he wishes the sponsors could have known how much their actions meant to his family and the long-term effects their act of kindness had on an immigrant couple's lives.

We (or our ancestors) were once immigrants in America, and our spiritual ancestors were once foreigners in a strange land too, struggling to find their way and forge a new life. Scripture calls us to love foreigners out of this deep sense of empathy. How can you show love and compassion for those who are new to your community? You never know what kind of long-term impact your simple act of kindness may have.

— *Kristin*

— Today's Act of Kindness —

Do something for someone who is a "foreigner" in your community, even if it's just offering them a kind word or a smile.

Neglecting God

[Jesus said,] "Take my yoke upon you. Let me teach you, because I
am humble and gentle at heart, and you will find rest for your souls.
For my yoke is easy to bear, and the burden I give you is light."
MATTHEW 11:29-30

God and I both know that this past month has seen a slip in quiet moments spent with my Savior. I've let the mundane ordinariness of life dim the sacred connection with my first love.

When I pull away from God, I find myself unable to be the woman I long to be in Christ. A spiral of guilt, striving, and failed expectations sucks me into a place I hate, one where God seems so far away. In these seasons I realize that, on my own, I am not a kind person—at least not in terms of biblical kindness. Without Christ, I am impatient, critical, and selfish with my time. While it is easy to be kind to those I like or love, the no-strings-attached sacrifice of time, energy, and money that Christ requires of his disciples feels like a chore when I stray from him. I am capable of showing Christ's love only when I am intentionally pursuing God, receiving spiritual renewal from him, and focusing on the sacred teamwork of Christ's light yoke.

As I sought God's forgiveness one morning for my recent distance from him, I was reminded of what Jesus told us about taking up his yoke and following him: we are promised rest for our weary souls when we walk closely with Christ, following his directives and his paths rather than the ones we create for ourselves. Jesus, in his grace, leads us faithfully in his way of kindness.

On our own, biblical kindness is impossible as a long-term way of life. However, when we intentionally set aside the time and energy to invest in our personal relationships with Christ—following his lead as we open our hearts, our homes, and our lives—we'll realize kindness is not a burden but a joyful and holy partnership.

— *Julie*

— Today's Act of Kindness —

Spend time listening to worship music, praying,
reading Scripture, and admiring God's creation.
Ask him to lead you in his way of kindness.

Encouraging Another's Talent

Encourage one another daily, as long as it is called "Today."
HEBREWS 3:13, NIV

My friend Jamie is a talented musician and singer. I have watched her use her talents to bless others since we first became friends in college. For Jamie, singing is more than just a hobby; it is a place where she finds purpose and renewal. But life recently has gotten a little crazy for Jamie, and some of her dreams have been put aside for the moment while she simply takes care of the day-to-day tasks that need to get done. As her friend, I hate to see this happen.

When a local talent event came up, I quickly texted Jamie with the information, encouraging her to audition. I reminded her how talented she is and how much I love to see her perform. She messaged me back saying she would try out for the event. A few days later I got another text with an attached e-mail showing that she was accepted to perform. We were both giddy with excitement. She was thankful for the opportunity to perform, but more than that, she was thankful for the reminder to keep doing something that she loves.

Calling out the talents and encouraging the dreams of others is one way we can extend kindness on a consistent basis. Everyone has something they're passionate about, and if we take the time to listen, we'll find out what it is. Scripture tells us to encourage one another daily, and reminding people to keep doing something they love is a great way to offer this encouragement. This is especially important when we see someone who is discouraged or has lost hope that they'll ever see their dreams come true. We can reignite a much-needed spark of hope at just the right time, pushing that person to keep trying and to keep pursuing all that God has for them.

— *Kendra*

— Today's Act of Kindness —

Be on the lookout for someone who is discouraged or has
not been using their talents, and take the time to encourage
and remind them of the talent God has given them.

Seeking a Compromise

How wonderful and pleasant it is when brothers live together in harmony!
PSALM 133:1

"Guess what!" my then-fiancé said to me over the phone, excitedly. "I bought a PlayStation 3 today!"

His pronouncement was met with silence on my end.

"Hello . . . ?" he asked after the pause extended to an uncomfortable length of time.

"How much did *that* cost?" I asked finally, feeling my voice tremble a little, with visions of flowers and photographers and wedding dresses scrolling through my mind. "We're saving for a wedding!"

"Oh," he said, pausing as he took in my unexpected reaction. "Well, it's a Blu-ray player too. I got it for the family," he tacked on at the end, a bit hopefully.

At twenty-nine, he wasn't used to having someone else sign off on big purchases. Years of living and working as an adult meant that he was pretty self-sufficient. Yet the prospect of marriage—and the joint bank accounts that came with it—required us to have some frank discussions about money. As a couple, we decided that if one of us wanted to buy something that cost more than our predetermined limit, we would give the other person the courtesy of a phone call first to discuss it.

Sometimes kindness, especially in marriage, requires us to adjust our expectations or rethink our natural inclinations. Sometimes it requires something as simple as a phone call. The Psalms talk about how wonderful it is when brothers (or, in our case, couples) live together in harmony, but a measure of kindness is needed in order to make compromises that lead to true unity. Financial considerations, career changes, and even parenting styles can clash. We need to be willing to discuss our preferences and beliefs and—when the occasion calls for it—to compromise with the other person in order to preserve unity.

Although we now joke about my husband's legendary "It's for the family" excuse for buying a video game console, truthfully, his willingness to consider my feelings and preferences went a long way toward smoothing our differences. And we really did get a lot of use out of that PlayStation!

— *Kristin*

— Today's Act of Kindness —

Are you in the midst of a difference of opinion with someone? Consider the issue from their perspective, and work to close the distance by suggesting a compromise.

A Quiet Support

*Moses' arms soon became so tired he could no longer hold them up. So
Aaron and Hur found a stone for him to sit on. Then they stood on each side
of Moses, holding up his hands. So his hands held steady until sunset.*

EXODUS 17:12

I once heard a keynote speaker share about not letting the green-eyed monster of jealousy steal what God has planned for your life. Her words forever altered how I view my role in God's Kingdom and in his bigger plan.

She spoke of her own experience with jealousy and how God had called her to daily prayer for a woman she envied. Obediently, she began continually praying for blessing and favor over her perceived rival, and her envy faded as she realized that there is no need for competition in God's Kingdom. She shared that we are each called to a unique journey, and the success of one does not require the defeat of another. Eventually, with her envy gone and a good dose of humility in its place, God began to use this speaker in ways that were beyond her wildest dreams.

Those words resonated deeply, and I've since found myself in the rare position of being the quiet prayer support for several women in ministry leadership positions. I've discovered that these women—all of them—periodically struggle. Their lives and their families are far from perfect, no matter how confident and put-together they appear to be. Having women who pray for them on a regular basis, who cheer them on without a glimmer of envy, is a blessing beyond imagination.

I love the story of Aaron and Hur holding up Moses' arms so that the battle being waged by the Israelites would be won. While Moses was the one God selected, it was the quiet support from Aaron and Hur that gave Moses the strength he needed to follow through. Whenever I pray for the deeply personal needs of women who are leading amazing ministries, I cannot help but think of Aaron and Hur quietly standing beside and lifting up Moses. My hope is that these prayers support my friends the same way that Aaron and Hur's physical assistance supported Moses' arms and spirit.

— Julie

— Today's Act of Kindness —

Pray for blessing, protection, and provision
over a woman who is a ministry leader.

Just Keep Talking through It

*Peter came to him and asked, "Lord, how often should I forgive
someone who sins against me? Seven times?" "No, not seven
times," Jesus replied, "but seventy times seven!"*
MATTHEW 18:21-22

Sometimes showing kindness to those who are closest to us—spouses, kids, good friends—is the hardest. Relationships are made up of imperfect people living life together and loving one another, however flawed they may be.

For a while my husband and I were having a particularly difficult time communicating with one another. Although we loved each other, misunderstandings were causing strain on our relationship.

I met with a good friend, who also happens to be a therapist. As I told her what had been happening in our relationship as of late, she stated, "Just keep talking through it. Don't stop, even when you don't feel like doing it. Just keep talking. Just keep showing up." I went home encouraged and with a renewed intention to not give up on our communication. Through several more weeks and a lot of talking and seeking forgiveness from each other, we were able to each realize where our miscommunications were taking place. We then spent the next several months adjusting our interactions to better communicate with each other without hurting—albeit inadvertently—the other's feelings.

In Scripture we find Peter asking Jesus how many times he should forgive someone, and I understand where he is coming from. Relationships can sometimes be hard, and I'd like to put a limit on how many times I should extend forgiveness toward those I love. But Jesus doesn't do that. He simply tells Peter (and us) that we are to offer others forgiveness as many times as they are in need of it. Although this can be challenging to carry out at times, it is comforting to know that we also are offered the same amount of unending forgiveness for our mistakes. We all need to offer others kindness through forgiveness, because the truth is, there are times when we need it extended back to us when we've erred.

— *Kendra*

— Today's Act of Kindness —

Offer forgiveness to someone you've been having
a hard time forgiving. Extend a bit of kindness
toward that person either in word or deed.

Go See a Movie

Worry weighs a person down; an encouraging word cheers a person up.
PROVERBS 12:25

One year my law firm hired a recent law-school graduate, and she spent her first two months of work studying for the two-day Minnesota bar exam. You can't practice law in Minnesota without passing the bar, and the thought of that two-day exam still makes me shudder. It was a miserable, stressful experience, and I have yet to meet an attorney who doesn't get a little twitchy when recounting their own bar exam experience.

When I was prepping for my bar exam, a mentor told me to go see a movie during the evening in between exam days, instead of trying to cram and study my notes one last time. Realizing the wisdom of that advice, I went to the cheap theater near my apartment and spent that evening watching a brainless romantic comedy, munching on popcorn and escaping for a few hours from thoughts of the next day's exam. My mentor was right; I arrived at the exam site the next morning feeling rested, relatively refreshed, and ready for day two.

As my new colleague's exam date drew near, I wondered how best to encourage her. Deciding to pass on the advice I had been given, I wrote her a note of encouragement and explanation, included the funds necessary for her and her husband to go see a movie, and sent it off in the mail.

When she joined the firm full time after passing her exam, she expressed her gratitude for the advice and thoughtfulness. She said that it made her feel encouraged and supported as she sat for the exam, usually an anxiety-inducing experience.

Life is too hard not to celebrate others as they stretch to reach difficult goals— whether they are physical, educational, or spiritual. Encouraging others as they face a difficult task takes just a moment of our time, but it gives the receiver a boost, reduces their anxiety, and allows us to have a tiny part in their larger story—just as a community of believers is meant to do.

— *Julie*

— Today's Act of Kindness —

Send a note of encouragement to someone
who is reaching for a big goal.

Balm for the Soul

Your words have supported those who were falling;
you encouraged those with shaky knees.

JOB 4:4

It was late in the evening when my friend heard the news that her daughter had died in an accident—and on this mother's birthday.

I'd spoken to this woman earlier that day, wishing her a happy birthday. I'd sent flowers too. Those actions felt hollow in the wake of such devastating news. I reached out to her quietly via text, letting her know I was thinking of her, that I cared for her and hoped she was doing okay. And then I waited.

On the one-month anniversary of her daughter's death, I sent her flowers again, telling her that she was loved, letting her know that I felt her grief and continued to mourn with her. When she left a voice mail on my phone, I could hear the sorrow in her tone and the tears causing her voice to tremble.

I've never lost a daughter, but I remember the terrible weight of grief I felt at age twenty-two when my sister, at just twenty-eight years old, died after a five-year battle with breast cancer. What I wanted most of all was for people to remember her—to recall how vibrant and wonderful she was, to never forget the life she lived and who she was. And in the ten years since then, I have always been so grateful when people have related to me the memories they have of her: the funny things she did, the thoughtful words she shared with them, the graceful way she carried herself despite her sickness. Whenever I have those conversations, each word spoken is a kindness to me, a balm to my soul that reminds me that life can still be good, even when it feels hard. The least I could do was try to provide that balm to my grieving friend.

The words we speak, the encouragement we give others, can support those who feel like they're falling. Our words have the power to comfort and heal those who are hurting today.

— Kristin

— Today's Act of Kindness —

Do you have a friend or loved one who is grieving?
Reach out to them in some way—with a phone call,
a bouquet of flowers, or a message—and let them
know that you are mourning their loss with them.

God's Fieldwork

Wake up and look around. The fields are already ripe for harvest.

JOHN 4:35

It was more than four years ago that my husband and I, with two toddlers and busy jobs, found ourselves sitting in a living room with four other families, each with young children, trying to decide whether or not we were going to launch a new church. After months of prayerful contemplation and frequent meetings, we responded to the call of God with a resounding yes and jumped into the adventure.

As my husband and I sat on our back patio one recent peaceful evening, we reflected on that simple yes, given without fully understanding the incredible journey of trust, faith, and spiritual growth we would undertake, and without fully understanding how difficult the journey would be at times.

We are so grateful we didn't delay saying yes to God, despite how crazy our decision looked to those around us at the time. We did not understand that our saying yes would be such a pivotal, defining moment in our lives. We now measure our lives in terms of "pre–church launch" and "post–church launch." We had no idea about the work God would do in our hearts and the way our faith would mature during the journey of launching Living Way Church.

Rarely does God wait until life is under control to invite us along on a faith adventure. Don't miss God's invitation to the proverbial fields ripe for harvest—the people around you who are searching for God—because you are too busy attending to earthly things that will fade away. If we are not careful, we will allow the temporary distractions in this life to become bigger and more important than the fields God has called us to tend. These are the plans that have eternal consequences for the lives around us, and it is up to us to wisely choose how we'll spend our time.

— Julie

— Today's Act of Kindness —

Prayerfully reevaluate your priorities, asking yourself which
items have eternal consequences and which items are temporary,
earthly distractions. Take a step to prioritize God's fieldwork first.

Back Problems

He comforts us in all our troubles so that we can comfort others. When they are troubled, we will be able to give them the same comfort God has given us.

2 CORINTHIANS 1:4

When the car skidded out of control while heading around the curve in the gravel road, careening onto its side in the ditch, I knew on impact that I'd broken something. As I hung from my seat belt in the rear of the car, sharp pain knifed through my back, and I wiggled my toes in panic, praying that my legs hadn't been paralyzed.

As sirens wailed in the distance and faces peered in at me, I felt profound relief at knowing I would be rescued. After I endured a couple of ambulance rides, a surgery, a week in the hospital, and three months wearing a back brace, my life settled into a new normal. But as a seventeen-year-old, I mourned the loss of experiences I'd never get to have. Marching band that summer—as well as the band trip to Kentucky with all my friends—was out of the question. So was football cheerleading in the fall. I was thankful for my restored good health, but I felt the deep ache of missing out.

A couple of years ago, a teenager I knew was diagnosed with scoliosis and told she would need surgery to correct her spine. Having had the experience of back surgery as a teenager, I felt keenly the pain and hardship she might encounter. So I made it a point to send flowers to her in the hospital. I also snagged magazines, nail polish, and treats to send her way during her recovery.

As children, we're often taught the Golden Rule, that we should do to others whatever we would like them to do to us. Although I would never wish the pain of a broken back on anyone, I was grateful that my experience could give me an insight into someone else's struggle. After all, I was able to use my knowledge of our shared experience to help our young friend through the challenge of her own recovery, even in a small way.

— *Kristin*

— *Today's Act of Kindness* —

Think of someone who could benefit from your shared experience. Use that experience to bless that person.

The Tradition of Rhubarb

The whole law can be summed up in this one command:
"Love your neighbor as yourself."
GALATIANS 5:14

Two Chinese families were joining us for their first-ever American barbecue on a Sunday afternoon in July, so the American families in our group brought quintessential barbecue fare as we define it here in Central Minnesota. For dessert, I made a rhubarb crisp with rhubarb plucked straight from my garden.

As we pulled out dessert, our Chinese guests said they had never seen rhubarb, and the conversation around the table turned to explanations of what it was. Fruit? Veggie? Herb? Stem? The debate raged on for ten minutes about its classification. Stories of how American grandmothers used rhubarb were shared around the table. Attempts to describe the plant turned into a foray into my garden for a specimen, and as we passed the leafy stem around the table, I remembered the childhood trick my father taught me.

Soon, small bowls of sugar had been passed out, the stem had been chopped up, and our Chinese friends were dipping their rhubarb into sugar and eating it fresh and raw—just as countless Minnesotans remember doing as children. We laughed, posed for funny photos with our sugar-encrusted rhubarb, compared notes and stories, and made memories.

This was my third American holiday hosting Chinese guests. I've learned that the best conversations and most poignant memories are made over simple traditions rather than attempts to impress our international guests with fancy cuisine. Sharing my life and my traditions becomes a bridge into conversations in which I catch a glimpse into the lives and traditions of others. Soon enough we are so busy sharing and laughing and comparing notes that we see one another's humanity first and foremost. Isn't that what it means to love another as yourself? To extend hospitality and friendship, and engage in conversation about what it means to live in different cultures. To reveal God in our thoughts, deeds, and words to those who come alongside us.

— Julie

— Today's Act of Kindness —

Invite someone from a different country or culture to share a meal.

When Kindness Feels Awkward

Don't just listen to God's word. You must do what it says.
Otherwise, you are only fooling yourselves.
JAMES 1:22

My friend Andrew was sitting in a coffee shop, working quietly, when he became aware of the two women talking at the table next to his own. He didn't mean to eavesdrop, yet he couldn't help but overhear the serious conversation happening as one woman told her friend that she had cancer. Crying quietly, she spoke about treatment options and the prognosis. She admitted that she would probably need to sell something to cover medical bills, and then she and her friend speculated on how easily she'd be able to sell her motorcycle to offset the costs.

Andrew ran out to his car, reached into his glove box, and pulled out some money, then returned inside. The women looked up as he approached.

"I'm sorry, but I couldn't help overhearing your conversation," he said apologetically. Handing the sick woman the cash, he offered her his concern and well-wishes. As the woman burst into tears, he told her to stay hopeful, hugged her, and left the shop.

A little more than an hour later, he had just finished up a meeting elsewhere when a colleague casually asked if he wanted to grab coffee. He agreed, but when they pulled into the parking lot of the very same coffee shop he'd left earlier, he felt dread twist his stomach. Seeing the women still sitting at the table, he asked his colleague if they could perhaps grab coffee somewhere else, feeling sheepish in having to admit that if he reentered the coffee shop, it could be awkward.

Relating the story afterward, he concluded with these words: "Doing kind things for other people can be awkward. People want to feel like they are in control, and putting yourself in certain situations can be uncomfortable because you don't always have control." Sometimes face-to-face encounters can feel discomfiting, yet we're told in Scripture to not just hear the Word but to act upon it as well. Refusing to do so may mean that our lives feel comfortable and yet are ultimately unfulfilling. We can combat this by choosing to step outside of our comfort zones to help others.

— *Kristin*

— Today's Act of Kindness —

Recognize and then overcome any feelings of awkwardness or discomfort you might feel in showing someone kindness in a face-to-face encounter.

The Big Picture

I am fully convinced, my dear brothers and sisters, that you are full of goodness.
ROMANS 15:14

Working with teens is challenging at times—like when my then-teenage husband, Kyle, wiped his cheese-covered fingers continually on his young youth pastor's couch, or when, instead of joining in with the youth group on a Wednesday night, he and another friend decided to hide out in the janitor's closet at church and listen to a basketball game on the radio. When Todd, the youth pastor, went to put the boys in their place (rightfully so), Kyle's friend's mother stopped him and very calmly told Todd that he'd have to lighten up and have a little fun if he ever wanted to engage the boys. Todd took her advice to heart and did just that, creating a lasting relationship with the boys that had a profound effect on their lives and faith.

Recently we hosted a reunion of my husband's youth group along with all the members' families. Their youth pastors came too, and it was a wonderful time of reminiscing and catching up on everyone's lives. My husband has told me what a huge impact Todd and his wife, Deb, have had on his life, and as I visited with them, it was easy to understand why. Kindness and caring and the ability to really listen oozed out of every conversation with them. But as they'll quickly tell you, these virtues developed over time and through lots of experiences that taught them how to extend God's love toward others, including those early experiences with my husband!

Remembering the big picture can be challenging at times—whether it's parenting our own kids, mentoring others, or just being in relationships with people. Everybody makes mistakes, and we all need guidance in life and understanding from others. Paul wrote many letters to the early church, often tempering his concerns with encouragement, confidently reminding his readers that they were full of goodness. Even though he faced challenges with other believers, he never forgot the bigger picture of drawing people closer to God through his teaching.

— Kendra

— Today's Act of Kindness —

Think about a particularly challenging relationship you are currently in. Take a step back and look at the big picture, and instead of criticizing, choose to commend this person.

Bless Those Who Hate You

*Bless those who persecute you. Don't curse
them; pray that God will bless them.*

ROMANS 12:14

I was on a rare coffee date with a dear friend, and our conversation turned to the never-ending violence in the news of late. Pausing as we contemplated this crossroads our world seems to be standing at, my friend began telling me the recent experience of a man she knows.

Daydreaming as he stood in the checkout line at the convenience store, he waited patiently as the woman ahead of him argued with the store clerk. With two credit cards declined, she noticed and misinterpreted this man's vacant gaze and slight smile as being directed at her. She laid into him, verbally attacking him and yelling profanities. Before he could respond with an explanation that he wasn't smiling at her misfortune, she stomped angrily from the store.

Approaching the sales clerk after the woman left, this man quietly said that he would like to put twenty dollars on a gas card for her. The cashier, shocked, asked him why he would do such a thing after the verbal abuse she had spewed. Overhearing the conversation, another gentleman standing in line stepped up and asked if he, too, could add twenty dollars to the gas card.

The two men then stepped outside and approached the woman as she got into her car, giving her the gas card and apologizing for the misunderstanding. She immediately burst into tears of remorse and relief—apologizing profusely for her conduct, asking for forgiveness, and explaining her circumstances. She had just been hired to start a new job but didn't have enough gas to get to her first day of work the next morning. She was discouraged, stressed, and desperate, and she had snapped.

With my friend's words lingering in the air, we both sat silent for several beats. This man had offered blessing in the face of angry words because he saw to the heart of the matter—a desperate person lashing out in the midst of her pain. That is hard to do, but think about what would happen if, as Christians, we made it a practice to respond to hurtful words with blessing. We could accomplish some pretty radical world changing if we followed that command.

— Julie

— Today's Act of Kindness —

The next time you are faced with someone else's anger,
respond with generous, over-the-top blessing.

August

Kindness for the Road

Whenever we have the opportunity, we should do good to everyone.
GALATIANS 6:10

My family and I like to travel. It's been important to both my husband and me to share memories with our kids through experiencing new things together. This past year we traveled by car from Minnesota to Seattle, and we decided to do kind acts along the way. We did this by leaving coffee gift cards with little notes for other travelers at rest stops, leaving notes of encouragement and extra tips for the people who cleaned our hotel rooms, and graciously letting people merge while driving.

It's been a fun experience to share with our kids as we wonder who will find our secret gifts and what they'll think when they stumble upon them. It's been a good way for my kids to see that we can bless people no matter where we are or what we're doing.

Being kind is a way of life and a different way of thinking, not just an action we perform every now and then. It's a habit we want to continue doing everywhere we go. It has also reminded us to be grateful for the work that others do each day—work that is often too easy to forget or ignore.

Looking for ways that we can bless other people along the way on a trip or in life is something we can all do. It doesn't matter if we travel far from our homes or not; we can all look for small ways to be a blessing in someone else's day. Scripture reminds us that whenever we have an opportunity, we should do good to everyone. Look at the activities of your daily life and see if there are ways to give others encouragement or kindness on a more regular basis. Where do you go and what do you do each day? These are the opportunities God has given you to be kind.

— Kendra

— Today's Act of Kindness —

Plan to do one small surprise act of kindness
for someone you see every day.

All Because of A. J.

*Don't let anyone think less of you because you are young.
Be an example to all believers in what you say, in the way
you live, in your love, your faith, and your purity.*

1 TIMOTHY 4:12

My husband noticed the student host wandering around a bit at the prom for students with special needs and then approached him to say hello. As they began to chat, the young man revealed, a bit sheepishly, that until that afternoon he had thought the prom was in St. Paul, not St. Michael. Despite knowing that it would double his drive time, he figured that since he had signed up and committed to volunteering, he would come anyway.

His name was A. J., and he talked animatedly of his plans to become a special education teacher after graduating from college and how much he loved working with his students every summer in the local adapted softball program. By the end of the night, he was mugging for the camera in the photo booth with the honored guests, having the time of his life.

Impressed with his character and his decision to volunteer at the prom despite the inconvenience of the drive, Tim contacted the head of A. J.'s adapted softball team the following week and asked if there was a way he could donate to the program.

The coach was surprised by Tim's phone call. "Not many people in the community know about our program. How did you hear about us?" the coach asked. As Tim explained about the prom for students with special needs and how A. J.'s story inspired him to want to help, the coach was clearly touched.

It can be easy to discount someone simply because of their age or experience. Yet Scripture tells us that just because someone is young doesn't mean they can't be an example to others. Despite A. J.'s youth, his desire to help others shone through. His character and commitment to helping others was the reason Tim went the extra mile to help an adapted softball team in another community, a program Tim likely would never have even known about without meeting A. J.

— *Kristin*

— Today's Act of Kindness —

Whose character impresses you? Go out
of your way to tell them so.

Short on Time

Your life is like the morning fog—it's here a little while, then it's gone.
JAMES 4:14

As a social worker for a hospice program, I spend a lot of time around people who are terminally ill, as well as with their families. It is one of the most rewarding jobs I've ever had, to be with people who are nearing the end of their lives and to watch them reflect on the years, spend time with their loved ones, make amends, and shrug off the small annoyances of life to allow space for what truly matters. They make space for things like warm hugs, soft smiles, small giggles, hand-holding, storytelling, reminiscing, listening, and sharing memories. It always reminds me that time is precious.

Recently my family and I got to visit my uncle and aunt while we vacationed in Washington. An avid outdoorsman, my uncle told us all about the area, taking us to his favorite spots on the ocean and telling us about many more areas to visit. But this gathering became even more precious to me as I watched my uncle stride slowly up the trail, seeming much more fragile than I remembered from past visits. Cancer had started to battle against his body and overall health. I listened more closely to the stories he told, especially the stories about his parents and his family growing up. I didn't want to miss the words and thoughts he shared, knowing I wouldn't have an infinite amount of time with him.

I texted my mom on my way home, and she wondered if she and my dad should visit as well. As I pondered my reply, I realized what is true for all of us: we never know how much time we have with those we love. We will never regret the time we spent with our loved ones, but we will certainly regret the time we missed. There is something to be said for not waiting, for speaking today with those we love, for extending kindness by reminding them how much they are loved. Because we know that our lives are like the morning fog, here for a little while and then gone, we should be encouraged even more to hold dear the people we love and to spend time with them today.

— *Kendra*

— Today's Act of Kindness —

Call, message, or visit someone whom you love.
Let them know how precious they are to you.

Rejecting Comparison

Always be eager to practice hospitality.
ROMANS 12:13

The first house Aaron and I owned was a 1960s two-bedroom rambler, whose exterior was painted an unforgettable shade of seafoam green. While our house was painfully retro instead of cool, it didn't stop us from inviting others in. We refused to compare ourselves with acquaintances living in far fancier houses. We viewed our house as a tool for ministering to others by throwing open our lives and inviting others to journey alongside us, and so that's what we did.

I still smile at the memories of parties we held in that tiny house. We had old friends, new acquaintances, and everyone in between squeezing inside for game nights or spilling out into the backyard for bonfires, their cars lining the length of the street. All the neighbors wondered about those two youngsters who lived in the little old lady's former house.

We even met our very best friends while we lived in that seafoam-green house. While we eventually outgrew that little house and moved just a bit down the road into something better suited to a growing family, I am so grateful that we decided early on never to let notions of whether our house was "good enough" for entertaining stop us from opening our front door. I think of all the fun we had, all the memories we made, and the deep and sustaining friendships we developed in that house simply because we refused to let materialism be a part of our decision-making process.

It was a lesson we learned early, and one I return to again and again. People crave personal relationships, time spent in community, and authentic friendships. I refuse to allow my possessions (or lack thereof) to stop me from offering relationship, community, and friendship to those around me. As Christians, we are repeatedly exhorted to show hospitality to others, and I am convinced that is because we are best set up to introduce others to Christ when we share meals, invite them into our homes, and open our lives.

Is the trap of comparison stopping you from showing hospitality? Prayerfully consider how you might overcome this trap today.

— Julie

— Today's Act of Kindness —

Whatever the state of your home, invite a friend or two
over for a meal, coffee, or just a life-giving chat.

From Great Loss to Great Gain

We know that God causes everything to work together for the good of those who love God and are called according to his purpose for them.

ROMANS 8:28

It was at a concert benefiting Place of Hope, our local homeless shelter, after we'd watched ballerinas dancing and heard a lovely soprano singing, that the announcement came. Place of Hope was in the midst of updating their women's wing, and they had decided to call it Katie's Club. Katie's Club—as in my sister's foundation. My sister's legacy. After watching a video about the impact Katie's Club has made over the past ten years, my family rose to step onstage, and I couldn't help but beam through my tears.

After the concert was over, I was approached over and over by strangers. They radiated sincerity, all offering condolences for my loss, all marveling that such a tragedy could result in something as wonderful and helpful as a new women's wing at Place of Hope. I was reminded once again of something Kendra, Julie, and I wrote a few years ago: only through great loss can we experience God's great gain.

In the past ten years, we have raised $200,000 through the foundation to support girls and women, to give them opportunities in Christian environments that they otherwise might not have had: providing them with an education, sending them to camp, assisting trafficked women, serving the homeless. But what's even more meaningful is that these opportunities have given them hope, choices, freedom. Those intangibles have made the burdensome weight of grief a little lighter, a little easier to bear. I'm so grateful that our pain over losing Katrina has given us the opportunity to accomplish something so much bigger than ourselves.

As I left the concert that evening, I felt blessed, thankful, and most of all, hopeful. Sometimes when we experience grief or tragedy, it can be hard to believe that God can truly cause everything to work together for our good. Yet if we allow him to, he can use our experience to teach us things or help others in ways we never could have imagined.

— *Kristin*

— Today's Act of Kindness —

Are you grieving someone? Do one kind action
as a tribute to their influence on your life.

When Coffee and Waffles Mean "I Love You"

*Love is patient and kind. . . . It does not demand its own way. It is
not irritable, and it keeps no record of being wronged.*

1 CORINTHIANS 13:4-5

As we drove the last few miles on our way home from vacation, my mind turned toward our house. Coming home from vacation is always hard for my family. We are all extra tired, grumpy, and a little out of sorts. This time I also knew that I was going to be walking into a house that was torn apart and turned inside out—with every piece of furniture shoved to the middle of every room and every item removed from the walls—in preparation for having the interior of our house painted while we were gone.

Walking inside, I noticed that the walls looked great, and I was grateful to have someone else doing the hard work. But the project wasn't finished, as I'd expected it to be. I sighed, knowing that I'd be going back to work the next morning with the house looking and feeling like a construction zone.

We had a snack, brushed our teeth, and then clambered over dressers and around bookshelves as we sought out our beds for the night. My husband was up and out of the house extra early the next morning, giving me a quick kiss and telling me he had lots of work awaiting him at the office. As the kids and I finished dressing, my mind turned to making breakfast in a barely functional kitchen.

I was standing cluelessly in the middle of the kitchen when my husband's smiling face appeared around the corner, his hands holding a large coffee from my favorite coffee shop and a box of frozen waffles.

His thoughtfulness cheered us all, but it especially touched my heart. My husband frequently shows his love for us by quietly meeting needs, by being slow to anger and frustration—even when it is deserved—and by not keeping score. He practices unconditional, agape love, and it makes me and our children feel absolutely cherished. Who do you know that could use an extra dose of unconditional love?

— Julie

— Today's Act of Kindness —

Shower a loved one—perhaps a parent, spouse, child, or sibling—
with the unconditional love described in 1 Corinthians 13.

Let It Go

Slander no one . . . be peaceable and considerate,
and always . . . gentle toward everyone.
TITUS 3:2, NIV

My husband and I took in around twenty children over the six years we provided foster care through our county. Most of the kids we took in were part of sibling groups, ranging in age from six months to seventeen years old.

When each child or sibling group came into our home, it was important for us to help them feel welcomed and comfortable as quickly as possible. To do this, we'd carefully help them go through their things, putting everything away in their rooms and never washing anything unless the kids asked me to. Scents can be very comforting, and we wanted them to be surrounded by familiar smells and objects. We'd also take them shopping for new clothes and shoes, and we'd always let them pick out one new toy or other item that they wanted.

We tried to listen a lot during those first days and weeks, and be sensitive to what would best help each child to adjust to their new environment. Although we were careful to set limits and safe boundaries with the kids, we never tried to change or correct behaviors in a way that would overwhelm them, especially in the beginning. We'd slowly teach them that certain things, like using vulgar language, weren't allowed in our home.

In our culture, being considerate of others is a bit of a lost art. It seems that people are not only easily offended but also quick to tell others when they are in the wrong. Sometimes this may be appropriate, but as Christians we should also be gracious to others, considering the person's circumstances or background and showing them kindness. Scripture tells us that we are to be peaceable, considerate, and gentle. We honor God when we are quick to love and let go of offenses rather than calling out others' faults or annoying habits.

— Kendra

— Today's Act of Kindness —

Choose to extend kindness to someone in your life
who annoys you or rubs you the wrong way.

Life-Giving Words

*The tongue can bring death or life; those who love
to talk will reap the consequences.*

PROVERBS 18:21

One year when I attended family camp, I had an encounter with God through someone else's words—although I wouldn't know just how meaningful they would be until much later in life. As I was waiting for my parents to finish their conversations after an evening meeting, one of the other moms approached me and told me that she believed I would write for God someday. In that time and at that moment, her words didn't mean much to me. Sure, I liked to write, but I was certainly no prodigy. My poetry and fiction attempts were, quite frankly, mediocre.

Yet over the years, her words would return to me again and again until they eventually settled into my bones, seeping into the very marrow of who I was and who I would become. The kindness of her words—and of her going out of her way to speak into my life, even though I was a stranger—had a lasting effect.

I think about other words that have spoken life or death to me, shaping me into who I've become: supportive words from my dad and a professor who both encouraged my writing, hurtful words from a bully that lingered for years, painful words during teenage breakups of friendships and relationships, the daily words of love and affirmation from my husband and children. All these experiences, whether the words were painful or affirming, made a lasting impression on me. They are words that I hear on repeat in the back of my mind; words that play on my deepest insecurities or bolster my confidence on days that it falters. Our words—with their power to heal or harm, to bring life or death—have profound, lifelong effects that are often impossible to gauge in the heat of the moment. We never know when our words might impact someone's life path or influence their calling. It's a sobering thought and a great responsibility. Do you regularly speak words of encouragement to the people in your life?

— Kristin

— Today's Act of Kindness —

Use kind words to encourage or lift up someone else.

The Gift of Quarters

*Give your gifts in private, and your Father, who
sees everything, will reward you.*

MATTHEW 6:4

One of my husband's favorite memories is of a self-driven adventure he embarked on when he was a teenager. It was a summer afternoon, and he found himself walking down the main street of a downtown area that was lined with bustling stores and restaurants and metered parking. For some reason (the "why" having faded with time), his pockets were filled with quarters, and so, on a whim, he began walking up and down the street, feeding expired meters.

The first time he told me this story, he smiled at the memory, and when I asked him why his teenage self had decided to pay meters, his response was simple: he had the quarters in his pocket, and he was able to help people avoid expensive consequences for the mere cost of twenty-five cents. He added how he loved the fact that he was feeding those meters secretly and that no one would know what he had done for them.

In a world intent on sharing far too much on social media, I find myself struggling to strike the balance between sharing acts of kindness with others in a genuine attempt to get them to join in and the caution set forth in Matthew 6. We are warned that publicly patting ourselves on the back for our good deeds is not pleasing to God and instead we are called to quietly meet needs, letting the knowledge of what we've done stay between us and God.

It's a careful balancing act, and one that requires prayer. Before I share about an act of kindness, I've learned to ask God to show me my heart's reasoning in wanting to share, trying to always keep in mind how easy it is to become prideful. While I do share some things because I want to encourage others, there are many quiet, secret acts of kindness that my husband and I do—keeping it a secret between us and God.

— Julie

— Today's Act of Kindness —

Perform a kind act secretly, taking joy in knowing
that God sees what you've done.

The Bucket List

*Do not despise these small beginnings, for the
LORD rejoices to see the work begin.*
ZECHARIAH 4:10

There is a group called the Bucket Brigade in our community that attempts to grant the final wishes of people with a terminal diagnosis. They get requests from individuals or family members and then pass these on to their community of supporters to see if anyone can help fulfill the dreams.

I found out about the organization several years ago and signed up to be on their e-mail list. Recently we got a message about a woman who had just a few months left to live and would really like to take a vacation with her family to the lake. The organization also requested gift cards to local grocery stores and pizza shops, and I thought this could be a perfect opportunity for my family to help. That night at dinner, I read the e-mail to my family, and together we talked about what we could do and what we'd like to donate, and then we prayed for the woman and her family. The next morning my kids made cards as I bought gift cards and wrote a check to help cover the cost of the woman's final vacation with her family. We sent it all off with a prayer and a blessing for her later that day.

I've come to realize that I don't have to take care of everyone or everything to make a difference. Deciding to help this woman didn't mean I had to cover every bit of the cost, but I did recognize that what my family could do, pooled with what others would also give, could add up to a whole lot of good. We don't have to be wealthy to be kind. The Bible tells us that we should not be discouraged by small beginnings and that God rejoices in just seeing us start. A kind word, a few dollars, and a simple prayer are often just what are needed in a particular situation. Don't miss the small ways that God may be asking you to make a difference in the life of someone else today.

— Kendra

— Today's Act of Kindness —

Look for a simple way that you could show a stranger kindness,
even if it's just with a smile or an encouraging word.

A Little Something Extra

Give, and you will receive. Your gift will return to you in full—pressed down, shaken together to make room for more, running over, and poured into your lap. The amount you give will determine the amount you get back.

LUKE 6:38

Clicking on the link to the devotional book we were planning to read for our women's Bible study, I paused, hand hovering over the mouse. I only needed a single copy, but I figured that someone else would come along who needed one, so I increased the order in my cart to two copies.

A few weeks later, the night of our first gathering arrived. As I busied myself setting out tea, coffee, and treats, and arranged my living and dining room chairs in a loose circle, I remembered to grab the extra copy of the book and tuck it next to mine.

Sure enough, we had just sat down and were making introductions when the woman sitting next to me admitted with a soft laugh that she hadn't been able to get the book yet. I didn't know much about her, only that she'd had to coordinate a ride to my house for the study but had wanted to attend despite the hassle. Snagging my extra book, I held it out to her and told her that she was welcome to keep it.

The gift, freely given, was small, yet I could tell she was touched. As her surprised eyes met mine, her quiet word of thanks was all I needed to know that I'd done the right thing in adding another book to my cart. The cost was minimal, but the reward felt sweet. Opportunities to share our excess can come in many forms, from something as small as an extra book, to a meal that we've doubled in size, to clothes in great condition that just don't fit anymore.

Sometimes we don't know what our simple act of kindness can do to ease another's burden, struggle, or busy schedule. What extras do you have available in your own life that could help alleviate someone else's challenges?

— *Kristin*

— Today's Act of Kindness —

The next time you make a purchase, consider picking up an extra for someone else who may need it, then give the gift quietly and freely.

A Redeemed Failure

We know that God causes everything to work together for the good of those who love God and are called according to his purpose for them.

ROMANS 8:28

Huffing and puffing two minutes into my hike up the steep switchback trail, I knew I was in serious trouble. In the months before our group of friends traveled to Colorado to climb a mountain as a fund-raiser, I hadn't trained enough to reach the summit.

Honestly, I didn't want to even attempt the climb. Praying, I told God that if someone offered to watch my children, then I'd know I should join my husband on the hike. Wouldn't you know it—that same afternoon of my prayer, one of our traveling companions offered, out of the blue, to watch our kids while my husband and I hiked.

So here I was, asking God why I was on a mountain I had no hope of summiting. As I panted upward toward the saddle summit, a mere quarter of the way to the top, I heard sobbing on the trail ahead. I pushed my tired legs and aching lungs to go as fast as I could, desperately praying about what I was going to find ahead.

As I reached the saddle summit, I encountered a tired and scared tween girl who had been separated from her hiking group. She later told me that I appeared around the bend just as she had finished praying to God for help. I struck up a gentle conversation and pulled out of my pack the candy bars meant for a summit celebration. I sat with her on a rock in the sun, nibbling on chocolaty goodness as we waited for her group to find us.

The reunion was filled with tears and gratitude. As the group disappeared back down the mountain, I found myself contemplating God's plan. I was on that specific mountainside that particular morning to answer that girl's prayer. I perceived my hike to be a failure, but God used it to meet someone else's need. God so often takes circumstances we perceive as failures, weaknesses, or tragedies and uses them to answer prayers, change lives, and reveal his glory to others.

Is there an area of your life where you've experienced failure lately? Pray that God would use this experience for your good or to meet someone else's need.

— Julie

— Today's Act of Kindness —

Watch for an opportunity to let God use
one of your failures for good.

Taking Care of Kids

Blessed are those who help the poor.
PROVERBS 14:21

My husband and I first heard about a child sponsorship program at a local concert. The musicians performing that night talked about the children they sponsored and encouraged others to sign up to sponsor a child themselves.

A booth was set up in the back of the room with pictures and information on children from around the world. My husband and I were deeply moved, and having no children of our own yet, we decided it would be a good thing for us to do before that season of life began. More than ten years later, and after becoming the parents to four children, we still sponsor the child we committed to care for that night. We've gotten to know him and his family over the years through letters and pictures, and he's seen our family grow and change as well. It has been a beautiful way for us to feel like we are caring for children as God does, not only by raising kids in our own home, but by supporting another child and another family.

Sometimes, in light of the many problems in our world, taking care of just one child or person can seem very insignificant, maybe even inconsequential. But I'm sure if you asked the young man we sponsor, he would tell you otherwise. If everyone were to take care of just one child, think of what a difference we could make regarding issues of homelessness, hunger, education, and medical care. We could truly change the world, one person at a time.

Have you ever sponsored a child or considered it? Even if you are not able to do so, we can all take the time to pray for children who are facing hardships or for an issue that affects children around the world. Scripture reminds us that those who help the poor are blessed, and so often God uses us as his vessels of kindness toward others. Sponsoring our child has reminded us each month of the plight of others around the world and how a simple donation can do a lot of good in one person's life.

— Kendra

— Today's Act of Kindness —

Sign up to sponsor a child, make a one-time
donation to an organization that cares for children,
or pray for children who are facing hardship.

Someone Else's Dream

*Each man must love his wife as he loves himself,
and the wife must respect her husband.*

EPHESIANS 5:33

"What are some of the most important things you've learned in your marriage?" The question was posed to Tim and me by a young couple who were getting married the following month.

My exact words escape my memory, but the gist was this: it's important to be honest, authentic, vulnerable, and above all, kind. Kindness requires us to see others as worthy and loved and made in God's image, despite their flaws. Kindness gives others the benefit of the doubt. And sometimes, kindness in marriage means supporting the other person's dream, even when it is not your own dream.

Several years ago, I decided to fulfill my goal of obtaining a graduate degree. I'll be honest—I picked a terrible time to start taking classes. Rather than bemoaning my decision to quit my job, or questioning the timing of starting school just as we were thinking of having a baby, or asking me what I was going to do with my degree afterward, my husband simply said yes. Despite the fact that it took me five years to finish—as I took breaks to have two children—and I stayed up late to write papers and talked about obscure topics like male hysteria in Richard Marsh's novel *The Beetle*—Tim supported me. And he was proud of me.

On my wedding day, it was easy to tell the world that I would love and cherish my husband always. But I didn't know then, as I know now and as our young friends will learn for themselves as the years go by, how challenging it is to truly love someone. Ephesians admonishes us to show love and respect to our spouses—just as much as we love ourselves.

Kindness in marriage can sometimes require us to make the sacrificial decision to be unselfish when our mate changes course in habits, interests, or career. That's not to say we are required to go along with every crazy scheme our spouses think up, but merely to show kindness in exhibiting love and respect, considering another person's preferences as much as we consider our own.

— Kristin

— Today's Act of Kindness —

Go out of your way to support your spouse's dreams.
If you are unmarried, show a friend or colleague that
you support them in a dream they are pursuing.

Just Call Me Jonah

The LORD spoke to Jonah a second time: "Get up and go to the great
city of Nineveh, and deliver the message I have given you." This time
Jonah obeyed the LORD's command and went to Nineveh.
JONAH 3:1-3

My heart sank as the moment passed; I instinctively knew that I'd blown it. I'd felt the Holy Spirit's gentle nudge to say something, but my fears about how my friend would take it and thoughts about whether I'd offend her made me hold my tongue until the moment of opportunity passed.

In the days following, I felt the heavy weight of regret and failure, and I feared that my lost opportunity would have eternal consequences. I sought the Lord in prayer, asking for forgiveness and a second chance—another opportunity to say the words I knew I was supposed to say in that moment. I prayed that my failure to speak up before would not impact the relationship this other person might have with Jesus.

God gently reminded me of Jonah—he ran from God's command and was tossed off a boat in the midst of a violent storm, swallowed by a big fish, and spit back up on the very land he had tried to flee. Jonah, acknowledging his sin, repented and went to Nineveh to accomplish what God had told him to do originally—to warn its citizens that the wrath of God was coming. The Ninevites heeded his words and repented. God gave Jonah a second chance, and he seized it.

It wasn't even two weeks later when my second chance came: a new opportunity arose for me to speak the words I had failed to speak before, and I leaped at the chance. Afterward I wept, thanking God for a second chance to follow through on his nudging.

Our God is the God of second chances. While we often consider this in the context of nonbelievers becoming believers, it holds true in my life as I try to reflect the glory of God, partly through intentional kindness. When I fail, when I blow it, when I mess it all up, I've learned to quickly approach God in prayer, asking for forgiveness and for a second chance to get it right. When have you brushed off God's leading recently?

— Julie

— Today's Act of Kindness —

Ask God for a second chance to accomplish
his purposes, and then follow through.

A Shining Light

Now you have light from the Lord. So live as people of light! For this
light within you produces only what is good and right and true.

EPHESIANS 5:8-9

My friend Andrea leads a Moms in Prayer group that meets on Tuesdays to pray for
their children, other students, teachers, coaches, and staff at several local elementary
schools. They pray for their kids to have good friends, that they would reach out to
include students who need friends, and that they would shine God's light to those
around them.

Each fall, the prayer group delivers bagels, cream cheese, and coffee to five local
schools, with a note saying who they are and that they've committed to praying
for the school and its staff and students. Two years ago, on the day they delivered
bagels, the women asked if they could pray for any of the office staff. Two women
came forward in tears, asking for prayer for specific things in their own lives. One
of them said, "No one has ever asked to pray for us before. Thank you." The group
of moms were able to pray in that school, that day, with two women who were
truly struggling.

About a week later, Andrea received an e-mail from the principal at one of the
elementary schools they had visited saying how grateful she was to know that there
was a group of moms praying for the school and everyone in it. She said she was in
tears at the kindness a group of women could display—even through something as
simple as bagels. Andrea and the other moms have received countless thank-yous
over the past few years from staff members who said they never realized how much
a simple, thoughtful gesture and the knowledge that people were praying for them
could help brighten their days.

Just as Andrea and the other moms pray for their children to be a light at
school, their kindness and intentional prayer for the staff at their local schools
provides a shining example too. We're called to live as people of light, as this group
demonstrates. In what ways can you shine the light of kindness into the lives of
those around you?

— Kristin

— Today's Act of Kindness —

Pray or do some other kind act for the
children and staff at a local school.

Letting Actions Speak

Let your good deeds shine out for all to see, so that
everyone will praise your heavenly Father.
MATTHEW 5:16

I had vastly underestimated the distance from our vacation condo to the small café up the road. I had convinced my international friend that it was just a quick walk, but instead we found ourselves walking along the roadside with a lot of unexpected time for contemplative conversation as we plodded along.

As we walked, we spoke about life. She is from another culture and was in the US for only a few short years. I'd become an informal cultural mentor as she navigated life in this country, and Aaron and I had made an intentional decision to welcome her into all parts of our life for those precious few years.

After finally reaching our destination and picking up some baked goods, we headed back. My friend turned to me and said, "I'm starting to think that people of faith are particularly kind."

I stumbled mentally, fumbling for words. Finally I said, "Well, we aren't always kind, because no one is perfect, but we try. . . . I try."

Early in our acquaintance, I learned that my friend had preconceived notions about Jesus, God, and faith in general, likely due to how religion is perceived in her culture. While I'd never hidden my faith from her, I'd always tried to be respectful in our conversations and not push Jesus on her. Instead, I invited her to live alongside me, to see the manifestation of Christ in my life and in my family. I trusted God to guide our conversations and was content to reveal my faith and my Savior through my actions and my life.

It's true that others often recognize our faith, whether they realize it or not, by our actions. If we are living as Jesus calls us to live, our actions and responses to those around us will shine, drawing them close and making them ask what we have in our lives that they do not. God's glory is often revealed more clearly in the actions of his disciples than through mere words.

— Julie

— Today's Act of Kindness —

Practice making sure that your actions, not
just your words, reveal God's glory.

A Trip to Iraq

Don't just listen to God's word. You must do what it says.
Otherwise, you are only fooling yourselves.
JAMES 1:22

It was a blog post about refugees living in Iraq that convinced my friend Samantha to take what some might consider a drastic step. The author's words about the hardships and suffering that the people displaced by war and violence were experiencing resonated with Samantha, and she felt the tug to do something—so strongly that she resolved to find a group that was going abroad to work directly with the refugees.

"I'm going to do this," she told her husband, showing him the post.

Several months later, she packed up and headed halfway around the world to help Yezidi families displaced by ISIS and living in the ongoing turmoil in the Middle East. For three weeks, she stayed in a trailer, living and working with refugees in an Iraqi village. Despite the discouragement of others who couldn't believe her decision to travel to such an unstable location, she made the decision and followed through. There was the potential for great danger on her journey—at one point, the car she was riding in was just a few miles from the border of the territory controlled by ISIS fighters—but she went anyway.

So often we hear about tragedies in the world and feel sympathy for the situation but don't believe that we can truly help. We might gather food supplies or donate to the Red Cross, but we don't think that one person can have an impact. But the Bible tells us that we are not just to listen to God's Word, but that we must also do what it says. When we feel called to do something, we should also follow through.

It would have been easy for my friend to decide to stay home with her husband and three children, living in the comfort of her Minnesota home. She could have justified her reasons for doing so, or found another way to help, yet she stood courageously by her convictions. For her, a genuine desire to help meant taking action and making a journey of several thousand miles. What journey might God be calling you to take today?

— Kristin

— Today's Act of Kindness —

Gather your courage and take one tangible step toward
doing something God is calling you to do.

You Are Beautiful

The LORD said to Samuel, "Don't judge by his appearance or height, for I have rejected him. The LORD doesn't see things the way you see them. People judge by outward appearance, but the LORD looks at the heart."

1 SAMUEL 16:7

Gathered together with my oldest, best girlfriends, I noticed our conversation turn to laughing and lamenting over how hard it is to find jeans that don't give us the dreaded "mom butt." As I gazed upon these women with whom I've wept uncountable tears, prayed audacious prayers, and laughed so hard that my sides ached the next morning, I saw not a few more wrinkles, a few more pounds, and a few more gray hairs, but breathtaking beauty.

Our culture tells us that beauty lies in striving to look eighteen for the next sixty years through Botox treatments and plastic surgery. The fashion industry uses sixteen-year-old models to walk runways, telling thirty-five-year-old moms that we must look like teenagers in order to be sexy.

Let us set aside these cultural notions of beauty. They are nothing but a mirage—an image we will chase forever through a desert with no hope of ever attaining the goal. We will starve ourselves physically, mentally, and spiritually, wasting our precious few days on earth running after an illusion.

Instead, let us *live* beauty. Can we embrace our bodies and all of the bumps and scars and wrinkles as signs of lives beautifully and fully lived, instead of forever wishing for bodies that pretend we've not lived at all?

As we meet our own eyes in the mirror every morning, can we see ourselves as our Savior sees us—as his beloved creation? Do we dare measure our beauty by looking inward and focusing on the condition of our hearts instead of on our outward appearances?

I imagine this is what Jesus would whisper into your soul as you glance into the mirror, if only you'd turn down the clanging, loud voices of our culture: Beautiful. *Beautiful.* BEAUTIFUL.

Believe it. Embrace it. Live it. And encourage the women in your life to live it too.

— *Julie*

— Today's Act of Kindness —

Tell your mom, your sister, a friend, or a coworker what you find beautiful about her according to God's definition.

What Are the Needs?

*Understand this, my dear brothers and sisters: You
must all be quick to listen, slow to speak.*
JAMES 1:19

Recently a friend challenged Kristin, Julie, me, and our readers to buy extra school supplies for kids in need as we approached a new school year. We took that challenge and asked others to join with us in this act of kindness.

Then another friend posted online about how her church was doing an event called the "Big Give" for those in the community who struggle with gathering school supplies. Each child would get a backpack and school supplies, but the church went even further, offering new clothes, winter coats, haircuts, and even a meal and games to make the whole day fun. What better way to help kids and families feel good about themselves and about going back to school than with these simple acts of kindness?

It's amazing what we can dream up and do in community with others. When I asked Rachel, the organizer of the Big Give, how she came up with the idea, she said that last year she went around to the different schools in her town, sat down with the principals, and asked them what their needs were. She didn't just guess or assume what others would need—she asked! As a result, she and her church put on an event that effectively met real needs.

Oftentimes we wonder what we can do, either individually or as a group, to help others in our community and show them kindness. One of the best ways to find out is to go out and *ask*. The Bible encourages us to be quick to listen and slow to speak. When we take the time to listen to others and find out what they really need, we can be even more effective by blessing them in ways that will benefit them most.

— *Kendra*

— Today's Act of Kindness —

Ask an individual or a group in your community to identify a
need that they may have, and then find a way to meet that need.

Behind-the-Scenes Kindness

The greatest among you must be a servant. But those who exalt themselves
will be humbled, and those who humble themselves will be exalted.
MATTHEW 23:11-12

I had volunteered to help out with the resource table at an amazing Christian women's conference, and I was so excited to be a part of the big things God was doing.

But as I watched other volunteers bustling about while I sat behind the confines of the resource table, I found myself longing to do more. Out of the blue, a stranger came striding up with an infant in her arms. "I need someone to hold this baby," she stated. I didn't hesitate. As I reached out my arms, this person explained that the child's mom was about to take the stage in a dramatic performance, and someone needed to hold her baby for approximately an hour.

Even though the baby had not been fed recently, she slept peacefully in my arms the entire time, and I guarded her as though she were my own. Her mom reclaimed her just as our table was deluged with questions and requests in between sessions, and I watched as they melted into the crowd—no names ever exchanged.

On my way home, I initially felt let down that I hadn't been able to play a bigger role at the conference, until a quiet thought interrupted my one-sided conversation with God. It suggested that my contribution to the conference was to hold that baby, standing in the darkened back of the auditorium behind the little resource table—allowing another woman to take the stage in a breathtaking performance used by God to reach a roomful of hearts and minds with the gospel.

I've returned to this lesson repeatedly when I start to wonder whether my small contributions, my small kindnesses have any eternal value. It's so true that God exalts the humble, and he humbles the ones who exalt themselves. I now simply ask God to use me on a daily basis and trust that the size of an act doesn't matter. It's what God does with our obedience that changes the world.

— Julie

— Today's Act of Kindness —

Find a small way to serve someone, and as you
do, pray that God would use it in a big way.

Mass Kindness

He handed the innkeeper two silver coins, telling him, "Take care of this man. If his bill runs higher than this, I'll pay you the next time I'm here."

LUKE 10:35

Tim hatched the idea and shared it with our leaders at church: What if we picked a day to do anonymous acts of kindness in the community? What if we split up all the grocery stores, gas stations, and coffee shops and had people in the church commit to paying for someone else's bill in a synchronized version of the "drive-thru difference"?

After a couple months of planning, the day arrived. We each did our own act of kindness that day, and then we watched with delight as the stories came in fast and furious on the local community's online message board:

> I went to get pizza with my boys. The cashier tells me there was a person in the store right before me who gave a $20 gift card to give to the next person. The person also left a note. Made me tear up. Whoever you are, thank you for putting a smile on people's faces.

> Came to study for a test I have tomorrow, and some kind, unknown person paid $5 toward my coffee purchase and left a card that said, "You are loved." Thank you for being so thoughtful.

> I had a similar experience at the grocery store. The man ahead of me in line gave the cashier a gift card for the next person, which was me. What a wonderful gesture and so much appreciated!

> We had this happen to us today! We received a note at a local restaurant this morning, and some kind person took care of our bill. There were nine of us. It brought tears to my eyes. So amazing.

People marveled at the kindness of the gestures and the handwritten notes left behind, and they speculated as to why so much was done anonymously on the same day. Sandwiched between stories of crime and complaints about neighbors, the stories of kindness received a disproportionate number of likes and shares. Although we are called to give generously, on this day, we felt just as blessed by the recipients' responses as we did by participating in the acts of kindness.

— *Kristin*

— Today's Act of Kindness —

Do the drive-thru difference, either by yourself or with a group of friends, by paying for the person behind you in line at a coffee shop or a store.

The Ring

We want you to know what will happen to the believers who have died so you will not grieve like people who have no hope. For since we believe that Jesus died and was raised to life again, we also believe that when Jesus returns, God will bring back with him the believers who have died.

1 THESSALONIANS 4:13-14

My sister Katrina was always a stylish woman. She loved to dress well and wear jewelry. In fact, she designed a ring early on in her marriage that became a favorite, one she wore every day. A few months after she died, my mom got a gift from my brother-in-law. Inside the box was the ring. Tears were shed as my mom put the ring on her own finger, a beautiful reminder of my sister.

But that wasn't the end of the story: my sister Kristin and I each received a box from my dad, and inside each box was a ring, just like Katrina's. We found out then that after she died, my dad went back to the same jeweler my sister had used, and he bought the last three stones the jeweler had of the type that was used in my sister's ring. He then had three more rings made—two for my sister and me, and the third to give to Katrina's daughter on her eighteenth birthday.

At this point we were all crying. We were so touched that my dad would think of such a thoughtful and kind gift to give my sister and me. I wear the ring to this day, a constant reminder of the sister I lost and the dad who has helped to keep her memory alive.

Do you have a special way to remember a loved one who has died? Maybe it's not a particular item, but a place that brings back memories, or a certain scent that reminds you of that person. No matter what helps us when we are lonely or missing someone, we can take comfort in knowing that Scripture promises us the hope of seeing our loved ones again. It's an incredible reminder of God's kindness for us as we grieve.

— Kendra

— Today's Act of Kindness —

Think of someone you know who is grieving, and do something to commemorate their lost loved one.

Don't Be a Fool

Fools vent their anger, but the wise quietly hold it back.
PROVERBS 29:11

"Seriously, I want to punch her in the nose!" I growled to my husband after recounting the ongoing saga involving a woman who was making my friend's life absolutely miserable.

Aaron, my even-keeled rock, looked me straight in the eye and informed me in a slightly stern yet mild tone that I would *not* be punching anyone in the nose.

Sighing, I slumped back in our living room chair. Of course he was right. As the conversation paused, words that had been spoken to me years ago in a similar situation floated to mind: *"Don't take up an offense on someone else's behalf."*

It is exceptionally hard to refuse to be offended. Yet, to be an effective Christian, it is absolutely vital that we take our anger and offense to God in prayer instead of letting them twist us up inside.

All those years ago, in that other situation, I heeded my friend's wise words. I refused to take up anger and instead started praying. As I turned to God, he preserved relationships that I was tempted to destroy. In the ensuing years, I've found myself sowing seeds of faith, of kindness, and of God into these women's lives. I've marveled at the work God has done through me in women I once harbored anger against, allowing it to burn slow and hot. Keeping a rein on my temper and keeping my lips zipped allows me now to reach out in kindness and love during difficult circumstances when people most need to see the love of Christ in action.

Because I'd experienced God's redemptive work when I refused to let anger have its way, I trusted him in this current situation. I committed to not be foolish and vent my anger but instead to quietly and fervently take my anger to God in prayer. I reminded myself to leash my tongue and guard my mouth, to speak no words I might later regret. And I looked forward to the day when I could reflect on this time and recognize the redemptive fingerprints of God at work in the midst of tension.

— Julie

— Today's Act of Kindness —

The next time you're tempted to hold a grudge against someone, practice quietly taking your anger to God in prayer. Then forgive that person and release your anger.

Outward Appearances

*The LORD doesn't see things the way you see them. People judge
by outward appearance, but the LORD looks at the heart.*

1 SAMUEL 16:7

If I'm honest, he's the kind of man I might eye a little warily now that I'm an adult. But as a child, I was unfazed by the grizzled old man with longish hair and tattoos who lived next door. After all, he had a soft spot for my sisters and me. Whenever our ragtag group appeared at his doorstep in the summer months, he would disappear inside the depths of his little house and emerge with a handful of ice-cream treats for us to eat outside.

As a child, I didn't know that he was a veteran, or that the service he performed for his country left him a little broken, a little changed. I didn't know that he coped by abusing alcohol, that he struggled to hold a job, or that he was alone. I only knew him for the way his face brightened when he saw us knocking at his door, how he kindly gave us treats that we ate in the heat of the summer sun, until they melted and ran down the sides of our grubby hands.

He could have sent us away, could have ignored our small knocks on the door. Instead, he took the time to think of us when he walked to the grocery store, stocking up on ice-cream treats the same way you would toothpaste or toilet paper.

Now, as an adult myself, I'm reminded that our appearance may reflect us, but it does not define us. Although people judge by outward appearances, God looks at the heart. It's true that a pretty exterior may be a mask that hides the ugliness inside. But it's just as true that a weathered appearance can easily cover a heart that tries, a person who loves—someone who is simply waiting for another person to knock on their door.

— *Kristin*

— Today's Act of Kindness —

Reach out to someone whose appearance intimidates you
a little. Share a kind word or a sweet treat with them.

Conversations about Kindness

*Direct your children onto the right path, and when
they are older, they will not leave it.*
PROVERBS 22:6

Settling into the hour-long drive to my parents' house with my children a captive audience in the backseat, I struck up a family conversation on kindness given and received. As we each took a turn sharing a story of doing something (or receiving something) kind, Aaron and I found ourselves entering into an unexpectedly wonderful conversation with our children.

After each story, we asked questions about how certain actions made others feel or added a comment that helped our children shift their perspective on a situation. We talked about successes and failures, what could have been done differently or better, what perhaps should not have been done at all.

My daughter shared a story of approaching a slightly older girl who was feeling excluded and inviting her to join her friend group. Her insights into the situation revealed maturity and reminded me that we often underestimate the ability of our children to understand concepts that adults sometimes struggle with. As she told her story, she explained that it doesn't matter if you are smaller, younger, or older than someone—you can still be kind and help them. How often do we, as adults, disqualify ourselves from reaching out to another because we believe we are too young, are too old, or don't have the right skill set? Hearing truth in the words of an eight-year-old is humbling, indeed.

As we expanded upon the stories that poured out, the conversation naturally turned to the biblical mandate on the lives of those who follow Christ to treat others kindly. We shared more about our own childhood experiences and how we show kindness now. We encouraged our children to think for themselves and to keep their eyes, ears, and hearts open for opportunities to show the love of Christ to those around them. It's the showing and the sharing with our children what lived-out Christianity means in our own lives that sets them up for a lifetime of walking with God.

— Julie

— Today's Act of Kindness —

Don't forget to include the children in your life in living out
intentional kindness. Share stories with them, encourage
them, and guide them in their own kindness journey.

It's Already Forgotten

Peter came to him and asked, "Lord, how often should I forgive someone who sins against me? Seven times?" "No, not seven times," Jesus replied, "but seventy times seven!"

MATTHEW 18:21-22

I knew immediately, even as the bitter words were coming out of my mouth, that I was wrong. We'd been traveling for several days with extended family, and as we made our last stop on our journey home, I broke. Angry words directed at my father-in-law spewed out before I'd even taken the time to think them through. We drove the rest of the way home in silence, my heart heavy with the words I'd just said.

As the first few days went by and we settled back in at home, I could not shake from my mind the unkind things I had said to Dave. I knew that I was wrong and that I needed to apologize. I hesitantly picked up the phone and called him, and my mother-in-law answered in her normal, cheery voice. I weakly asked if Dave was around and if I could talk to him for a minute.

"Sure!" She responded, and I heard her call for him.

He picked up the phone, and immediately I burst into tears. As he waited for my crying to subside, I tried to speak through my tears. "I'm so sorry for what I said," I blurted out between sobs. "It wasn't right of me to say those things."

He interrupted me with his usual calm voice. "It's all right," he stated. "I'd already forgiven you. It's been forgotten."

I let out the long sigh I'd been holding inside for days, as the weight of guilt lifted off my shoulders. His words sank deep into my heart, offering relief and a mended relationship with him.

Dave's words are ones that I have thought of often when I'm faced with some unkindness or slight toward me. Even in Scripture we see Peter asking Jesus how often we must forgive someone. Jesus' reply is very telling: "Seventy times seven!" I understand this to mean that we are to offer forgiveness as often as someone needs it. Although challenging, it's a kindness we are not only encouraged but commanded to offer to others. Whom do you need to offer forgiveness to today?

— Kendra

— Today's Act of Kindness —

Forgive someone that you have been holding a grudge against, even if they have not asked for it.

Good Intentions

It is sin to know what you ought to do and then not do it.

JAMES 4:17

I have an embarrassing confession to make: sometimes my good intentions suffer from a lack of follow-through. Like the time I bought baby items for a local diaper drive and then didn't drop them off in time, or the time I picked out flowers online to send to a grieving daughter and forgot to finish the purchase, or the time I sent my nephew his graduation card nine months late. I am full of good ideas, but I will be the first to admit—to my chagrin and my husband's everlasting frustration—that sometimes I just forget to do things.

One year, I had the idea of doing something in conjunction with my oldest daughter's birthday. There's a birthday-box program where you can send shoeboxes filled with certain items to children in poverty-stricken communities around the country. I looked it up online, contacted the program, bought the items, and put the boxes together with my children. And then those four bright boxes sat in my office for more than a year. I never took them to the post office, never sent them. Kindness fail.

Oh, sure, I eventually used one of the boxes to take cookies to our new neighbors, and I gave away the toys and books to children in need locally. But my original intention was never realized, much to my shame.

I know that people say it's the thought that counts, but in my mind that's a little disingenuous. It lets people like me feel good about unfulfilled intentions. Scripture says that it is a sin to know what you ought to do and then not do it. I can understand this, because in my mind, my failure has nothing to do with what I'm giving away and everything to do with the attitude of my own heart. When I don't follow through, I'm not considering someone else and their needs, but my own priorities. I will never be perfect, but I can commit to prayerfully trying to do better and make good on my intentions one at a time.

— *Kristin*

— Today's Act of Kindness —

Think of one kind act you've been meaning to do but have yet to follow through on. Stop procrastinating and do it.

What It Means to Be Blessed

When someone has been given much, much will be required in return; and when someone has been entrusted with much, even more will be required.

LUKE 12:48

A few days ago, I found myself engaged in a deep conversation with my daughter about what it means to be blessed. We spoke of Queen Esther, the woman whose stunning beauty put her in the king's palace at the precise moment necessary to save her people from slaughter because of her deep faith and courage to speak up when the time was right. Turning to the New Testament, we discussed the scriptural concept that significant responsibility accompanies the resources, talents, and gifts God has given us. The greater our gifts, the greater our responsibility to use those gifts to further God's Kingdom.

Those were the words bouncing around in my head a few days later as I read about unthinkably young girls being raped by rebel soldiers halfway around the world. And those were the words that pounded in tandem with my rapidly beating heart as I read of minor girls being sex-trafficked in the heart of my own community.

If you are a woman and a citizen of the United States, then you are a part of the tiny percentage of women who have more freedom, more power, and more of a voice than any other group of women in the history of the world. You and I are among the most blessed of any generation of women *ever.*

In light of these historical and global perspectives on blessing, the real question is this: since we have received and been entrusted with much in the way of freedoms and resources, what is required of us in return? What is our obligation to our sisters half a world (or three blocks) away who have no voice, whose bodies and souls are being mistreated in indescribable ways?

What are we called to do, in this moment, with our great blessing of freedom, of voice, of financial resources? Friends, we are the Esthers in this story and of this time. We must show the same courage and faith to speak up, to stand up, to step up at such a time as this.

— *Julie*

— Today's Act of Kindness —

Choose one way to help victims of sex trafficking.
You could volunteer with a local organization that
fights trafficking or make a purchase from a company
that employs women who have been victims.

Inclusive Kindness

Jesus replied, "'You must love the LORD your God with all your heart, all your soul, and all your mind.' This is the first and greatest commandment. A second is equally important: 'Love your neighbor as yourself.'"

MATTHEW 22:37-39

When I first met my good friend Myndee, I honestly was a bit bothered by her. It wasn't that she wasn't kind—in my mind, she was a little *too* kind. As part of a leadership team we were on together at a local church, Myndee was constantly assessing our programs to make sure the women who didn't grow up in church or who might be far from God would still be comfortable being a part of our groups. She wanted all women to feel welcome.

I don't know why exactly this bothered me so much, especially since it's a really good intention. Maybe it's simply that I'd never been part of a group that truly considered what those outside the church might think or feel if they came to our group, so this was a brand-new concept for me. But over the years I have come to not only appreciate but deeply value my friend's constant sensitivity to those who may be far from God, struggling with their faith, or even wondering if they believe in God at all. She does all this without compromising what she believes, and she speaks truth while wrapping it completely in love. This enables her to implement Jesus' command to love God and then love others, no strings attached.

Have you ever been part of a community that welcomed others in, even those who were searching? Maybe you're part of one now. Even if not, we can each create a safe place of community for those who have questions about faith, who are trying to find God's love and grace. Jesus said that the second greatest command, next to loving God, is showing love to our neighbor, and he puts no parameters on *who* our neighbor is. Whether it's opening our homes, inviting others to be a part of a group, or just showing kindness to coworkers, we can all be inclusive.

— *Kendra*

— *Today's Act of Kindness* —

Include someone who may be far from God or
just in need of some kindness at work, at church,
or in another community you're a part of.

The Kindness of Time

Teach us to realize the brevity of life, so that we may grow in wisdom.
PSALM 90:12

My father-in-law, Al, was forty-eight when my husband was born, and he retired from his career at United Airlines during Tim's childhood in Colorado. My husband was always an athlete who loved to play football and baseball, but the joke in his family is that for as many practices and games as Tim attended, Al attended one more.

On the day of that practice, Tim was home sick but had a science project due. His science teacher happened to be one of his football coaches, so Al dropped off the project while the coaches and team were on the field practicing. Even though Tim wasn't there, Al decided he might as well stay and finish watching the practice. Afterward, they had a good chuckle over the fact that Dad had gone to a practice his son hadn't been able to make it to.

Even now, one thing that makes my husband smile is recalling the way his father made it a point to attend every practice and game that Tim had in high school. Every single one. In fact, Tim says that he felt like his Dad was part of the team, standing on the sidelines with the players. When Tim went on to play football at a college in another state, Al flew across the country or drove hours in a rental car to attend his games. Al's subtle, quiet support of his son's passion for sports was an outward expression of the love he had for his child. The kindness of Al's attention wasn't showy, but steady—his effort to show up and be present more meaningful than any expensive gift could ever be.

It probably wasn't always convenient for Al to sacrifice his time, but his faithful showing up was one of the highlights of Tim's childhood. Recently we found out that Al's own father, who died when he was in high school, had made it a point to do the very same thing for Al when he was a child. His father's early passing left an indelible impression on him of the importance of time and the brevity of this life. Years later, the legacy of time was one that he passed along to his son, who now makes it a point to show that same kindness and sacrifice to our daughters.

— Kristin

— Today's Act of Kindness —

Give someone the gift of your time.

September

Strong Will, Strong Love

Love must be sincere.
ROMANS 12:9, NIV

I had to laugh just a little when the e-mail arrived in my in-box. Elise's teacher, who is very kind and by all accounts an excellent teacher, had this to say about our daughter's first few days in kindergarten: "She is a free spirit and strong willed. How does she respond to you at home when you ask her to do something she really doesn't want to do?"

To be honest, we're still working on it. After all, this is the child who swung from the curtains in her bedroom and pulled her bookshelf out of the drywall by climbing it one too many times. She's our negotiator, the one who likes to wheedle her way into going out for frozen yogurt. She's full of "great" ideas, and she often asks me if I'm feeling generous. She's independent and fearless, and she likes to have the last word.

But as a mother, there are times when I find it difficult to know how to parent such a strong girl. One night we had a particularly challenging bedtime. Finally, my husband reached his limit and had to go downstairs for a break.

Without pause or hesitation, Elise announced, "I still love Papa."

Even in the midst of our chaos, I stopped in amazement. This child, this strong girl who runs with the boys at the bus stop and beats her mom to the mailbox—she loves fearlessly, unashamedly, unconditionally. She loves without reserve, regardless of whether someone else earns or deserves it. Couldn't we all use a little dose of that kind of fearlessness?

Kindness requires our *unreserved* love. Because, to be honest, God's kindness to us is an undeserved love. Elise's love is sincere, and it shows. Just like love, our kindness should not be conditional, dependent on our circumstances. Instead it should be a reflex, a choice we've turned into a habit. Our love should be sincere, and our impulse to show kindness even more so.

As a mom, I want to raise strong girls with strong hearts who become strong women who change the world. For as small as Elise is, she's already changing mine.

— *Kristin*

— Today's Act of Kindness —

Go out of your way to love someone who is difficult to love.

Mean Girls

Anyone who belongs to Christ has become a new person.
The old life is gone; a new life has begun!
2 CORINTHIANS 5:17

"You are just such a kind person!"

A neighbor recently paid me this compliment, and although I appreciate her kind words, I know that in reality, it's not always true.

Just the other day I was talking with someone about her high school reunion, and I said that I'd love to attend my next one since I've never been to any of them, but I would probably need to make some apologies while there. Although I had many friends, got good grades, and was involved in a lot of activities in high school, the truth is that there were several people that I was not very kind to. Looking back now, many of the "mean girl" things that I said or did had much more to do with the insecurities I felt deep inside than with the people I gossiped about. Even so, this doesn't excuse the behavior. I've been a mean girl at times, and making it right with those I've harmed is something I long to do.

I know that God's forgiveness is complete and that he no longer sees me as the mean girl of my youth. I imagine we all have moments that we are not proud of or that we are even a bit embarrassed to admit to, as I do. Unkind words we've spoken to others, actions we've taken that we later regret—these things can color our view of the past, but they don't have to disqualify us from sharing kindness today.

Learning to be kind is a bit of a process, but it's one we all need to go through. The Bible tells us that anyone who belongs to Christ has become a new person, that our old lives are totally gone, and that we've been given new lives. This means we don't have to let old memories or thoughts from our past hinder our ability to share kindness today. We all deserve a fresh start.

— *Kendra*

— Today's Act of Kindness —

Seek forgiveness from someone you may have hurt in the past.

Uninhibited Joy

Shout with joy to the LORD, all the earth! Worship the LORD with gladness.
Come before him, singing with joy. Acknowledge that the LORD is God! He
made us, and we are his. We are his people, the sheep of his pasture.
PSALM 100:1-3

My daughter's small voice swelled as it rose above those around her in worship one Sunday. I watched as she poured her whole self into the effort—mind, body, and spirit. Her voice wasn't perfectly tuned, and yet it was a joyful noise from her heart—and it was beautiful.

The general state of womanhood often weighs heavy on my heart, and when it does, my mind returns repeatedly to that memory of my daughter. When did I, my friends, and most women I know first lose that uninhibited joy? When did we start being unkind to ourselves, quietly berating ourselves for our imperfections, hiding pieces of ourselves away?

This attitude isn't just about raising our voices in song—it seeps into every area of our lives. We hesitate to do things that might reveal imperfection or weakness, whether physical, mental, or simply imagined. We hide those things that we deem to be less than perfect about ourselves.

What would it look like if every Christian woman stopped declining and instead jumped into the fray of life with God-inspired fearlessness? What example would we paint for all other women if our love for Christ overshadowed our self-doubt? If we lived with that kind of joy, think of the unspoken witness we could be for Christ's transforming love, and think of the energy we would have to live lives of exceptional, intentional kindness.

I think we would turn this world upside down if every Christian woman set aside her insecurities and embraced opportunities and adventures with both hands. We expend energy when we belittle and hide parts of ourselves, energy that is far better spent on looking outward, reaching toward other women in intentional kindness.

I can't help but imagine what that joy would feel like in our hearts and what it would look like to those watching. This is who God intended us to be—fearless, joyful noisemakers who worship and serve and seek God with all our hearts, minds, and strength.

— Julie

— Today's Act of Kindness —

Prayerfully consider how you may need to stop
hiding your faith and your joy in Christ.

The Hands and Feet of Jesus

Give all your worries and cares to God, for he cares about you.
1 PETER 5:7

I tucked the note and gift card into the envelope, then penned the address of a stranger on the front. Earlier that week, I had seen a message posted on a Facebook group I'm in about how a woman and her family were struggling financially and looking for ways to economize. I reached out to ask for her address and sent her some encouragement.

The gesture didn't take much time on my part, but the note I received in return was worth any small sacrifice. It read, "I got your card. It came at a perfect time. I had actually spent quite a while that morning lying in my bed crying, not knowing how we were going to get through this. I came down the stairs, and the envelope was sitting right on the counter. I opened it, and I felt God clearly saying, 'How could you think I wouldn't take care of you? What makes you think I've changed after all this time?' Thanks for being such a great friend—even though we've never met!"

Her words resonated with me because there have been many days that I've felt the same way: days when it seems easier to cry about a situation and wonder how I'll survive it than to actually face it; days when I feel like I'm failing and God doesn't care enough to help. Yet it's often in the moments when I feel most desperate that I am reminded of God's faithfulness—like the day I was struggling to successfully parent one of my strong-willed children, only to receive a message from a friend admitting her own struggle with her child and asking for resources to help her remain calm in these difficult moments. I'm not always calm with my own daughter, but I appreciated the sweet sentiment and expression of solidarity arriving on a day I needed to hear it.

Scripture tells us that we can give all our worries to God, but sometimes when we're in the midst of a hardship, it can be difficult to believe he truly does care. Yet I've found that when I choose to trust him, he often uses others to encourage me to keep doing so. We can be that encouragement for others too; we just have to keep our eyes open for opportunities.

— Kristin

— Today's Act of Kindness —

Send a note to someone who is struggling
and in need of encouragement.

Cards for Cops

A cheerful look brings joy to the heart; good news makes for good health.
PROVERBS 15:30

When a police officer was shot and killed in the line of duty in a small community near ours, it rattled many people. He left behind four young children. It was senseless and heartbreaking, and it left me casting about for a way to show support.

That next Sunday, I hauled out blank paper and markers, and I had an age-appropriate conversation with the older kids in my Sunday school class about what it means to live in a community and what it means to support those who risk their lives to protect ours.

As we engaged in a wide-ranging conversation about ways to show the love of Christ to others, we drew and colored and wrote out prayers for the officers in that small-town police department. Kids never fail to impress me with their grasp of intentional kindness and their natural generosity. Hearing them talk about how we can make Jesus tangible for people around us was fascinating and heartwarming.

When class was over, I couldn't help but get a bit misty-eyed as I read the heartfelt words of thanks and blessing my class had spilled out on paper. Their pictures were funny and sweet, and some of them were completely random, but their words conveyed the lesson I had hoped they would soak in during our art and conversation time. They prayed for, thanked, and wrote blessings for the officers and their families. Their words were more than I could have hoped for when the idea occurred to me early that morning.

I bundled up the papers and attached a little note explaining that the cards were from a Sunday school class, put them into a manila envelope, said a prayer over the package, and put it in the mail.

The people in our community who serve others—law enforcement officers, nurses, EMTs, firefighters, teachers, social workers, and the list goes on—pour out their hearts and are often in need of some cheer and good news in the midst of working in difficult situations. Do you know someone in one of these roles who could use some encouragement?

— *Julie*

— Today's Act of Kindness —

Write out a prayer for the first responders in your community, and then send it to them.

A Simple Celebration

Be happy with those who are happy.
ROMANS 12:15

My parents were married at a local courthouse by the justice of the peace, right after they graduated college. In between court cases, with lawyers waiting for the next trial, my parents took the monumental step of marriage with just a few close friends in attendance at the sacred event.

My mom's best friend, Mary, was one of the witnesses for the wedding. When Mary's mother heard about the small ceremony they'd planned, she invited them over afterward for a time of celebration and toasting their marriage. She said that they "simply had to do something to celebrate the occasion," especially because the couple's families could not be there to celebrate with them. It really touched my mom that someone else cared enough to celebrate with them and wanted to be a part of their happy day. It may have been a simple act of kindness for my mom's friend and her family to initiate and then perform, but it impacted my mom greatly, creating warm memories from that day that she still remembers fondly, as well as memories of the friends who helped to make it so special.

We are encouraged to be happy with those who are happy. Celebrating alongside of someone who is experiencing a joyous occasion or success is just as important as offering support as they go through a challenging or difficult time in life. We don't even have to be particularly close to someone to celebrate with them. Sending a note of congratulations to a coworker who got a promotion, sending flowers to a neighbor who's getting married, or attending the graduation party of someone who goes to your church—these are all ways to show kindness. Letting someone know that we are happy for them or proud of them is one way to show God's love. People will remember what we did to join in their happy times just as much as they will remember our support during their hard times.

— *Kendra*

— Today's Act of Kindness —

Take time to celebrate someone's success or happy occasion.

I Once Was Blind

Suppose you see a brother or sister who has no food or clothing, and you say, "Good-bye and have a good day; stay warm and eat well" — but then you don't give that person any food or clothing. What good does that do? So you see, faith by itself isn't enough. Unless it produces good deeds, it is dead and useless.

JAMES 2:15-17

Each week when I went to drop off my daughter in the toddler room at church, the childcare worker would be there, arms outstretched. My daughter Noelle was a bit of a mama's girl and was usually stuck to my side, so this worker was ready each week for a quick handoff so I could race out of the room.

One day, an e-mail arrived in my in-box. Whenever there's a need in our church community—if someone has a new baby, is ill, or has experienced grief—it gets filtered and sent out through the Hope Team. This time, the request was for meals for a family whose little boy was experiencing unexplained seizures. I didn't recognize the family's name, but since we are part of such a large church community, that is often the case. I signed up for a date on the meal schedule, then thought little more of it.

The next week, as I rang the doorbell to deliver my baked ziti and salad, the person who opened the screen door was none other than the volunteer from my daughter's classroom. She thanked me for the meal, and we chatted for a bit about her son's challenges, but the whole time I felt ashamed. How could I have seen her each week and never realized the struggles she was facing? At church, all I had noticed was my own clingy child, my own desire to escape so I could sit in peace in the adult service. I hadn't asked the volunteer about her own children—I hadn't even asked her name.

Kindness often requires us to look beyond ourselves. It does little good for us to express our faith and yet be blind to the needs of those around us. In fact, Scripture says our faith is useless if we don't meet others' needs with our actions. Whose needs might you be blind to?

— *Kristin*

— Today's Act of Kindness —

Listen closely to those around you, ask questions, and investigate. As you hear of needs you were previously blind to, step up to meet those needs.

When God's Plans Are Bigger

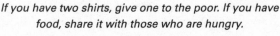

If you have two shirts, give one to the poor. If you have food, share it with those who are hungry.

LUKE 3:11

As my best girlfriends and I gathered together for a rare girls' dinner out, we decided ahead of time to leave our waitress with a gift as a random act of kindness—a coffee gift card and a delicious-smelling candle in a cute pink gift bag. It wasn't until our *male* server arrived that we realized we had seriously miscalculated. As he left, we sheepishly leaned in close to discuss our girlie gift and prayerfully decided to let the evening play out.

Before our waiter could return to take our order, another server approached us with an apology on her lips, telling us that our waiter had left due to a family emergency and that she would be taking over for him.

After she left with our orders, we began going through our purses. We pulled out cash, grocery and gas gift cards, and anything else we thought could be helpful to our first server and stuffed all of it into our pretty pink gift bag. As we finished dinner, we gave the gift to our replacement server and told her that we'd come to the restaurant that night with the intention of leaving a fun gift for our waitress. We apologized for the pink bag and the half-used grocery gift cards, but told her that our hearts went out to our waiter in his emergency and asked if she would please make sure he received our gift. Teary eyed, she agreed.

As we approached the front to pay, the manager intercepted us, thanking us for our gift and promising to give it to our waiter. Before we walked out the door, we stopped and prayed as a group for the man and for his family. We thanked God for the sacred opportunity to be his hands and feet by sharing what we had—even when it didn't turn out as we had expected.

— *Julie*

— Today's Act of Kindness —

Carry an extra grocery or gas gift card in your wallet
to give away when an opportunity arises.

Connected Community

Always be eager to practice hospitality.
ROMANS 12:13

My family and I showed up to a barbecue late in the afternoon, the hot summer sun still beating down. As we strolled up the driveway with a fruit salad in hand, we watched as kids launched themselves down the Slip 'N Slide in the backyard overlooking the lake while adults sat on the deck or in the shade and chatted. Besides our hosts and one other couple, we didn't know anyone. But actually, that was the point.

A few weeks earlier, one of the couples had sent us this message:

This weekend we had a couple over for dinner. They have kids the same age as all of ours; we had a great time together. You guys would like them. This got me thinking: next time we all hang out we should each invite one family that isn't plugged into community with similar-aged kids as a way to connect our families to each other.

I have to admit that I'm kind of a hermit, and though I enjoy meeting new people, I feel more comfortable hanging out with "my" friends. I know that Scripture tells us to always be eager to practice hospitality, but if I'm honest, I'm not always eager to invite strangers into my home. Yet I remember how Tim and I prayed for good friends when we moved into our community and how glad we were to develop strong, lifelong friendships with other couples. So, after thinking about it a bit more and agreeing it was a good idea, we decided to have a barbecue and all invite folks who attended our church but weren't necessarily plugged into a group of friends yet.

Later, to my homebody shame, I realized it had been a marvelous night. It was fun to chat with the other moms about babies and summer plans, the kids played well together, and we all left happy and exhausted.

— *Kristin*

— Today's Act of Kindness —

Be on the lookout for someone who may not be plugged into
a community, then take one step toward including them.

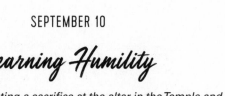

Learning Humility

If you are presenting a sacrifice at the altar in the Temple and you suddenly remember that someone has something against you, leave your sacrifice there at the altar. Go and be reconciled to that person. Then come and offer your sacrifice to God.

MATTHEW 5:23-24

I went off to college at seventeen. I was a somewhat proud, opinionated kid who didn't like to admit when I was wrong. I was also blessed to have some good friends, a few of whom I lived with during the four years of school.

One time I got angry with my roommate, who was also a friend, over the petty issue of dirty dishes that had been left in the sink and whose turn it was to clean them. I said some not-very-nice words and left the house.

I called my mom later, telling her what I had done and how I felt bad about the way I'd treated my friend. I ended by saying, "It's just really hard for me to go back and apologize." Expecting my mother to sympathize with me on how hard apologizing is, I was surprised when she responded by saying, "Well, you had better get over that, because there is no way you will ever be able to have relationships or a marriage without being able to say, 'I'm sorry.'"

I hung up, struck by my usually soft-spoken mother's strong response to my inability to ask for forgiveness. Realizing she was right, I went home and apologized to my friend, repairing our relationship.

Although apologizing for angry words over dishes may seem to be a trivial thing, it's a lesson I still remember to this day. Being willing to admit when we are wrong and to seek forgiveness from others, regardless of the situation, is a necessary part of any close relationship. Scripture tells us that if we have sinned against someone else, we must find a way to reconcile with that person before we can be reconciled to God. It takes much more strength and humility to apologize than it does to blow something off or ignore a person or issue. It's not always easy to do, but the results are worth it.

— Kendra

— Today's Act of Kindness —

Think of someone you have put off apologizing to. Pray that God would give you the words to say, and then apologize.

Becoming Peacemakers

God blesses those who work for peace, for they
will be called the children of God.
MATTHEW 5:9

As unfair accusations spewed across the universe of Facebook, I longed to hit back, to defend myself and others emphatically in that very public forum. Finding my words taken out of context, my motives questioned, and my good intentions misunderstood by others and then twisted into something hurtful and mean was devastating. Then when a multitude of others suddenly joined in the public fray, taking sides without knowing all the facts and without knowing the parties involved, half a dozen people on both sides of the issue were left bleeding blue Facebook blood.

I prayed about how to respond—and when I say "pray," I mean I mostly sobbed. I trusted God to know my heart in those moments, because words utterly failed me. While I prayed, I held still. I zipped my lips, took no action, and sought out God.

After the initial swirl of emotion settled, I sensed a deep hurt beneath the anger of some of the others involved, and after three days had passed, I was sure of my next steps. I sent private messages to several people, extending gentle invitations to meet for coffee so I could give them a sincere apology for hurts caused unintentionally.

Whom did I find sitting across from me over coffee? Vulnerable, wounded people who are *good and decent and kind.* People who shared fears of their own as we spoke, whose tear-stained cheeks revealed that we are far more alike than we are different. Our meetings ended in hugs and promises to join forces, to be united rather than divided—and that has held true. I've found allies instead of foes, and we've worked hard together on projects to make our community a stronger, better place.

Being a peacemaker is not for the faint of heart. It involves facing conflict head on, laying down our own rights, and searching beneath angry words for a raw wound and a tender heart. God blesses those who seek peace, who do the quiet, difficult work of reconciliation. When we choose to be peacemakers, we are called the children of God.

— *Julie*

— Today's Act of Kindness —

The next time you find yourself in a heated debate, choose to intentionally look through conflict to see the hurt the other person is carrying. Respond to that hurt instead of fueling the fire.

Meal-Centered Giving

Whether you eat or drink, or whatever you do, do it all for the glory of God.
1 CORINTHIANS 10:31

One year while on a weekend vacation to Chicago, my husband and I saw a homeless man on a downtown street corner. Tim never likes to miss an opportunity to bless a homeless person, especially when he has a spare minute, so he stopped to chat with the man. We happened to be on our way to eat famous Chicago-style hot dogs, so as they finished chatting, my husband told the gentleman, "I'll be right back, and I'll come back with some food."

After we had finished our own meal, Tim purchased a bag of food and a drink for the man, and we stopped by on our way back to our hotel. Amazed, all the man could do was repeat, "You came back. They never come back. People say they will, and they don't."

Food is such an essential part of everyday life that it's easy to think of kind acts that revolve around providing food for others. From the meals made for people struggling with medical illnesses or emergencies or for families adjusting to life with a new baby, to cookies given to welcome new neighbors or to thank school staff members, it's often food-centered giving that can mean the most. Food is practical and comforting and needed, yet oftentimes all it requires is for us to make the effort to double our own dinner, purchase a little extra, or have something as simple as pizza or sandwiches delivered. Recalling someone else and their own needs and then showing up can go a long way toward meeting their needs.

The man's gratitude over something as small but as essential to life as a simple meal—even a meal of hot dogs and fries—was a good reminder that we don't always have to do big or extravagant things to show kindness. But whatever we do, we need to do it all for the glory of God and for the purpose of showing his love.

— *Kristin*

— Today's Act of Kindness —

Buy a meal for someone else.

The Knowing Woman

We are God's masterpiece. He has created us anew in Christ Jesus,
so we can do the good things he planned for us long ago.
EPHESIANS 2:10

Even in my earliest memories, I remember how my father called me by the meaning of my name just as often as he called me by my actual name. Anytime I came to him with something new I had learned or some new truth I had gained from the Bible, my dad would say, "Well of course you have that insight, you're the knowing woman." Many of the things I told him as a child probably weren't *that* insightful, but he never failed to remind me that I was "the knowing woman," speaking to the person he knew I could be, not just the one I was at the time.

As I've grown to be an adult, I can now see that this affirmation—my dad constantly telling me who I was—has had a significant impact on my life, the things that I do, and the way I think about myself. I have confidence that I may not otherwise have gained because of my dad's continual calling me a wise person.

As I look at my own children and other people I'm in close relationship with, I'm reminded of how valuable it is to speak what we believe is true about a person, even if it is not fully evident in someone's character or actions at the time. Scripture reminds us that we are God's masterpiece, created anew in Christ Jesus, so we can do the good things he planned for us. Because of this truth, we have the ability to call attention to others' strengths and gifts, even while they are still being developed—just as my dad did for me. We can extend kindness, encouragement, and vision, not just by looking at someone's current character, but by speaking what we believe God will develop in them in the future.

— Kendra

— Today's Act of Kindness —

Encourage someone by pointing out a character
trait you see God developing in them.

A Warm Home

When a stranger sojourns with you in your land, you shall not do
him wrong. You shall treat the stranger who sojourns with you as
the native among you, and you shall love him as yourself.

LEVITICUS 19:33-34, ESV

My friend was asked to open her home to an international guest for two nights, and she gladly extended an invitation. The guest was simply folded into her family, and they spent that first afternoon and evening doing the mundane, normal stuff involved with living in an American household with a couple of children and pets.

After the youngsters were tucked in for the night, the conversation turned to the guest's hometown and her stay in this country. They began to explore the commonalities and differences in their cultures from opposite sides of the globe.

At some point during the conversation, my friend's guest paused, and with a sweep of her hand, gesturing widely across the room, she said, "This is what I want someday." She went on to explain that she has stayed at fancier homes during her travels, but, as she explained, "Your home is *warm*."

Warm. The word was spoken with a bit of a wistful sigh and was clearly a compliment. "Warm" looks beyond the surface trappings and focuses on the condition of the heart of the house, on the intangibles that make up a family and a home. What the guest identified as "warm" was my friend's very intentional kindness through hospitality and her family's heart for welcoming others into their life. They seek to reveal Christ, in part, through opening their home and their hearts.

In a culture that is often fixated on outward appearances and on keeping up with the Joneses, God cares far more about the internal cultivation of our hearts. Good things ultimately flow from hearts that are overflowing with goodness. The condition of our hearts will leak out in the most unexpected places and ways—so strongly that strangers from distant lands may sense it, even if they cannot put precise words to what they see. It is the reflection of the hearts of those who love and follow God that results in a home that is *warm*.

— Julie

— Today's Act of Kindness —

Take the temperature of your home as a
reflection of the hearts within it. If it is not warm,
prayerfully consider what needs to change.

Kindness to Strangers

Don't forget to show hospitality to strangers.
HEBREWS 13:2

Not long ago there was a story on my local news channel detailing a tragic loss a father experienced when his house burned down and five of his children died in the fire. As I sat listening to the account, I had tears running down my cheeks. I could only imagine what he must have been feeling as a parent.

My daughter happened to be walking through the room at the time, and as she stopped to ask me what was the matter, I hesitated to tell her just for a moment. It can be hard to face the pain in this world, and often I want to shield my kids from the realities of life. But instead, on this night, I decided to tell my daughter about what I had just heard. We then talked about what we could do to help. The first thing we did was pray. Next my daughter decided to make a card, and we sent it along with a donation to a fund that had been set up in the family's name to help cover the costs of the funerals and the items that had been lost in the fire. Even though we didn't know this man personally, and we never did find out exactly what happened to him or the rest of his family, it felt good to help someone in their time of need.

We hear stories on a daily basis of others who are suffering in our neighborhoods, in our cities, and around the world. Rather than telling us to tune it all out, Scripture encourages us to show hospitality to strangers. We may not be able to help with everything, but if we'll be sensitive to follow God's leading, we'll find ourselves in places where we can reach out to strangers and show them the kindness and love of Jesus.

Have you ever sent encouragement or support to a stranger? Or maybe you've received kindness from someone that you did not personally know. How blessed did you feel that someone you'd never even met would reach out in support?

— *Kendra*

— Today's Act of Kindness —

Offer encouragement or support to a stranger who
is going through a challenging circumstance.

Killer Shoes

His peace will guard your hearts and minds as you live in Christ Jesus.
PHILIPPIANS 4:7

In the past, whenever I was intimidated, I would reach for my "killer shoes." My killer shoes were not particularly expensive, but they were magnificent. They reminded me of a Monet painting, with creams and pinks and rose colors all blending together. Unfortunately, they hurt my feet like no other pair of shoes I've ever owned.

The last time I wore those heels, I was headed to a charity event that required formal attire. I was more than a little insecure about the evening, so I slipped on those heels, hoping they would give me confidence and courage.

I did fine at the event, but my feet throbbed so badly by the end of the evening that they continued to hurt most of the next day. As I later reflected on the event and on my shoes, I realized that I had intentionally chosen something painful to hide my insecurity that evening instead of taking it to God in prayer.

I know I'm not the only one who does this. I see people hiding their insecurities behind all sorts of things—food, exercise, makeup, or trendy clothes. While none of these things are inherently bad, they become bad when we won't or can't choose something different—when we hide behind them in an effort to quiet our fears rather than taking our fears directly to God.

But we cannot be effective Christians when we are making unhealthy choices to cover up our insecurities instead of seeking God. We cannot live lives of long-term intentional kindness when we are seeking security and peace outside of Christ. We don't have the energy to invest in intentional kindness while we are busy hiding our insecurities. It's not healthy, and while we may succeed for a while, eventually we'll pay the price in our health, in our relationships, or in our spiritual walk. When we give our fears to God in prayer, he guards our hearts and minds, giving us his peace—which is far better than the temporary relief we feel when we hide.

Seeking God's peace and overcoming insecurity is a journey, not a destination, and I find that I still need to remind myself to seek God first when I am feeling insecure, even long after my killer shoes were sent to Goodwill.

— Julie

— Today's Act of Kindness —

Consider whether insecurity is holding you back from
expressing kindness to others. Take your insecurity to God
and confess it to a friend. Then do an act of bold kindness.

Monday-Morning Blues

Kind words are like honey—sweet to the soul and healthy for the body.
PROVERBS 16:24

Depressed after a weekend of carousing with friends, Tim, who was in his early twenties at the time, sat hunched over on a bench outside the airport, looking blearily into space as he waited to be picked up. A young man sat down next to him, and they fell into casual conversation in the way that strangers do while traveling.

As they chatted, the stranger noted Tim's red eyes and haggard appearance. He admitted that he used to have a lot of weekends like the one Tim had just had, but that he'd become a Christian and lived his life differently now. His tone was sympathetic and nonjudgmental, and the conversation continued on from there to other topics.

Before too long, the stranger's ride arrived. He swung his bag into the car, then turned back to Tim and stuck out his hand. "I'm praying for you," he said, shaking Tim's hand firmly. And then, with a wave, he left.

Years later, the conversation is still vivid in my husband's memory. Tim wasn't a Christian at the time, but on that day, the man's offer to pray for him hit him deep inside. Maybe if Tim had heard these words the day before or the day after, they wouldn't have mattered as much. But in the midst of his Monday-morning depression, when life felt like it was at an all-time low, the man's words came at just the right time. Scripture says that kind words are like honey, and in that situation, Tim felt them like a balm for his soul.

It's easy to put off kind acts or words. Life is busy, and there always seem to be reasons or excuses to delay. Yet you never know when the words you've been nudged to say or the act you've felt led to do might be exactly what someone needs that very day.

— *Kristin*

— Today's Act of Kindness —

Take a minute to pray about who you can
encourage, then do it without delay.

SEPTEMBER 18

Simple Solutions

If someone has enough money to live well and sees a brother or sister in need but shows no compassion—how can God's love be in that person? Dear children, let's not merely say that we love each other; let us show the truth by our actions.

1 JOHN 3:17-18

A few years ago I read a blog post about children in Africa whose feet were infected with jiggers—tiny fleas that burrow into the skin, causing pain and difficulty walking, and in extreme cases, requiring amputation or causing death. But there was a very simple solution to this problem: shoes. If the children just had shoes to wear, they would not get jiggers so easily.

After reading about this problem, I found an organization called Sole Hope that is helping to resolve the issue. Sole Hope provides advocates with instructions on how to make shoe kits, and the kits are then sent over to Uganda, where they are put together to make shoes for kids. The organization even makes it a fun group activity, encouraging people to have shoe-cutting parties.

That is exactly what my family and I decided to do one late summer day. We sent out invitations, welcomed others to join us, set up tables and food and drinks in our garage, and made a party out of cutting out shoe parts for children overseas. My kids still remember and talk about the experience—such a practical and tangible way to show kindness to others.

Is there an organization or cause that is dear to your heart? Have you thought about how you could gather a group to support this organization, or have you asked what their needs are and prayed for them? Scripture asks us a question that cuts straight to the motivation of our hearts: if we have money to live, and we see someone else in need and show no compassion, how can God's love be in us? We are called to love others with our actions, not just by the things that we say.

— *Kendra*

— Today's Act of Kindness —

Do some research on tangible ways you can help an organization that is supporting others, and then take action to assist this cause.

Bless a Teacher

Don't look out only for your own interests, but take an interest in others, too.
PHILIPPIANS 2:4

At the beginning of every school year, Grandma Connie—Aaron's mom—sends a note of encouragement containing a check to pass on to each of our children's homeroom teachers. A retired teacher herself, she knows teachers often spend their own money to outfit their classrooms and to provide extras for their students.

As we approached the last week of school, my son's teacher sent out invitations to a kindergarten graduation ceremony for her class. Connie joined my husband and me as parents and grandparents packed into the classroom to watch the ceremony.

Our chairs were set up in a semicircle around the perimeter of the classroom. The students, each wearing a graduation cap made from construction paper and decorated during art class, proudly walked a red carpet (made of paper) to take a turn standing on a small podium before receiving a hug and a diploma from Ms. Zhoung and posing for a photo.

Ms. Zhoung's love for her students—which had been evident in so many ways all year long—was never more clear than in how special she made each of them (and their parents) feel on their last day of kindergarten.

After the last student graduated, we were invited to stay for celebratory cake and juice. As Ms. Zhoung greeted our family, she thanked Connie for the check and told her that she had used it to purchase the large sheet cake celebrating her students' graduation.

Connie's act of kindness was used so beautifully by Ms. Zhoung, a woman who encouraged, corrected, and showered love on my son and his classmates all year long. She poured herself into her students, and her use of the money for their graduation cake was a beautiful reminder of the multiplied good that happens when we intentionally look out for the interests of others.

— Julie

— Today's Act of Kindness —

Do something unexpectedly kind for a teacher.

274

When Tuna Shows God's Love

The faithful love of the LORD never ends! His mercies never cease.
Great is his faithfulness; his mercies begin afresh each morning.
LAMENTATIONS 3:22-23

My friend Carol's husband, Geary, had just lost his job. With three kids and no money saved up in the midst of the economically depressed 1980s, it was a bad situation for their family.

One day, Carol felt the Lord prompting her to make a grocery list and place it on her windowsill. "I put the list on the window, and we just prayed," she said. A day later, a woman Carol had never met—someone who had heard about Carol's family from a mutual acquaintance—showed up at her house with a carload of groceries.

"I was blown away. I'd never experienced anything like that," she told me years later, still marveling over the situation. "She left, and as I began to unload the groceries, I got to the two cans of Chicken of the Sea tuna, and I *knew*. Shocked, I went and got my list—everything that was on there was in these bags. We didn't even know what we were doing, and God was faithful to us." More than thirty years later, Carol can still recall how she felt, how one woman's kind act of bringing groceries to her in a time of need was additional evidence that God loved and cared for her family in their distress.

We know that the faithful love of the Lord never ends and his mercies never cease, yet when difficulties arise, it can be easy to become fearful or question whether God truly does love us. As Carol found, if we continue to trust God, we will see that he is faithful to us. It's not that life will suddenly become easy or we won't experience hardship, but we will learn to rest easy in the comfort of his love, trusting that he will provide. The kindness and provision we experience in the hard times of our own lives is something we can then turn and bless others with later on.

How has God been faithful to you?

— Kristin

— Today's Act of Kindness —

Encourage someone else with your story of God's faithfulness.

We All Need a Boost

Trust in the LORD with all your heart; do not depend on your own understanding. Seek his will in all you do, and he will show you which path to take.

PROVERBS 3:5-6

"Mom, give me a little boost," my son instructed me. He was newly off training wheels and had just graduated to a bigger bike. I steered my bike closer, bent down, and gripped his handlebar as he put his feet on the pedals and then took off down the bike path.

I didn't physically boost him—I didn't need to. He was doing it all on his own—the balancing, the surging forward under his own strength. He just needed me next to him for a little boost of confidence.

We'd been playing this game for about two weeks. At first, he did need me. He needed that push forward while he balanced and figured out the pedals. But then I'd been gradually holding less tightly and pushing less forcefully, until this day when I simply balanced the bike during his takeoffs.

At one pause during our seven-mile ride, he turned to me as he stood there straddling his bike and said, "Mom, I'm okay. I can do it." And he did. He started off pretty wobbly, but he soon straightened out and began steadily pedaling.

As we pedaled along the trail that meandered through woods and fields and over swollen streams, I contemplated those last few "boosts" and realized that I'm not so very different from the four-year-old biking superstar pedaling furiously just ahead of me.

A life of intentional kindness can sometimes be extremely difficult. It requires me to trust God in the bigger picture when what I'm seeing makes no sense, and it often requires me to step outside of my comfort zone. The beautiful thing is that I don't walk this journey alone, and I can (and should) turn to prayer when I'm in over my head and in need of a boost. We are promised that we can trust God, even when we can't clearly understand what he is accomplishing in a situation, and that God will show us the path to take.

— Julie

— Today's Act of Kindness —

Find a passage of Scripture that boosts your confidence, then write it down and tuck it in a place you can see often. Share it with a friend who also needs a boost.

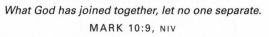

Celebrating Together

What God has joined together, let no one separate.
MARK 10:9, NIV

Two couples in our friend group had big anniversaries on the horizon—one couple had been married for fifteen years, the other twenty. We decided to take a trip together to celebrate.

About a week before the trip, I secretly messaged family members of both couples to find out what kind of wedding cakes and flowers they'd had at their weddings. Unbeknownst to our friends, I called a local baker from the town we'd be traveling to and ordered two small cakes, mini replicas of their wedding cakes. When we arrived, my friend Julie (who was also in on the secret fun) stopped at a local florist and picked up flowers of the types used in their wedding bouquets.

On our second night together we celebrated their anniversaries with a favorite meal, wedding flowers on the table, and the cakes for dessert. We spoke an anniversary blessing and prayer over each couple, intentionally taking the time to celebrate and remember God's goodness toward them. We all shed a few happy tears as we reminisced about all the life that had happened over the past several years.

Relationships are worth celebrating, whether they are marriages, friendships, or family ties. Rejoicing over the life that is shared together is important, especially when things get hard, life gets busy, and people mess up or make mistakes. Scripture tells us that what God has joined together, no one should separate, reminding us of our commitment and the value God places on faithful relationships.

Do you know a couple who have been married for a long time, have walked through difficulties together, and are still able to love each other with kindness and respect? Let's not forget to celebrate with them! It's important to not only pray for others who are walking through a hard time but to also pray for and bless those who are doing well.

— *Kendra*

— Today's Act of Kindness —

Send a message or a note of encouragement, prayer,
and blessing to someone who is married.

The Cat Ladies

Two people are better off than one, for they can help each other succeed.
ECCLESIASTES 4:9

I left the house for a mere three hours on a Friday to take my kids to the pool, and by the time I returned, Tim had temporarily adopted a stray cat. A bag of food, a dish of milk, and a kitty bed were strewn across the surface of our deck, while the newly named Kit Kat lay contentedly purring in Tim's lap.

Kit Kat had appeared in our yard a few weeks before, and we hadn't thought much of it, assuming she was one of the neighbors' cats. But on this day, noticing that her ribs were showing and she clearly wasn't being looked after, Tim decided to feed and care for the affectionate cat while trying to locate the owner via social media.

After a few days, Tim had bonded with Kit Kat. Whenever he returned home from working out in the morning, she'd be just outside the door waiting for him to feed her. When he returned from work later in the day, she'd be waiting for him again. Yet he continued to look for an alternative home for her, knowing that although I love cats, I wasn't ready to have one in the house permanently with a newborn to take care of as well.

Whenever Tim had questions about taking care of her or figuring out a long-term placement, he'd post in an online message board. A group of women that Tim affectionately dubbed his "cat ladies" would always respond with knowledge and encouragement, thanking him for his concern for Kit Kat, and he both appreciated and relied on their expertise.

Before too long, Tim took Kit Kat to the vet for a checkup and was shocked to learn that she was pregnant. He turned to his cat ladies for advice, and they once again offered suggestions and resources. Eventually, Kit Kat went to a good home when one of the veterinary technicians decided to adopt her.

Despite the fact that Tim was a stranger, the women on the message board took the time to share their knowledge with him. Ecclesiastes says that two people are better than one, because they can help each other. Tim's willingness to ask for help—and the kindness of strangers to provide it—paid off.

— *Kristin*

— Today's Act of Kindness —

Help someone with a project or problem they are puzzled by.

Finding Peace

*I am leaving you with a gift—peace of mind and heart. And the peace
I give is a gift the world cannot give. So don't be troubled or afraid.*

JOHN 14:27

"When is the last time you stopped and actually spent time thanking God for what happened on the cross?"

The question caught me a bit off guard, although it shouldn't have. My husband and I were visiting a church in the middle of a last-minute, unplanned, child-free, two-night dash to the North Shore of Lake Superior, and this question was simply a riff on the theme I'd been contemplating all weekend. It had been a busy year, and my husband and I found ourselves juggling more than we'd intended to. We'd been craving a break, a reprieve, a little time to breathe deeply and just pause.

If you've never been, the North Shore area of Lake Superior is rugged and majestic, and it can also be a little dangerous. Hiking through towering conifer forests and up rocky outcroppings, observers can perch far above rivers carved deep into rocky canyons. And everywhere you look, you cannot help but notice both gorgeous vistas and beautiful, tiny details.

It is when we stop running through our regular days, lift up our eyes, and simply soak in the moment that we find God. And it is when we stop and thank God for the work of the cross that everything else gets put back into perspective. That intentional pause in the midst of busy days allows us to remember that we exist for a reason, that we have a calling on our lives that goes beyond our own well-being, and that Christ, in his kindness, promises us his peace in the midst of any storm so that we need not be fearful or anxious.

When you take the time to slow down, soak in the beauty of God's creation, and rest in his peace—a gift the world cannot give—then you will find the energy and the ability to pour out kindness into the lives of those around you.

— Julie

— Today's Act of Kindness —

Visit a place that reminds you of the bigness of God,
and spend quiet time reflecting on what it means
to have the gift of his peace in your life. Then find a
way to pass that peace on to someone else.

When Kindness Offers Comfort

He comforts us in all our troubles so that we can comfort others. When they are troubled, we will be able to give them the same comfort God has given us.

2 CORINTHIANS 1:4

My sister passed away while I was in my first year of graduate school. My program was small, with only forty people in our group, so we knew each other quite well. When Katrina was in the hospital, close to death, I contacted one of my professors who was an expert in children's mental health. I asked her the best way to have my niece and nephew—who were only six and four at the time—see and say good-bye to their mother. She immediately responded by offering me kindness and support, while also giving me suggestions on the best way to help my grieving family members.

Her words and wisdom were a lifeline to me during what was one of the most difficult times in my life. Weeks later, when I returned to class, I was offered hugs and condolences by my classmates and professor. As we began to discuss our final projects that would be due soon, my classmate Jackie politely interrupted, suggesting to the professor that I should be given a "free pass" from the assignment because of all that I was going through. My professor turned toward me with compassion in her eyes and silently nodded agreement as everyone else voiced affirmation of my friend's suggestion. A weight lifted off my shoulders as tears slipped down my cheeks, and I looked around at my classmates, so thankful for this group of supporters I was privileged to be a part of.

We don't always notice or can't always see the heavy burden someone else may be carrying in life. Sometimes people may be dealing with a mental illness, a physical illness, or a challenging family situation. The Bible reminds us that we've been comforted by God so that we can give out the very same comfort to others when they are in need. Pray that God would give you the sensitivity to notice when someone is deeply burdened. Who in your life needs some kindness through comforting words today?

— Kendra

— Today's Act of Kindness —

Listen and offer compassion and comfort to someone who may be carrying a heavy burden in their life.

A Conversation with a Teacher

He heals the brokenhearted and bandages their wounds.
PSALM 147:3

I gripped the phone tightly in my hand, willing myself not to cry. It was just two weeks into the school year, and my daughter's teacher had called to update me on her progress and talk about some challenges she was having in school.

I tried to respond to her questions and comments in calm, measured tones, but eventually I felt myself crack, tears running down my face as I listened to her words, feeling each one like a blow to my heart.

Finally she paused. I took a deep breath for composure, and my voice wavered a bit from my tears as I tried to respond. I could hear the care and concern in her voice when she said, "Kristin, let me tell you something: I have a daughter who learns *just like yours* does. For years, I felt guilty because I am a teacher and I still didn't know how exactly to help her learn best. And you know what? She is an adult now and is doing great. Your daughter will, too; she will figure things out and be just fine."

"Thank you," I said, too choked up to say more. In that moment, I felt a burden lifted from my heart. Yes, our family had some challenges ahead of us that we'd need to work through. But who doesn't?

My daughter's teacher certainly wasn't required to tell me anything about her personal life or her own child's struggle. Although we had met once before in person, she wasn't a close friend or confidante. Yet her willingness to admit her own struggle spoke volumes to me in a way that little else could have in that moment.

Sometimes when we are brokenhearted over a challenge, all we need is for someone to say, "Yes, me too." It's okay to admit our heartache or our brokenness and let ourselves be healed by the love of God and the love of others in the process.

— *Kristin*

— Today's Act of Kindness —

Allow yourself to be vulnerable with someone you know who is struggling. Share a "Yes, me too" moment to encourage them.

Kindness Isn't Safe

Let us run with endurance the race God has set before us.
HEBREWS 12:1

Safety. Left to my own devices, I would build a life around that word. The notions of comfort, predictability, and consistency are what I gravitate toward. While that type of life may sound incredibly boring to the adrenaline junkies out there, it sounds soothing and perfect to this risk-averse scaredy-cat.

These past few years I've found myself standing near the edge of my safe little bubble more and more frequently—confronted with invitations placing me just beyond my comfort zone, facing situations that make me distinctly unsettled, unsure, and most definitely nervous.

As I prayerfully consider and then accept each invitation, it is always done with sweaty palms, butterflies in my stomach, and a hesitating step or three. I don't like uncertainty. I don't like the unknown. I don't like being out of control. But I *love* my Savior, and I've come to learn that when I'm following his invitation, he will catch my step off the cliff.

Jesus isn't safe. He never was. His time on earth was spent turning the religious leaders of that day upside down and inside out. He was constantly doing the unexpected, hanging out with those considered unworthy, unclean, unremarkable. And he hasn't changed. He invites us to do the same, especially when it comes to incorporating kindness into our lives.

Anyone can be kind to people they already like, people who look like them, believe like them, act like them. But what happens when Jesus calls us to be kind to those who have been unkind to us, who look nothing like us, who come from far-flung countries with vastly different beliefs? That's when kindness can be scary and intimidating and make you feel extremely vulnerable.

While I *really* don't like doing scary things, I love finding Jesus standing on the edges of my comfort zone inviting me (and anyone who is willing to say yes) to take that next big step. More than anything, I want to run my individual faith race with endurance, with trust, and with the right attitude.

— *Julie*

— *Today's Act of Kindness* —

Do an act of kindness that is outside of your comfort zone.

Giving Our Best

Whatever is good and perfect is a gift coming down to us from God our Father, who created all the lights in the heavens.

JAMES 1:17

Over the years I've had the privilege of collecting items for numerous charity events. I am always pleasantly surprised by the generosity of others. Most people give such nice things with such kindness, and it is always encouraging and uplifting to witness.

But there is also always a portion—a small portion—of donations that are less than great. In fact, if I'm honest, they're awful. Now, I am not talking about an old sweater that was once loved but doesn't fit anymore or that's just not trendy. I'm talking about things like used makeup, soiled bedsheets, half-used bottles of lotion, stained or hole-riddled clothing—all items I've seen donated. Things that really should just be thrown into the trash.

Although this is not the bulk of donations received, could I put out a gentle reminder to us all? Give the good stuff. Don't donate things that really should just be thrown away. I tell this to my kids all the time: we want to give people our best, not our worst.

I recently heard from a friend who wanted to donate items to an event for single moms in her area. Instead of just looking in her closet or asking close friends, she called several local retailers asking if they would be willing to donate new clothes. A couple of the stores agreed, and my friend said it was fun dropping off items that still had new tags on them. I love that sometimes kindness is purely practical and other times kindness is extravagant.

Putting ourselves in the shoes of the person receiving the gift or donation is one way to gauge whether or not what we're giving is appropriate. Asking ourselves, *What would I really like to receive?* can help us to navigate our giving. We know that anything good or perfect is a gift that comes from our Father in heaven, so let's be sure to pass on the goodness and kindness that God has gifted to us. Let's give the good stuff.

— Kendra

— Today's Act of Kindness —

Donate something that you'd consider to be the "good stuff" to a person or a local organization that could use it.

Three Weeks in the NICU

I am giving you a new commandment: Love each other.
Just as I have loved you, you should love each other.
JOHN 13:34

My oldest daughter arrived six weeks early, two weeks after I went into preterm labor and was put on bed rest at home. Although I am profoundly grateful for the care we received during the extra time we spent in the hospital postbirth, I'll be honest in saying that spending time in the NICU was exhausting. Seeing my tiny five-pound baby in the layette, surrounded by beeping machines, felt scary. It was a part of motherhood that I hadn't even thought I might experience, as the many hours I spent in chairs at her bedside were a far cry from the cozy scene at home I had imagined. Most of my daughter's three weeks in the NICU were spent developing her sucking skills, and she and I cried many tears together in those days until she figured it out.

Through the hardship, though, our time in the NICU gave my husband and me an appreciation for what other parents with premature babies experience, and the encouragement we received while there made such a difference for our spirits. From the ornament the nurses made with our daughter's footprints stamped on it, to the wrapped gift given to us by the March of Dimes, to the kind words the NICU's volunteer "grandma" spoke to us, each small action made us feel loved and made our time there more bearable.

Years later, the words from John about loving each other just as Christ has loved us resonated for Tim and me when the opportunity arose to help a mom on bed rest. She was expecting twins and was put on bed rest in the hospital for more than a month. We were able to drop off a meal and a care package to her husband and other children, who were still at home. Later, after her premies were born, we bought tiny outfits for them and popped those in the mail too, to let them know they remained in our thoughts and prayers. Even though our daughter's early days were hard and exhausting, I'm so grateful for our own experience and what it taught us about loving others in such a uniquely difficult situation.

— *Kristin*

— Today's Act of Kindness —

Reach out to help someone who is in the hospital
or who is struggling with a medical issue.

There's Room for Everyone

We know that God causes everything to work together for the good of those who love God and are called according to his purpose for them.

ROMANS 8:28

As writers and bloggers, we've had the privilege of meeting other women who like to write and blog as well. We've found wonderful communities, online and in person, of like-minded women who encourage and lift up one another on their writing journeys. When one fellow writer recently asked if I'd be willing to promote and be a reference for her upcoming book, my response was, "Of course, it'd be an honor!" I was so excited to be a part of her team. Though I also had a dream of writing a book someday, I wasn't at all jealous that she'd achieved the same dream sooner than I had. I was, simply, genuinely happy for her.

I once heard a speaker say that jealousy is not of God, and if he's given you a dream, you don't need to be jealous of what he's called anyone else to be doing. He has enough dreams to go around for everyone! This speaker's words birthed a motto that I've come to live by: there's room at the top for everyone. If we are pursuing all that God has for us, we can be confident that he knows our hearts' desires, that he has placed them within us for a reason, and that he will bring them to fruition in his timing. Believing this frees me up to be outward focused and able to cheer on and extend kindness to those around me as they pursue all that God has for them.

Do you believe that God has a plan for everyone's life? If so, there is no reason to be jealous of others. God promises to work everything together for our good and according to the purposes that he has for us. We can trust his plan for our lives, just as we can trust his plans for those around us.

— *Kendra*

— Today's Act of Kindness —

Think of a person whom you are sometimes tempted to be jealous of. Pray for that person and find a way you can encourage them on their journey.

October

We're All in This Together

Blessed are the peacemakers, for they will be called children of God.
MATTHEW 5:9, NIV

There has been some racial tension in my community over the past few years. We've had an influx of refugees to our town, and it has created some misunderstanding and fear about those who are different from us. After a serious incident happened at our mall, a flurry of social media buzz began. Many posts were rooted in negativity and fear, demanding that something be done, that our leaders step up and take some kind of action. As I sat with a heavy heart for my community, I began to pray and ask God, *How can I be a person of peace in this situation? What can I do, however small, to make things better?*

Kyle and I sat down with our children later that night and told them what had happened. We explained that the actions of the person who caused the incident were wrong, but that does not mean we blame or hate an entire group of people because of what he did. Each person is an individual, we said, and we don't need to be afraid because God will never leave us. We then talked about how we could be peacemakers in our community and in our schools.

Countless times in the Bible we are told not to fear. This can be challenging when faced with all that is happening in our world, but we always have a choice about what we will do and how we will act and respond. Jesus said that the peacemakers are blessed, for they are the children of God. This sounds simple enough, until we are faced with a situation that is anything but peaceful. As Christians, what should be our response to the hate and discord that is so often around us? I believe that we should follow Jesus' example. We speak words of love and not hate. We speak words of hope and life, not death. We respond in kindness, even when it is undeserved. We remember that we all have a part to play. We remember that we are all in this together.

— Kendra

— Today's Act of Kindness —

Think of a way, either in word or action, that you
can bring some peace to your community.

Rescued

When God's people are in need, be ready to help them.
ROMANS 12:13

It was a regular weeknight as I sat in the parents' viewing area of tae kwon do class. My phone rang, and seeing that it was my husband, I stepped outside into the chilly autumn air to take the call. The news was bad. The car was dead, and he was stranded on the side of the road two hundred miles from home.

Calling my dear friend Jenny, I explained the situation and asked if one of her older kids could handle a midweek babysitting gig so I could go pick up my husband. Halfway through our conversation, I heard her husband's voice quietly in the background before she repeated his offer to me—Carl was willing to go get Aaron so I could keep the kids on task and on track and get them into bed at a normal time.

After more discussion, that was the plan we finally settled on. With a grateful heart, I laughed and asked Jenny whether or not she realized that she and Carl have had to come to my rescue on more than one occasion when Aaron has been out of town.

Our families' lives have been so intertwined over these last dozen years that I sometimes forget we are not actual blood relatives. Because Aaron and I do not have family close by, they have become our default family—the ones we call when we are locked out, the ones who give up an evening to retrieve my hubby from halfway across Minnesota, the ones we can spend a whole week with—two couples and seven kids crammed in a small house near the shores of Lake Superior—and still leave as good friends.

For years we've quietly come to one another's rescue, in big things and small, with no scores kept. Just as we are encouraged to do in Scripture, we've met one another's needs during times of discouragement or times of hardship, or even when we've just needed an extra set of hands to move something heavy. While I cannot speak for Jenny and Carl, living in community with fellow Christians who go out of their way to help us during those hard moments in life has been life-giving to our spirits and our faith.

— Julie

— Today's Act of Kindness —

Watch for an opportunity to "rescue"
someone in your church this week.

Project Pencil

*Let's not get tired of doing what is good. At just the right time
we will reap a harvest of blessing if we don't give up.*
GALATIANS 6:9

"This is my fourteenth one!" someone crowed from the other side of the room. Looking up from my list of school supplies, I glanced over to see a preteen boy smiling widely, arms raised as he held a black-and-white backpack aloft.

We were in the midst of packing up items for Project Pencil, an initiative that provides school supplies for local kids in need. Not-yet-filled backpacks rested on the floor, while tables set up around the room were stacked with an organized jumble of notebooks, pencils, markers, crayons, folders, and much more. Kids and adults strolled around the room, eyes focused on school supply lists and hands busy adding items to backpacks they carried.

Within an hour of my arrival, the project was completed. As I walked to the front door with the event organizer, she marveled over how quickly the sorting had gone and how much she's seen the project grow. In the past three years, they went from coordinating forty backpacks for area children to more than three hundred backpacks.

"It's kind of my baby," the organizer said, biting her lip as though it were a confession. As I assured her that it was a great project, valued by the community and something others were happy to help with, I also wondered why she felt the need to speak almost apologetically about her passion for such a project. As we said our good-byes and I headed into the parking lot, I thought about how easy it can be to get discouraged when it comes to helping others. The needs can be so great and the workers so few. We might even think that our efforts are small, something to feel apologetic about. Yet God reminds us not to get tired of doing what is good, because at just the right time we will reap a harvest of blessing. This woman—*one* person—now impacts more than three hundred local children each year.

What acts of kindness have you felt nudged to do that appear to be small on the surface? One person's actions can snowball and make a huge difference.

— *Kristin*

— Today's Act of Kindness —

Donate school supplies or choose another
"small" action to be faithful in.

International Kindness

She extends a helping hand to the poor and opens her arms to the needy.
PROVERBS 31:20

Not long ago, Julie, Kristin, and I received an e-mail from Work of Worth, an organization that works with artisans from developing countries and sells their products for a fair price in the United States and other countries. They wondered if we would want to curate a collection of goods with their organization. Of course we were completely honored to do so, wanting to support women around the world who are trying to make a living to provide for their families.

We picked out our favorite items, wrote blog posts about them, and then shared on social media about this outstanding organization (in addition to purchasing many items ourselves). We continue to support Work of Worth and regularly let our readers know of the wonderful things they and other organizations like them are doing around the world to help people provide for themselves and their families.

There are so many great organizations doing good around the world. Kindness is not something we want to do just at home—we should also take care of those we do not know and may never meet. Whether it's through buying jewelry, clothing, shoes, or scarves, we can all find a way to support such organizations. They are providing work and a way for many to make a living, enabling them to care for their families even while living in communities that have very few resources or jobs available. Kindness can certainly start at home, but it should not end there.

Scripture encourages us that a virtuous woman will extend a helping hand to the poor and will open her arms to the needy. We all have the opportunity to do this in a variety of ways. What causes around the world concern you most? Who could you help today through prayer or financial support, perhaps through a donation or by purchasing a fair-trade item?

— *Kendra*

— Today's Act of Kindness —

Find an organization that is doing something to
further a cause or issue that you are passionate
about, and see how you can get involved.

Revealing God's Love

*Let your good deeds shine out for all to see, so that
everyone will praise your heavenly Father.*
MATTHEW 5:16

It started with a quick e-mail from Doug, a work acquaintance, letting me know that our former coworker's father had died. He was wondering whether I knew how she was doing. Before I knew it, I'd e-mailed a response asking Doug if he and his family would like to join forces in putting together a gift basket for her. After sending out the invitation, I paused for a moment, wondering why I was inviting someone I didn't know very well to participate in a gift that I intuitively knew had God's hand on it.

I later learned that, at the same moment when I was stealthily leaving the gift basket on our colleague's doorstep, she was telling her husband that every last one of her friends had abandoned her during her father's long illness, and that no one remained. Also unbeknownst to me was how perfectly God put together every gift in that basket, so much so that it sang out to her the existence of God and his love for his children.

She called me late that night to share the details of how perfectly God had orchestrated that gift, and she asked me to share it all with Doug. While I promised to generally share her thanks with Doug, I told her that the details were her story to share, not mine, and that he needed to hear from her how God had used us to encourage her.

Considering all that transpired, I realized that God used that gift in three ways. First, to reveal his love to a woman who was feeling abandoned. Second, to reveal himself to Doug and his family through the incredible timing and the perfectly chosen items in the gift basket. Third, as a reminder to me of the importance of inviting others to journey alongside of me, especially when I feel the nudging of God. It seemed so simple, providing a tangible gift of love for someone walking through a hard time, but God used this good deed to proclaim his glory and love and to draw others to praise him.

— *Julie*

— Today's Act of Kindness —

Invite someone you do not know well to join you in a kind act.

No Cash Allowed

You must each decide in your heart how much to give.
And don't give reluctantly or in response to pressure.
"For God loves a person who gives cheerfully."

2 CORINTHIANS 9:7

It was a weekday, and every line at Costco's card-only gas station was several cars long. My husband, Tim, was in between work appointments, pumping gas into his Jeep Grand Cherokee, when he overheard a man in the lane next to him pleading with the gas station attendant to let him pay for his gas with cash, as he had forgotten a card. The attendant declined, reiterating the card-only policy.

Making a quick decision, Tim walked over and interrupted their disagreement by sticking his debit card into the card slot at the man's gas pump. "Here you go," he told the man.

"Are you serious?" the man asked him, mouth open with astonishment. "I can pay you cash!"

Tim told him no thanks, that it was okay, then returned to his car and drove away from the gas station.

No matter whether we're giving of our time, talent, or treasure, each act of kindness we do is an intentional decision. Some of those decisions are made on the spur of the moment, and others are made over time, requiring us to use planning and intention. Yet however we choose to give and whomever we choose to bless, one of the only requirements God has for us is that we decide *in our own hearts* how much to give. He would much rather have us give cheerfully and sincerely than in response to someone else's urging, or because we feel guilty or think we "have" to give to a certain individual or organization.

In that moment at the gas station, Tim's habit of kindness led him to a spur-of-the-moment decision to bless someone else and to meet a need he didn't plan for and didn't see coming. He didn't feel pressured to give in that moment, but he gave cheerfully and of his own will.

Have you ever felt pressured to give? If so, how did that experience contrast with a time when you gave cheerfully?

— *Kristin*

— Today's Act of Kindness —

Watch for a spur-of-the-moment opportunity
to provide for someone else.

Interrupted

I heard the Lord asking, "Whom should I send as a messenger to this people? Who will go for us?" I said, "Here I am. Send me."
ISAIAH 6:8

As I sat in church one Sunday, my pastor illustrated my preferred way of living with the most beautiful arrow—a perfectly straight black line drawn across the whiteboard. I could easily predict the course of travel, and there were no obstacles in the direction the arrow was pointing. The illustration was, to me, soothing, predictable, safe. His next drawing, I'll admit, made me uncomfortable. It was a curving line that looped and weaved and turned in lazy circles even as it moved forward. It was messy, twisted, and chaotic.

His point was that God most often moves in our lives in twisting, unpredictable ways. Are we okay with allowing him to interrupt our carefully coordinated schedules? Are we willing to set aside our to-do lists, our plans, our agendas for the sake of his plan? Are we willing to be interrupted by God?

As my children and I wait at the bus stop each morning, I've started praying over our days—that we would each learn to feel the quiet nudge of the Holy Spirit and that we would pause whatever we're doing to respond obediently. I pray that we would know that when God asks us to move, he will arrange our lives so that the important things still get done.

I never want to hold so tightly to my preconceived view of my day that I ignore the call of God as he seeks someone to send. I want always to be the woman who raises her hand and says, "Here I am, Lord. Send me!" when I feel that gentle tug on my heart to walk over, to say something, to step into the gap for someone else. I desire to be a woman who welcomes and responds willingly to God's interruptions.

— *Julie*

— *Today's Act of Kindness* —

Ask God to interrupt you, and listen for his invitation
to show kindness in an unexpected way.

A Safe Person

*Always be humble and gentle. Be patient with each other, making
allowance for each other's faults because of your love.*
EPHESIANS 4:2

"Why do you and Julie bicker so much?" Kyle asked me one evening as we were heading home from a dinner with Julie and Aaron.

"We're not bickering so much as we're working out what we think about things," I replied.

As I thought more about his question, I realized the reason for our "bickering" was even deeper than that. Julie is someone I can share thoughts and struggles with, who listens without judgment, and who talks through ideas with me. She loves me like family, and I love her the same way. She is safe, and I trust that she would not hurt me intentionally. As I considered all the things I love and appreciate about Julie, I wondered, *Am I a safe person for others? Am I someone who listens and loves without judgment or fear of rejection?* I certainly hope I am. I may not demonstrate these things perfectly, but they're qualities I want to strive for.

Sometimes it feels like the world is full of people who can be harsh, unforgiving, and cold, making it easy to give in to the negativity that surrounds us. Scripture is quick to remind us that we are always to be humble, gentle, and patient with one another, graciously making allowance for one another's faults and mistakes. This sounds a lot like my friend Julie. This sounds a lot like a safe person who will love people well despite their faults or imperfections. It may not always be easy to love people the way that Jesus asks us to, and at times, showing kindness seems to go against our natural instincts or the way we would really like to treat people. But God's command is very clear, and although we may follow it imperfectly, we should each strive to be a safe person for the people in our lives.

— Kendra

— Today's Act of Kindness —

Look for an opportunity to be a safe person for your family
members, coworkers, or even strangers that you encounter.

Building Bridges

Treat them [foreigners] like native-born Israelites, and love them as you love yourself. Remember that you were once foreigners living in the land of Egypt.

LEVITICUS 19:34

There's an area of the state where I lived for several years that has an increasingly large immigrant and refugee population, many of whom are from the war-torn country of Somalia. In a predominantly white area, this has caused tensions to rise as people confront a culture and religion that is different from their own.

Recently a friend of mine was at a local pharmacy. She overheard a Somali woman at the window next to her having a hard time understanding why her health insurance card didn't cover the whole cost of the medicine she needed. She was short by eleven dollars. The pharmacist asked if she had any money to make up the difference in cost, and the woman said no. The pharmacist then asked if she could return later to pay for the medicine, and she simply shook her head. She looked scared and confused, and my friend thought about how horrible it must be to be in a foreign land, to not really understand the language, to have no money and no transportation.

Moved to action, my friend paid for this woman's prescription. She told me that the pharmacist looked at her with surprise, making my friend think that pay-it-forward actions must not happen very often for Somalis in her community.

The Somali woman, when she understood that her medicine had been paid for, looked relieved and grateful. It made my friend want to bless and take care of others who may not always feel welcome. "We have to make an effort. We have to get better at reaching out. We have to build bridges toward peace," she told me.

It's not always easy to see the ways we can actively work to build bridges in our own communities, but doing so can be as simple as reaching out to someone who differs from you in their social or economic background, culture, or religion. As with so many other acts of kindness, you can start small and see where it leads.

— *Kristin*

— Today's Act of Kindness —

Do an act of kindness for someone who may
not feel welcome in your community.

A Different Kind of Birthday Gift

Give generously to the poor, not grudgingly, for the LORD your God will bless you in everything you do.
DEUTERONOMY 15:10

I was recently visiting with my friend Tammy as she recounted the story of her daughter's ninth birthday. She told me that right before Megan's birthday, they received a World Vision catalog in the mail, filled with ideas for practical things you could donate to others around the world, such as livestock, medical supplies, or school supplies. She suggested to her daughter that instead of presents, they ask party guests to bring a donation. Then they'd take time at the party to pick things out of the catalog to send to people who were in need. Her daughter readily agreed to the idea.

My friend went on to explain, "The day of the party came, and because it was fall, we did a lot of outdoor games like three-legged and gunnysack races. While we were having pizza, the kids sat down in groups. I showed them the catalog and reminded them that instead of gifts, they had brought money with them that we were going to pool together to buy items for families around the world."

While the kids spent time deciding what they would like to give collectively, Tammy and her husband, Troy, announced that they would match the amount that was given. Tammy told me what stood out to her the most was how "amazing it was to watch and listen while the kids talked about the items in the magazine. It was like they got it—they understood that there are folks who are less fortunate or who live very differently than we do, and we can impact them."

We are encouraged to give generously and happily to the poor, not grudgingly. Part of the blessing of this kind of giving is that it can become contagious. I am sure that those children, if asked, would still remember Megan's birthday party where they got to pick out gifts for those in need. Oftentimes, our giving can start a wave of giving in those around us, and showing someone else generosity and kindness on your birthday is a perfect way to do so.

— *Kendra*

— Today's Act of Kindness —

To commemorate your birthday or some other special occasion this year, donate a gift to someone else.

Kindness Isn't Enough

*You must commit yourselves wholeheartedly to these commands that
I am giving you today. Repeat them again and again to your children.
Talk about them when you are at home and when you are on the
road, when you are going to bed and when you are getting up.*

DEUTERONOMY 6:6-7

Pulling into the drive-thru line at the coffee shop, I asked the kids if we should pay for the next car. A chorus of cheers went up from the backseat, with squirming and excited giggles of anticipation as we watched a red sedan pull up into the line. As we paid and drove away, the kids' eyes were glued to the rear window, hoping to catch the magical moment when the driver received the good news.

"Okay, who wants to pray for the woman in the red sedan?" I asked as I glanced into my rearview mirror. Suddenly my rowdy peanut gallery turned suspiciously quiet. When continued silence met my second request for prayer, I recognized a disconnect in my children: they felt the joy of doing the random kind act but were reluctant to bow their heads in prayer for the person we'd just blessed.

It's often easier to buy someone a cup of coffee and check off our good deed for the day than it is to set aside time and energy to pray for that same person. Meeting a temporary physical need frequently requires less of an investment than meeting a spiritual need through intentional prayer.

Living a life of kindness is not about simply performing random acts of kindness for the thrill of it and then continuing on with our lives. The point of living with intentional kindness is to be a physical manifestation of the love of Christ, to tangibly reveal God's love through actions, and to practice our faith on a daily basis.

Realizing that my kids needed to be reminded of what biblical kindness means, we had a conversation about kindness, God, and prayer, and how these things must be intertwined in our lives. As I intentionally guide my kids through what it means to live out their faith, I trust that God will take these conversations and this faith journey my family walks, and tuck it deep into their hearts. My hope is that they will continue to follow this path with God even as adults.

— Julie

— Today's Act of Kindness —

Include a child you know and love in a kind act, and then
talk to them about the meaning of biblical kindness.

Stopped on the Side of the Road

My sheep listen to my voice; I know them, and they follow me.
JOHN 10:27

My friend Steve was driving on a local highway one morning when he saw a man and his beat-up pickup truck stopped along the side of the road. Both looked as though they'd seen hard times. Steve stopped to ask if the man needed help, but the man told him that he'd already called a towing company and planned to have it towed to a local repair shop. Since the situation was under control, Steve drove off and went about his day.

Later that day, Steve ended up driving by the repair shop, as it was located close to his home. He noticed that the same pickup truck he'd encountered that morning was parked outside, and he felt God nudging him to go in and pay for the man's repair. Heeding this prompting, Steve stopped inside the auto-repair office and asked the man behind the counter how much the repair for the truck was going to cost. When Steve admitted that he wasn't the truck's owner, the worker looked a little puzzled, but he obliged and told him the amount. Steve then gave the worker enough cash to cover the cost of the repairs. The worker asked if Steve wanted him to tell the customer who had paid the bill, but Steve declined.

"No thanks," he said. "Just tell him that I hope his week gets better."

There's a passage in the Bible where Jesus says he is the Good Shepherd and his people are the sheep who follow him. "My sheep listen to my voice," he says. If I'm honest, sometimes it's easy to ignore the still, small voice of God. When God nudges us to do something that takes us out of our comfort zone or costs us in some way, it can be harder to heed the call than to ignore it. Yet if we obey, he will work in and through us to bless others.

— *Kristin*

— Today's Act of Kindness —

Ask God to tell you how you should bless others. When you feel nudged, obey.

The Apprentice

Work hard and serve the Lord enthusiastically.
ROMANS 12:11

As a friend and I talked over lunch, our discussion turned to the e-mail request I'd sent out with respect to meeting a local need. The response was generous and immediate—it seemed that everyone just needed a little nudge, needed someone to take charge and make the suggestion. But still, it bothered me that no one else had acted in the first place to take up the cause.

As we talked about the lack of initiative but the enthusiastic response to the invitation, we wrestled with why so many people don't simply act when they see a need instead of waiting to be invited along. Fear of failure, fear that they'll accidentally offend someone—she and I named a variety of thoughts that might cause someone to stand still rather than move toward a need.

The fact of the matter is that Christians are called to movement, not to status quo and complacency. Serving God invariably means serving people, and that calls us to step forward and step up, especially when others are reluctant to do so. We are in apprenticeship—*discipleship*—under Jesus as we learn to live and love according to his example set forth in Scripture.

It's important to understand that apprentices don't learn solely by reading and listening, but also by doing—by mimicking the master's movements, making mistakes, being corrected, and trying again. Electricians do not become masters of the trade by watching videos or reading manuals alone. They learn under the careful tutelage of a professional, in a personal relationship consisting of encouragement and correction. And isn't that the way we learn to serve God—through a personal relationship with Christ? A relationship in which reading Scripture is our vital instruction and in which we are also called to action?

Once we start practicing living out the teachings of Christ, it becomes easier and easier to initiate the e-mail, to be the first voice raised either in petition or defense, to be the first person to reach out a hand. We are called to work hard and serve the Lord enthusiastically, and being the person who steps up first and invites others to follow along is part of that mandate.

— Julie

— Today's Act of Kindness —

When you see a need, invite others to help meet it
instead of being the person invited to join in.

A Daughter's Pictures

God blesses those who mourn, for they will be comforted.
MATTHEW 5:4

The dad of a young teenager from our church died unexpectedly. He was in his thirties, close to my husband's age. As a family, we reached out to offer the girl and her grandparents our condolences.

One day, while visiting their home, Tim noticed that the daughter had tacked up pictures of her dad on the wall. A picture of the two of them on a swing together when she was a little girl, her face filled with joy. One of her as an older child, reaching over to give him a giant kiss on the cheek while he hugged her. A more recent one of the two of them, arms slung around each other's shoulders, smiling faces pointed toward the camera. Tim asked if he could borrow the pictures, and she agreed.

A few months later, he returned them to her for her birthday, with a few important changes: he'd had the photographs professionally matted and framed at a local store, with a plaque underneath the photos engraved with her father's name, date of birth, and date of death. Surprised and pleased, she posed for a picture of herself holding the frame and posted it on social media, thanking Tim for the thoughtful birthday gift.

When someone has experienced loss, it can be hard to know what will comfort them in their grief. It's easy to feel helpless or unequipped to say anything that would be truly meaningful to the person who is mourning. Thankfully, we know that God blesses those who mourn, because he comforts them. It's okay if we don't know exactly what to say, but it can be easy to find things to *do* simply by looking for opportunities. What mattered most to the person who is gone? What matters most to the person who is mourning? Taking the time to extend kindness by doing something that commemorates the grieving person's loved one in a tangible way can offer comfort that lasts long after the action itself has been done. It's a beautiful example of the everlasting comfort God provides for those who mourn.

— *Kristin*

— Today's Act of Kindness —

Commemorate someone's loss in a tangible way.

Hidden Notes

Worry weighs a person down; an encouraging word cheers a person up.
PROVERBS 12:25

"You guys, there's some kind of little note in here!" my friend Savannah heard the young woman in the bathroom stall next to her tell her friends.

Smiling to herself, Savannah knew what the girl would find: a note card with a Bible verse on it, tucked into an envelope along with some chocolate. Earlier that day, she and some friends had purchased the items, assembled the little gifts, and then tucked them all over their large college campus in little nooks and crannies, in out-of-the-way places, and even in bathrooms for other students to find.

The girl's friends wanted her to wait to open the envelope so they could see too, but in her excitement she opened it without them, exclaiming over the note and chocolate. "I guess there really are good people in the world," the girl said as she exited the bathroom.

When Savannah placed the gifts of encouragement anonymously, she wasn't looking for affirmation or credit—she didn't even think she would get to know what happened to them. In fact, she had placed this particular note in the bathroom many hours earlier, and it was happenstance that it got opened while she was in the room.

Yet not only did she get to overhear someone's reaction, but amazingly, her friends reported back to her that even though they'd hidden only sixty treats on a campus of more than sixteen thousand undergrads, they overheard people in their classes talking about the hidden gifts. The girls' motivation to let others know that they are loved by God and by others showed that, as Proverbs notes, an encouraging word really can cheer someone up. Taking time out of their busy schedules to assemble small gifts for strangers and distribute them anonymously was a simple way to quietly show others love. Even actions we perceive as small can have a big impact.

— *Kristin*

— *Today's Act of Kindness* —

Leave an anonymous encouraging note in a bathroom or another out-of-the-way place for someone else to find.

Inexperienced

Don't let anyone think less of you because you are young.
Be an example to all believers in what you say, in the way
you live, in your love, your faith, and your purity.

1 TIMOTHY 4:12

"How could anyone so young really know about grief? You haven't lived enough yet."

The words stung and hung in the air as I sat in a grief training session for new hospice workers. She spoke the words as if to anyone, but I knew she meant them for me. Younger than everyone else in the group by at least twenty years, I had just taken my first social-work job at a local hospice agency.

As I was fresh out of college and inexperienced, my supervisor sent me to a conference to help me feel equipped and prepared to visit people in their homes, and here I sat, shamed for nothing other than my age. Tears welled up in my eyes as I swallowed the lump in my throat, too embarrassed to reply, thinking of my sister who had been given the diagnosis of cancer only a couple of years earlier and all the joys and heartaches we'd known during her treatments.

I went home after the conference, and when she asked, I told my supervisor of my experience. She was shocked that someone could be so ignorant as to believe that a young person would not know what loss was all about, and her indignation over such an insensitive statement gave me the confidence to do my job anyway. She met with me weekly that year, asking how I was doing and offering me invaluable wisdom that I still cherish today.

Sometimes it is easy to disregard the young as too inexperienced or unknowing, but the Bible is clear that we shouldn't think less of anyone just because they are young. Young people can still be an example to all believers in the things they say and in the way they live. It seems that God values the young people who are just starting out their journeys, and so should we. Yes, they may need guidance, but they also may have fresh ideas and insight that we all need to hear.

— Kendra

— Today's Act of Kindness —

Take the time to respectfully listen to the thoughts or
insights of someone who is younger than you.

The Musical Nutcracker

*Give, and you will receive. Your gift will return to you in full—pressed down,
shaken together to make room for more, running over, and poured into
your lap. The amount you give will determine the amount you get back.*

LUKE 6:38

Whisking into the craft store with my kids in tow, I was surprised—but not
shocked—to see Christmas decor filling the shelves and spilling out into the center-
aisle endcaps. Halloween hadn't even passed and already retailers were stocking
merchandise geared toward the Christmas season.

After I completed my mission, my son asked to stop by the nutcrackers. Sighing
internally, I agreed and watched as the kids happily race-walked over to the massive
display of nutcrackers of every size, shape, and style. Upon catching up, I noticed
that they were cradling a musical drummer-boy nutcracker and whispering excitedly to one another about how much their beloved music teacher would love such
a gift.

They turned to me, and their plea slipped out: "Can we please buy this for Ms.
Kruse's Christmas present?" This request was followed by the logic that, because
Ms. Kruse loves nutcrackers and loves music, this musical nutcracker would be the
perfect gift for her.

While I secretly wondered whether their music teacher really loves nutcrackers
so much, I recognized that my children were doing exactly what my husband and
I try to instill in them—thinking thoughtfully and generously of someone else and
then turning those thoughts into tangible actions.

As silly as it felt leaving the store with a musical nutcracker when it was not even
close to Christmas, I was reminded that I need to recognize when God is working
through my kids and encourage that rather than shut it down. Aaron and I want
our kids to be generous, and that means we actively fan the flames of generous,
abundant giving when we see the desire in them. We have witnessed, time and
again, that generous, faithful giving returns to us in ways that are immeasurably
more than what we first gave away, and we want to keep teaching this to our kids.
We cannot outgive God, and he always returns our gifts in full.

— *Julie*

— Today's Act of Kindness —

Look for ways to fan the flames of generosity in a child's life.

The Hope We Have

You have sorrow now, but I will see you again; then you
will rejoice, and no one can rob you of that joy.

JOHN 16:22

"How did you feel when you lost the baby?" My sister's voice was quiet, almost a whisper.

I paused, trying to collect my thoughts and the breath that had just left my lungs in a rush. She had just experienced her own loss, and I knew she was hurting. "I was heartbroken," I said, feeling the pain all over again. "Even though we still had Elise, I grieved that baby."

It was soon after experiencing the joy of finding out that I was pregnant with our first child that I had complications and had to race over to the emergency room with Tim. After a few tests and a couple of clinic visits, we found out that I had actually been pregnant with twins, and I had miscarried one of them. Even though I knew this was "common," it certainly didn't feel commonplace to me.

The next week, I was visiting with a family friend who knew about our loss. Squeezing my hand, she said, "Now your sister has someone to watch over." Tears pricking my eyes, I thanked her and smiled, feeling comforted by the thought. My sister had died several years earlier, but the thought of her watching over my little one in heaven brought me profound comfort. I'm not sure whether that's true of heaven or not, but I took comfort in the underlying premise that this life is not the end for believers. The woman's kind words—her recognition of both my sorrow and the hope that we have of seeing loved ones again someday—felt like a balm.

Years later, as I searched for something to say to comfort my other sister in her own loss, I remembered this experience of receiving comfort and felt the desire to pour it back out to her. I recalled the Lord's words: "You have sorrow now, but I will see you again; then you will rejoice, and no one can rob you of that joy." These words contain a hope and a promise, one we as Christians can cling to even amid the storms of grief that come our way in this life.

— Kristin

— Today's Act of Kindness —

Find a way to encourage someone who
has recently experienced loss.

God around a Fire Pit

You are a chosen people. You are royal priests, a holy nation, God's very own possession. As a result, you can show others the goodness of God, for he called you out of the darkness into his wonderful light.

1 PETER 2:9

Halloween has become quite a thing at our house over the past few years. Although I know people have many different ideas about the celebration of Halloween, we've decided as a family that it can be a wonderful way for us to get to know our neighbors even better.

Each year we buy full-size candy bars, as well as supplies for s'mores and hot chocolate, and we set up our fire pit right in the middle of our driveway. From late afternoon through the evening, we welcome kids of all ages and their parents to warm themselves by the fire and help themselves to a treat. This has become an event that our family looks forward to every year. We've had hundreds of visitors, many of whom come year after year, remembering the house that has the fire and good treats.

Although there are things about Halloween I dislike (for example, I hate anything that's scary), we've talked with our children about the opportunity Halloween gives us to extend kindness while also getting to know our neighbors better. Our children realize this is another way we can reach out to our community, showing the love and light of Jesus by welcoming others to our home.

We don't have to like everything about a holiday or celebration to find ways as Christians to share the love of Christ with those around us. The truth is that we are a chosen people, God's very own possession, created to show the goodness of God to others. Looking for opportunities to engage the world around us is important if we want to make an impact on others' lives. Every kind step we take opens the door for relationships to grow.

— Kendra

— Today's Act of Kindness —

This Halloween, find one thing you can do to go above and beyond to show kindness and the love of God to your neighbors.

Love Yourself as You Love Others

*Don't you realize that your body is the temple of the Holy Spirit,
who lives in you and was given to you by God? You do not
belong to yourself, for God bought you with a high price.*

1 CORINTHIANS 6:19-20

Sitting in the parking lot outside the medical clinic, I clutched the phone, trying not to sob as I told my husband the news: "I got the test results: there is actually something medically wrong with me, and I have a prescription."

It had been years since I had felt truly good—full of energy, ready to conquer the world. The previous winter had been particularly difficult, with feelings of hopelessness and fatigue, and my husband's words, said with wistful sadness, continuously echoed in my head: "I just want my Julie back." It was his words that finally made me reach for the phone to schedule an appointment with a clinic specializing in women's health issues.

It turned out my testosterone levels were near zero and my other hormone levels were extremely low too. As the nurse practitioner rattled off a list of symptoms associated with my test results, it felt as though she had been watching footage of my life over the course of the last several years.

While I find it relatively easy to extend grace to others for their shortcomings, I struggle to give myself that same grace. I often expect perfection of myself in situations where I would be quick to forgive the imperfection in another, and the voices in my head are always quick to compare my secret worst to another's public best. As I've reclaimed my life through a careful rebalancing of my hormones and making other lifestyle changes, I've worked on extending the same grace to myself that I extend to others.

Secretly despising our bodies, our talents, and our skills is not how Christ calls us to live. Our bodies are his temple, bought at a high price—and we are to treat ourselves accordingly. Anything less and we cheapen Jesus' sacrifice on the cross and sabotage the plans God has for us and also for us to reach others.

— Julie

— Today's Act of Kindness —

Practice extending grace to yourself instead
of secretly beating yourself up.

Talking to Strangers

A word fitly spoken is like apples of gold in a setting of silver.
PROVERBS 25:11, ESV

My dad is someone who always seems comfortable chatting with strangers and friends alike—the clerk in the checkout line, the lady standing next to him in the produce aisle. He'll call up an old friend he hasn't seen in twenty years, just to say hello and shoot the breeze. He's a born talker. Being somewhat shy myself, I've always admired this gift and skill. Although I try to smile and say hello to those I don't know when I'm out in the community, it's not always as effortless as I'd like it to be, and I'm always impressed when I see it modeled so well in others.

My mother-in-law, Elaine, has the same skill my dad does, always offering a friendly word to those around her. She explained to me that she learned it from her parents. When she was a little girl growing up in Michigan, she noticed how often her mother, Jean, said hello to people, and she asked her mom if she knew the people she said hi to. One day, when her mother was feeling philosophical, she explained why she always acted the way she did:

> Say hello with a warm smile to at least three people you don't know every day, whether you're at the grocery store or the park or just walking down the street. You'll never know if they need a smile or a kind word or encouragement at that moment. Just assume that they do.

I love that idea—assume that everyone needs a kind word, and be intentional with your compliments. Scripture tells us that an encouraging word is like an apple of gold—nourishing and valuable—and God makes it clear throughout the Bible that words have the power to heal or destroy. Something as simple as saying hello and offering a sincere compliment can impact someone far beyond the moment, just when they may need to hear it the most.

— *Kristin*

— Today's Act of Kindness —

Say hello to three people you don't know, and compliment
a stranger regarding something you genuinely admire.

That's Not My Experience

When God our Savior revealed his kindness and love, he saved us, not because of the righteous things we had done, but because of his mercy.

TITUS 3:4-5

Not too long ago I was privy to a conversation about a young woman known mutually in our family, whose recent life choices seemed like poor ones. Her choices to reconnect with a boyfriend who had previously abused her and to turn down a good job in her chosen career field left others wondering, *What was she thinking?* One woman in our family finally stated, "I just don't understand how she makes these poor choices!"

But that's when another woman reminded us all that this young woman had grown up in a chaotic and somewhat dysfunctional home, and that, to her, these choices might be seen as "normal," no matter how unhealthy they appeared to the rest of us.

In that moment, I realized this young woman has had quite a different life experience than I have. And that conversation got me thinking about the compassion (or lack thereof) I show toward other people. It's easy to think, especially if you grew up in a loving environment, that others should know how to make good or healthy choices in life, but that is simply not always the case. People, for better or worse, often follow similar paths to what they've experienced, because it's what is familiar to them. And the truth is, even if you grow up in a healthy environment, you can still make poor choices in life.

The Bible reminds us that Christ revealed his kindness and love toward us, saving us, because of his mercy. He offers us new life, despite our poor choices. When we remember all that God has forgiven us for, it is easier to extend that same grace toward others. And who knows? Our kindness could be just what someone else needs to experience to help them make healthier choices in their own life or to remind them of how much God loves them.

— Kendra

— Today's Act of Kindness —

Think about someone who has been making poor choices lately in life. Is there some way that you could pray for them and then offer them some encouragement on their journey?

Hug It Out

Be kind to each other, tenderhearted, forgiving one another,
just as God through Christ has forgiven you.
EPHESIANS 4:32

My children have learned that there is nothing that will bring down the wrath of Mom faster than their turning on one another with unkind words, harsh tones, or physical touch that's meant to cause pain or fear.

I have zero tolerance for treating loved ones in ways that are unloving or unkind (even if he is sometimes a pesky little brother and despite the fact that she can be a bossy big sister). We may get angry with one another, but we do not undermine the loving relationships we have in our family—at least not within Mom's keen earshot.

It is relatively easy to be kind to random strangers because we don't have to live with them every day. The real test is learning to be kind to the people you do life with day in and day out, year after year—especially when they mess with your doll collection, throw leaves at you while you're walking the dog, or are forever bossing you around. We frequently learn kindness (or its opposite) from our interactions with our siblings, and I want those interactions to be positive and affirming.

My mom is a wise woman, and she used to make my two brothers and me hug one another after a disagreement. I realized at an early age that I just couldn't hold on to my anger when I was attempting to squeeze the life out of—I mean, hug—my little brother. I'd try my darndest to stay mad, but it never worked. It didn't work for my brothers, either, and soon we'd be laughing and playing, the cause of the argument forgiven and often forgotten. I've adopted the same hug-it-out strategy in my house, and it works just as well now as it did then.

The more we practice the actions of showing kindness and forgiving quickly, the more tenderhearted we will become toward others. What better place to practice these qualities than right at home with our own families?

— Julie

— Today's Act of Kindness —

The next time you feel frustrated with someone
you love, give them a bear hug instead.

Sacrificial Giving

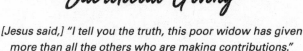

[Jesus said,] "I tell you the truth, this poor widow has given
more than all the others who are making contributions."
MARK 12:43

A friend once confided in me these wise words:

> I often do things for people I don't know. I'm not doing it for praise or to
> look good. I do it because I know if I were in their shoes, it would be a
> huge blessing. We often experience a very tight budget, and I know what
> it feels like to worry about how much gas I have in the car, or whether we
> have enough groceries to get us through until next payday. We have also
> been blessed with times of plenty, and even though we don't have "extra,"
> we have more than many, so I often sacrifice to give some to others.

For my friend, her husband, and their four children, their own hard times as a
family have spurred them to help others. So they've bought groceries for families
who are struggling to make ends meet, brought meals for the homeless, and purchased Christmas presents for other families—all because they know what it's like
to be in a position where life feels a little precarious.

There's a story about giving that Jesus tells in the Gospel of Mark. Observing
rich people who put large amounts of money in the collection box, Jesus then sees
a poor widow drop just two small coins inside the box. Gathering his disciples, he
tells them that the poor widow has given more than the rich people have, because
they are giving just a small portion of what they have while she is giving all she has
to live on.

Perhaps the widow, like my friend, gave more because she knew firsthand what
it's like to live on less. She knew what empty cupboards and a slim income feel like
when you're raising a family amid job transitions and financial difficulties. It's a
sacrificial kind of giving. Yet it honors God when we are faithful in times of plenty
and in times of want, when we give from sincere hearts.

— Kristin

— Today's Act of Kindness —

Find a way to give sacrificially, whether it's
a gift of money, time, or talents.

An Unexpected Cheerleader

A cheerful look brings joy to the heart; good news makes for good health.
PROVERBS 15:30

Turtling along. That's what I was doing approximately one and a half miles into my first 5K. I was technically running, but the average person walks faster than my running pace at that point. I wanted to finish the race without walking, no matter how slow my running—er, turtling—pace.

It was at about the two-mile mark that I realized the finish line was not where I thought it was going to be. In fact, I'd severely miscalculated, and in that moment, I felt as though I might have to run forever. That may sound a bit ridiculous, but it seems that running makes me think ridiculously overdramatic thoughts.

Discouraged and still turtling, I whispered to God that I wanted—*needed*—to finish this race without walking. It wasn't but a few moments later that, refusing to give up, I plodded on past the place I had mistakenly thought was going to be the finish line. An older gentleman standing along the trail clapped loudly and said two simple words as I passed: "Good job!" As crazy as it sounds, my eyes immediately welled up with tears as I met his gaze, gave him a determined nod, and kept putting one foot in front of the other.

He couldn't have known it, but his encouragement came at my lowest moment in the race, and his words buoyed up my flagging spirit. His cheerful look brought me joy, and in that moment, I picked up my pace and knew I was going to reach my goal.

His simple encouragement cost him nothing—in fact, I doubt that he even remembers giving me a clap and a cheer—and yet, he was the pivot point in my race, responsible for the moment when my mind-set switched from "I think I can" to "I know I can." His kindness in that moment is burned into my memory.

It is so easy to share a smile, a cheerful look, an encouraging word with others—and the cost of that small gesture (nothing) often has an outsize impact on the receiver.

— *Julie*

— Today's Act of Kindness —

Encourage a stranger with a smile and a word of encouragement.

The Not-So-Spiritual Gifts

If your gift is to encourage others, be encouraging. If it is giving, give generously. If God has given you leadership ability, take the responsibility seriously. And if you have a gift for showing kindness to others, do it gladly.
ROMANS 12:8

"People like *me* love people like *you*. I'm terrible at putting together gifts," the conference speaker confided as she thanked me for the basket I'd put together for her.

"Oh—really? Thank you!" I said, feeling a little flustered. The speaker was well known, someone whose books I have read and whose TV show I have seen, and her words felt like a much greater gift than the one I'd given her.

I like to put together gifts and gift baskets, but I don't exactly see it listed among the important spiritual gifts like prophecy, teaching, encouragement, or leading. It might even seem materialistic or vain, considering the shopping I have to do to accomplish it or the way I try to make the whole basket look pleasing to the eye. It doesn't feel special or holy. So most of the time, I don't feel special or holy either. My friend Julie can say and write beautiful prayers, and my sister Kendra is a wonderful, inspiring speaker. My dad is a born teacher, and my friend Carol is both a leader and an encourager. Compared to all of these giftings, mine feels humble, maybe even a bit useless.

Yet in rereading the passage in Romans that discusses spiritual gifts, I am struck by two things: "If it is giving, give generously" and "If you have a gift for showing kindness to others, do it gladly." Giving is a gift too, and so is kindness. Rather than dismissing the gifts we have, we need to recognize them as God-given. Downplaying their importance ensures that we won't find ways to use them to bless others.

What gifts and talents do you have? Perhaps you've downplayed them, thinking them not holy or spiritual enough. How can you use them to encourage others?

— *Kristin*

— Today's Act of Kindness —

Think of a gift you have, perhaps one you've always thought wasn't very special, and use it to bless others.

Less Is More

Don't worry about tomorrow, for tomorrow will bring its own worries. Today's trouble is enough for today.

MATTHEW 6:34

"Life is busy right now."

"I just don't have time."

"I'm so stressed."

"I wish time would slow down."

These are all statements I've made at one time or another in my life. We live in a world where, if we are not careful and intentional, our days and months and years will go by with very busy schedules but very little connection with others.

I am beginning to learn that we need to clear some space in our schedules for kindness to happen. It's not that we have to get rid of everything—we all need to work and take care of necessary daily tasks—but if we really want to prioritize connecting with and helping others, we need to be willing to clear some of the busyness away.

For example, when a young man's car wouldn't start in the grocery store parking lot, I offered to let him use my vehicle for a jump. Another time, some little children with the woman at the table next to mine spilled a large pitcher of water, and I quickly went to help clean up the mess. These are examples of small opportunities to act that are easy to overlook and pass up if I don't take the time to slow down. Keeping a slow pace allows me to carve out space to show kindness to others when it's most needed.

I regularly need the reminder not to worry about tomorrow, for tomorrow will bring its own worries. We should focus simply on today. Less worry. Less stuff. Less busyness. Somehow when we do let go of these things, we find so much more peace and love and kindness in our hearts, which we can then give out to others. What nonessential things can you remove from your schedule in the coming month? Is there anything that's hindering your connection to God and to others that needs to be removed?

— *Kendra*

— Today's Act of Kindness —

Pray that God would give you wisdom to see what you can remove from your plate. Then keep your eyes open for opportunities to show kindness.

The Miserable Plane Ride

Sympathize with each other. Love each other as
brothers and sisters. Be tenderhearted.
1 PETER 3:8

I was on edge, to say the least. My daughter, who was about twelve months old at the time, was screaming on an airplane and wouldn't stop. Despite her angelic-looking blonde hair and innocent face, her big, blue, tear-filled eyes were a source of misery for everyone in the rows around us on the long flight. I had plied her with food, drinks, and toys. I had passed her back and forth with my husband. I had bounced her, rocked her, and tried everything I could think of, but still she screamed. She was tired and just wanted to be put down, not held on my lap where she was required to be.

I felt helpless against the looks of displeasure radiating toward me from disgruntled passengers. Embarrassed and trying to hold in tears of my own, I had my head tucked down toward my chest when I felt a hand gently touch my shoulder.

"I'll take her," a woman seated behind us offered kindly, a smile on her face. She had been playing peekaboo with Elise earlier. Normally, I wouldn't hand my child to a stranger, but figuring we were in an enclosed area and there wasn't any harm in letting her hold her for a moment, I gratefully lifted my aching arms and passed her over to the woman.

Immediately, Elise became enthralled with the woman's necklace, tugging at it and staring at it intently. They played more peekaboo, and Elise bounced on the woman's lap. I felt myself relaxing as the crying stopped and laughter ensued. When the woman passed Elise back to me about ten minutes later, the respite had been enough to help me calm down and face the rest of the ride. The woman's attitude was clear: she sympathized with the frustration I felt, and her tenderheartedness moved her to action. Her kindness in the face of tears—mine and my daughter's—was enough to bolster my hope that things could get better.

— *Kristin*

— Today's Act of Kindness —

Speak words of encouragement or take action to show
someone that you sympathize with their circumstances,
offering hope that things will get better.

Kindness Speaks the Truth

I prayed to the LORD, and he answered me. He freed me from all my fears.
PSALM 34:4

"God's got that baby right where he wants her. You don't need to worry; she's safe now with you. If you want to pray for anybody, you should be praying for her mother—that's who's going to need your prayers."

These were the words spoken to me by Dennis, a colleague of mine, after our daughter Jasmine was placed in our home for foster care. I'd frequently stop by his office for encouragement, and Dennis spoke faith into our situation when very few other people had the ability or gumption to do so. He believed what he was saying and would speak truth to me with such conviction that I believed it too, and that was something I really needed during that time. This particular day, Dennis opened my eyes to the truth that I needed to be praying for my daughter's birth mother, especially considering her own challenging life circumstances. I realized he was right, so I did just that—over the years as my daughter grew up, I continued to pray for her safety and well-being and that she would sense and know God's love.

Oftentimes in life, we or those we love face hard or challenging situations that seem to have no end in sight. When we are unsure of the outcome, we can hang on to hope by confidently praying to the Lord and resting assured that he will answer. He will free us from all our fears as we trust in him. This becomes the hope that we have, even in the midst of tumultuous circumstances: to know that God is with us, he will answer us, and he offers to free us from our fears. We then can offer this same comfort, this same kindness, to those around us by speaking faith and truth into the hard situations they face. Who do you know that has been discouraged or fearful lately? What hope could you offer to them?

— Kendra

— Today's Act of Kindness —

Ask the Lord to show you someone who is discouraged or fearful, and then do something to bolster their spirit and encourage them to find hope in the Lord.

Listening Well

Understand this, my dear brothers and sisters: You must all be
quick to listen, slow to speak, and slow to get angry.
JAMES 1:19

"How's the nannying job going?" I asked Savannah, a young friend who feels more like a daughter to Tim and me, one day after work.

"Great!" she said. "I really like the kids. The mom is nice too." Hesitating a little, she added, "I feel bad for the daughter, though. Last week, she was talking on and on and her mom finally said, 'I'm sorry, I'm just not listening to you.' That would be hard for me to hear. The daughter talks to me all day long too, but she seems so happy about it. I feel bad that the mom doesn't listen, so I do."

I couldn't help but agree. I remember how when I was growing up, my own mom would listen to whatever my sisters and I had to say. We could prattle on and on about the kids at school or their parents, and we'd always know that she would listen intently and wouldn't gossip about what we told her or go running to talk to the other parents about it. She listened well, and we knew we could trust her to keep a confidence.

James admonishes us to be quick to listen, and sometimes, listening is all that's required to be kind. It can be easy to get sidetracked by our smartphones, the TV, or our own interests. Life can get so busy that we feel unequal to the task of getting dinner on the table and helping kids finish homework, much less taking the time to really listen to them. Yet we underestimate the value of something as simple as attention and what it conveys to another person: *You matter to me, and the things you care about matter to me as well.* Who in your life do you tune out or give noncommittal, one-word responses to? Who needs the benefit of your kind, listening attention?

— *Kristin*

— Today's Act of Kindness —

Practice the art of listening well by giving someone
the kindness of your undivided attention.

A Genuine Thank-You

*Love each other with genuine affection, and
take delight in honoring each other.*
ROMANS 12:10

"Single-handedly running the household isn't very relaxing," I wryly responded to my husband's question about how the evening before had gone. His chuckle echoed through the phone during our early morning check-in while he was on a work trip halfway across the country. My words held no bite and were instead an understated acknowledgment of all the tasks, big and small, my husband quietly handles week in and week out in our family.

The weeks that he is gone I notice his absence in myriad ways. Not only do I miss my best friend, but I miss his set of hands to help with household work and his pair of eyes on our kids. I always end up with a renewed appreciation for all the tasks he takes on in our lives that I normally don't have to think about, let alone figure out how to accomplish. We are a true team, and with young kids, we both pitch in without a second thought as to what work traditionally "belongs" to which gender. We just get it done.

But that doesn't mean that a genuine thank-you isn't important, especially in a marriage. My husband and I have learned that life ebbs and flows, and there are times when one of us simply has to pick up additional tasks for a week or two while life is busier than normal for the other. It's amazing how far a kiss, a hug, and a genuine thank-you goes during those busy weeks. The simple acknowledgment of the other's efforts to fill in the gaps, to pick up the slack, to take a few things off the plate of the other when work or ministry require extra time is a quiet reminder that we are on this journey together.

We honor one another when we recognize the role we each play in our marriage and in our household. That acknowledgment, I believe, has helped us forge a marriage of genuine affection and a love that is deeper today than it was on our wedding day.

Honoring those whose lives intersect our own goes far beyond children and marriage—siblings, parents, coworkers, and friends may also provide us with critical support, and we, in turn, can find ways to ease their burden during especially busy weeks.

— Julie

— Today's Act of Kindness —

Honor someone in your life by picking up
the slack in their busy season.

November

Loving Children You'll Never Meet

Wherever your treasure is, there the desires of your heart will also be.
MATTHEW 6:21

Brenda approached me four years ago, asking if the children's ministry program at our church would like to participate in Operation Christmas Child by packing shoe boxes filled with a mixture of necessities that would then be sent all around the world. Of course I responded with a resounding *yes!*

What I didn't know was that Brenda is pretty much an Operation Christmas Child shoe-box professional. She knows how to make every last square inch of a shoe box useful and spends the entire year gathering items to be tucked into the boxes—items that will benefit not only the child who receives them but also that child's entire family. Toothbrushes, pencils and paper (with a pencil sharpener), soap, toys—these all find a place in the shoe box, along with a handwritten note from the child sending the gift.

In early November, Brenda takes over our Sunday school classes, showing videos and sharing explanations of how these packages make their way into the hands of children across the globe, many of whom have never before received a gift. She brings what can be an abstract concept to life for our kids, and we then spend a few Sunday mornings packing and wrapping shoe boxes. Our church subsidizes some of the supply costs and covers postage, allowing our kids to pack a towering pile of shoe boxes as part of the experience.

Brenda has overseen this project with our church's kids every year for the past four years, but she has been running this quiet campaign in her own family for decades. The time, money, and effort she has poured into what has to be hundreds upon hundreds of shoe boxes over the years leave no doubt that the desire of her heart is to reach out to kids all around the world with the message of Jesus through a shoe box full of gifts.

The question I've begun asking myself is what my budget and finances reveal about the desires of my heart. Do they reveal a heart overflowing with generosity that extends beyond the walls of our church? Do they reveal Christ's influence on my priorities? Or do they reveal that I have work yet to do? This is convicting, hard stuff. But Scripture is clear: the way we spend and handle money reveals what is most important to us.

— Julie

— Today's Act of Kindness —

Volunteer to buy items or help assemble
packages for kids who lack basic supplies.

A Thankful Heart Is a Kind Heart

Always be joyful. Never stop praying. Be thankful in all circumstances,
for this is God's will for you who belong to Christ Jesus.

1 THESSALONIANS 5:16-18

Each November our family is intentional about celebrating Thanksgiving and listing all the things we are thankful for during the month. Our kids even make a paper chain that we hang in our kitchen, listing the things they are thankful for on the links. Each evening we add several more links to the chain.

Nothing is too big or too small to be thankful for—food, clothing, shelter, snowboarding, air to breathe, clean water, grandparents, friends, teachers, shoes, a warm house, family—on and on the list goes. Our kids can be creative (one is thankful for cooked vegetables because they're healthy) or profound (my oldest is thankful for laughter).

We can certainly express thankfulness any time of year, but during November we try to be especially intentional about taking the time to ponder all the things we are thankful for, all the ways we've been blessed, and all the things God has done for us during the year. I am amazed that the more I think about what I am thankful for, the kinder I am to those around me. It's as if my patience and understanding increase along with my gratitude.

No matter what we've experienced or what we are currently going through, there is always something to be thankful for. Are you grieving? Think about all the ways God has comforted you in the past. Are you experiencing financial strain? Remember how God has provided for you before. Are you dealing with strained relationships? Consider how God is bringing healing, even if it is just to your own heart.

Although it's not always easy to do, we are told to be joyful, to never stop praying, and to be thankful in all circumstances. It seems that a grateful heart is a kind heart, one that can allow us to extend outward the thankfulness we feel in our own hearts.

— *Kendra*

— Today's Act of Kindness —

Make a list of all the things you are thankful
for, and then encourage someone else who
may be struggling during this season.

Responding to Hatred with Love

[Jesus said,] "But to you who are willing to listen, I say,
love your enemies! Do good to those who hate you. Bless
those who curse you. Pray for those who hurt you."

LUKE 6:27-28

The unthinkable happened in our community when ten people were randomly stabbed in a shopping mall by an angry young man who happens to be of Somali descent. With his motives still unclear, my community was reeling from religious and racial tensions laid bare, grappling with our collective loss of innocence, fearful that hateful rhetoric would spill into yet more senseless and random violence.

As I processed the violence that struck so close to home and the chaotic aftermath that splashed across the national news, I prayed about what my response might be, what Scripture required of me and my family. Tears lingered close to the surface, and I wrestled with Christ's clear mandate to do good to those who hate us, to bless those who curse us, and to pray for those who hurt us.

After much prayer and many tears, my conclusion was this: while we should not be naive, responding with radical kindness tempered with divine wisdom is what sets Christians apart from the rest of this fear-filled world. How else do we reveal the character of Christ but through our forward-reaching actions when everyone else pulls back in hate and fear? This world desperately needs to see Jesus, and by being willing to listen, love our enemies, and pray for those who hurt us, we can be a reflection of Christ, even in the face of violence.

My small, forward step of faith in response to this violent act was to send out an e-mail to all my coworkers with a simple lunch invitation. With a Somali leader (and personal friend) serving as our guide and interpreter, we walked across the street from our law firm and into a marketplace owned, run, and frequented by our local Somali population. We went there to eat lunch together and maybe build a bridge or two. My dream is simple: I want to see people from my law firm traipsing across the busy intersection for lunch on a regular basis—a visual symbol of two cultures living fearlessly side by side.

— Julie

— Today's Act of Kindness —

Take a small forward step of faith toward
a real or perceived enemy.

Weekly Shots of Kindness

Share each other's burdens, and in this way obey the law of Christ.
GALATIANS 6:2

"Hi! Come on in," my neighbor Monica said with a bright smile, opening the front door to welcome me in and then quickly closing it behind me to shut out the Minnesota cold. Out of the corner of my eye I could see her youngest son peeking around the kitchen island at me, his blond hair sticking up and blue eyes wide, her three other boys already off at school for the day.

The trip to her house was one I'd been making every week. My oldest daughter was premature, and each successive pregnancy required me to get weekly shots in my hips for twenty weeks—five months' worth of shots that left me limping for a day or two afterward—to help extend my pregnancy to full term. When I found out I was pregnant with our third child, I was thrilled, but since I was no longer working in the same city as my clinic, I was worried about making it all the way to my appointments every week. Hesitantly, I reached out to my neighbor Monica. As a nurse in the birthing area of a local hospital, she graciously agreed to give me my shots.

That's how I found myself, week after week, tromping through the snow to stand at her door, enter her home, and get my shot. She took time out of her schedule—early in the morning, during lunch, or even in the evening—on the same day each week to make sure she could administer them for me.

Sometimes it can be hard to know exactly how we can share one another's burdens. Yet in the case of my sweet neighbor, she managed to do exactly that. I know there were some weeks that it was surely an inconvenience to squeeze me into her schedule, yet not once did she ever seem to be anything but kind and patient and happy to see me—and I was so thankful to have the burden lifted.

— Kristin

— Today's Act of Kindness —

Do something to intentionally ease someone else's burden.

When Plans Change

You must grow in the grace and knowledge of our Lord and Savior Jesus Christ.
2 PETER 3:18

My mother loves traditions. She is always the one who keeps family gatherings going every year, especially during the holidays. One year, there was a man at our church who did not have family in the area and needed assistance in meeting several needs. As the fall began, my husband and father would help by giving him rides, buying him groceries, or gathering things that he needed for his apartment.

As Thanksgiving approached, he told them one day that he did not have anyone to spend the holiday with, as his family would not be in town. When the story was relayed back to my mother and me, I watched as she took it all in, wondering how she'd respond. She simply sighed and said, "Of course invite him, no one should be alone for Thanksgiving." I knew this was a hard thing for my mother to do, not because she is not an incredibly kind and gracious person—she is—but because change has always been a bit difficult for her, especially when it comes to family traditions. Even so, she said yes to what was uncomfortable. Thanksgiving came, and we had a wonderful time with our welcomed guest, who was so grateful to have a family to spend the holiday with.

Sometimes we are challenged in our faith and relationship with God to do things that are outside of our comfort zones or that are different from what we are accustomed to doing. But to love God means that we must grow in the grace of Jesus, and one way to do that is to offer kindness to others, even when it's uncomfortable or a new experience for us. Don't miss the growth that God may bring you, just like he did for my mother when she said yes to something new. You never know how God will use your kindness to change you and bless another person.

— *Kendra*

— Today's Act of Kindness —

Invite someone who may be alone this holiday season
to a celebration or gathering you are attending.

After the Funeral

Pure and genuine religion in the sight of God the Father means caring for orphans and widows in their distress and refusing to let the world corrupt you.

JAMES 1:27

A friend and colleague of Tim's passed away unexpectedly at age forty-five. I knew Steve from work meetings and was always charmed by his kind nature, Southern drawl, and big laugh. He had a larger-than-life personality, and the sudden nature of his passing at such a young age was a shock on many levels. Tim, especially, was hit hard by the gravity of the situation and the way it struck a chord with us: how easily it could be my husband, or me, or one of our children. How life can change in an instant through a heart attack, a car accident, a diagnosis. How often we take this life for granted.

My husband and many of his coworkers traveled to Louisiana to attend Steve's funeral, and their presence filled half the church. But it was when Tim returned home after the funeral that I was moved to tears yet again: his coworkers had banded together and collectively raised more than $50,000 for Steve's widow and her children, which would be used to establish savings plans so the kids would be able to attend college. In the months that followed, Tim's coworkers continued to reach out to Steve's wife and her children. They attended their home football games. They took the oldest son hunting. They comforted their friend's family as they grieved, and they remained a constant presence in their lives as they learned how to live a new normal.

Part of living out our faith and showing love to others means caring for orphans and widows. Tim's coworkers are a prime example of how a person or group can do so—not simply with a few words of sympathy hastily spoken, but through repeated actions that show the sincerity of shared grief and continued love and care for those who have experienced loss.

— *Kristin*

— Today's Act of Kindness —

Find a way to do a tangible act of kindness for a widow or orphan.

The Doll Dress

We should help others do what is right and build them up in the Lord.
ROMANS 15:2

My daughter and I were in the car when the topic arose. She adores the American Girl doll that her grandma and aunt gave her several years ago, and she has been happily receiving clothes and accessories for her doll on birthdays and at Christmas. She asks to bring her doll whenever she goes to play at a friend's house, especially when her friends also have similar dolls.

As we chatted, my daughter mentioned in passing that she had given away one of her doll's outfits—and not just any of them, but a beautiful, expensive dress. Surprised, I started thinking of a nice way to tell her that she needed to get the dress back, until my daughter's explanation stopped me in my tracks.

She explained that she gave the dress away because her friend didn't have beautiful clothes for her doll—in fact, her friend really didn't have a whole lot to dress her doll in and didn't have a dress at all. My daughter noticed and simply gave the dress to her. She explained how much her friend loves the dress, how beautiful her doll looks in it, and how much fun they had playing with their dolls and pretending that they were in old-fashioned times.

As my daughter's explanation washed over me, my irritation faded. Swallowing my words of censure, I instead complimented her thoughtfulness, her generosity, and her kindness. She did exactly what my husband and I pray that our children will do—she saw a need and met it with generosity. And it wasn't a big deal to her—it was simply part of the ebb and flow of her life. She didn't mark the occasion as something extraordinary but simply as an ordinary kindness shown to a friend she loves.

We are called to build up one another in the Lord, helping and supporting others in doing what is right. I will not, cannot, censure my daughter for giving a good, generous gift of her own accord to someone else. I will not stifle the Holy Spirit's gentle nudge in her young life, and instead, I will cheer her on every step of the way.

— Julie

— Today's Act of Kindness —

Look for someone who is doing the right
thing, and then celebrate them.

The Prewedding Phone Call

He will once again fill your mouth with laughter and your lips with shouts of joy.

JOB 8:21

My friend Andrea was busy setting up at the reception hall the night before her wedding, when her mom handed her a phone. "It's Cody, calling from Italy," she said, walking away.

As Andrea chatted on the phone with her brother, he congratulated her on her upcoming marriage and said he wished he could be there to celebrate. But since he was in the military and currently stationed in Italy, the ticket price was too high to fly him, his wife, and their young daughter home for the wedding. Andrea said she understood, although she wished it had worked for them to come, as the family hadn't seen them for two years.

As they continued to visit on the phone, Andrea's mom walked back around the corner, holding a little girl. Andrea glanced over and then did a double take, unable to believe what she was seeing. It was her niece! Andrea dropped the phone on the floor and ran around the corner to find her brother—the same one she'd thought was still in Italy. Andrea's mom had secretly paid to fly the three of them home just in time for the wedding. Leaving the reception hall, they went that night to get an extra bridesmaid dress and a flower girl dress to include the newly arrived family members in the wedding the next day.

We often think of showing kindness to others in terms of helping someone who is in a tough place in life—whether they are homeless, grieving, or otherwise in need. Yet laughter and joy are also from the Lord, and so we are encouraged to join with others when they are experiencing happy occasions in their lives. Taking part in another person's happiness and celebrating with them in a joyous time is a beautiful way to show kindness and demonstrate that you care. In what ways can you show kindness to those who are celebrating something in their life?

— Kristin

— Today's Act of Kindness —

Celebrate a recent joy—a new baby, a job promotion,
a new marriage—of someone you know.

Years of Wisdom

Wisdom belongs to the aged, and understanding to the old.
JOB 12:12

Right before my eighty-two-year-old neighbor blew out the candles on the little cake my kids and I had brought him to commemorate his birthday, he said, "I'm really thankful for good friends."

He had recently moved away from our neighborhood to an apartment complex for elderly people, and although we understood his reasons for wanting to move, we missed him. He had been a fixture in our neighborhood, sitting outside each afternoon and evening on nice days, giving my kids treats, and taking the time to sit and talk with anyone who came to visit. He loved my kids and always made time to listen to their stories or to watch them dance or play. I found that I enjoyed just spending time with him, and I valued his advice and his knowledge of the area where we live. He added a richness to my family's life that we wouldn't have otherwise had, simply by being willing to share all of who he was with us.

Sometimes it's easy to overlook the elderly, but the Bible reminds us that they have earned great wisdom and understanding. We who are younger can learn a lot about how to handle issues in our lives now by listening to those who have walked this road before us. Or perhaps you are on the other end of this spectrum, wondering if the younger generations even care about what you have to say. It may not be true of everyone, but many do find value in your words and the wisdom you have to offer. The older I get the more I want to listen to those who are further along in life than I am. Don't miss the value of gaining wisdom from those who are more experienced than you and spending time with the older generation. It is not only kind but also a wise thing to do.

— *Kendra*

— *Today's Act of Kindness* —

Ask advice from or offer encouragement to
someone who is older than you.

Giving the Good Stuff

The people rejoiced over the offerings, for they had given freely and wholeheartedly to the LORD.

1 CHRONICLES 29:9

In a concrete, windowless room at the back of the sanctuary, we toiled over bins and boxes, putting together bathroom- and kitchen-themed gifts to give away during the main sessions at the retreat for single moms. The items had all been donated or bought for that purpose, and we had fun putting together fifty eye-catching, beribboned baskets of joy.

I was later mortified when one of the women who received a basket pointed out very quietly and very kindly that the hand lotion she received in her basket had previously been opened. My heart sank. I thought I had checked over all of them so carefully—in fact, I had thrown away several items for that very same reason—but in my haste to get the giveaways finished, I must have missed one.

When you work with donated items, this is a scenario that arises more often than you would think. "These clothes didn't sell at my garage sale, so I thought I would give them to you" is something I've heard many times. I bite my tongue and thank the giver kindly, but inside I think, *Please don't give me your junk.*

All too often, I've found that folks think nothing of giving the ripped, stained, or discarded items they don't have a use for anymore. What if, just once, we gave our best? What if we donated new clothing to the homeless shelter instead of our discarded items? What if we gave food to the food pantry that we would normally buy for our families, rather than the cheapest cans we find at the grocery store?

I'm not suggesting that the brand should matter or that cheaper food isn't perfectly acceptable to eat. Rather, I'm suggesting that we consider the heart of the matter and ask ourselves, *Am I giving my best? Am I giving freely and wholeheartedly, or am I giving my leftovers?*

— *Kristin*

— Today's Act of Kindness —

Resolve to give the best you can the next time
you have the opportunity—be it the best crayons,
food, clothing, or something else entirely.

Be the Support

Moses' arms soon became so tired he could no longer hold them up. So Aaron and Hur found a stone for him to sit on. Then they stood on each side of Moses, holding up his hands. So his hands held steady until sunset.

EXODUS 17:12

My friend Jenny has always been a huge support not only to me but to all the women in our close circle of friends. She's not showy or loud, but she has the ability to make people feel like they matter simply by the way she listens and the way she gets involved in and engaged with activities they're doing. She often offers to help in any way that she can and simply makes herself available when someone needs a friend. On the surface, few people may realize, see, or value all that she does, but for those of us who *really* know her, she is a steady rock, offering safety, friendship, and support to those around her.

Do you have a friend like Jenny in your life? Maybe you are that person, wondering if you really make any difference in the lives of those around you—Jenny has told me she often has those thoughts. But I am quick to remind her that having someone who will stand with you, even quietly, through all the good and bad times of life, remaining a stabilizing force in the midst of chaos, is something we all need desperately. Kindness can be large and loud at times, or it can come in the quietest of ways: a simple hug, an encouraging smile, a squeeze of the hand, a reassuring presence—these things all count as kindness, and they all matter.

The Bible offers a wonderful story of friendship and support. In the Old Testament, Moses needed to hold his arms up, and as long as he did, the Israelites would continue winning the battle they were engaged in. As soon as his arms fell, they'd begin to lose. Noticing this, Moses' friends, Aaron and Hur, held his arms up so that his hands would hold steady and the Israelites would win. What a beautiful picture of the kindness we can show to one another, holding each other up when someone is weary or weak.

— Kendra

— Today's Act of Kindness —

Come alongside a friend who may need help holding their hands steady, and offer them encouragement.

Intentional Kindness during Advent

Blessed are those who are generous.
PROVERBS 22:9

Tired of Christmas being hijacked by too many gifts and stores targeting our children with ads for the newest, latest, and greatest, my family now focuses on the sacred meaning of the Advent season. We do this by intentionally giving with abundant generosity through a variety of kind acts in the weeks leading up to Christmas.

While some of our acts of generosity are done quietly and secretly, we've discovered the joy of partnering with others in blessing those around us. We've included our extended family, Sunday school classes, and churches in our kind acts, and we love the community and encouragement we've found. It feels like we're a part of something bigger than just our family.

If you are looking for inspiration for how to fit this into your own Christmas season, know that kind acts during Advent can be done daily, once a week, or as one big kind act every Christmas season.

It is so fun to hear all the ways in which our friends and families join us in living out the command to be generous with others. My friend Becky and her family have adopted the one-big-kind-act model. She and her husband buy gift cards to a local grocery store, put them into sealed Christmas cards, and then allow their child to hand out the cards to strangers who are walking into the grocery store on a busy Saturday morning. They give no hint as to what is in the card, and their child delights in knowing that he is choosing who gets the gift cards.

The possibilities for incorporating kind acts into your Advent and Christmas season are endless. It's a time of year in which hurting people generally ache even more, and opportunities abound for reaching out to others as a tangible expression of God's love, inviting people into relationship with him. We are called to look out for others, not just ourselves, and kindness during the Christmas season is a beautiful way to point toward our Savior.

— Julie

— Today's Act of Kindness —

Ask a family member or friend to join you in an act of kindness.

Shifting Perspective

You should remember the words of the Lord Jesus:
"It is more blessed to give than to receive."
ACTS 20:35

Several years ago Aaron and I began incorporating random acts of kindness into our family's Advent traditions. It started as a conversation between Kendra, Kristin, and me at a local coffee shop one fall weekend afternoon. We were complaining about how our culture's commercial view of Christmas was impacting our children's attitudes in a way that we didn't like and didn't want to promote. At some point, our conversation switched from complaining to discussing how to take back the sacredness of the Christmas season. We walked out of the coffee shop that afternoon with the rough framework for Advent acts of kindness and have been refining what it looks like for our individual families every year since.

For my family, it began with a perspective shift about what Christmas is and what it is not. I began talking with my young children about Christmas in terms of Jesus' birthday—because it's true and also because my kids already understood that we *give* presents instead of *receiving* presents on someone else's birthday. As part of the explanation, we scaled back (significantly) the celebration of Christmas when it came to presents under the tree and scaled up the kindness and giving we do at Christmastime. When Christmas was explained in terms of birthday celebrations, our kids went along with our perspective shift from getting to giving without complaint.

We try to have only three or four gifts under the tree for each child on Christmas morning. We'll tuck a few small things into their stockings, but that's it. Christmas morning is still a magical time in our household, and honestly, none of us have missed the extra gifts.

This simple change in perspective has helped us shift Christmas from a season of *getting* to a season of *giving*. As we've given, we've found ourselves blessed beyond measure by the people we've met, the stories we've heard, and by how God has worked through us to accomplish his will.

— Julie

— Today's Act of Kindness —

As you begin planning what the Christmas season will look like for your family this year, consider how you can tangibly realign the focus away from getting and onto giving.

The Hotel Room

Don't forget to do good and to share with those in need.
These are the sacrifices that please God.
HEBREWS 13:16

My friend Andrea was ready to fly to Minnesota with her fifteen-month-old daughter, Emma, when severe weather delayed them at a small airport in West Virginia. By the time they finally boarded the plane, the toddler had fallen asleep in Andrea's arms, waking only when Andrea tried to shift Emma to her stroller after landing in Detroit. Two young men, cousins named David and James, were sitting across the aisle from Andrea, and they offered to help.

Because of the delay and their 11:00 p.m. arrival in Detroit, they all received hotel vouchers for the night. David pushed the stroller while James called the hotels listed on each of their vouchers to secure rooms. It was then that they hit another snag—the same storm that had delayed their flight had stranded many other travelers in Detroit, and even though everyone had received vouchers, Andrea's assigned hotel was already full. The cousins' hotel wasn't, so they offered to give Andrea their voucher.

However, there was yet another snag when they realized that the name on the voucher required them to show identification in order to check in. David and James insisted on taking the shuttle with Andrea and Emma to the hotel, where they then planned to check in to their room, give it to the girls, then return to the airport to spend the night in hard plastic chairs.

When they all arrived at the hotel and explained to the front desk employee what the guys were insisting upon doing—giving up their room for Andrea and Emma—the clerk not only secured David and James a room too, but he also comped both rooms. Although she never saw the cousins or the clerk again after the hotel check-in, Andrea says she's never forgotten their kindness.

All too often, it's easy to ignore acts of kindness that require us to sacrifice something. We believe that we don't have enough time or money, or perhaps we reason that someone else will do it. However, when we share with those in need, our sacrifice is what pleases God.

— *Kristin*

— Today's Act of Kindness —

Give up something (time, talent, or money)
for someone who needs it.

Inspiration for Advent

If someone has enough money to live well and sees a brother or sister in need but shows no compassion—how can God's love be in that person?

1 JOHN 3:17

We are called to be the walking embodiment of God's love—his presence revealed in tangible form. One significant way we reveal God's love to others is by sharing our resources (time, talent, and treasure) to meet the physical needs of those around us.

Kendra, Kristin, and I have started a tradition for our families in which we combine the holiness of Advent with our call to reveal God's love through acts of kindness during the days leading up to Christmas. While we always leave room for the Holy Spirit to move us in a different direction on any particular day, we generally plan out our acts of kindness sometime in mid-November.

Planning ahead while being flexible and willing to shift plans at the nudging of the Holy Spirit is key, at least for us, in successfully following through on our kind acts. Additionally, we intentionally do our acts of kindness to impact four different geographic regions: our local community, our state, our nation, and the world.

Broadening our perspectives to include the family down the street, the trafficked girl halfway across the world, and everything in between initiates important conversations about what it means to be blessed simply by living where we do. It allows us to switch between tangible acts of kindness (typically local in nature) and abstract acts of kindness (typically national or global), and it gives us parameters that help keep us from getting stuck doing the same kind acts year after year.

We also balance our kind acts across the financial spectrum—some of the acts we do are free or low cost, and some require a significant financial investment. This allows my husband and me to demonstrate for our kids that we can show compassion and generosity in many different ways. While it might be tempting to focus on the free or low-cost forms of kindness, God specifically calls us to financially care for those who have less than we do, and sharing our financial blessings is an important part of my family's Advent observation.

— *Julie*

— *Today's Act of Kindness* —

Incorporate both the regional perspective and the full financial spectrum as you plan out your own kind acts during Advent.

Let us think of ways to motivate one another to acts of love and good works.
HEBREWS 10:24

Not long ago I received a call from a social worker in my county, who was wondering if I'd be willing to share with a group of potential foster parents about my experience as a foster parent myself. Without hesitating, I said, "Yes! I love to talk to others about fostering children in need." A few weeks later, I had the opportunity to meet with the group, answer their questions, speak about the joys and fears associated with fostering, and give them an honest overview of what it's like to be a foster parent.

As I spoke with the parents during and after the meeting, it was encouraging for me to share all the challenging and joyful parts of being a foster parent while also listening to their stories and answering questions as best I could. I could see the excitement in the attendees' eyes—excitement that mirrored my own—as we all shared our desire to care for kids who really need it. We left thanking one another for the support we all felt on our foster-care and adoption journeys.

No matter what we're doing or in what stage of life we find ourselves, we all have wisdom that we can use to encourage one another. There are many ways that we can motivate one another to acts of love and good works. Is there something in your life that you are passionate about? Perhaps there are issues happening in our world that deeply concern you. Sharing what you know with others who have the same concerns not only encourages them but shows kindness by letting them know they are not alone in their convictions. We are called to support one another, and sharing what you know or have learned through your life experiences is valuable and worth mentioning to others who are on a similar path. You just might motivate them to do good works of their own for the same cause.

— *Kendra*

— *Today's Act of Kindness* —

Share your experience with someone else who is on a similar journey or who is passionate about the same issues as you are.

No Freezers in Spain?

The very hairs on your head are all numbered.
MATTHEW 10:30

"Do you have freezers in Spain?" I heard my husband ask Inez, a teenage exchange student who was spending the summer with friends of ours. As she paused, either to collect her thoughts or to make sure she'd heard his strange question correctly, I couldn't help but interject.

"What?" I found myself squawking from across the kitchen, a bit embarrassed on his behalf. "Why would you ask that?"

"It's not a dumb question," he said, defending himself. "A speaker I was listening to talked about how people who live in Europe buy fresh ingredients from the market and don't typically use freezers."

Although we gave him a hard time—and Inez clarified that yes, her family does have a freezer—afterward I regretted making him feel bad about it. For as clumsy as his question felt to the rest of us, I was glad that he asked it. Perhaps it was a small question about a little detail of life, but I appreciated his effort to get to know someone whose everyday life is quite different from his own.

All too often when we see people among us who have a different cultural background, religion, or even political perspective, we don't care enough to show genuine interest in them. We don't take the time to get to know or understand them for who they are. Instead, we lump them into groups with other people and make generalizations that just might be incorrect.

God knows us so personally and loves us so deeply; we should follow his example in our relationships with others. If God can take the time to count the hairs on our head, surely we can take the time to get to know people beyond a cursory, surface evaluation, regardless of whether or not they own a freezer.

— *Kristin*

— Today's Act of Kindness —

Take time to get to know someone who has a
background that differs from your own.

A Nudge from the Holy Spirit

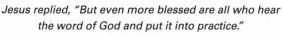

*Jesus replied, "But even more blessed are all who hear
the word of God and put it into practice."*

LUKE 11:28

As my hand reached for the restaurant door handle, I sensed the Holy Spirit say, "*No.*" I've learned to recognize the way the Holy Spirit whispers into my soul, and I've learned to trust his voice, but still, I was surprised by this.

Though I had originally come to the restaurant to purchase a gift card for a friend, I drove out of the parking lot empty-handed, momentarily wondering if I had heard God correctly. This act of kindness had sent me significantly out of my way, and here I was driving away without the card because at the very last second I was told no and then prompted to give my friend cash instead.

After writing a note of prayer and encouragement, I enclosed the money, saying that it was intended to be used for a dinner out with her husband, but that they should use it in whatever way they wanted or needed.

What I didn't know was that every afternoon that week, my friend had begged her daughter's preschool provider for just a little more time, just until the end of the week, to get the deposit together for her preschool spot. On the drive home from her meeting with the preschool, she had cried out to God about their finances and had asked him to provide for her family even as her family was taking care of others. Medical bills for an extended family member had piled up, and she and her husband had been paying down those bills, leaving their savings depleted. These were the things I did not know as I quietly left my card with a little gift on her doorstep. As it turned out, the cash in the card was enough to cover the preschool deposit.

When she called to tell me the story, we both wept—she, because God heard and answered her cries for help, and me, in humble gratitude for that whisper from the Holy Spirit. God knows better than we do what someone else needs, and being open to changing our plans at his nudging will bless us and others.

— *Julie*

— Today's Act of Kindness —

Carefully listen for the Holy Spirit's prompting
as you plan a kind act for today.

Everybody's In

Peter replied, "I see very clearly that God shows no favoritism."
ACTS 10:34

My aunt and uncle took in many foster kids and adopted several others during the seventies and eighties. Many of the children were racially different from them, and people would sometimes make comments about the children's race or heritage. My aunt said that she would often choose to overlook people's words, because if she tried to argue, the commenters would simply get defensive.

But there was one occasion when her kids were at a neighbor's house playing, and the neighbor let all the kids join in except for one—my adopted cousin. As soon as my uncle heard what had happened, he quickly went to the neighbor's home and very calmly told him, "You either let all my kids join in and play or none of them."

As I listened to my aunt recount the story, I was proud of the hard work she and my uncle did all those years ago. It wasn't just that they were willing to take in children and give them a home, but that they also treated each child as family. My aunt and uncle understood that every person, no matter their background or heritage, has value and worth in God's world, and so every person was valuable to them, too.

In our world today we are still faced with people who are biased or prejudiced against other people groups. Our response as Christians should be similar to God's, showing no favoritism. In God's eyes, we are all equal. Everybody's in, and no one will be left out because of their race or heritage—*everyone* who calls on the name of the Lord will be saved. We have a choice not only in how we think about people who are different from us but also in how we treat them. The Bible tells us countless times that God's kindness and love are for everyone, indiscriminately, and so should ours be.

— *Kendra*

— Today's Act of Kindness —

Combat discrimination in your own heart or your community
by doing a kind act for someone who is different from you.

The Secret Snowplowing

Jesus replied, "'You must love the LORD your God with all your heart, all your soul, and all your mind.' This is the first and greatest commandment. A second is equally important: 'Love your neighbor as yourself.'"

MATTHEW 22:37-39

"No one ever offers to help," the woman, an acquaintance from church, said. There was anguish and even a hint of anger in her voice. Sitting across the table from her at a French restaurant for dinner with several other girlfriends, I could hear the frustration she felt. She was a young wife and mother, and her husband's job required him to be gone for long periods of time.

As we talked about the challenges she faced as the only parent in the home during those weeks, she admitted that, by and large, our Minnesota winters brought some of the toughest hardships. When storms would come, snowdrifts piled high in the driveway, and with two children to care for, she often struggled to find the time to clear it. Early in the morning or late at night, she'd have to squeeze in time between her job, meals, and bedtime to shovel the snow off her driveway and sidewalk.

Her neighbors were busy people, with demanding jobs and families to care for. She would see them outside, clearing their own driveways, while hers sat neglected. They were nice people, and it was a pleasant neighborhood, yet no one ever offered to help. No one saw her need.

The next winter, recalling her story, we secretly contacted a snow-removal service and arranged for her driveway to be plowed each time it snowed. It was nothing more than a simple phone call, some money out of our blessing budget, and a few minutes out of our day, but when the service called and told her the news, she cried.

When Jesus tells us to love our neighbor as we love ourselves, it's meant both figuratively and literally. I'm sure this woman's neighbors were busy with their own lives, and no one was intentionally trying to be unkind. Perhaps they had simply never noticed her need. But I've found that when you look for opportunities to be kind, they are always there.

— Kristin

— Today's Act of Kindness —

Look for something kind you can do for a neighbor.

Comfort the Sick

I [the Lord] will bandage the injured and strengthen the weak.

EZEKIEL 34:16

I have a friend who had cancer many years ago. Although she is healthy now, she still has annual checkups, and even though she doesn't fear the cancer returning, it is always a bit nerve racking to go through the tests all over again. I decided a couple of years ago that I would make a care package for her to take to the hospital every year, including magazines, a coffee gift card, chocolates, and a note telling her I'm praying for her—all the essentials she'll need while there. I leave it on her doorstep each year before her appointment, just to let her know I'm thinking of her and praying for her.

And each Christmas season my kids and I bring coffee gift cards, crayons, and coloring books up to the children's floor at our local hospital and leave these gifts for the nurses to give away to parents who need a few minutes' break and kids or siblings who could use something to do. When asked if we'd like to leave our names, our kids say, "No, just tell them it's from someone who cares." It takes just a bit of planning and a few hours out of our day to buy and deliver the materials, but we know these gifts mean so much to families who find themselves with a child in the hospital, especially at Christmastime.

It's sometimes easy to forget the struggles that people are facing, especially if they are long-term illnesses, but remembering to show kindness to those who are ill is important. The Lord says that he'll bandage the injured and strengthen the weak. What a promise we have and what comfort we can find in these words, whether it's we ourselves or others around us who are ill. We can partner with God in his promise to strengthen the weak by showing his kindness and encouraging others as they walk through seasons of sickness.

— Kendra

— Today's Act of Kindness —

Put together a gift for someone you know who is ill, or bring a gift to your local hospital for someone who may be in need of encouragement.

Just in Time

*If you keep quiet at a time like this, deliverance and relief for the Jews
will arise from some other place, but you and your relatives will die. Who
knows if perhaps you were made queen for just such a time as this?*
ESTHER 4:14

Many years ago, my aunt Delpha and uncle Jim and their three small children had just moved to a small cabin in the northern woods of Minnesota. They didn't have running water yet, much less a phone.

Delpha and her brother Michael, who was visiting at the time, were at home late one evening when her husband's uncle Rod came down from his place, which was a short ways away. He had received a phone call on Delpha's behalf, and he hurried over to tell her the news. Her mother had experienced health problems for several years, and although she was only in her midforties, her recent bout with pneumonia had taken an unexpected turn.

"Your mother is dying," he said. "If you want to see her, you need to go now."

Delpha's mother lived hundreds of miles away in North Dakota. Rod, recognizing that the young family might not have the funds to cover the cost of gas, gave her money to pay for the trip. She thanked Rod, and then Delpha and Michael drove all through the night back to North Dakota. They arrived in the morning just in time to see their mother in the hospital. She died that very day.

In the Old Testament story of Queen Esther, Esther is told by her relative Mordecai that perhaps she has been placed in a position of power "for just such a time as this"—specifically, when her people, the Jews, needed to be saved from death. Her circumstances gave her a unique advantage in helping others, but it was up to her to recognize and follow through on it.

Sometimes, God puts us in specific places or intersects our lives with others so that we can bless or encourage them at just the right moment. If Rod hadn't visited Delpha that evening and provided the funds for the trip, the two siblings never would have made it in time to see their mom.

What kind act have you felt nudged to do? Perhaps the opportunity has been placed in your path for such a time as this.

— *Kristin*

— Today's Act of Kindness —

Whatever act of kindness you have felt led
to do, stop putting it off and do it.

An Unlikely Friend

*[Jesus said,] "But I say, love your enemies! Pray
for those who persecute you!"*
MATTHEW 5:44

"What are you working on?" I asked my seven-year-old daughter casually. She was perched at our kitchen island, art supplies tumbling over each other haphazardly as she dipped a paintbrush into vibrant watercolors. Leaning closer, I read the words on her picture: *Merry Christmas, Emma! Love, Elise.*

"You mean Emma from the bus?" I clarified, a bit alarmed. "As in, the Emma that's not very nice to you?"

"Yep," she said. "I thought she would like a picture."

I complimented her on the butterflies she was painting in a rainbow pattern, but my thoughts were in turmoil. The previous month, I had held my daughter in my arms while she told me in a pained whisper that Emma, a second-grader, greeted her each day on the bus with a mocking tone and had made it a point to pick on her. Although Elise can present a stoic face to the world, she is sensitive and feels things deeply, and I knew she was bewildered by the ugly attention. I couldn't help but think, *Why would she want to give a drawing to someone who had been mean to her? Why would she expose herself to the risk of rejection or more ridicule?* But, knowing that her mind was made up, I decided to pray over the situation and let it play out.

A week later, Elise bounded home after school to report how much Emma had liked her picture. "Emma told Daniel that she got it from her *friend!*" she said exuberantly, cheeks flushed from the cold and her excitement. Despite my doubts, she had managed to turn the little girl from a bully into a friend.

I was proud of her bravery and yet humbled by my own uncharitable thoughts. We're called to show kindness even when people are unkind, to forgive others "seventy times seven" (Matthew 18:22), and even to pray for our enemies, but there are days when those seem like impossible feats. Yet sometimes, the only way to remedy a situation is to reach out to the other person, even when it's hard or feels uncomfortable. Who knows? They may even become an unlikely friend.

— Kristin

— Today's Act of Kindness —

Go out of your way to be kind to someone
who has been unkind to you.

Consistent Kindness

Never tire of doing what is good.
2 THESSALONIANS 3:13

My sister Katrina was the mom of two young children, battling breast cancer in her midtwenties. Many times she had very little energy as she went through treatments that tried to rid her body of the cancer. The women at our church decided that they'd like to help her during this season. They signed up to do things like watch her kids and bring meals for the family. One woman even volunteered to come and clean her house every week.

I often think of that woman who showed up to do the unlovely work of cleaning my sister's house from top to bottom. She quietly worked for several hours every week, with no fanfare or crowds to see her work. Even as other volunteers dwindled, meals slowed, and babysitting ended, Carol persisted, continuing with her devotion to Katrina. I realize now that this was one of the biggest blessings my sister received during that difficult time and has remained one of the most profound acts of continual kindness I remember from her illness.

We may never know what our consistent acts of kindness will do in the lives of those around us. Kindness doesn't have to be showy or pretty or done in front of others to matter. My sister's clean house became a testament to me of someone who was willing to regularly show up and love someone else, even when others had stopped.

We all have things that we are good at or that are second nature to us, whether that's cooking, offering encouragement, praying for others, or even cleaning. We can offer these gifts to those who are going through a challenging time. Scripture encourages us to never tire from doing good; sometimes that means we are to offer occasional help, but other times we may need to persist and show up on a more regular basis. Carol understood that her offering to show up week after week was needed, and it created a deep impact over time. We, too, must understand and harness the power of continually showing up for someone else.

— Kendra

— Today's Act of Kindness —

Think of someone who may need assistance on a consistent basis, and choose a way to extend kindness to them regularly.

Sharing Thanksgiving

For I was hungry, and you fed me. I was thirsty, and you gave me
a drink. I was a stranger, and you invited me into your home.
MATTHEW 25:35

My friend Wanda is from China, and we met when our daughters were in kindergarten together. Her daughter was learning English as a second language, and my daughter was learning Chinese as a second language. Our daughters became fast friends—chattering excitedly in a strange mix of English and Chinese, never realizing that they were doing something extraordinary in the eyes of the adults watching them.

Knowing that Wanda was in the United States alone with her daughter, I asked Aaron's extended family if perhaps we could invite them for Thanksgiving. One thing I love about Aaron's family is their willingness to invite others into our celebrations. Between Aaron and his sister extending invitations, you never know who you might find gathering around the extended Fisk family's Thanksgiving table, regardless of whose house we are at that year.

The year Wanda joined us was the year I hosted—and I was left in charge of the turkey for the very first time. Until that year I hadn't thought about how Thanksgiving in America is very traditional, but every family serves dishes that are different and delightfully unusual. Our Thanksgiving with Wanda was filled with explanations of what wild rice is, what a "hot dish" is, and why we cook turkeys only once a year. We discussed traditions, talked about foods that make our cultures unique, and giggled as we took a selfie with my first turkey—which was a little on the dry side. We weighed the pros and cons of Black Friday, football, and postdinner naps. It was a great time, and that particular Thanksgiving remains one of my favorites.

Sharing our families and lives can be as easy as inviting people into our holiday celebrations, into our family's unique traditions, into community over a meal. There is something intimate about sharing food that just cannot be replicated in other settings. God knew this, and Scripture is replete with commands to feed strangers and invite people into our homes. It is hard not to grow close to the people we invite into our homes, who sit at our tables and pass the salt as we discuss ordinary things.

— Julie

— Today's Act of Kindness —

Invite someone new to Thanksgiving this year.

Speaking Truth with Kindness

As iron sharpens iron, so a friend sharpens a friend.
PROVERBS 27:17

"I've been praying about this and I really felt like I needed to say something to you about it," my friend nervously stated over the phone as we were talking one day. She went on to tell me about something I had done that she felt wasn't right.

As her words came through graciously over the phone, tears sprang to my eyes. I knew that she was right. As I talked through the issue with her, I found grace and mercy mixed in with her words, and I felt a weight lifting off of me.

I hung up the phone so grateful for a friend who could speak to me honestly about something I needed to be corrected on, while doing it completely in love and without judgment. I left the conversation feeling better about who I was and like I had worked through an issue that I had become blind to seeing for myself. My friend took a chance by speaking honestly to me, knowing I might have been offended by her words, and I was thankful for her bravery.

There may be times in life when we feel that someone around us needs to be corrected, but we should always make sure that we are speaking to them from a place of love and not from resentment or anger. Scripture reminds us that "as iron sharpens iron, so a friend sharpens a friend." I was so grateful that my friend took a chance to speak to me honestly about a concern, therefore sharpening me. We need to be willing to do the same for those around us. Kindness can often come through in our honesty toward others, when we speak in love and with genuine concern for the other person.

Do you have a good friend to share your life with, who has a line of sight into your choices? Do you have a friend who will speak honestly to you, even if it's hard, in an effort to sharpen you? If so, thank God for them today. If not, consider what you might need to do to build that kind of friendship.

— Kendra

— Today's Act of Kindness —

Send a note of thanks to a friend who has
sharpened you in some way.

Big Tips and Family Traditions

Wherever your treasure is, there the desires of your heart will also be.

LUKE 12:34

Each year, after the Thanksgiving meal has ended and the turkey and mashed potatoes have been put away, our friends George and Kylee and their three children pile into the car and head to a local restaurant for dessert. When they leave, they give the server a big tip—much more than is typically given—along with their sincere thanks. It's a treasured family tradition. They love to bless someone who has to spend their holiday working, whatever the reason—whether because that person needed the money or just couldn't get the day off to be with family.

As a mom, it's easy to think about doing kind acts with my kids on regular days when we have the time, when it works with our schedule, and when it doesn't require too much additional effort. But in the busy rush of big holidays like Christmas, Thanksgiving, or Easter, it's easy to focus on my own children, the comfort I enjoy, or our immediate or extended family's expectations of what the day will hold. Yet I love the idea of making kind acts as much of a family tradition as lefse and meatballs on Thanksgiving or cinnamon rolls on Christmas morning are for us—something we can look forward to that becomes ingrained as a long-lasting tradition.

Rather than worrying about buying another Thanksgiving pie or more stocking stuffers for my children, I want to remember that my pocketbook should follow not just my own heart but the heart of Jesus. After all, Scripture says that where we choose to spend our money reveals the inner desires of our hearts. Investing in others—like giving a big tip to a server on Thanksgiving—speaks not only to the heart of what the holiday is truly about but also to the heart of what God desires for us, his children.

— Kristin

— Today's Act of Kindness —

Find someone who is working on a holiday—an airport worker, a gas station attendant, or the waitstaff at a restaurant—and do something kind for them.

Looking behind the Hurt

Look, I am sending you out as sheep among wolves.
So be as shrewd as snakes and harmless as doves.
MATTHEW 10:16

I've heard it said before that hurt people hurt people. While that adage doesn't justify the behavior, remembering it shifts my perspective from the behavior itself to the *why* behind the behavior. When I see the human being behind the action, I can better think through what my response ought to be instead of responding with hurtful words or actions of my own.

I couldn't help but reevaluate this perspective after my daughter, a small girl with a fierce sense of justice, witnessed a wrongdoing on the playground during recess and stood up to the perpetrator. Later that day, the perpetrator got even by shoving her into a set of lockers. I later learned that this particular student has a propensity for violence and is outside of the standard classroom for a good portion of the day, and I couldn't stop the fear that snaked through my heart.

What do we teach our children at these moments? The world is filled with potentially dangerous people whose actions physically hurt others. Do we look away from injustice in these circumstances? Do we respond to violence with violence of our own? These were the thoughts that rolled around in my head as I tossed and turned during the early morning hours, praying about my daughter's situation.

While individual circumstances will require different responses, my wrestling eventually reminded me that Jesus intentionally sent us out as sheep among wolves with the admonition that we are to be as shrewd as snakes and as harmless as doves. This guidance applies to every person or experience we have in our lives.

That is the biblical wisdom I shared with my daughter as she navigated the situation with this student, knowing that later it would impact the way she navigates the world. I warned her to be wise and aware and smart about when and how she engages (or chooses not to engage) but to always remember that there is very likely a hurting person behind hurtful actions. We can show compassion without condoning wrong behavior. Looking for the hurt underneath someone's words or actions often gives us a different perspective on a situation, enabling us to respond with divine discernment.

— Julie

— Today's Act of Kindness —

Practice being wise and gentle in your interactions,
even when someone hurts you.

Kind Applause

Encourage one another and build each other up, just as in fact you are doing.
1 THESSALONIANS 5:11, NIV

My daughter Jasmine has loved to dance since she was a little girl, so we researched dance studios in our area to find the one best suited to her. As winter came, we decided to attend a special performance put on by the studio, showcasing all the dancers who would be performing solo or in small groups for the upcoming spring competition season.

The dance numbers were moving along beautifully when one young girl got up to do her dance. Several moments into her performance she froze, unsure of what to do next, seemingly forgetting her next move. As the crowd realized what was happening, they began to applaud, offering her encouragement to continue. The girl began to cry, the music stopped, and we heard Ms. Melinda (her coach and the owner of the studio) above the crowd's cheering, encouraging this girl that she could do it and coaxing her to start again.

I watched as the young girl walked off to the side of the stage, where her coach hugged her, offered her reassurance, and sent her back out. The music started again, and people began to cheer loudly. When the dancer reached the part where she'd frozen in fear, you could hear Melinda's voice above the crowd, shouting, "Get it, girl!" And she did. As the applause increased, many were on their feet, and she finished her dance with a huge smile of success on her face. I had tears in my eyes from the support all these parents offered to this young dancer.

Sometimes encouragement can be hard to come by, especially when we make mistakes. We live in a world where failure is often avoided at all costs, and success in everything is what we strive for. But the reality is, we all fail at some point. When we encourage one another and build each other up, especially after a failure, we demonstrate some of the greatest kindness we can show to another person.

— Kendra

— Today's Act of Kindness —

Offer encouragement to someone who has been
discouraged or experienced a failure lately.

The Unadopted

God decided in advance to adopt us into his own family by
bringing us to himself through Jesus Christ. This is what
he wanted to do, and it gave him great pleasure.
EPHESIANS 1:5

Every year, Place of Hope, a local homeless shelter, runs an adopt-a-family program during Christmas. It's one of our favorite things to do as a family during the season: choose gifts for our adopted family off the wish lists, wrap presents, and deliver them to the shelter.

One year, I opened an e-mail with a list of yet-to-be-adopted families attached, along with a few notes from the director. I downloaded the attachment and scanned the details. There were six families still waiting, as well as several singles. One potential adoptee was a guy who said he didn't have much contact with his family but still wanted to send them a small gift.

As I read a bit further, my heart sank.

"I have ten more single guys," the e-mail said. "Do you want them all?"

My family had been participating in this program for a while when we found out that not everyone gets adopted. Although the directors, a kind couple we've worked with many times, try to give everyone a present, it usually ends up being something small, like a gift card. By and large, the unadopted people are single males in their middle years. Many are veterans; all have fallen on hard times.

When I first heard this, my heart broke a little. So now my family adopts the unadopted. If I'm being honest, it's not as much fun. Grown men want denim jeans and Carhartt jackets, electronics and underwear, not ponies and puzzles and Thomas the Tank Engine toys. Yet when I think about the love God showed us when he adopted us into his family, I am reminded that he didn't adopt us because he had to but because it gave him great pleasure. The heart of God is one that takes utmost pleasure in adopting everyone, including the forgotten, the misfits, the ones who recognize their need for grace and mercy. So now, when I mull over what color socks or what kind of work boots to purchase, I think to myself, *I'm choosing to do this for someone else, and it is my great pleasure and honor to be able to do so.*

— *Kristin*

— Today's Act of Kindness —

Who do you know that is "unadopted"
or forgotten? Do a kind act for them.

December

Off to the Races

Come, let us worship and bow down. Let us kneel before
the LORD our maker, for he is our God.
PSALM 95:6-7

I don't know about you, but I generally dread December 1 because, in my mind, it's the official start of the holiday season. I use the phrase "holiday season" specifically because it embodies all of the obligations and traditions that, when you stop and really think about it, have nothing to do with the sacred birth of our Savior. But nonetheless, all these obligations fall on me.

For example, everyone has a holiday party: the community organizations where my husband and I volunteer, our workplaces, our friends. On top of parties, there are Christmas cards, Christmas cookies, our hunt for a real Christmas tree, our yearly outing to see the Christmas lights at that one house on that one corner that sets one hundred thousand lights to music. These traditions get layered on top of already-busy schedules involving school and sports and work.

All these extra traditions, on their own, are fun and joyous and filled with giggles, messes, and memories. But when they're all piled up in the short few weeks between December 1 and Christmas morning, I can't help but start feeling like a bad mom, a bad wife, and a bad Christian for not juggling this month with a cheerful smile, a cute apron, and Pinterest perfection.

In response to all the busyness this season brings, I've discovered that when I make a conscious effort to focus more on Advent—preparing my heart and mind for Christ's birth, and helping my family to do the same—and less on the never-ending to-do lists, I strike a better balance. Finding extra moments to withdraw from the rat race and simply sit in the presence of Christ—worshiping, remembering the significance of Christ's birth, and kneeling before the Lord—makes me a better mom, wife, and friend during the rest of the busy day. I am better able to handle the tasks of the holiday season with kindness rather than frustration, because my heart and head are focused on Advent.

— Julie

— Today's Act of Kindness —

Fill yourself up by spending time with Christ
during Advent, and allow that fullnes to flow out
as kind words and actions toward others.

Kindness Returned

A man reaps what he sows.
GALATIANS 6:7, NIV

For the past couple of Christmas seasons, my family has made one of our acts of kindness to bring small gifts to two special ladies who work at our local grocery store. Both of the women work at the checkout counter, and without fail, they are quick to greet us, smile, and ask how we're doing.

That first year, seeing these two women became the highlight of our shopping trip. I'd bundle up my youngest child, Eleanor, and hurry off to do our weekly shopping. As soon as we'd enter the store, the friendly clerks would warmly greet us both by name and take time to visit with us. This continued all year long, week after week. We realized what a consistent blessing they were to us and how they most likely didn't get thanked too often for the job they did, so we thought they would be the perfect recipients for one of our acts of kindness. The kids made cards, and I bought chocolates and wrote nice thank-you notes, and then we brought our gifts to the ladies. These women were surprised by our presents and thanked us wholeheartedly while I stumbled over my words, attempting to tell them how much their kind and welcoming greetings had meant to us each week.

We planned to bring goodies to our friends at the grocery store again the next year. When Eleanor and I walked in with our gifts, one of the ladies rushed off to the employees' break room, saying that she had something for my daughter. It was a birthday present—a couple of books—because she knew how much Eleanor liked to read. I stood stunned for just a moment, blessed by such a thoughtful gift. While Eleanor spent the rest of the grocery store trip looking through her books, I realized how easily kindness can be returned to you when you give it away.

Have you noticed how kindness begets kindness? We often reap what we sow, and as a result, kind acts can cause others to reach out with their own kind acts, creating a snowball effect and encouraging others to extend kindness.

— Kendra

— Today's Act of Kindness —

Think of someone who has shown you kindness,
and find a way to return kindness to them.

DECEMBER 3

An Unlikely Delivery Crew

If you love only those who love you, what reward is there for that? . . . If you
are kind only to your friends, how are you different from anyone else?
MATTHEW 5:46-47

It was Halloween, and my husband was making the trick-or-treating rounds in our cul-de-sac with our children. They were thrilled to dress up like Rainbow Dash and the Little Mermaid, and they wanted to keep ringing doorbells and getting candy. Deciding to venture out further into the neighborhood, they stopped by the home of some neighbors we'd never met. As our daughters tugged on Tim's arms, anxious to go on to the next house for more candy, he chatted with the woman who answered the door. She told him about some health problems she'd been experiencing and how she was worried about some test results. He listened to her story, and after saying good-bye, he left her home resolved to pray for the woman and her health.

A couple of months later, as we were brainstorming ideas for acts of kindness we could do as a family during the month of December, he had the idea to check in on the neighbor and see how her health was doing. With a poinsettia in hand and our children once again in tow, he walked along snowy sidewalks to his destination. The girls rang the bell, but the door was answered this time by a man who looked a little harried and somewhat confused.

"Thanks," he said abruptly, not allowing Tim to get a word in as he took the poinsettia from Tim's arms and closed the door.

A bit stunned, Tim and the girls came home and related the story. "I think he thought I was a delivery man," Tim said, bemused. "But why would I have brought children along?"

Shrugging a bit, we decided not to worry too much about it and went on with our day. Yet it was hard to explain this incident to our children. Why are we kind to people who don't seem to notice or care? We reminded them (and ourselves, as well) that we are to show kindness to everyone, not just those who are kind in return. We asked them, "Didn't we have fun picking out pretty flowers?" Yes, we did, they replied. "And wasn't it fun to go for a short walk with Papa, out in the snow?" Yes, it was, they agreed. Even when things don't turn out the way we expect them to, we can find ways to be thankful for the gift of giving itself.

— *Kristin*

— *Today's Act of Kindness* —

Give something without expecting anything in return.

DECEMBER 4

With Open Arms

This is my commandment: Love each other in the same way I have loved you.
JOHN 15:12

Kyle and I recently spent the weekend with some of my college friends, another married couple. We made the several-hour trek up to her parents' place in the woods, which they lovingly refer to as their "shabin" (something in between a shed and a cabin) to spend time together, relax, and reminisce. We spent the unseasonably warm winter weekend walking their land, riding four-wheelers, playing cards, and sitting by the bonfire, all while catching up on life from the past almost-twenty years.

As we talked about all that had happened over the past decades, I felt a sense of love and comfort I'd missed from these friends for quite some time. Life had taken us down different paths, and I wasn't in contact with these friends like I'd once been. But their response to me was one of open arms, of kindness, of welcoming me back in as if I'd never been away. It felt good to be remembered, to be loved by others with whom I have so much history, to laugh and reminisce about old memories that only these dear friends would know.

There are times in our lives when relationships end, sometimes for good reasons, but there are also times when we simply go in different directions and fall out of touch with those we were once close with. Sometimes in order to love one another the way Jesus loves us, we need to rekindle a friendship or reconnect with those we've lost contact with simply because life has gotten busy, causing us to drift apart. Sometimes the comfort we need comes from those who know us best, who have been with us the longest, who know our faults and love us still, and who carry out Christ's command to love others in the same way that he has shown love to us.

— *Kendra*

— *Today's Act of Kindness* —

Ask God to show you whom you could reconnect with. Send
them a few words of encouragement or a note of kindness.

The Candy Bombs

You have been taught the holy Scriptures from childhood, and they have given you the wisdom to receive the salvation that comes by trusting in Christ Jesus.

2 TIMOTHY 3:15

"What are we doing today, Mom?" my girls asked me early one morning, climbing on top of the tufted orange living room chair and stretching eager arms as far as they could to reach the Advent tree hanging on the wall. It's a common question in our house in the month of December, as each individual slot in the tree is filled with a different activity for the day: a kind act, a Christmas project, an adventure we'll have as a family.

It was a weekend, so on that day we were going to "candy bomb" the local hospital's parking lot. We put together little bags of candy and added handmade tags to them, wishing the recipients a merry Christmas. Then, after bundling up against the cold, Tim and the girls headed to the local hospital, where the girls worked their way methodically from car to car, placing the bags under windshield wipers with Tim's help.

All too often, it's easy to exclude our children from acts of kindness. For example, Tim and I might give to a charity without taking the time to explain it to the kids. I've found that I need to be more intentional about including them. Teaching the Scriptures to children helps them later to have the wisdom to trust and believe in Jesus. As someone who grew up in the church, I can still remember the verses I memorized through Pioneer Girls. Verses like "For God has not given us a spirit of fear" (2 Timothy 1:7) played over and over in my mind when I thought I saw a ghost in my room or when a thunderstorm boomed too loudly. Those early lessons gave me a foundation upon which to trust in Jesus. Now a parent myself, I see that the principle of kindness and how that plays out in our lives is yet another great way to teach children about God's undeserved grace and mercy, and the boundless love he has for us—all while having fun together as a family. And if some of the lessons include candy? All the better.

— *Kristin*

— Today's Act of Kindness —

Brainstorm fun kindness-centered activities
to do with the children in your life.

The Worst Kind of Thief

"Don't sin by letting anger control you." Don't let the sun go down
while you are still angry, for anger gives a foothold to the devil.
EPHESIANS 4:26-27

My friend's father, having been admitted to the hospital, was slowly dying. His body was worn out and simply began shutting down, and the doctors could do nothing to stop it. As hard as it was for her to watch her loved one fade, the real tragedy in this story lies in the angry grudge this man nursed for years against his adult daughters. Rejecting their peacemaking efforts, he preferred holding tightly to perceived hurts over pursuing reconciliation. Every part of his life was colored by his unforgiveness, and this hurt his Christian witness to the nonbelievers in their extended family.

It wasn't until his final weeks that he reconciled with his daughters, sons-in-law, and grandchildren. While my friend and her sister heard repeatedly about how wonderful it was that their family was reunited and made whole on this father's deathbed, I couldn't help but cry hot, angry tears. Forgiveness, while better than never, came too late for a hundred family holidays and too late to leave behind beautiful memories made up of small moments—the ones that become the most precious because of their very ordinariness. The loss of precious memories broke my heart for my friend.

Unforgiveness is a thief. It steals precious time, it destroys our Christian example, and it consumes us. How can we live lives that reflect the character of God and that intentionally pour out mercy and kindness to the people around us when we have hearts festering with unforgiveness?

Does it surprise us that God knows this and, while acknowledging that we will be angry, warns us not to let anger control us? He even commands us to deal with our anger before the sun sets and before we go to bed. God knows that unforgiveness eats us up from the inside out and will cost us precious years and a compromised witness.

Instead of allowing anger to fester, take it to God, asking him to help you forgive—whether or not the other party deserves it. God cannot use you to your fullest potential if your heart is holding on to unforgiveness.

— *Julie*

— Today's Act of Kindness —

Choose to forgive an old hurt and let go of a grudge.

God at the Gas Station

Now all glory to God, who is able, through his mighty power at work within us, to accomplish infinitely more than we might ask or think.
EPHESIANS 3:20

It was an icy, cold day in early December, and it was our family's turn to post an act of kindness for the day on social media. As our car crunched over snowy, icy roads on our way into town, Tim and I brainstormed kindness ideas. We eventually concluded that we'd like to bless someone in the military since it was the anniversary of the bombing of Pearl Harbor.

"What are the odds we're going to find a person in the military, in uniform, on a day like today?" Tim mused.

To be honest, it seemed unlikely. After all, the population of the town we were cruising through was only a little more than seven thousand. And on such a gloomy winter day, no one seemed to be out and about. We prayed that God would reveal someone for us to bless.

We pulled into a gas station to fill up our tank and sat waiting patiently for an opportunity to bless someone. To our delight, within just a few minutes, a man in uniform pulled up to the gas pump. Tony, a husband and father with a bright smile, was in the navy, and he was heading to Florida for six months. Although he originally seemed surprised by Tim's request to allow us to pay for his gas, Tony agreed and stood chatting for a few minutes about his family and experiences in the armed forces. My husband shook Tony's hand, pumped his gas, and thanked him for his service. As Tim hopped back into our vehicle, rubbing his hands together to restore their warmth, he told me that it was one of his favorite things that we've done for someone else.

Sometimes my prayers to God feel more like a last-ditch effort rather than my first response. I believe that God answers prayer, but sometimes I try to do things on my own rather than turning to him first. Yet it's experiences like this one that remind me, time and again, that God is able to work through us to accomplish more than we can imagine. In return, our faith and our trust in God can be bolstered even by the smallest details of life, as his love for us shows up in unlikely places.

— *Kristin*

— Today's Act of Kindness —

Thank someone who has served and protected our country or communities. This could include servicemen or servicewomen, police officers, or firefighters.

Acknowledging Loss and Providing Comfort

Praise be to . . . the Father of compassion and the God of all comfort,
who comforts us in all our troubles, so that we can comfort those in
any trouble with the comfort we ourselves receive from God.

2 CORINTHIANS 1:3-4, NIV

My husband and I always knew we wanted to have a large family. We'd already birthed one child, opened our home to foster kids, adopted another, and were waiting for more, so when I found out I was once again pregnant, Kyle and I were very excited that we'd be growing our family even more.

Everything was fine for the first several weeks, and then without any warning, I lost the baby to miscarriage. I was sad and upset, quickly letting close friends and family members know what had happened. Everyone seemed to understand my feelings and offered me comfort and support.

Months later as Christmas was approaching, we were invited to dinner at my in-laws' house. When I walked through the door, my eyes immediately fell on their fireplace mantel, now covered in red stockings for each of the grandchildren. As we removed our boots and coats, my daughter looked up and asked who the small, white stocking in the middle of the fireplace was for. My mother-in-law looked at me, then at my daughter, and said that it was for the baby we had that was now with Jesus in heaven. My eyes filled with tears as all those months later she remembered and quietly commemorated our loss.

So many people are suffering loss and heartache, and although initially we may send encouragement or comfort, how often do we then just move on with life, forgetting the loss? Maybe you know the pain of loss yourself and wonder, *Does anyone else even remember or care?* I am so thankful that, even if no one else knows, God sees and remembers our pain. He promises to comfort us in all of our troubles, but he doesn't stop there—he then encourages us to offer comfort to others, just as we've received it from him. You never know the comfort your kindness may bring to another.

— Kendra

— Today's Act of Kindness —

Offer comfort to someone who needs it.

The Joy of Glitter Glue

*Whatever you do or say, do it as a representative of the Lord
Jesus, giving thanks through him to God the Father.*
COLOSSIANS 3:17

Really, when it comes down to it, the glitter glue was the deciding factor for my three- and five-year-old girls. Our mudroom closet is filled to bursting with art supplies and activities for us to use during the long winter months, including the notoriously messy-but-desirable glitter glue.

One day, as part of our daily acts of kindness during the Advent season, we decided to become Bheveni DreamCatchers. Bheveni is a small community in the African country of Swaziland. An organization called Children's HopeChest was asking people to sign up as "DreamCatchers" to help raise funds to build a new community center. At the time, the children of Bheveni gathered in a small building for lessons, singing, and learning, but only about sixty people were able to stand inside shoulder to shoulder, so many would end up sitting outside in the hot sun. We wanted to help change that reality.

With that in mind, my girls pulled out construction paper, markers, and glitter glue to decorate empty mason jars. We spent the afternoon decorating the jars, which then sat on our counter for the next few weeks. In them we collected change—from my husband's pockets, from my purse, and "commissions" the girls received for doing small chores around the house. Within three weeks, our family had collected $200 for the children of Bheveni—all thanks to a little excitement over glitter glue.

Sometimes we can get so caught up in the seriousness of the needs facing us that we can forget to add a little fun to giving. We are called to give thanks in all circumstances, including the happy ones! We honor God when we have fun helping others. And with a little intentionality, even something as simple as craft time with children and chores around the house can be used to bless others—glitter glue optional.

— *Kristin*

— Today's Act of Kindness —

Gather your spare change and give it to a worthy cause.

A Gift to Give Away

*Dear children, let's not merely say that we love each
other; let us show the truth by our actions.*

1 JOHN 3:18

Every Christmas one of each of my children's presents is to choose something they would like give to someone else. Leading up to the holiday, we look through catalogs from charitable organizations from which you can purchase items for donation—things like farm animals, school supplies, clean water, and so on. We encourage our children to prayerfully consider whom they'd like to give to each year.

It's wonderful to see their excitement and compassion for others as they decide what gift they'd like to give—one year it might be a goat and chickens, the next it could be a clean water well. They often spend hours scouring the magazines and circling their favorite options, before deciding on the one they want to give that year. No matter what they decide, Kyle and I discuss with the children how this will be a blessing to the person receiving the gift and how we are blessed to be able to give it.

This act of kindness and remembering others in need has in turn allowed our kids to feel empowered to give toward something they are passionate about in a very tangible way. Setting an example of giving on a regular basis shows our kids that this is part of our everyday lives, not just reserved for special occasions, and although we may be more intentional at certain times of the year, we keep trying, and we don't berate ourselves when we've missed opportunities to show kindness or give to others.

If you haven't been intentional about doing something kind for someone else lately, it's okay—today you can start again. Think about how you can incorporate your own family or friends and their passions into your giving. Consistency, rather than perfection, is our goal as we seek to live out Scripture's command to show our love for others through our actions.

— *Kendra*

— Today's Act of Kindness —

Find an organization that gives tangible gifts to those in
need, and purchase an item you feel passionate about.

Cross-Cultural Community

*There is no longer Jew or Gentile, slave or free, male and
female. For you are all one in Christ Jesus.*
GALATIANS 3:28

Several years ago my church supported our local Hispanic community by allowing them to hold their own church services in our building. They are a wonderful community of people, and as Christmas approached one year, I wondered if our church could do something more to support them.

I talked to their pastor and found out what their big needs were, and then our church decided to hold a blessing service for them. It was a wonderful cross-cultural morning as we worshiped and prayed together, celebrating Jesus and getting to know one another. It was such a success that we continued our relationship with this community, helping with needs as we heard of them and blessing families with practical things—clothing, furniture, and household items.

But with all of the things people donated and along with all the encouragement we received to keep going, there were a few people who weren't happy about our desire to help this Spanish-speaking church. A few voiced concerns because some of the recipients couldn't speak English or hadn't been in the US very long. As I sat in my living room, feeling discouraged by these comments, I opened my Bible and was reminded that in God's eyes, there is no longer Jew or Gentile, slave or free, male or female. There is no longer English-speaking or Spanish-speaking. We are all one in Christ Jesus. This passage renewed my desire to continue on with what we were doing, assured that God was pleased with our efforts.

Have you ever been questioned about helping others? Maybe someone has been critical of a people group you've had a desire to help. Even Christians can hold prejudices against others or have biases against those who are different from them, but we can't let this discourage us. Our love may not be perfect, but thank God that his is. If we are following what he's asked us to do and loving those he's asked us to show kindness to, we can continue confidently and can prayerfully release any criticism we receive to him.

— *Kendra*

— Today's Act of Kindness —

Show kindness toward a people group who often face criticism.

Winter-Weather Blessings

If you help the poor, you are lending to the LORD—and he will repay you!
PROVERBS 19:17

Minnesota winters can get bitterly cold. The students in my community are expected to go outside for recess unless the wind chill has caused the temperatures to dip into subzero territory. This means there are plenty of wintry days when elementary-aged children are bundled up and sent out on snowy playgrounds to burn off pent-up energy before returning to warm classrooms.

With two children in elementary school, I've learned how desperately schools appreciate donations of extra sets of boots, snow pants, mittens, and warm hats. They are needed not only for kids whose parents have a hard time affording these items, but also as backups to lend out on the occasions when children, my own included, have traipsed out of the house with only one mitten or without a hat—or when their snow pants have become temporarily lost in the bottomless pit otherwise known as the school's lost and found.

Because children seem to always mysteriously lose one mitten the same way my dryer eats single socks, I've started picking up a few extra sets of mittens, hats, boots, coats, and snow pants during Black Friday sales, on spring clearance racks, and at garage sales, and I also stash away the items my kids outgrow seemingly overnight. As our weather turns from brisk autumn days into snowy winter mornings, I bring the extras to the school office or to a trusted teacher, knowing that they'll get the items into the hands that need them most.

Because there is no end to the need, when we take care of children or of the poor—no matter who they are, where they are from, or what their parents believe— we are actually lending to God, and he is generous beyond measure when repaying us. He may not return the cost to us mitten for mitten, but he will meet our physical and spiritual needs when we are generous.

— Julie

— Today's Act of Kindness —

Take care of the children in your community by donating
winter clothes to a local school or homeless shelter.

Strength in Numbers

*Two people are better off than one, for they can help each other
succeed. If one person falls, the other can reach out and help.*
ECCLESIASTES 4:9-10

My brother-in-law Marin is from Romania, a country in Eastern Europe. When we'd gather as extended family, he'd tell us stories of what it was like to grow up and live in the poor conditions of rural Romania at the time. His life, we found out, had been quite different than ours. Harsh winters and poor housing, along with few ways to get necessary supplies to make things better, have led to a hard life for his family members still living in that poor area.

As Christmas drew near one year, he and my sister-in-law approached our family with an idea. What if we took the money we would normally spend on each other's gifts and, instead, pooled our resources to buy pigs and other food for Marin's family in Romania? We thought it was a wonderful idea. Each family gave what they could, and in the end we were able to collect enough money for his family to buy several months' worth of food. Each year since then, we have continued to send Christmas wishes and money to his family in Romania.

You don't have to know someone from another part of the world to be able to send money or needed items. One friend told me that she and her extended family decided to adopt another family in need in their own community for Christmas. They pooled their resources and bought the family a new washer and dryer along with personal gifts for each family member. She said the people were overwhelmed because they hadn't expected to be given such a wonderful Christmas present. My friend said it was by far her family's favorite Christmas memory.

Because two are better than one, joining forces with those around us to bless someone or help out with a problem, either locally or across the ocean, can make all the difference in someone else's life. We were meant to do life and show kindness in community because there is strength in numbers.

— *Kendra*

— Today's Act of Kindness —

Find others that you can join forces with to bless
someone else this Christmas season.

Strangers among Us

You must not mistreat or oppress foreigners in any way. Remember, you yourselves were once foreigners in the land of Egypt.

EXODUS 22:21

Aaron and I each come from a long line of pastors and missionaries, and I treasure our faith lineage. My cousin Lisa, currently serving as a missionary in Japan, recently shared with me her story of being newly married and arriving on the mission field in a tiny village in Mexico many years ago. I was struck by how timely and instructional it was for me, now living in a community with a large influx of refugees.

This Mexican village had no running water or electricity, and Lisa found herself struggling with the language and trying to figure out how to survive in such a primitive environment. The entire village was full of curiosity at this strange young couple who had come to live among them and yet were so woefully unprepared for even the most obvious tasks of survival. Still, they welcomed Lisa and her husband, Gary, into their community.

They taught Lisa how to wash clothes on a rock in the river and invited her to share their lunches. They taught her how to turn her oil drum into a wood-burning stove to cook corn tortillas and how to shop for and cook with local ingredients. They showed them how to find the trail and where to safely climb down the cliff face to get fresh spring water for drinking. Even the children got involved by teaching her how to swim in the ocean and dive through the waves so she wouldn't drown.

She was a foreigner in a foreign land, and the locals opened their hearts with kindness and graciousness. She and Gary were there to share the love of Christ with the villagers, but the villagers seemed to already have Exodus 22:21 figured out—they came alongside Lisa and Gary with love and gentle teaching.

Lisa's story of how these villagers supported and encouraged them caused me to stop and consider in a new light how I respond to those who are new in my country. Our spiritual ancestors were once foreigners too, and we're called to treat foreigners today with compassion and respect.

— Julie

— Today's Act of Kindness —

Do something especially kind for someone
who was not born in your country.

We Need You

Keep on asking, and you will receive what you ask for. Keep on seeking, and
you will find. Keep on knocking, and the door will be opened to you.
MATTHEW 7:7

I paused as I got ready to share a message on social media in mid-December, reading it through once more before pressing the "post" button. I had received the list of unadopted families earlier that morning, but knowing my family couldn't handle it all ourselves, I asked for help:

> We need you! Each year, Place of Hope homeless shelter adopts families and individuals in need. Again this year, there are a few families who have yet to be adopted, and with the deadline looming, we would love to have everyone receive gifts. There are a couple of families left, but the majority of folks are single or couples without kids. A quick glance over their wish lists shows that although some dream of big electronics, most are asking for gift cards from places like Coborn's or Walmart and necessities like socks, razors, and sleepwear. Would you be willing to take on a single person, couple, or family? Wrapped presents need to be dropped off by Friday. Also, please share this with others!

Within hours, the information had been shared by several friends on their Facebook pages, and I received a flurry of messages in response. By the following day, all the remaining families had been adopted by friends and acquaintances, near and far. The most thoughtful message came from an old high school friend, now living and working in Zurich, who offered to send a bank transfer if someone else was willing to do the shopping locally.

One friend, after adopting a family that Christmas, messaged me again the next fall. "How can we do this again?" she wondered. "My family and I would love to adopt a family each Christmas. Who should I contact?"

Sometimes, all kindness requires of us is to bring awareness to others. I didn't need to buy gifts for all of the remaining families myself—I simply had to ask others to help fill the gap. When we are persistent, when we keep seeking, knocking, and asking, we can be sure that God will answer us. What needs are you aware of that you can bring to the attention of others?

— Kristin

— Today's Act of Kindness —

Raise awareness of a need, and ask others
to help you work toward meeting it.

DECEMBER 16

A Pattern of Giving

Give as freely as you have received!
MATTHEW 10:8

"I know a family that has taken in some boys. They need clothes, and immediately I thought of you," my neighbor explained over the phone one cold winter evening as I listened to the story of her friends. "It sounds like the boys are the same sizes as your kids. Is there any way you could help?"

"Of course I can," I said and headed upstairs to sort through my boys' closets. I found plenty of items that were still in good shape but were too small or that we had too many of.

A few weeks later another neighbor asked if I had any extra baby items I could give to a friend of hers, a new immigrant in our area, who was in need of all the basics. Again, I dug through closets, looking for things that I had too many of or that I wasn't using anymore to give to another mom who needed them more than I did.

This has happened several times over the past few years—neighbors or friends asking for items that we no longer need but that could be useful to someone else. I consider it a huge compliment that they would think of me and ask if I could give to someone in need, knowing that I'll be willing to help.

We all have the ability to answer Jesus' command to give as freely as we have received. Do you know someone who freely gives of what they have? Think about the character traits you admire about them. Perhaps they are kind, grateful, or humble. Are you someone who is able to give easily to others when asked, or do you find it hard to part with things even if you do not need them anymore? Even if we have a more difficult time with giving freely, we all have the ability to grow in this area, and as we do so, to develop these traits that we admire in others.

— *Kendra*

— Today's Act of Kindness —

Give something away to someone who needs it more than you do.

Stuck

Dear brothers and sisters, never get tired of doing good.
2 THESSALONIANS 3:13

At the end of an especially difficult day, I turned onto our side street after picking up my two young children from day care. It had snowed the night before, and the snowplow had buried my driveway entrance with at least a foot of heavily compacted snow while we were gone. I managed to plow the minivan through the snow at the bottom of the driveway, only to find my tires spinning uselessly as I tried to drive up the remaining fifty feet at a slight incline and into the garage.

After slipping and sliding back down the driveway, I was fed up. I threw open the van doors, grabbed my kids, and—in my suit and heels—carried them through the three inches of snow blanketing my driveway and into the house. My van, having slid to a stop at a crazy angle, was a humiliatingly silent testament to all my neighbors that my day had been lousy and that I'd lost my battle against the snow.

About twenty minutes later, I heard a knock at the door. It was my neighbor—a father and grandfather—who lived two houses down. He had his snowblower with him: he had taken care of the snow left behind by the plow and had started up my driveway. With the help of his snowblower and his pushing the back of the van, I was able to get the van up the driveway and into the garage.

The fact that my neighbor noticed my catawampus parking job and helped me—a young mom with toddlers—warmed my heart and redeemed a rotten, no-good day.

His simple kindness still flashes across my mind and brings a smile to my face as I pull into my driveway on snowy days. It is amazing how a simple act of kindness can have a lasting impact on someone, even years later. When I start to wonder whether "doing good" actually does any good in a world that feels crazy, I remember how I felt that snowy day, and I'm encouraged to keep going. Let's not tire of doing good, knowing that a simple kindness can have an outsize impact on someone's life.

— *Julie*

— Today's Act of Kindness —

Help a mom who seems a bit frazzled.

Puppy Love

*I am giving you a new commandment: Love each other. Just as
I have loved you, you should love each other. Your love for one
another will prove to the world that you are my disciples.*

JOHN 13:34-35

My middle daughter, Jasmine, has always had an affinity for animals. Whenever
we visit a home with pets, she will stay with the dog or cat, spending time with it
and showing it love. It's as if animals offer a comfort to her like nothing else does.
One winter, while visiting a friend who had a new puppy, we once again saw how
Jasmine loved the dog, and we decided it was time for our family to get one of our
own. We searched the Internet for a local breeder and surprised our kids with a
new puppy.

Kyle and I are not particularly animal people. It had never crossed our minds
to get a pet before Jasmine came into our lives. Whenever I had to take the puppy
outside in the middle of cold Minnesota winter nights, I would think about what
comfort the puppy was offering my daughter—how she'd lie by him at night, pet-
ting him and whispering to him. I would remember that often we do things for
others, even sacrificially, because we see that it benefits them.

Jesus' love for us is so great, and his most important commandment to us is a
reflection of that: we are to love each other just as he has loved us, because that is
how we will prove to the world that we are his disciples. Sacrificial love is not easy.
Even with our children or other loved ones, putting their needs above our own
comfort is challenging at times. We must certainly maintain balance in also taking care of ourselves, but we must make sure that in doing so, we are still showing
God's love and kindness toward those around us, even when there is no personal
benefit we will gain from it.

— *Kendra*

— Today's Act of Kindness —

Do a kind act that does not benefit you.

Do for One

*I tell you the truth, when you did it to one of the least of these
my brothers and sisters, you were doing it to me!*
MATTHEW 25:40

In the background, carols crooned about white Christmases and holy nights. Earlier in the day, I'd marveled over the sun dog shimmering in rainbow arcs around the sun. It was December, and life seemed beautiful and magical once again.

Evening settled in, and I felt cozy and warm even as I cleaned up dinner, while art supplies left over from the day's projects slid haphazardly across the counter and the baby squawked for more supper, thumping her arms on her high chair. My husband and older two children had just left the house to go bell ringing for the Salvation Army, so with a moment to myself, I paused to look at the news.

A headline caught my eye, and I found myself reading about war and bombings, the lives of innocent women and children lost. Suddenly my cheery kitchen, the Christmas music, the comfort—it all seemed like a mockery in the face of such tragedy. *How insignificant our acts of kindness are,* I thought helplessly, hopelessly. *How can it be that I have so much and others have so little, simply because of where we were born?* I felt burdened by the weight of that unbearable truth.

I was reminded of what Andy Stanley has said: "Do for one what you wish you could do for everyone." And I was reminded of how two thousand years ago, shepherds on a hill came to worship a baby. And later, how wise men brought gifts to a child. These were small kindnesses in the moment. Yet they would eventually have a profound impact on the Christmas story and how we respond to it. We never know the ripples our small acts of kindness will have on the currents of history.

— *Kristin*

— Today's Act of Kindness —

Instead of feeling overwhelmed by your inability to fix everything that's wrong in the world, thank God for the people and situations you do have the ability to help. Then make a move toward doing for one what you wish you could do for all.

The Christmas Wreaths

Whenever we have the opportunity, we should do good to everyone.

GALATIANS 6:10

When I was a child, every winter my family would load up our car and make the eight-hour trek to my grandparents' house in North Dakota to celebrate Christmas. My parents would have spent the previous couple of months making wreaths that they would sell to make extra money for Christmas presents and travel. One year, my parents had a surplus of wreaths that, although beautiful, just hadn't sold.

As we packed up our car that year, my dad decided to bring the extra wreaths with us, believing God would show us what to do with them. We arrived at my grandparents' house, and while enjoying the days leading up to Christmas, we had conversations about what to do with the wreaths. Finally, someone suggested we distribute them to the residents of the local nursing home, and my parents readily agreed.

When we walked through the doors later that evening, I watched as my dad explained to the staff what we were doing, and they smiled and nodded, agreeing that it was a great idea. We went from room to room, my dad knocking on the doors, greeting each resident, saying "Merry Christmas," and offering a wreath to hang on the door. Many thanks were offered and jokes and merriment were shared as we slowly made our way around the home. As we neared the end, my dad wiped tears from his eyes as he told me of a few residents who said it was the only gift they'd receive that year. This became a distinct memory for me of what kindness toward others can do not only for the person receiving the kindness but for the giver as well.

We are encouraged that whenever we have the opportunity, we should do good to everyone, looking for opportunities throughout our days to extend goodness and kindness to others. On the surface this may seem easy, but it takes intention on our part to notice needs and look for ways to use what we may already have, even something like extra wreaths, to be a blessing to someone else.

— Kendra

— Today's Act of Kindness —

Give something away that you have an extra of.

Pet Shopping

*God is working in you, giving you the desire and
the power to do what pleases him.*
PHILIPPIANS 2:13

Hugo, Shortcake, Mrs. Buffy. As I scrolled down the list of pets available for adoption on the Happy Tails Rescue website, my children kept pointing at the pictures, exclaiming over them, and asking me to read the details of each pet. The dogs were cute, they said, but they missed our temporary pet Kit Kat, and so they kept gravitating toward the cats.

"They're so cute, Mom! I wish we could have one!" their little voices chorused.

I smiled, agreeing, but tempered my response with the reminder that we weren't in the market for a permanent pet.

That didn't mean we couldn't dream a little, though. Snuggled up together on the couch, my kids sat on either side of me while we talked about the pros and cons of cats and dogs. Then we got down to the real business of the day: shopping for the animal rescue's needs. That morning when I had read out our kind act of the day, written on a small slip of paper taken from our Advent tree, the children were overjoyed at the thought of helping these sweet animals. I endured as much kid excitement as I could take before giving in during the baby's nap time that afternoon. Finding the link for the animal rescue's online wish list, we clicked over to Amazon, buying puppy pads, food bowls, and cat chews to be sent directly to the rescue's location. We talked and made decisions together about what items we should choose, the kids' excitement palpable with every click.

"That was fun, Mom," Elise said when we were finished. "I'm glad we could help those dogs and cats."

"Me too," I agreed. It hit me that nothing about this kind act felt frustrating or difficult—in fact, it was a joy. The more we help others and show the people (and pets) in this world kindness, the more God will work in us, giving us the desire and the power to do what pleases him.

— Kristin

— Today's Act of Kindness —

Find a way to show kindness to animals today.

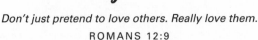

Watching for Pauls

Don't just pretend to love others. Really love them.
ROMANS 12:9

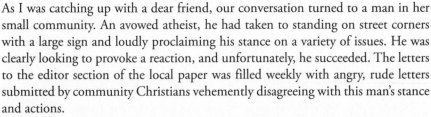

As I was catching up with a dear friend, our conversation turned to a man in her small community. An avowed atheist, he had taken to standing on street corners with a large sign and loudly proclaiming his stance on a variety of issues. He was clearly looking to provoke a reaction, and unfortunately, he succeeded. The letters to the editor section of the local paper was filled weekly with angry, rude letters submitted by community Christians vehemently disagreeing with this man's stance and actions.

My friend's position on the entire situation struck me as particularly wise. She was irritated at the Christians who were publicly berating this individual. She was frustrated by their misunderstanding of what it means to engage with nonbelievers in a respectful dialogue—one that invites others into a relationship with Christ rather than shutting down conversation and living up to the (sometimes rightfully earned) reputation of Christians as hateful individuals.

She told me that this man had been attending local churches and listening to the gospel, and had even subscribed to my friend's blog in which she explores faith, life, and what it means to be a Christian.

"Julie, this man is *Paul*—you know, before he met Christ," she said, with frustration evident in her voice. Although he proclaimed to have no faith, his actions revealed an inner battle as he continued to engage and listen, and he was clearly being drawn toward Christ. Her words made me stop to think about the potential Pauls in my own life—how do I treat people with whom I disagree, especially those who do not share my faith?

We are called to be loving toward people, to *really love* them, even when we do not agree with their message, and perhaps *especially* when we do not agree with their message. This is hard stuff, and I often wrestle with putting it into action. It is my prayer that I would not miss the Pauls of this generation, and that I would recognize those who are seeking God (even if they do not yet know it), take a deep breath, and engage in conversation with respect and empathy.

— Julie

— Today's Act of Kindness —

Think of someone you know who is a potential Paul. Pray
for them and extend them some extra kindness.

411 Children

Whatever is good and perfect is a gift coming down to us from God our Father, who created all the lights in the heavens. He never changes or casts a shifting shadow.

JAMES 1:17

Four hundred and eleven. That was the number of underprivileged kids that walked through the Kids' Hope Shop at the homeless shelter on a December evening. They stood outside in a line wrapping around the building, blowing on their hands and stomping their feet to ward off the chill. Once inside, they walked through a Nativity scene, enjoyed a lasagna dinner, and then entered a large room full of donated items for parents, teens, and smaller children. They chose items for each of their family members, wrapped them, and took them home to put under the tree for Christmas.

I was part of the wrapping crew. Hugely pregnant, I stretched my back and smiled at the children in line, waiting their turn to wrap gifts. Some children hurried through their gift wrapping with reckless abandon, joyously grabbing tags and bows to adorn them. Others were deliberate, almost unsmiling in their determination to choose exactly the right wrapping paper for each family member, with small, grubby hands firmly placing crooked tape and writing names on tags in shaky handwriting.

After I'd spent more than three hours standing there wrapping gifts, my feet were protesting. I took a short break and then headed back. After another couple of hours, we were finally finished cleaning up. As we left, I couldn't help but whisper to Tim, "I love this event. It's one of my favorite nights of the year." Nodding, he agreed, reaching over to take my hand in his as we drove away from the shelter toward home.

Nights like that remind me of God's love for us; experiences like these are good and perfect gifts that come from God. And it makes me think: *Isn't our ability to help others, to show kindness, to spread love, a gift in itself?* Despite the hours spent helping to wrap other people's gifts, the joy it brings to me to help others is a precious gift beyond measure, yet another reflection of how God lavishes us with gifts and delights in seeing us do the same for others.

— *Kristin*

— Today's Act of Kindness —

Give someone a gift, and thank God for
the opportunity to bless them.

Senior Bowling

Is there any encouragement from belonging to Christ? Any
comfort from his love? Any fellowship together in the Spirit?
Are your hearts tender and compassionate? Then make me truly
happy by agreeing wholeheartedly with each other, loving one
another, and working together with one mind and purpose.

PHILIPPIANS 2:1-2

One year as Christmas approached, our friend Carl contacted a local nursing home wondering if there was something he and his family could do for the residents over the holidays. The staff quickly responded that, yes, there was something they could do. Several residents did not have family that lived in the area and wouldn't be expecting any visitors over the holidays. They then asked if he'd like to come and bowl with the residents on Christmas Eve (bowling being one of their favorite activities).

Our friend said yes, and as he relayed the conversation to Kyle and me, he asked if we'd like to join their family. We immediately agreed. We explained to our own extended families that we'd need to move our Christmas Eve gathering around a bit and then planned to meet our friends.

As we walked into the nursing home a few weeks later, the facility was quieter than usual, with many residents out with family members. The activities coordinator brought us into the gathering room where we'd bowl together. We spent the next couple of hours bowling and cheering each other on. The kids set up the pins after each ball was thrown, and we passed out flowers and treats that we'd brought for the residents. It became a favorite memory my kids still talk about today.

As Christians, if we've received any encouragement, any comfort from God's love, or any fellowship from his people, then we should, in turn, love one another and work together with one mind and purpose. Acts of kindness are good things to do on your own, but gather a friend or two and somehow the excitement grows exponentially. Just as our friend Carl invited us to join what his family was already doing, we can do the same with our kind acts. Who could you ask today to join you?

— Kendra

— Today's Act of Kindness —

Invite someone to go with you to do something
for a local nursing home—stop by with treats,
visit the residents, or ask to join an activity.

Strong and Courageous

Have I not commanded you? Be strong and courageous.
Do not be afraid; do not be discouraged, for the LORD
your God will be with you wherever you go.
JOSHUA 1:9, NIV

I sometimes grow frustrated seeing Jesus repeatedly portrayed in pastoral scenes with the requisite woolly lamb in his arms or surrounded by a posse of peaceful youngsters. Yes, Jesus frequently embodied gentle compassion. But he was made of far sturdier stuff than the wimpy Jesus I so often see depicted in portraits.

Today we celebrate the birth of an audacious, bold Savior who stood up for the weak and who turned the religious leaders of his day upside down and inside out. They considered him to be a renegade, but he was actually a leader who offered forgiveness, calling the forgiven ones to leave behind their sinful ways.

He expected his disciples to be just as audacious. After his death, they were sent out into unknown places and lived lives that, even by the standards of that age, cannot be defined as comfortable or ordinary.

Being kind is often, I think, viewed by our American culture the same way as those portraits of Jesus: passive, naive, and—dare I say it—weak. Do not be fooled by our culture's skewed understanding of kindness. We are not called to wimpy kindness; we are called to intentional kindness—the kind that requires us to lay down our lives; to sacrifice our time, talents, and treasure for others; to love the unlovable, stand up for the downtrodden, and wade into the muck of life. We are called to kindness that requires strength and courage as we get shoved far outside our comfort zones.

When we view life through the lens of biblical kindness, we will act in counter-cultural and radical ways. And isn't that exactly what Christ calls us to—to live so differently from those around us that others seek us out to find out what we have, that they might have it too? As we live differently from those around us, we are not to be fearful or discouraged, but instead to be strong and courageous because the Lord our God goes with us wherever we go.

— *Julie*

— Today's Act of Kindness —

Celebrate Christ's birth with an especially
courageous act of kindness.

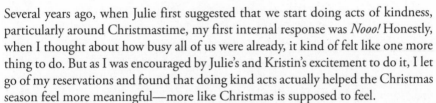

Not Just One More Thing to Do

Do everything with love.
1 CORINTHIANS 16:14

Several years ago, when Julie first suggested that we start doing acts of kindness, particularly around Christmastime, my first internal response was *Nooo!* Honestly, when I thought about how busy all of us were already, it kind of felt like one more thing to do. But as I was encouraged by Julie's and Kristin's excitement to do it, I let go of my reservations and found that doing kind acts actually helped the Christmas season feel more meaningful—more like Christmas is supposed to feel.

Then one year, Kristin had the idea that after Christmas, we should do a whole year of kindness. Every day we would do a kind act for someone else, and again I thought, *Nooo!* Although I could imagine doing acts of kindness during the Christmas season, it just seemed like a lot of work to continue them throughout the whole year. Who really needs one more thing to do? But after a little discussion about what it would look like, I agreed to do it with them, however grudgingly, and again I found out the most amazing thing (something you've probably discovered for yourself by this point): over time, the kind acts simply became a part of who I am. They were no longer separate acts I had to fit into my day, independent of everything else I had to do. They became a natural expression of love and care toward others, which only enhanced what I was already doing in my life. Doing intentional acts of kindness added a new dimension to my faith and love for God that I had not experienced before we began.

Deciding to add kind acts to our days can feel like adding one more thing to an already-full to-do list. But when we do *everything* with love, we have the opportunity to extend kindness toward others during the course of our normal days. We just might find that we are not only following God's command to love, but that doing so gives our spirits a sense of fulfillment, reminding us of what is truly important.

— *Kendra*

— Today's Act of Kindness —

Come up with a small way to show kindness to someone
in the places you are already going. Buy someone a cup
of coffee, share a treat, or leave an encouraging note.

Confidence Keepers

A gossip goes around telling secrets, but those who
are trustworthy can keep a confidence.
PROVERBS 11:13

While keeping confidences is an integral part of my job as an attorney, I long ago learned the value of being a person who listens without repeating what I've been trusted with. Many times, people simply need to speak out loud as they process a scenario and don't need any particular input from me other than being actively present, actively listening. After we've hung up the phone, or after we've given one last hug outside the coffee shop before jumping into our cars, I have decisions to make about the information I've learned.

And unless it is necessary to share in order to protect or help someone in danger, I don't repeat it.

In a culture that overshares and encourages "friendships" that can be better defined as "frenemies," letting interesting tidbits go unspoken requires swimming against the cultural tide. It requires guarding our words and our tongues and checking our hearts before deciding to share.

Do I fail at this? *Yes.* Sometimes I do. But I strive to practice the art of secret keeping, and I find that it gets easier and easier to let the things I learn in confidence stay there, unspoken and not repeated.

Don't get me wrong, there are certain things that must be shared, that could do great harm if left unspoken and secret. I'm talking here about the things that do harm *when repeated*—that expose a woman in her weakness, in her worst moment, in her vulnerability. I'm talking about sharing things about another person that are calculated to show our superiority or to raise our social standing within a group by exposing someone else.

We, as people who love and follow Christ, are called—*are required*—to cover one another with grace. This means we choose not to expose another's struggle for all the world, our church congregation, or our circle of friends to ridicule behind polite smiles and secret snickers. We are called to unity, not division. When we are people who can listen compassionately without repeating what we've heard and who let juicy gossip die instead of repeating it, it builds community, builds up those around us, and sets us apart as trustworthy.

— Julie

— Today's Act of Kindness —

The next time you hear a secret you feel tempted
to repeat, practice keeping it to yourself.

The Gift of Gratitude

The LORD has told you what is good, and this is what he requires of you:
to do what is right, to love mercy, and to walk humbly with your God.

MICAH 6:8

Glancing over toward my husband, I noticed that he was crying. He is a strong man with a tender heart. It was near the end of the evening at the retreat for single moms, and as a breakout speaker talking about finances later in the weekend, he was one of the only men present in the room. As he reached over to the row ahead of us and hugged the director of the retreat, he tried to say something to her but couldn't quite manage to choke it out amid the tears.

When I asked him about it later, he said he wanted to tell her thank you for letting him be a part of the event.

He and I both have a special place in our hearts for single moms. I wasn't raised by one, but my husband was. His mother was a strong woman who taught him to be thoughtful and courteous, loving and respectful. As a family, we've invited single moms and their children to live with us for a few months while they get back on their feet. We've bought appliances, covered mortgage payments, and taken care of medical bills—not because of how great we are, but because of how great God is.

Seeing my husband's tears, and knowing the heartfelt emotion behind his words, I was struck by how generosity changes the person doing the giving. When we obey God's commands to do what is right, to love mercy, and to walk humbly with him, we get to participate in his greater story for each other. Whenever I think of the things we've been allowed to accomplish with God's help, the acts of kindness that we've had the great privilege to do, I can't help but pray, *Thank you, God, for letting us be a part of this.*

— *Kristin*

— Today's Act of Kindness —

Spend time thanking God for the acts of kindness he
has allowed you to take part in this year and the ways
in which they've impacted the lives of others. Pray that
he would continue to multiply these kindnesses.

Bringing God to Work

The Holy Spirit produces this kind of fruit in our lives: love, joy,
peace, patience, kindness, goodness, faithfulness.

GALATIANS 5:22

My husband runs the human resources department at a company in our commu-nity. He has been there for a little less than two years, and he spent the first several months in his new position inviting people out to lunch. Managers, supervisors, team leads—every week he was buying coworkers lunch all around town. Yes, you read that correctly. My husband was not only inviting coworkers out to lunch, he was *buying* every one of them lunch. Upon seeing our credit card statement those first few months, I quietly swallowed my objections, knowing that he was wisely and intentionally investing in developing relationships and that this up-front cost would yield dividends later.

He periodically picks up coffee and donuts for his staff, drives hours to attend funerals for coworkers' parents, quietly pulls someone aside to share an insight that will allow that person to shine in the spotlight. His job often has him working hard behind the scenes to smooth out misunderstandings, bolster someone's confidence, or help individuals navigate conflict in a healthy manner that pushes the company forward rather than creating internal weaknesses.

My husband is prayerful in his approach to difficult situations, and while he wouldn't necessarily shout it from the rooftop, he intentionally practices the fruits of the Spirit within his workplace as a part of the essential functions of his job. He is a peacemaker and joy-bringer, and he works to encourage attitudes of patience and kindness in those who are leading others.

This approach to human resources has paid off. Because he has proven himself trustworthy and a team player, he is able to have quiet, difficult conversations with integrity and trust. His actions stem from his heart and his faith, whether or not others always recognize it. As he practices patience and kindness, and as he strives to create a work community filled with love and peace, he is quietly bringing God to work with him every single day.

— *Julie*

— Today's Act of Kindness —

Start bringing God to work or school with
you through the fruits of the Spirit.

Serving Up Kindness

You yourself must be an example to them by doing good works of every kind.

TITUS 2:7

One winter my friend Christa decided to start helping out at the Meals on Wheels program that delivers hot meals to elderly residents in her community. She told me that she had an itch to give more of herself away, even to complete strangers, and that she hoped to shine the light of Jesus into their lives.

She also told her three boys that they would be helping her when summer came around. Initially, the boys had grumbled and even asked what they'd get paid for helping, but as she and her husband, Jason, explained to them the importance of serving others (and that staying home wasn't an option), they begrudgingly agreed. The boys ended up thoroughly enjoying themselves, and as the summer went on they were engaging in conversation with the elderly people and even at times arguing about who would get to carry the trays.

She went on to tell me, "This once-a-week serving is not fancy, and it goes unnoticed by many. We believe that including our boys in this small act of kindness will stick with them as they grow into young men who will have a greater desire to see love and kindness in the world around them."

Christa is an example of doing good works of every kind, leading her family by her godly example. She began a pattern of being the hands and feet of Jesus in her community, and then she took the time to show her children how to do it as well. We don't have to be parents to set a good example for others. We all have other people who are observing our lives and actions, and the best way to "tell" them to do some act of kindness is to do it ourselves and then ask others to join us.

— *Kendra*

— Today's Act of Kindness —

The next time you do an act of kindness,
invite someone else to join you.

Kind Thoughts, Starting with Yourself

Kind words are like honey—sweet to the soul and healthy for the body.
PROVERBS 16:24

While coming up with some goals for the new year, I realized that many of the things I wanted to accomplish—while very good things—came from a place of being unhappy with myself. I began to see that many of the thoughts I was having about myself were critical and condemning.

These thoughts I allowed in were things I would never say to anyone else, or even *think* about anyone else. But somehow, I had no problem saying these things to myself. For example, I would never ask someone, "Why can't you just lose those last ten pounds?" Yet I feel completely justified in asking myself this question on a regular basis.

I often berate myself for saying the wrong thing, when I would totally offer grace to someone else in the same situation and tell them not to give it another thought. I can be hard on myself when I make a mistake, but I would offer mercy to another when they mess up, even reminding them that no one is perfect.

This year I have decided that this double standard of kindness needs to stop. It will be a hard habit to break, I'm sure, and it will take time, but if I want my kindness toward others to be truly effective, I have to start by being kind to myself.

Often it seems that unkindness will creep into our thoughts unchallenged. We can go months or even years thinking unkind or critical things about ourselves privately without even realizing it. Because we know that kind words are like honey—sweet to the soul and healthy to the body—the truth is simple: we all need kind words and actions. We can begin by assessing how we treat ourselves. Don't let yourself be bullied by your own thoughts. This year, let's take control of what we think about ourselves and be willing to extend grace, love, and mercy to ourselves first, just as we would to another.

— *Kendra*

— Today's Act of Kindness —

When you find your thoughts toward yourself being
critical, stop and respond in kindness instead.

Advent Acts of Kindness

The idea behind Advent Acts of Kindness is simple: to change the focus during the Christmas season from *consumption* to *compassion*. With that purpose in mind, each year our families do one kind thing for someone else, every day, from December 1 through December 25. This is not meant to be "one more thing" to add to the Christmas to-do list. Rather, it's a way to revel in the joy of doing something unexpected for another person, no strings attached. Slow down, savor the moment, and enjoy the season of Advent as you prepare to celebrate the birth of our Savior.

1. Write encouraging notes to place inside your children's school lunches.
2. Buy or make treats for your coworkers.
3. Send cards and supplies to servicepersons or veterans through organizations like Operation Gratitude and the USO.
4. Babysit (for free) for a single mom or a young couple who need a night out.
5. Leave water, pop, and granola bars on your front porch for the delivery person.
6. Join with other parents to pay off the school-lunch deficit at a local school.
7. Buy toys for Toys for Tots or another local organization. If you have children, let them help choose a toy.
8. Leave microwave popcorn and a few dollars on a Redbox machine for someone else to rent a movie.
9. Bring Christmas cookies or homemade gifts to your neighbors. If you have children, let them be the delivery elves.
10. Send a card of encouragement to a child who is ill through a program like Post Pals.
11. Fill a carafe of coffee and drive around your community passing out cups to the homeless, to people waiting at bus stops, or to people working outside on a cold winter day.
12. Bring cookies to a local nursing home, then go out of your way to thank the employees and visit with residents.

13. Leave crayons and coloring books in the waiting rooms at your local hospital, and bring coffee gift cards to hand out to parents.
14. Drop off boxes of tissues at local schools to replenish their supplies during cold and flu season.
15. Go caroling in your neighborhood or at a local nursing home.
16. Volunteer to make a meal at a local Ronald McDonald House or other establishment that helps families cope with ongoing medical challenges.
17. Partner with Seed Effect or another microfinance organization to help fund a loan.
18. Offer to pick up an elderly church member for a Sunday service.
19. Donate food or extra linens to a local humane society or animal shelter.
20. Bring goodies for the workers at your local grocery store or gas station, or pay for their treat of choice while you're checking out.
21. Help assemble baskets of food items for children who receive free lunch to take home with them over the long holiday break.
22. Offer to run errands for someone who is elderly or ill or who has a new baby.
23. Donate to organizations like the Salvation Army that help pay for people's heat during the cold winter months.
24. Write a note to a local place of business, recognizing an employee by name and thanking them for the excellent service they provided.
25. Invite someone who may be lonely over for dinner during the holiday season.

Beyond "How Was Your Day?"

How to Discuss and Practice Kindness with Your Kids

As busy moms with a combined total of nine children ranging in age from toddlers to teens, we know it can be a challenge to find time to talk about kindness as a family. Several years ago, in an effort to connect each day, we began to make family dinners a central part of our day. In between asking our kids to eat their veggies and pass the butter, we talk about the day's highs and lows . . . and we sneak in the "big" questions. We talk about kindness and about how God calls us to show love to others. We talk about how people around the world are hurting or hungry and what we can do to help.

Learning from our experiences, we've come up with a list of practical things for your family to discuss—whether it's over the dinner table, in quiet early-morning moments, or during occasional snatches of free time on the weekends. As parents, we've been surprised at how well our kids have responded to these kindness discussions and made kindness their own pursuit. It's been easier than we thought to incorporate the truths of Scripture into our everyday lives. We pray that it will be the same for your family as you work through these ideas together.

1. What does it mean to be kind? How is being *kind* different from being *nice*?
2. Why do you think Jesus asks us to treat other people with kindness? Can you think of a time when Jesus showed kindness toward someone else?
3. Read Luke 10:25-37. How did the Samaritan show kindness to the injured man? For each way the Samaritan was kind, discuss and choose a correlating kind act you can do as a family.
4. Think of a time when someone was unkind to you. How did that make you feel? Have you forgiven the person who hurt you? Think of a time when you were unkind, perhaps even to a sibling or family member. Have you apologized for your unkindness? How can you work toward repairing that relationship? How can you be kind to them in the future?

5. Read Matthew 5:43-48. Why do you think Jesus tells us to love our enemies? Do you think this would be easy or difficult to do? What are some ways to show kindness to people who are not always kind to us? (This can also be an appropriate time to talk about being kind while not allowing others to harm or bully you.)

6. Read Galatians 5:22-23, and start a daily kindness poll about the fruits of the Spirit. Each night at dinner or before bed, have each family member list at least one kind thing they observed (or did) that day. Discuss how each act reflects one of the fruits of the Spirit.

7. Have each person in your family think of one way they can be kind at home, and then implement it: help an adult make dinner, help a sibling clean up their room, or take care of pets without being asked to do so.

8. Read Matthew 25:31-46. How does this story encourage us to treat others?

9. Look for acts of kindness in the world around you. As a small craft project, encourage your children to look through newspapers and magazines and cut out stories about people helping others or being kind in some way.

10. Read 1 Thessalonians 5:18. How is being thankful related to being kind? How are things like encouraging others and being grateful important in our efforts to be kind? Who can you say thank you to throughout your day? (As a fun game, see if kids can keep track of how many times they thank people in a single day.)

About the Authors

Julie Fisk first discovered her passion for teaching and empowering others as a practicing attorney. She loves to use that passion to encourage women to be strong and courageous in their individual faith journeys through her writing and speaking and through quiet conversations over steaming cups of coffee. Julie and her husband, Aaron, are committed to living out the commandments to love God and love others in their daily lives, and they are raising their children to do the same. Julie loves trotting the globe with her family, pulling weeds in her heirloom-vegetable garden, running 5K races (only if she is running with friends), and tromping through the woods with her children and their rescue dog, Peanut.

Kendra Roehl is described by her father as a "defender of the weak" and is always looking for those who fall through the gaps and are in need of help. Her natural inclination toward the hurting has segued first into a career as a clinical social worker, then as a foster and adoptive mom, and now as a writer and speaker. Kendra writes and speaks regularly in her community and at her home church, and she volunteers as an adviser for Bridging the Gap, a Christian women's organization in Minnesota. Kendra loves lazy evenings at home with her family, playing spirited card games with friends and neighbors, and dreaming about trips to take with her husband.

Kristin Demery is married to her best friend, Tim, and is a mom to three girls. A grammar geek and Jane Austen addict, Kristin has a background in journalism that has led to many roles, from managing a social networking site for moms to working as an editorial assistant for an academic journal. Kristin's work has been featured in diverse publications, including the *St. Cloud Times*, *ROI Business* magazine, *USA Today*, and *(in)courage*. She's an adviser, editor, and writer for Bridging the Gap, a statewide women's ministry in Minnesota. Kristin loves staying up way too late, spending sun-soaked days at Madeline Island with her family, sipping campfire mochas, thrifting, and gift giving.

You can find Julie, Kendra, and Kristin on their blog at
www.theruthexperience.com.

Do-able. Daily. Devotions.

START ANY DAY THE ONE YEAR WAY.

For Women

| The One Year® Home and Garden Devotions | The One Year® Devotions for Women | The One Year® Devotions for Moms | The One Year® Women of the Bible | The One Year® Coffee with God |

| The One Year® Devotional of Joy and Laughter | The One Year® Women's Friendship Devotional | The One Year® Wisdom for Women Devotional | The One Year® Book of Amish Peace | The One Year® Women in Christian History Devotional |

CP0145

For Men

The One Year®
Devotions for
Men on the Go

The One Year®
Devotions for Men

The One Year®
Father-Daughter
Devotions

For Families

The One Year®
Family
Devotions, Vol. I

The One Year®
Dinner Table
Devotions

For Couples

The One Year®
Devotions for
Couples

The One Year® Love
Language Minute
Devotional

The One Year® Love
Talk Devotional

For Teens

The One Year®
Devos for Teens

The One Year®
Be-Tween You
and God

For Personal Growth

The One Year®
at His Feet
Devotional

The One Year®
Uncommon Life
Daily Challenge

The One Year®
Recovery Prayer
Devotional

The One Year®
Christian History

The One Year®
Experiencing God's
Presence Devotional

For Bible Study

The One Year®
Praying through
the Bible

The One Year®
Praying the
Promises of God

The One Year®
Through the
Bible Devotional

The One Year®
Book of Bible
Promises

The One Year®
Unlocking the
Bible Devotional

TheOneYear.com

CP0145

Do-able. Daily. Devotions.

START ANY DAY THE ONE YEAR WAY.

Do-able.
Every One Year book is designed for people who live busy, active lives. Just pick one up and start on today's date.

Daily.
Daily routine doesn't have to be drudgery. One Year devotionals help you form positive habits that connect you to what's most important.

Devotions.
Discover a natural rhythm for drawing near to God in an extremely personal way. One Year devotionals provide daily focus essential to your spiritual growth.

It's convenient and easy to grow
with God the One Year way.